SCRIPTURE STUDY

FOR LATTER-DAY SAINT FAMILIES

THE DOCTRINE AND COVENANTS

SCRIPTURE STUDY

FOR LATTER-DAY SAINT FAMILIES

THE DOCTRINE AND COVENANTS

Dennis H. Leavitt and Richard O. Christensen
with
Bruce L. Andreason, John S. Bushman, Dean E. Garner, Lynn H. Hatch,
Nihla W. Judd, Todd A. Knowles, and Andy McArthur

DESERET
BOOK
SALT LAKE CITY, UTAH

Biographical sketch photos courtesy Church Archives, The Church of Jesus Christ of Latter-day Saints.

Library of Congress Cataloging-in-Publication Data

Leavitt, Dennis H.

Scripture study for Latter-day Saint families : the doctrine and covenants / Dennis H. Leavitt and Richard O. Christensen ; with Bruce L. Andreason . . . [et al.].

    p.   cm.
    Includes bibliographical references and index.
    ISBN 1-59038-283-8 (pbk.)
    1. Family—Religious life. 2. Mormon Church—Doctrines. I. Christensen, Richard O. II. Andreason, Bruce L. III. Title.

BX8643.F3L43 2004
289.3'2--dc22   2004008815

Printed in the United States of America   54459
Malloy Lithographing Incorporated, Ann Arbor, MI

10 9 8 7 6 5 4 3 2 1

CONTENTS

CONTENTS

CONTENTS

CONTENTS

CONTENTS

CONTENTS

INTRODUCTION

In modern revelation the Lord declared, "I have commanded you to bring up your children in light and truth." (D&C 93:40.) In February 1999, the First Presidency sent a letter to members of the Church throughout the world with the following instruction: "We call upon parents to devote their best efforts to the teaching and rearing of their children in gospel principles which will keep them close to the Church. The home is the basis of a righteous life, and no other instrumentality can take its place or fulfill its essential functions in carrying forward this God-given responsibility." (First Presidency letter, February 11, 1999.)

One of the best ways to fulfill this responsibility is through family scripture study. "Just as the best meals are home cooked," Elder M. Russell Ballard said, "the most nourishing gospel instruction takes place at home." (*Ensign,* May 1996, 81.) Elder Howard W. Hunter taught, "Families are greatly blessed when wise fathers and mothers bring their children about them, read from the pages of the scriptural library together, and then discuss freely the beautiful stories and thoughts according to the understanding of all." (*Ensign,* November 1979, 64.) This book is the second in a series designed to help Latter-day Saint families enhance teaching moments when studying the scriptures together. The first book provided resources to use in studying the Book of Mormon, the keystone of our religion. This book provides ideas to use in studying the Doctrine and Covenants, which President Ezra Taft Benson called the capstone of our religion. (See *Ensign,* May 1987, 83.) The importance of studying the Doctrine and Covenants is further emphasized:

"Perhaps no other book is of such great worth to the Saints as is the Doctrine and Covenants; it is their book, the voice of God in their day. The revelations therein are true and men are commanded to search them. (D&C 1:37–39.)" (Devere Harris, *LDS Church News,* January 7, 1989.)

What You Will Find in This Book

Every effort has been made to make this book simple to use, even for children. As you thumb through its pages, you will notice that it follows the Doctrine and Covenants sequentially. Creative teaching ideas have been provided for every section in the Doctrine and Covenants. It also includes ideas for Official Declaration—1 and Official Declaration—2, Joseph Smith—History, and the Articles of Faith.

You will find many helpful and exciting tools in this book. In addition to the teaching ideas, historical background is provided for each section, as well as many biographical sketches of people mentioned in the Doctrine and Covenants who played a key role in the restoration of the gospel. Additional biographical information can be found in Susan Easton Black's *Who's Who in The Doctrine and Covenants.*

Object lessons, activities, scripture insights, prophetic statements, discussion questions, stories, and many other learning aids are provided to help your family unlock the scriptures and deepen their testimonies. You will find yourselves having enjoyable and inspirational experiences with the scriptures in your family.

How to Use This Book

This resource is intended to help families improve upon the traditional family scripture study method of having each person simply take turns reading a verse. This book is designed to help families actually study the scriptures, working at a pace that will help give them insightful interaction, ask meaningful questions, and gain insights throughout the Doctrine and Covenants. Many families have found success using this resource book in a way that allows all family members to take turns planning and leading the family scripture-study session.

It is most important to note that this is a resource book. Do not feel obligated to use every idea. Think of the book as a buffet of scripture teaching ideas from which you can pick and choose as part of your daily scripture diet. Simply review the material for the section or verses you are studying and, with the aid of the Spirit, select those teaching ideas you feel will most help your family. Help your children use this book so they will teach the family also.

In this book, each section of the Doctrine and Covenants is divided into shorter scripture blocks that have a unifying message or theme. The scripture reference is listed first, followed by a simple question or statement. The question or statement gives you an idea of the topics discussed in that particular section. As you read these questions and statements, you can quickly find a topic your family might need to consider.

You will also see an icon or small picture. These icons are quick visual prompts to let you know what kind of teaching ideas are suggested for that section. Though many lessons use more than one teaching approach, the icon identifies the major approach for that set of verses.

This is the activity icon. It lets you know your family will be actively involved during the lesson. The activity might be drawing pictures, creating projects, taking a quiz, or making a list. Some activities might be more involved than others and may require preparation in advance.

This is the insight icon. It lets you know that questions, cross-references, side-by-side comparisons, or other teaching methods will be used to lead your family to find insights in the scriptures.

This is the object lesson icon. Simple objects or experiments can draw the mind to see spiritual parallels in the scriptures. We have tried to keep the object lessons simple so they can be used with children of various ages.

This is the quotation icon. It identifies teaching suggestions that use quotations, usually from General Authorities, to help us understand a doctrine or scriptural concept or help us apply important principles in our lives.

This is the story icon. It points to a story used to help teach a block of scripture. Sometimes the story is a personal one told by a family member. Sometimes you will find a case study that develops a situation where answers can be found in the scriptures. You may even find a story told by a General Authority. Sometimes the story simply inspires you to do better.

This is the writing and scripture marking icon. It identifies activities that are designed to allow your family to write their impressions and feelings in their journals. Pondering and expressing thoughts in writing is helpful in making gospel principles and doctrines part of our thinking and actions. Marking the scriptures personalizes them so family members can remember what was important to them.

Helping Your Family Become Students of the Scriptures

This book assumes that each family member will have his or her own scriptures and journal. The teaching ideas invite everyone to participate in scripture study. There will be a lot of searching in the pages of your scriptures. Often you will be asked to look for things in a block of scripture that you might mark, list, or discuss. As you study in this manner, your scriptures will become a handbook for life. On subsequent visits to these scripture pages, the marked verses and marginal notes will remind family members of principles they have learned.

Do not be afraid to slow down as you study. Elder Henry B. Eyring taught, "We may be nourished more by pondering a few words, allowing the Holy Ghost to make them treasures to us, than to pass quickly and superficially over whole chapters of scripture." (*Ensign,* November 1997, 84.) Elder D. Todd Christofferson said, "For the gospel to be written in your heart, you need to know what it is and grow to understand it more fully. That means you will study it. When I say 'study,' I mean something more than reading. It is a good thing sometimes to read a book of scripture within a set period of time to get an overall sense of its message, but *for conversion, you should care more about the amount of time you spend in the scriptures than about the amount you read in that time.* I see you sometimes reading a few verses, stopping to ponder them, carefully reading the verses again, and as you think about what they mean, praying for understanding, asking questions in your mind, waiting for spiritual impressions, and writing down the impressions and insights that come so you can remember and learn more. Studying in this way, you may not read a lot of chapters or verses in a half hour, but you will be giving place in your heart for the word of God, and He will be speaking to you." (*Ensign,* May 2004, 11; emphasis added.)

You might also find the following suggestions helpful:

- When possible have a set time for scripture study: each morning, at dinnertime, or each night.
- Make sure each family member has his or her own set of scriptures, marking pens or pencils, and a journal.
- Begin with prayer and invite the Spirit.
- Adapt teaching ideas to the different ages and learning levels of family members.
- When you come across difficult words, be sure to stop and define them.

What Blessings You Can Reap

Imagine what might happen as a result of studying the scriptures together as a family. What value might there be in an increased understanding of the scriptures? What would it mean to young and old alike to be comfortable and conversant with the scriptures? Elder Neal A. Maxwell taught, "The igniting in our youth of a love for the holy scriptures is to ignite a fire that will probably never be extinguished. After all, our youth can take their scriptures and their understanding thereof with them long after parents, bishops, and advisers, of necessity, are left behind." (*Ensign,* April 1985, 10.) Notice these promises given by President Ezra Taft Benson: "When individual members and families immerse themselves in the scriptures regularly and consistently . . . testimonies will increase. Commitment will be strengthened. Families will be fortified. Personal revelation will flow." (*Ensign,* May 1986, 81.)

We hope you find this book useful. We hope it will bless you and your family. It is our wish that you might find some keys to unlocking the scriptures and feasting upon the words of Christ. (See 2 Nephi 31:20.) We feel the following counsel from the Lord has application to family scripture study: "Be not weary in well-doing, for ye are laying the foundation of a great work. And out of small things proceedeth that which is great." (D&C 64:33.)

DOCTRINE AND COVENANTS 1: THE LORD'S PREFACE

Historical background: *Although this revelation is designated as section 1, it was not the first revelation received or recorded by the Prophet Joseph Smith. It was actually received November 1, 1831, and fits chronologically between section 66 and section 67. (See "Chronological Order of Contents" in the front of the Doctrine and Covenants.) The Lord directed that this revelation be placed at the beginning to serve as a "preface" or introduction to the rest of the book. (See D&C 1:6.) As you read this section, watch for the things the Lord warns us to beware of.*

Doctrine and Covenants 1:1–7
A voice of warning

Have family members find the "Chronological Order of Contents" in the front of the Doctrine and Covenants. Ask someone to explain what is meant by a "chronological order." (It refers to the order in which the revelations were received or recorded.) Have your family find where section 1 fits chronologically. Ask, "Why does section 1 appear as the first section in the book if it was received between sections 66 and 67?"

To help answer that question, have your family read the heading to section 1 and also verse 6. (It was given by the Lord to be the preface of the book.) Ask, "What is the purpose of a preface?" (To state the purpose of the book.) Share the following statement by President Ezra Taft Benson: "The Doctrine and Covenants is the only book in the world that has a preface written by the Lord Himself." (*Ensign,* November 1986, 79.)

Read together D&C 1:1–7 and discuss the following questions:

- What is the first word in section 1 of the Doctrine and Covenants?
- What does "hearken" mean? (To pay careful attention, to heed.)
- Who is speaking? (The Lord.)
- To whom is He speaking? (All men.)
- According to verse 4, what kind of a voice will be raised? (Voice of warning.)
- How will this voice of warning be taken to all people? (By "the mouths of my disciples.")

Ask your family to find words in these warning verses that might make people feel uncomfortable; then discuss what they mean. (For example: "none to escape," "rebellious shall be pierced," "secret acts shall be revealed.") Invite your family to look for "warnings" the Lord gives "unto all people" as they study this section and the rest of the Doctrine and Covenants.

Doctrine and Covenants 1:8–16, 37–38
Give heed to the prophets

As a family, sing or read the hymn "We Thank Thee, O God, for a Prophet" (*Hymns,* no. 19) or "Follow the Prophet" (*Children's Songbook,* page 110). Read together D&C 1:8–14 and ask your family what kind of responsibility they think a prophet feels. Tell them that Joseph Smith said, "It is an awful responsibility to write in the name of the Lord." (*History of the Church,* 1:226.) Share the following incident:

"Soon after President Spencer W. Kimball had moved into the office of President of the Church, Elder Boyd K. Packer went to him to get his approval for an article he had been asked to write. He found President Kimball seated at his desk weeping. Concerned, he asked, 'President Kimball, what is the matter?' 'I am such a little man for such a big responsibility!' was the quiet response." (Lucile C. Tate, *Boyd K. Packer: A Watchman on the Tower,* 187.)

Give each family member a pencil and paper and ask them to write down two things our living prophets have recently counseled us to do or not

BIOGRAPHICAL SKETCH: JOSEPH SMITH JR.

Joseph Smith Jr. was born December 23, 1805, in Sharon, Vermont. He was the third son born to Joseph Smith Sr. and Lucy Mack and had five brothers and three sisters. On a beautiful day in the spring of 1820, Joseph knelt in prayer and asked the Lord which church was right. Joseph received a glorious vision of God the Father and His Son Jesus Christ, who told him, among other things, that the true church was not then on the earth. Three and a half years later, the angel Moroni appeared to Joseph and told him of a book written on gold plates, which Joseph later translated into the Book of Mormon. Acting under God's direction, Joseph Smith Jr. and five other men officially organized the Church of Jesus Christ on April 6, 1830. Through this latter-day prophet, the Lord restored many eternal truths. Joseph and his older brother, Hyrum, were killed by an angry mob at Carthage, Illinois, on June 27, 1844. John Taylor wrote, "Joseph Smith, the Prophet and Seer of the Lord, has done more, save Jesus only, for the salvation of men in this world, than any other man that ever lived in it." (D&C 135:3.)

do. Have them share the things they wrote. You could also read the message from the First Presidency in the beginning of the *For the Strength of Youth* pamphlet.

Invite someone to read aloud D&C 1:38 and discuss what that scripture tells us about the voice of prophets. Then read together D&C 1:15–16 and ask what the Lord had to say about the people in 1831. Invite family members to share some ways we "walk in our own way" today.

Share the following quotation from President Gordon B. Hinckley about the disintegration of the family in modern society: "I lift a warning voice to our people. We have moved too far toward the mainstream of society in this matter." (*Ensign*, November 1997, 67.)

Discuss the following questions:

- What kinds of things is our family doing to follow the prophet?
- Are there ways our family may have "moved too far toward the mainstream"?
- Are there things in your individual life you could change to better follow the prophet?

Doctrine and Covenants 1:17–28
Joseph Smith was called to . . .

Ask your family what they think the word *calamity* means (a disaster). Read together D&C 1:17–19 and ask what the Lord did because He knew "the calamities which should come upon the inhabitants of the earth." (Called Joseph Smith and gave him commandments.)

Invite family members to read verses 20–28 and mark the word *that* each time it occurs and the word *and* each time it begins a verse. Explain that these words identify the reasons the Lord gave commandments or revelations to Joseph Smith. Have family members share the reasons as they find them. These could include:

- "That every man might speak in the name of God." (Verse 20.)
- "That faith also might increase." (Verse 21.)
- "That mine everlasting covenant might be established." (Verse 22.)
- "That the fulness of my gospel might be proclaimed." (Verse 23.)

- "That [His servants] might come to understanding." (Verse 24.)
- "And inasmuch as they erred it might be made known." (Verse 25.)
- "And inasmuch as they sought wisdom they might be instructed." (Verse 26.)
- "And inasmuch as they sinned they might be chastened, that they might repent." (Verse 27.)
- "And inasmuch as they were humble they might be made strong, and blessed from on high, and receive knowledge from time to time." (Verse 28.)

To help personalize this message, tell your family to reread verses 24–28 and substitute their own name or "I" in place of the word "they" each time it occurs. Ask your family what these verses teach us about the Lord's love for us.

Doctrine and Covenants 1:29–33
With whom is the Lord well pleased?

Write the following "true or false" statements (without the answers) on a paper for all to see:

1. Joseph Smith was able to translate the Book of Mormon by the power of God. (True.)

2. There is only one true and living church upon the face of the whole earth. (True.)

3. The Lord is well pleased with every member of the Church. (False.)

4. The Lord cannot look upon sin with the least degree of allowance. (True.)

5. Those who are unrepentant shall lose the Spirit and the light they have already received. (True.)

Have family members silently read D&C 1:29–33 looking for the answers. When they have finished, give each person a turn to answer the following questions:

- What kinds of things do Church members do that keep the Lord from being "pleased" with them?

- What can our family do to help the Lord be "well pleased" with His Church?

Doctrine and Covenants 1:34–39
Prophecies shall be fulfilled

Read together D&C 1:34–35 and share the following statements:

"That was given 140 years ago. Is there anyone here that doubts but what *this* is the day that the Lord was referring to, when the devil has power over his own dominion? Everywhere it seems as though a wave of wickedness is about to engulf an unrepentant world." (*The Teachings of Harold B. Lee*, 10; italics added.)

"What a pitiable thing it would be if that ended there, for we can see the power of the adversary in the world and the destruction that is being wrought by those who are his emissaries." (George Albert Smith, in Conference Report, April 1943, 92.)

Have a family member read aloud D&C 1:36. Then share with your family the rest of the statement by President George Albert Smith: "What a promise, but it is all conditioned upon our righteousness, not on anything else, not upon our wealth nor our strength in numbers, not upon our isolation from the world, but upon our righteousness." (George Albert Smith, in Conference Report, April 1943, 92.)

Ask, "What did President Smith say we must do to receive the promised blessing?" (Be righteous.) Have a family member read aloud D&C 1:37. Ask your family the following questions:

- How is searching the scriptures different from merely reading them?
- What does the Lord say about His "prophecies and promises"?
- How might searching the Lord's words help us obtain His promises?

Share an experience with your family of a time when you "searched" the scriptures and received a blessing from the Lord.

DOCTRINE AND COVENANTS 2: ELIJAH'S MISSION

Historical background: Joseph Smith wrote, "On the evening of the . . . twenty-first of September, after I had retired to my bed for the night, I betook myself to prayer and supplication to Almighty God for forgiveness of all my sins and follies, and also for a manifestation to me that I might know of my state and standing before him; for I had full confidence in obtaining a divine manifestation, as I previously had one. While I was thus in the act of calling upon God, I discovered a light appearing in my room." (Joseph Smith—History 1:29–30.) Joseph then proceeds to tell us of his visit with Moroni. Some of Moroni's instructions to Joseph are found in D&C 2. Notice how essential Elijah's mission is to the whole human family

Doctrine and Covenants 2:1–3
Has your heart turned?

Share the following story: Ann Temperance George and her husband, John Doney, sailed from England to America on April 19, 1856, on the *Samuel Curling* with their toddler, Ann. Little Ann became sick at sea. Her parents prayed that her life could be spared until they reached land. Their prayers were answered, and they buried their little daughter in Toledo, Ohio. ("Life Sketch of Ann Temperance and George Doney," in Daughters of the Utah Pioneers Museum archives, Salt Lake City, Utah. Submitted by Ora Lowe Geddes Marstella of Layton, Utah, March 1999.) Ask:

- If you were related to John and Ann, how could you help them be an eternal family?
- What kind of work might be involved in order to go to the temple for them?
- How might this experience affect how you feel about this family?
- What made all of this possible?

If possible, display picture 404 from the Gospel Art Picture Kit that illustrates the appearance of Moroni to Joseph Smith in his bedroom. Read together Joseph Smith—History 1:30–32 and discuss what it was like when Moroni appeared in Joseph's room. Invite someone to read aloud D&C 2:1. Ask:

- What did Moroni tell Joseph Smith would be revealed to him? (JS—H 1:38.)

- What priesthood power would Elijah reveal to Joseph Smith? (Sealing power.)
- When would this priesthood power be revealed? (Before the coming of the great and dreadful day of the Lord.)

On a the left-hand side of a sheet of paper write "Great Day"; on the right-hand side, write "Dreadful Day." Have your family write down reasons why the Savior's Second Coming will be great for some people and dreadful for others. Ask what they can do to make sure it is a great day for them.

Read together D&C 2:2–3 and ask:

- What promises did the Lord make to our fathers? (They would be taught the gospel and have eternal families—see Abraham 2:11.
- Why is it so important that children's hearts turn to their fathers? (See footnote 2b.)
- Why do you think "the whole earth would be utterly wasted" if families were not sealed together before the Lord's coming?

Share the answer given by Elder Jeffrey R. Holland: "No family ties would exist in the eternities, and indeed the family of man would have been left in eternity with 'neither root [ancestors] nor branch [descendants].' Inasmuch as . . . a sealed, united, celestially saved family of God is the ultimate purpose of mortality, any failure here would have been a curse indeed, rendering the entire plan of salvation 'utterly wasted'" (*Christ and the New Covenant*, 297–98.)

Testify that this doctrine of turning our hearts to our fathers is so important that it has been often repeated in the standard works. (See Malachi 4:5–6; 3 Nephi 25:5–6; JS—H 1:37–39; D&C 2.) Consider doing any of the following activities that would be appropriate for your family:

- Compile a storybook of experiences of individuals from your own family history and find out if their ordinance work has been done.

- As a family, take the names of your ancestors who need ordinance work done to the temple. Family members over the age of twelve can participate in baptisms for the dead with a temple recommend.

- Invite your ward family history consultant to teach your family how to search for ancestors who need to have ordinance work done.

DOCTRINE AND COVENANTS 3: THE LOST MANUSCRIPT

Historical background: September 22–December 1827: *During these months Joseph obtained the Book of Mormon plates and Urim and Thummim from the Angel Moroni. Conspiring people who had heard about the "gold plates" sought to steal them from the Prophet. Joseph and Emma moved to Harmony, Pennsylvania, in order to work on the translation in peace.*

December 1827–February 1828: *As time passed, Martin Harris visited Joseph Smith in Harmony. Joseph had written some of the characters from the plates and their translation on a piece of paper. Martin took them to a Professor Charles Anthon at Columbia College in New York. At first the professor certified that the characters and translation were correct, but when he heard they had come from gold plates delivered by an angel, he tore up the certificate. (See Joseph Smith—History 1:64–65 and compare Isaiah 29:11–14.)*

April 12–June 14, 1828: *During this time, Joseph and Martin made considerable progress in translating the plates. Martin felt the need to show his wife the translated pages so she would be satisfied that he was involved in an inspired work. Three times Martin asked Joseph to inquire of the Lord. The answer to the first two requests was no. But after Martin pleaded with Joseph to ask a third time, the Lord said yes. However, Martin was given strict instructions concerning to whom he could show them. (See* The Papers of Joseph Smith, *1:10.) Martin made a covenant to keep these instructions, took 116 pages of the manuscript, and went to Palmyra. Martin did not keep his solemn promise, and the 116 pages were lost.*

July 1828: *Shortly after Martin left for Palmyra with the manuscript, Emma gave birth to a baby boy, who lived only a few hours. Emma's life was threatened by complications associated with the birth. Joseph spent all his efforts nursing her back to health. Once he believed Emma would be all right, he began to worry about the status of the manuscript. Consequently, he made the 100-mile journey to Palmyra to seek out Martin. After learning of the loss of the 116 pages, Joseph returned to Harmony, where he received the chastisement, counsel, and comfort found in the revelation recorded in D&C 3. Moroni then left with both the Urim and Thummim and the plates. (See Lucy Mack Smith,* History of Joseph Smith, *135.) Look for how important it is to rely on the Lord.*

BIOGRAPHICAL SKETCH: MARTIN HARRIS

Martin Harris was born May 18, 1783, in New York State. Shortly after his marriage to Lucy, he met Joseph Smith and became very interested in his work of translating the Book of Mormon plates. He acted as scribe for the Prophet until he was involved in the loss of 116 pages of the translation. In June 1829, he was chosen as one of the three witnesses of the Book of Mormon and mortgaged his farm to finance its publication. Though he was later disfellowshipped, spending thirty-two years away from the Church, he always maintained his testimony of the Book of Mormon. At the age of eighty-six he desired to visit Utah, and Brigham Young sent him money for the trip. During his visit, Martin was rebaptized, on September 17, 1870. Nearly five years later, he passed away while living in Cache County, Utah.

Doctrine and Covenants 3:1–4
Why should we trust the Lord?

Put your family's scriptures in a place in your home other than where you normally have family scripture study. Blindfold a family member and tell him or her to go get the scriptures. Only give help if the person asks for it (such as saying where the books are located or which way to turn), without letting the person get hurt. Keep track of how long the person takes to find the scriptures. Then have another family member start from the original spot and find the scriptures—without being blindfolded. Time how long it took. Ask family members to specifically describe why the one took longer than the other.

After gathering your scriptures, have your family read D&C 3:1–4. Ask them how the activity they just did relates to the ideas in these verses.

Share with your family the historical background to section 3 found in this book and the section heading to D&C 3. Ask:

- What do you suppose were Joseph's biggest worries at that time? (His wife's health and the safety of the manuscript.)
- What did Joseph learn from D&C 3:1–4 that may have comforted him in regard to his worries?
- What things in D&C 3:1–4 may have caused Joseph to feel some remorse?
- How were Joseph and Martin like the blind-folded family member?
- If Joseph Smith were to come to our scripture study today, what do you think he would tell us he learned from this experience?
- How does it make you feel to know that the Lord's work cannot be "frustrated"?
- What does this teach us about the plans we make?

Write the following on a piece of paper so all can see it: "If I want to be successful in life it would be better to trust _____ than _____." Invite your family to fill in the blanks from what they learned from D&C 3:1–4 so the sentence states a true principle. (Possible answers could include *the Lord* and *man*, or *the Lord* and *my own wisdom*.) What truths do we learn about God in these verses that strengthen our faith to live this principle?

Doctrine and Covenants 3:5–15
What are the fiery darts of the adversary?

If you have a dart from a dart game, bring it to family scripture study. If you do not have a dart, show them this picture. Hold up the dart so your family can see it. Ask them what darts are used for.

Be sure that hunting is mentioned. Explain that some people use small darts dipped in poison to kill small animals and birds for food. Have a family member read D&C 3:8 and ask:

- Who else uses darts?
- What do you think is meant by "fiery" darts? (Attacks and temptations from Satan.)
- What is the only way we can be saved from these "fiery darts"?

Read together with your family D&C 3:5–15 and have them look for the "darts" in Joseph Smith's life. Then discuss the following questions:

- What were the fiery darts of the adversary used against Joseph Smith? (See verse 4, 6–9, 14–15.)
- What privilege did Joseph lose "for a season"? (The ability to translate—verse 14.)
- What positive promise was given to Joseph? (See verse 10.)
- What are some of the fiery darts that Satan throws at us today?
- What must we do if we have been affected by Satan's fiery darts? (See verse 10.)
- How can trusting in the Lord help keep us out of harm's way?

Give each family member a sheet of paper (or have them write in their journal) and a pencil. Have them write about a recent "fiery dart" they have experienced and what they can do to be healed from its wound and be protected in the future.

Doctrine and Covenants 3:16–20
The Lord always keeps his promises

Invite your family to think of the last promise they made to someone. (You might have a willing family member share the promise.) Ask:

- Why do we make promises?
- What do we call promises we make with Heavenly Father? (Covenants.)
- Why is it important that we keep our promises and covenants?

Take turns reading D&C 3:16–20 and ask the following questions as you read:

- What did the Lord promise He would do for His people? (Give them knowledge of the Savior—verse 16.)
- To whom did the Lord make that same promise in verses 17 and 18? (The descendants of the Nephites and Lamanites.)
- How will the Lord keep His promise? (By preserving the Book of Mormon record.)
- What part can we play in helping the Lord to fulfill this promise? (Do missionary work.)

DOCTRINE AND COVENANTS 4: A MARVELOUS WORK

Historical background: In February of 1829 Joseph Smith's parents, Joseph Sr. and Lucy, made the 100-mile trip from the Palmyra area of New York to Harmony, Pennsylvania, to visit their son and his wife, Emma. It was during that visit that Joseph Sr. asked his son to seek direction from the Lord on his behalf. The Prophet inquired of the Lord and received the revelation in section 4. Joseph Fielding Smith said of this revelation, "[It] is very short, only seven verses, but it contains sufficient counsel and instruction for a life-time of study. No one has yet mastered it. It was not intended as a personal revelation to Joseph Smith, but to be of benefit to all who desire to embark in the service of God." (Church History and Modern Revelation, 1:35.) Watch for the qualities that best prepare us for missionary work.

BIOGRAPHICAL SKETCH: JOSEPH SMITH SR.

Joseph Smith Sr. was born July 12, 1771, in Topsfield, Massachusetts, the son of Asael and Mary Duty Smith. The 1790s found him in Vermont, where he married Lucy Mack in Tunbridge in 1796. There they settled on a farm and began their family of eleven: a male child that died shortly after birth (1797), Alvin (1798), Hyrum (1800), Sophronia (1803), Joseph Jr. (1805), Samuel Harrison (1808), Ephraim (1810), William (1811), Catherine (1813), Don Carlos (1816), and Lucy (1824). Because of financial difficulties, the Smiths moved several times in the first 20 years of their marriage. In 1816, they moved to Palmyra, in western upstate New York—which was then part of the American frontier.

Joseph Sr. believed in the revelations of his son, and he told young Joseph to follow the instructions he had received by revelation. (See JS—H 1:49–50.) Joseph Sr. was baptized the day the Church was organized, April 6, 1830. He later became one of the eight witnesses to the Book of Mormon and the first patriarch in this dispensation. He traveled hundreds of miles as a missionary and suffered persecutions along with others of the Saints in first decade of the Church. He died September 14, 1840, in Nauvoo, Illinois.

Doctrine and Covenants 4:1–7
What is the question?

Read the historical background for this section to your family. Tell them that although we know this revelation came because Joseph Smith Sr. sought direction from the Lord, we do not know his specific question (or questions). What we do have is the answer.

Write the following questions on a piece of paper that can be displayed as you study D&C 4: What? Who? Where? Why? When? How? Have everyone read D&C 4 silently and then try to write at least one question that begins with each of these six "question words." All questions should be answered by one or more verses in D&C 4. (For example, "How are we to serve God?" [With all our heart, might, mind, and strength—verse 2.])

When everyone has finished, give each family member a turn to ask a question and have the rest of the family answer it. You may want to discuss the following ideas as they come up in your discussion:

- "Heart, might, mind, and strength" symbolizes our whole selves. "Heart" represents our desires and loves; "might" represents our will; "mind" represents our intellectual abilities; and "strength" represents our physical abilities.
- Doing God's work allows us to be blameless before God and brings salvation to our souls. (See also Jacob 1:19.)

When you have finished, discuss the following:

- Which quality or personal characteristic in this revelation is your favorite? Why?
- Tell of a time when you have seen a family member demonstrate one of the characteristics mentioned in this revelation.
- Tell of a time when you have seen another Church member demonstrate one of these important qualities.

Consider sharing your testimony with your family about the joy and blessings that come from serving the Lord.

Doctrine and Covenants 4:1–7
Memorize the section

Tell your family that full-time missionaries are often asked to memorize this entire section—although the revelation applies to all who are engaged in God's work. Have family members do an "MTC" experience by memorizing D&C 4 together. You may need to learn a verse or two each week and say it aloud as a family several times before dinner, family prayer, or scripture reading until the entire section is memorized.

DOCTRINE AND COVENANTS 5: RECEIVING A WITNESS

Historical background: "Having humbly repented of his folly which brought upon him the charge from the Lord of wickedness, Martin Harris again sought the Prophet Joseph Smith and pleaded for the privilege to become one of the three witnesses which were spoken of in the Book of Mormon. (2 Nephi 27:12–14.) It was in the summer of 1828 when the manuscript was lost and in March 1829 when Martin again pled with the Prophet for this great privilege of being a witness. The Lord hearkened to his request and the Lord gave the revelation known as section five in the Doctrine and Covenants." (Joseph Fielding Smith, Church History and Modern Revelation, 1:35–36.) *Notice what the Lord teaches Martin Harris about repentance.*

Doctrine and Covenants 5:1–10
The Lord's testimony to Martin Harris

Ask your family to look at the section headings for D&C 3 and 5 and figure out how many months after the loss of the 116 manuscript pages this revelation was given to Joseph Smith (about 8 months). Ask your family to read D&C 5:1 to themselves and look for why Martin Harris requested this revelation. Explain that part of the Lord's "witness" to Martin was the Lord's own testimony of the calling of Joseph Smith.

Have your family take turns reading aloud D&C 5:2–10. Ask someone to summarize the Lord's answer to Martin's request for a witness that Joseph had the plates.

Share the following story with your family and invite them to think about how the story compares to what the Lord said to Joseph Smith and Martin Harris in D&C 5:5–10:

"It is said that during an epidemic of cholera in a great city, a scientific man proved to his own satisfaction, by chemical and microscopical tests, that the water supply was infected, and that through it contagion was being spread. He proclaimed the fact throughout the city, and warned all against the use of unboiled water. Many of the people, although incapable of comprehending his methods of investigation, far less of repeating such for themselves, had faith in his warning words, followed his instructions, and escaped the death to which their careless and unbelieving fellows succumbed. Their faith was a saving one. To the man himself, the truth by which so many lives had been spared was a matter of knowledge. He had actually perceived, under the microscope, proof of the existence of death-dealing germs in the water; he had demonstrated their virulence; he knew of what he spoke. Nevertheless, in a moment of forgetfulness he drank of the unsterilized water, and soon thereafter died, a victim to the plague. His knowledge did not save him, convincing though it was; yet others, whose reliance was only that of confidence or faith in the truth that he declared, escaped the threatening destruction." (James E. Talmage, *Articles of Faith*, 99–100.)

Ask:

• How is this story like the Lord's answer to Martin Harris?

- Why were those who believed in the scientist's words saved but the scientist was not?
- Why does a spiritual witness of Joseph Smith's calling have more saving power than seeing the plates? (A testimony comes by faith and the Spirit, which leads to righteous actions, whereas physically seeing something only satisfies human curiosity.)

Ask your family to write in their journals of a time they received a witness that Joseph Smith was a prophet of God. Offer the opportunity for family members to share their feelings or what they wrote.

Doctrine and Covenants 5:11–20
How important are witnesses?

Ask your family to imagine they are lawyers in a courtroom. Ask:

- What is the purpose of bringing witnesses to the stand?
- What kinds of things might witnesses be asked to testify of?
- How difficult would it be to prove your case if you had only one witness?
- How would additional witnesses make your case stronger?

Read D&C 5:11–15 aloud and have your family look for how many witnesses of the Book of Mormon the Lord said He would call (Joseph and 3 others). Tell your family they will learn more about the fulfillment of this promise when they study D&C 17.

As a family, read the testimony of the three witnesses found at the beginning of the Book of Mormon and evaluate the strength of their testimonies as if you were a judge in a courtroom. Read D&C 5:16–20 together and look for the blessings and curses that come from accepting or rejecting those witnesses and why. Share the following statement from Joseph Fielding Smith:

"The effect of the testimony of the three witnesses is the power of salvation to all those who believe and accept the Gospel. On the other hand, it is the power of damnation to all those who, after having heard it, reject it. . . . Therefore, they are left without excuse, and their sins are upon their own heads (D&C 88:81–82)." (Joseph Fielding Smith, *Church History and Modern Revelation,* 1:37.)

Doctrine and Covenants 5:21–35
The blessings of being corrected

Briefly discuss the following questions:

- When was the last time someone corrected you?
- How did it make you feel?
- What are some reasons people correct others?

Read D&C 5:21–22 to your family and ask:

- What was Joseph Smith commanded to do?
- What blessings was he promised if he obeyed?

Take turns reading D&C 5:23–32 and have your family look for the following:

- What did the Lord say was Martin Harris's problem?
- What was Martin commanded to do?
- What blessings was he promised if he obeyed?

Share the following story, which helps us know how Martin responded to God's counsel:

"Martin was possessed of a somewhat arrogant and egotistical spirit, and without doubt it took this long period of probation and mental suffering to give him the experience which such a nature as his needed. Even after his sincere and earnest pleading to be one of the Three Witnesses, and the request had been granted, the Prophet said to him before they started for the woods 'Martin Harris, you have got to humble yourself before your God this day, that you may obtain a forgiveness of your sins. If you do, it is the will of God that you should look upon the plates in company with Oliver Cowdery and David Whitmer.' Before this purpose was accomplished the angel appeared to the two other witnesses after Martin Harris had withdrawn from them, as he seemed to be a hindrance to the presence of the holy messenger. Later he also beheld the messenger and exclaimed:

"'Tis enough; 'Tis enough; mine eyes have beheld; mine eyes have beheld.' (Doc. Hist. of the Church, Vol. 1:55.)" (Joseph Fielding Smith, *Church History and Modern Revelation,* 1:81.)

DOCTRINE AND COVENANTS 6: OLIVER COWDERY RECEIVES DIRECTION

Historical background: Oliver Cowdery had been boarding at the home of Joseph Smith Sr. while he was teaching school in the Palmyra area of New York. When he learned that Joseph Smith Jr. had received an ancient record, he traveled to Harmony, Pennsylvania, to meet the Prophet. He arrived on April 7, 1829, the same day this revelation was received. Watch for the specific gifts promised Oliver Cowdery if he remained faithful.

Doctrine and Covenants 6:1–13
What makes a person rich?

Ask your family what they think makes a person rich, and how they might identify a "rich" person. Have your family silently read D&C 6:1–7 and then discuss the following questions:

- What great "harvest" is the Lord speaking of in these verses? (Missionary work.)
- Why is sharing the gospel with others such a "great and marvelous work"?
- What are the Lord's faithful servants promised in verse 3? (Everlasting salvation.)
- According to verse 7, what makes a person rich?
- Why would "eternal life" and "everlasting salvation" be better than earthly riches?

Have family members take turns reading aloud D&C 6:8–13. Have them look for those things Oliver Cowdery was commanded to do in order to do "much good." Share ideas of how this counsel can apply to us by discussing these questions:

- Why do you think desire plays such a key role in "doing good" in this generation?
- What work in God's kingdom can we "assist to bring forth"? (See verse 9.)
- What special "gifts" (see verse 10) have you been given to help accomplish God's work?

- Why is it important to "inquire" (see verse 11) when trying to share the gospel with others?
- What "good" can you do in order to obtain the blessings mentioned in verse 13?

Share your testimony about the importance of gaining salvation, and encourage your family to seek for that most important gift.

Doctrine and Covenants 6:14–24
"Did I not speak peace to your mind?"

Ask family members to briefly write down one thing that happened to them yesterday that they think no other family member would know about. When everyone has finished, ask the following questions:

- How common is it for you to have experiences that only you know about?
- Do you think any family member could guess what you wrote on your paper?
- Who, besides yourself, knows about that event and what you wrote on your paper? (God.)

Tell your family that Oliver Cowdery had an experience while living in Palmyra, New York, that he had not shared with anyone. He explained, "After [I] had gone to [Joseph Smith's] father's to board, and after the family had

BIOGRAPHICAL SKETCH: OLIVER COWDERY

Oliver Cowdery was born October 3, 1806, in Wells, Rutland County, Vermont. He became a schoolteacher and taught in Manchester, New York, for the Joseph Smith Sr. family. While there, he heard of Joseph Smith through the Prophet's brother Hyrum, and he made a visit to see Joseph. They met April 5, 1829, and two days later Oliver began serving as scribe to Joseph in the translation of the Book of Mormon. Sections 6, 8, and 9 are directed to him. On December 5, 1834, he was ordained assistant president of the Church. He was with Joseph during many spiritual events, including the following:

- Restoration of the Aaronic Priesthood by John the Baptist.
- Restoration of the Melchizedek Priesthood by Peter, James, and John.
- Organization of the Church on April 6, 1830.
- He was one of the three witnesses of the Book of Mormon.
- He saw the Savior with Joseph in the Kirtland Temple.
- He received priesthood keys from Elijah, Elias, and Moses. (See Daniel H. Ludlow, *A Companion to Your Study of the Doctrine and Covenants,* 351.)

Sadly, he did not remain true to the Church. He was excommunicated on April 12, 1838, for differences with Joseph. After 11 years of being plagued by financial problems and illness, he repented and returned to the Church. In October 1848 he was rebaptized.

Never once did he deny his testimony of the Book of Mormon—even during his 11 years of apostasy. Before he could act on his plans to head west with the Saints, he died March 3, 1850, in the home of David Whitmer.

communicated to [me] concerning [Joseph] having obtained the plates, that one night after [I] had retired to bed [I] called upon the Lord to know if these things were so, and the Lord manifested to [me] that they were true, but [I] had kept the circumstance entirely secret, and had mentioned it to no one." (Account related by Joseph Smith in *History of the Church,* 1:35.)

Read D&C 6:14–24 as a family. Look for evidences that show the Lord knew about Oliver Cowdery's experience, even though no one else did. When you have finished, discuss some of the following questions:

- What would this experience teach you about Joseph Smith? (That he was a true prophet who could receive revelations from God.)
- What would this experience teach you about God?
- If you were Oliver Cowdery, what phrases would have given you comfort? Why?
- What feelings did Oliver Cowdery experience from the Holy Ghost? (Enlightenment [see verse 15]; peace [see verse 23]; a witness of truth [see verse 24].)
- How are these feelings similar to the times when you have felt the influence of the Holy Ghost?

Invite family members to write down an experience when the Lord answered their prayers. Ask them to keep this experience in their journals, so they can refer to it later in their lives.

Doctrine and Covenants 6:29–37
What are some blessings that come to those who do good?

Ask your family to imagine that someone is trying to convince them that it is all right to make bad choices. What might you say to someone with that attitude?

Now invite your family to do the following activity "silently" for the next several minutes:

1. Read D&C 6:29–37.

2. Ponder what those verses teach about being "good."

3. Write in your journal an answer to this question: "What are some blessings that come to me when I choose good"?

Invite family members to share what they wrote. You could give family members a CTR ring and encourage them to always "Choose the Right." Testify of the blessings that come as we choose to serve the Lord in goodness.

Doctrine and Covenants 6:5–36
What must I do to receive revelation?

Ask your family what they might do to prepare for the following activities:

- Take a test in school.
- Play in a sporting event.
- Go on a date.
- Receive revelation.

Share the following statement from Elder Boyd K. Packer:

"It is good to learn when you are young that spiritual things cannot be forced.

"Sometimes you may struggle with a problem and not get an answer. What could be wrong? It may be that you are not doing anything wrong. It may be that you have not done the right things long enough. Remember, you cannot force spiritual things." (*Ensign,* November 1979, 19.)

Tell your family that D&C 6 has many principles we can follow to prepare ourselves to receive spiritual blessings. Ask your family to read the following verses and identify what they suggest we do to prepare ourselves to receive revelation: D&C 6:5, 6, 8, 11, 20, 36.

Discuss your family's discoveries and talk about ways your family can improve in these areas.

DOCTRINE AND COVENANTS 7: ANSWERS ABOUT JOHN THE BELOVED

Historical background: Joseph Smith wrote, "During the month of April I continued to translate, and [Oliver Cowdery] to write, with little cessation, during which time we received several revelations. A difference of opinion arising between us about the account of John the Apostle in the New Testament, as to whether he died or continued to live, we mutually agreed to settle it by the Urim and Thummim and the following is the word which we received." (History of the Church, 1:35–36.) This revelation stands as a testimony that God answers our questions and can clarify our misunderstandings as we approach Him in prayer.

Doctrine and Covenants 7:1–8
"What desirest thou?"

Ask each family member to respond to the first question below and then discuss the second question together:

1. If you could be granted one special wish, what would it be and why?

2. Would that wish change if the Lord were the one granting your wish? Why or why not?

Read D&C 7:1–2 together as a family. (See also John 21:20–23.) Ask:

- To whom did the Lord grant a special wish?
- What did John desire?
- What do you think about John's desire?

Have a family member read the section heading for D&C 7 and the historical background above. You might also explain that the Savior offered a similar opportunity to his disciples in America. (See 3 Nephi 28:1–12.)

Ask your family to read D&C 7:3–8 and look for answers to the following:

- What reason did John give as to why he wanted to continue to live on earth?
- How long was John told he could tarry?
- What was Peter's desire?
- What was the Lord's response to both John's and Peter's desires?
- What else was given to Peter, James, and John? (Verse 7.)
- Where is John serving the Lord today?

To help answer the last question, share the following prophecy from Joseph Smith: "John the Revelator was then among the Ten Tribes of Israel . . . to prepare them for their return from their long dispersion, to again possess the land of their fathers." (*History of the Church*, 1:176, footnote.)

Refer again to the desires family members spoke about earlier. Ask them to show by raise of hands how many would like to go to the celestial kingdom. Tell them President Brigham Young said, "The men and women, who *desire* to obtain seats in the celestial kingdom, will find that they must battle every day" (*Journal of Discourses*, 11:14; emphasis added), and Elder Neal A. Maxwell added, "Therefore, true Christian soldiers are more than weekend warriors" (*Ensign*, November 1996, 21). Ask family members what they can do to show their righteous desires and demonstrate that they are more than "weekend warriors."

DOCTRINE AND COVENANTS 8: THE GIFT OF TRANSLATION

Historical background: In the first revelation given to Oliver Cowdery, he was told, "Behold, I grant unto you a gift, if you desire of me, to translate, even as my servant Joseph." (D&C 6:25.) This section came as a revelation to Oliver because he continued to desire the fulfillment of that promise. (See also the historical background for Doctrine and Covenants 9. Both revelations deal with this matter.) Watch for what the Lord teaches about how revelation works.

Doctrine and Covenants 8:1, 12
Does God know your name?

 Talk about some of these questions with your family:

- Do you like it when people remember and call you by name? Why?
- Share a time when you were surprised that someone knew your name.
- If someone knows your name, what does it tell you about him or her?

Read D&C 8:1, 12 aloud and ask:

- How does the Lord address Brother Cowdery?
- How do you think that may have made Oliver feel?

- How do you feel knowing that God also knows your name?

You might consider comparing these verses to Joseph Smith—History 1:17 where God calls Joseph Smith by name.

Doctrine and Covenants 8:1, 5, 8–11
What are some requirements to obtain and exercise spiritual gifts?

Place on the floor several objects, pictures, or labels of things that you think your family members would desire (money, food, sporting event tickets, vacation package, and so on). Ask them which of those items they desire the most and why. Then ask:

- What are some things you desire more than these?
- What would you say is your greatest desire?
- What effort or "price" is required if you were to obtain what you most desire?

Have family members scan the section heading to D&C 8 and look for what Oliver Cowdery desired. Take turns reading D&C 8:1, 5, 8–11. As you do, have each person find and mark the things that are a requirement for putting a gift of the Spirit into operation. Discuss what your family finds, and talk about why those things are important.

Reread verse 10 and ask:

- What does "trifle" mean? ("To treat someone or something as unimportant.")
- Why would it be important for Oliver not to trifle with the gifts he is given?
- What else was Oliver not supposed to do? (Ask for things he shouldn't)
- What does this teach us about receiving spiritual gifts?

Doctrine and Covenants 8:2–4
What is the "Spirit of Revelation"?

Write the following sentence on a piece of paper for your family to see. Be sure to leave out the words in parentheses.

"The spirit of (<u>revelation</u>) is when the Holy Ghost speaks to my (<u>mind</u>) and (<u>heart</u>)."

Then have your family search D&C 8:2–4 and find the words that fit in the blanks and complete the sentence. You might invite someone to draw a picture of a mind and a heart on the paper with your sentence.

Ask your family to suggest some ways the Holy Ghost communicates to our hearts and minds. (For example, you may discuss how ideas, thoughts, or clear impressions are communications from the Holy Ghost to our minds, and how feelings, impressions, or tender nudges could be communications from the Holy Ghost to our hearts.)

Share an experience with your family when you felt the "spirit of revelation" in your life. Consider inviting other family members to share their experiences with the Spirit.

Doctrine and Covenants 8:5–12
What were Oliver Cowdery's spiritual gifts?

Display a package wrapped up as a gift and have your family share memories about receiving a favorite gift. Have them read silently D&C 8:4–9, underlining the gifts the Lord gave to Oliver. The following statement may be helpful:

"There was another gift bestowed upon Oliver Cowdery, and that was the gift of Aaron. Like Aaron with his rod in his hand going before Moses as a spokesman, so Oliver Cowdery was to go before Joseph Smith. Whatever he should ask the Lord by power of this gift should be granted if asked in faith and in wisdom. Oliver was blessed with the great honor of holding the keys of this dispensation with Joseph Smith, and like Aaron did become a spokesman on numerous occasions. It was Oliver who delivered the first public discourse in this dispensation." (Joseph Fielding Smith, *Church History and Modern Revelation*, 1:48.)

DOCTRINE AND COVENANTS 9: OLIVER TRIES TO TRANSLATE

Historical background: In the spring of 1829, with Oliver Cowdery's help, the translation of the Book of Mormon continued at an accelerated pace. In addition to being Joseph Smith's scribe, Oliver asked for and received permission from the Lord to translate. (See D&C 6:25.) Oliver made an attempt but was not successful, and the gift was taken from him. Doctrine and Covenants 9 was given as instruction to Oliver after his failure to translate. Notice what the Lord teaches about the process of receiving revelation.

Doctrine and Covenants 9:1–4
The Lord changes Oliver's calling

Ask your family to name various Church callings and who presently serves in those callings (for example, Who is the bishop? Who teaches primary? Who is the librarian?)

Read together Article of Faith 1:5 and talk about how callings come from the Lord. Ask:

- Do you think the people in your ward knew they would be called to those positions? Why or why not?
- How long do you think these people will serve in their present calling?
- Who decides when people are called or released from callings?

Take turns reading D&C 9:1–4 and ask:

- What calling had Oliver desired? (See the section heading for D&C 8 if needed.)
- What did the Lord ask Oliver to do at this time?
- How do you think Oliver felt about not being able to translate?
- What did the Lord mention to Oliver about future callings?

Have one family member read aloud Matthew 26:39 and another read aloud 3 Nephi 11:11. Discuss the following questions:

- Did the Savior ever get a calling He didn't really want?
- What did He do about it?
- How might the Savior's example have helped Oliver Cowdery during this experience in his life?

- What blessings come to us when we faithfully fulfill the callings we receive from the Lord?

Doctrine and Covenants 9:5–9
How does revelation come?

Wrap a warm blanket around one member of your family. Have that person write down one word they would use to describe that feeling. Next, wrap the blanket around another family member and have him or her write an answer to the same question. Continue doing this until all have had a chance to write. Then take turns sharing what each person wrote.

Have your family read the section heading for Doctrine and Covenants 9 and the historical background section above. Have them explain what Oliver Cowdery struggled with at this time. Explain that after this struggle, the Lord taught Oliver one way that revelation is received. Tell your family you want them to compare the process of revelation with the "blanket" activity they just finished.

Study the scriptures in the chart on the next page together as a family. Fill in information in the other columns as family members discover it.

Remind your family that there are many feelings that accompany the Spirit of the Lord. It may not feel the same for each person, nor may it be exactly the same each time we feel the Spirit. Share with your family some experiences you have had when you have felt the Lord's Spirit. Allow family members to express how they feel when the Spirit is present. Remind them that just

Scripture Reference	Some ways I may feel the Spirit of the Lord	Some things I can do to receive the Lord's Spirit
D&C 9:5–9		
John 14:26–27		
D&C 8:2–3		

as we use different words to describe the feeling of being wrapped in a warm blanket, we also use different words to describe the times when we feel the prompting of the Holy Ghost.

Doctrine and Covenants 9:10–14
Why was Oliver Cowdery not able to translate as he wanted to?

Show your family some writing in a different language. (These may come from different books, assembly instructions, or the Internet. Or you can use the sample below.) Ask one family member to try to translate it. When they are unable to do so, talk about why they cannot.

> Parece que a maioria de nós tenta resolver os problemas sozinha, contando com a própria força. E, na verdade, o Senhor ordenou que orássemos quanto a todas as coisas.

Read D&C 9:10–14 and ask your family to look for reasons Oliver Cowdery could not translate as he wanted to. Ask:

- Why was Oliver not able to translate? (Fear—see verses 10–11.)
- What is the opposite of fear? (Faith—see also Matthew 14:24–31 for another example of a person who feared.)
- What blessings could still come to Oliver if he obeyed the Lord? (See verses 13–14.)

Ask your family to list some of the things the Lord would like them to do that may seem too difficult to accomplish (such as speak in church, teach a class, go on a mission). Ask:

- Why might it be easy to "fear" those things?
- How can we gain greater faith to obey the commandments, even if they are difficult?
- What does 1 Nephi 3:7 teach us about this principle?

DOCTRINE AND COVENANTS 10: REPLACING THE LOST MANUSCRIPT

Historical background: The historical background to D&C 3 contains most of the history leading up to D&C 10. You should review it again. After Joseph Smith received the revelation in D&C 3, he gave up the Urim and Thummim to Moroni. After a space of time (perhaps seven or eight weeks), Joseph again received the Urim and Thummim from Moroni. He inquired of the Lord and received the revelation found in D&C 10. (See History of the Church, *1:23.)*

Section 10 is not found immediately after section 3 because this revelation had been mistakenly dated May 1829. When Elder B. H. Roberts determined that the actual date was late summer 1828 as a part of editing the History of the Church, *it was determined to put the more accurate date in the section heading. The decision was also made at the next reprinting of the scriptures to leave it as section 10 rather than move it next to section 3 and alter the numbering of the rest of the sections of the Doctrine and Covenants. (See Lyndon Cook,* The Revelations of the Prophet Joseph Smith, *17.) Watch for how the Lord's knowledge of the future foils Satan's plan.*

Doctrine and Covenants 10:1–33
Conquering Satan

Ask your family, "In time of war, what is the value and role of a good spy?" (A spy can help reveal the plans and strategies of the enemy.) Have one family member read aloud Alma 34:23, and another read aloud Moroni 7:12. Ask:

- Who is our greatest enemy?
- In what ways have you seen this enemy at work?

Review the history related to D&C 3 and the loss of the 116-page manuscript and ask:

- In what ways had the enemy partially succeeded in the instance of the 116 pages?
- What allowed Satan to get the manuscript away from Joseph?
- If you were Joseph Smith in this instance, what would you want to do or know now?

Tell your family that having been humbled by his experience in losing the manuscript, Joseph was prepared to be taught about overcoming the influence of the adversary. In his mercy, the Lord provided the revelation in D&C 10, which "spies" on the plans and tactics of Satan. Encourage your family to look not only for what this revelation might have meant to Joseph Smith but also how it teaches truths that can help anyone who is tempted by Satan.

Take turns reading D&C 10:1–9 and then discuss the following questions:

- Why did Joseph Smith lose his gift for a time?
- What do you think "your mind became darkened" means? (Verse 2.)
- Why did the Lord call Martin Harris a "wicked man"? (See verses 6–8.)
- What are some things the Lord has "entrusted" us with that are sacred? (For example, our bodies, our covenants, our family.)
- In what ways have you seen people "deliver" these things "unto wickedness"?
- According to verses 1–2, what will be the consequences?
- According to verse 5, how can we escape the attacks of Satan?
- According to verse 6, what does Satan seek to do?

Tell your family that D&C 10:10–33 identifies many ways Satan sought to destroy Joseph Smith.

Most of them are also ways he seeks to destroy us. Take turns reading verses 10–33 aloud and have your family look for: (1) Satan's purposes and (2) the ways he seeks to accomplish those purposes. When someone has identified one, have the person say "Stop" and then tell it to the family. Then have the entire family suggest ways they have seen the effects of these purposes and tactics today.

Some family members may become concerned or fearful about the influence of Satan. Consequently, you may want to share with your family the following statement from President James E. Faust:

"We need not become paralyzed with fear of Satan's power. He can have no power over us unless we permit it. He is really a coward, and if we stand firm, he will retreat. The Apostle James counseled: 'Submit yourselves therefore to God. Resist the devil, and he will flee from you' (James 4:7). And Nephi states that 'he hath no power over the hearts' of people who are righteous (1 Nephi 22:26).

"We have heard comedians and others justify or explain their misdeeds by saying, 'The devil made me do it.' I do not really think the devil can make us do anything; certainly he can tempt and he can deceive, but he has no authority over us which we do not give him.

"The power to resist Satan may be stronger than we realize. The Prophet Joseph Smith taught: 'All beings who have bodies have power over those who have not. The devil has no power over us only as we permit him. The moment we revolt at anything which comes from God, the devil takes power' (TPJS, p. 181). He also stated, 'Wicked spirits have their bounds, limits, and laws by which they are governed' (HC, 4:576). So Satan and his angels are not all-powerful." (Ensign, September 1995, 4.)

Have each family member share one thing learned from this study of D&C 10:1–33 that will help him or her overcome Satan.

Doctrine and Covenants 10:34–45
How did God frustrate the plans of the enemy?

Place on the floor next to each other a stack of five plates and a stack of two plates. Have your family turn to "A Brief Explanation About the Book of Mormon" in the front pages of the Book of Mormon. Read together the paragraph that begins "1. *The Plates of Nephi*." Ask:

- In what way could these plates on the floor represent something in the paragraph we just read?
- How did these two sets of plates differ from each other?

Explain to your family that as Nephi was recording the history of his people on the large plates, the Lord commanded him to make another record (the small plates) covering the same period of time. Read together 1 Nephi 9:3–6 and ask:

- According to verse 5, why did Nephi have to make two sets of plates?
- What role do you think Nephi's beliefs, expressed in verse 6, had on his decision to make the second set of plates?

Quickly review the information given in the historical background above and the section headings to Doctrine and Covenants 3 and 10. Make six strips of paper. In large letters write on one of them: "The Large Plates—The Book of Lehi" and place it on the larger stack of plates. Write on another strip: "The Small Plates of Nephi" and place it on the smaller stack of plates. Then read together D&C 10:34–45. As you read, have the family look for:

- What the Lord told Joseph Smith to do about the part of the translation that was lost.
- What the Lord said was on the "plates of Nephi." (See verses 38, 40, 45.)
- What the Lord said about the "Book of Lehi." (The large plates of Nephi—see verse 44.)

As your family finds things about the plates of Nephi and the book of Lehi, have someone write it on one of the strips of paper and place it on the appropriate stack of plates. Ask:

- Based on what we read in these verses, which set of plates would seem to be more valuable to us? Why?
- When we consider how everything turned out, what does that teach us about the Lord?

Tell your family that one thing this incident teaches us about the Lord can be expressed in an idea repeated in D&C 10. Have them find a common word in D&C 10:34–35, 43 that describes the Lord. Then have them underline the phrase "here is wisdom" in both verse 34 and verse 35, and then "I will show unto them that my wisdom is greater than the cunning of the devil" in verse 43. Finish by rereading 1 Nephi 9:6, and share your testimony that Nephi's faith was certainly accurate. Ask, "How do you think this principle can bless our family?"

Doctrine and Covenants 10:46–52
Answers to prayers of faith

In preparation for studying these verses, discuss with your family the following questions:

- Why do we pray before we study the scriptures together, before family home evening, and so on?
- Can you think of a time when the prayers of many people were united for a specific purpose? (For example, a ward fast, a family emergency, in the temple, or a national crisis.)
- How would you feel if you knew that many people were praying for you?
- Can you tell about a time when you felt the power of prayers on your behalf?
- What are some things we can and should pray for?
- Have all of your prayers been answered at

the time and in the way you wanted? Why or why not?

Read together D&C 10:46–52 and make a list of all the things the Lord said the Nephite prophets prayed for. Ask:

- How do the things they prayed for relate to us?
- How long did it take for their prayers to be answered?
- How are their prayers being answered?
- What words or phrases describe the way they prayed? (They prayed in faith.)

Elder Richard G. Scott gave the following counsel that helps us understand what it means to pray in faith: "Faith in Christ means we trust Him; we trust His teachings. That leads to hope, and hope brings charity, the pure love of Christ." (*Ensign*, May 1994, 7.) After sharing this statement with your family, ask them how D&C 10:45–52 demonstrates that ancient Nephite prophets prayed with faith.

Write the following statement where all can see it: "If I want the Lord to answer my prayers, _____." Invite your family to complete the statement by summarizing what we should learn about prayer from D&C 10:45–52. Have a scribe write their statements down, along with the verses from D&C 10 that seem to teach that truth. After a week, review this list of truths and invite family members to share how it has blessed them over that time.

Doctrine and Covenants 10:52–70
Purposes of the Book of Mormon

 Have your family suggest:

- Questions people have about the Book of Mormon. (For example, "Where did it come from?" "What's it about?")
- Reasons why people resist or do not accept the Book of Mormon. (For example, "The Bible is all of God's word; there isn't any more.")

Appoint a family member to be a scribe and record these questions and reasons.

Divide the family into two groups. Have each group read D&C 10:52–70 and determine ways these verses could help answer the questions and concerns you listed about the Book of Mormon and the Church.

Choose two people to role play and practice answering people's questions about the Book of Mormon and the Church. Have the "investigator" ask questions like: "What is the Book of Mormon?" "Why do we need it?" "What does it contain?" "What if I already have a Church?" "What do you believe about Jesus Christ?" Have the other person answer by using the teachings found in D&C 10. Other family members can offer help and suggestions if needed. Encourage your family to look for opportunities to teach people about the Book of Mormon and the Church and to be more confident in doing so.

DOCTRINE AND COVENANTS 11: "HYRUM, MY SON"

Historical background: Shortly after Joseph Smith and Oliver Cowdery received the Aaronic Priesthood from John the Baptist (see D&C 13), Samuel Smith came to Harmony, Pennsylvania, to see his older brother. Joseph and Oliver told Samuel about the restoration of the priesthood and showed him the pages they had trans- lated from the plates. Samuel received his own witness of the truth of the work and was baptized.

"Returning to his father's house under an elation of spirit that acceptance of the gospel had brought to him, Samuel evidently excited increased interest in the ever enlarging work of his Prophet brother, for Hyrum Smith hastened from Palmyra to Harmony in order to inquire of the Lord concerning these things reported by Samuel, and to learn what his relationship to the then unfolding work was to be. The Prophet inquired, through the Urim and Thummim, and obtained for him a revelation." (B. H. Roberts, A Comprehensive History of The Church of Jesus Christ of Latter-day Saints, *1:181–82.) Notice what the Lord teaches Hyrum about preparing for a mission.*

Doctrine and Covenants 11:1
What is the marvelous work about to come forth?

Have someone read D&C 11:1 and ask if anyone recognizes the words in this verse. Have family members quickly review D&C 4:1 and 6:1. (See also D&C 12:1; and 14:1.) Ask:

- Why do you think these words appear in so many of these early revelations?
- What "great and marvelous work" do you think the Lord is referring to? (Answers could include the Book of Mormon transla- tion and the restoration of the priesthood, the gospel, and the true Church.)

- What was "marvelous" about the coming forth of the Book of Mormon?
- Why is the restoration of the priesthood and the Lord's true Church "great and mar- velous" to you?

Explain that the phrase "a marvelous work is about to come forth" is not found again in the scriptures after D&C 14:1. Read D&C 11:1 again to your family but insert the word "has" in place of "is about to." Testify of the wonderful thing the Lord has done in bringing forth the Book of Mormon and restoring His kingdom upon the earth.

BIOGRAPHICAL SKETCH: HYRUM SMITH

Hyrum Smith was born on February 9, 1800, making him five years older than his brother Joseph. From the beginning of the Restoration, Hyrum was one of Joseph's most faithful supporters and was baptized by Joseph sometime in June 1829. Hyrum was one of the Eight Witnesses of the Book of Mormon and was later ordained to positions of trust in the Church. Joseph wrote of his brother, "I could pray in my heart that all my brethren were like unto my beloved brother Hyrum, who possesses the mildness of a lamb, and the integrity of a Job, and in short, the meekness and humility of Christ; and I love him with that love that is stronger than death." (*History of the Church,* 2:338.) Hyrum suffered with his brother in Liberty Jail and later died as a martyr with him in Carthage Jail on June 27, 1844. (See D&C 135.)

Doctrine and Covenants 11:2–9
What are the Lord's object lessons?

Show your family a rock and ask them to name some ways it can be used to teach gospel principles. (Jesus is the rock, build your house upon a rock, and so on.) Read together D&C 11:2–9 and have your family identify any objects the Lord used to illustrate an idea to Hyrum Smith. After the objects are identified, ask, "What do you think the Lord wanted Hyrum to learn from these objects?" Below are some of the objects and some of the truths they illustrate:

- Two-edged sword. (God's word is like a two-edged sword that cuts both ways: it can bless us as we use it properly, or it can hurt us if we use it improperly or ignore it.)
- Field that is white. (When the wheat is ripe and ready to harvest, the head of the wheat turns a golden white color. People who are ready to hear the gospel are like wheat ready to harvest.)
- Sickle. (A sickle is a tool used to harvest wheat. The Lord also refers to missionary work as a "harvest." Missionaries harvest with scriptures, prayer, faith, and charity.)

- Knock on a door. (Prayer is like knocking on the Lord's door—see Matthew 7:7.)
- Riches. (The worldly focus on temporal riches, but the Lord offers us true eternal riches.)

Ask family members to choose one of the objects that has the most meaning to them. Invite them to draw this object in their journals and write a paragraph on what the object means to them and how they can better their lives from its use.

Doctrine and Covenants 11:10–11
What was Hyrum's gift?

Ask someone to read D&C 11:10–11. Ask, "How would you like to know more about Hyrum Smith's gift?" Tell your family that Hyrum's grandson, Joseph Fielding Smith, wrote the following concerning this gift: "The Lord declared that Hyrum Smith had a gift. The great gift which he possessed was that of a tender, sympathetic heart; a merciful spirit. The Lord on a later occasion said: 'Blessed is my servant Hyrum Smith; for I, the Lord, love him because of the integrity of his heart, and because he loveth that which is right before me, saith the Lord.' (D. and C., 124:15.) This great gift was manifest in his jealous watch care over the Prophet lest some harm come to him." (*Church History and Modern Revelation,* 1:52.) Ask:

- What is a tender, sympathetic heart?
- What do you think is a merciful spirit?
- Who do you know that has these same attributes?
- How can a person develop these attributes?

Challenge your family to be more tender-hearted, sympathetic, and merciful to each other and everyone else they know.

Doctrine and Covenants 11:12–27
How do you prepare for a mission?

Have a family member read aloud D&C 11:15. Ask your family what that verse says Hyrum had a desire to do. (Missionary work.) To find out why Hyrum had not yet been called, divide your family into pairs. Have each pair search D&C 11:12–27 together and mark the things the Lord wanted Hyrum to do to prepare before he could be a missionary. While they are searching, write "Preparing for a mission" on the top of a piece of paper.

After a few minutes, have each pair take turns sharing what they found and writing it on the paper. Your list might include the following items:

- Learn to trust the promptings of the Spirit, which will lead you to do justly, walk humbly, and judge righteously. (Verse 12.)
- Learn how the Spirit can "enlighten your mind" and "fill your soul with joy." (See verses 13–14.)
- Attend church and learn the doctrine. (Verse 16. Note that at that time the Church had not yet been organized.)

- Keep the commandments. (Verses 18, 20.)
- Stay close to the Lord. (Verse 19.)
- Learn God's word found in the Bible and the Book of Mormon. (Verses 21–22.)

Challenge your family to prepare to serve missions, whether as full-time missionaries, member missionaries, or as future full-time couple missionaries.

Doctrine and Covenants 11:21–22
What is so important about personal scripture study?

Before scripture study, prepare two pitchers —one empty and the other full of juice, punch, or water. Keep the full pitcher out of sight. Place the empty pitcher in front of your family. While passing out a cup to each family member, explain that they can all enjoy a refreshing drink before scripture study. When they recognize and point out that the pitcher is empty, invite someone to read D&C 11:21–22. Ask:

- What do these verses have to do with the empty pitcher?
- Are there people in the world who are thirsty for the things of the Spirit?
- How is an unprepared Church member or missionary like an empty pitcher?
- How can we quench people's thirst if our pitchers are empty?
- How can we fill our pitchers? (Daily scripture study.)

Invite your family to write the following in their scriptures above verse 21: "The Lord can't pour from an empty pitcher!" Serve your family the drink from the full pitcher and challenge them to fill their pitchers by daily scripture study.

DOCTRINE AND COVENANTS 12: ASSISTING IN THE WORK

Historical background: *Joseph Smith became acquainted with Joseph Knight Sr. while working for Josiah Stoal in 1825 (see JS—H 1:56.) Apparently, the Prophet told Joseph Knight about his sacred experiences, and Brother Knight believed. On September 22, 1827, when the Prophet Joseph went to retrieve the gold plates from the hill Cumorah, he and Emma rode in a wagon loaned to them by Joseph Knight, who waited anxiously at the Smith home for news of their success in obtaining the plates.*

In May of 1829, Joseph Smith and Oliver Cowdery were spending as much time as possible on the translation of the Book of Mormon in Harmony, Pennsylvania. Joseph Smith wrote, "[Joseph Knight] heard of the manner in which we were occupying our time, [and] very kindly and considerately brought us a quantity of provisions, in order that we might not be interrupted in the work of translation by the want of such necessaries of life; and I would just mention here, as in duty bound, that he several times brought us supplies, a distance of at least thirty miles, which enabled us to continue the work when otherwise we must have relinquished it for a season. Being very anxious to know his duty as to this work, I inquired of the Lord for him." (History of the Church, 1:47–48.) The result of that inquiry was what we now have as D&C 12. Notice how the Lord feels about missionaries and missionary work

Doctrine and Covenants 12:1–2
What is sharper than a two-edged sword?

Write or print the words "Truth" and "Error" on a strip of paper so that there is some space between the "h" in "Truth" and the "E" in "Error." On the other side of the paper, write or print the letters from the words "Truth" and "Error" all mixed together (for example, Terrurtohr). Show your family the mixed letters and ask if they can determine what it means. Then take a pair of scissors labeled "The Word of God" and (looking at the back of the wordstrip) cut the paper exactly between the "h" of "Truth" and the "E" of "Error." Turn the papers over and place the two words apart from each other so the whole family can see them. Read together D&C 12:1–2 and ask how this demonstration relates to the verses. (The word of God cuts through the confusion and makes the difference between truth and error clear.)

Invite family members to give examples of how the world is often confused about what is right and what is wrong. Ask:

- Why are the scriptures and the words of living prophets the right place to look to clear up the confusion about what is right and wrong?
- What issues have become clearer because of the "great and marvelous work" of the Restoration? (The importance of the family, the nature of the Godhead, the plan of salvation, and so on.)

Invite family members to share a time when the scriptures, the words of the prophets, or the whisperings of the Holy Spirit helped them see more clearly during a personal choice in their lives. Have your family write Helaman 3:29–30 next to D&C 12:1–2 in their scriptures. Ask someone to read Helaman 3:29–30 aloud. Share your testimony that if we listen to and follow the word of God, we will have the power to see the difference between truth and error, overcome the tricks and traps of Satan, and be led to happiness and eternal life.

Doctrine and Covenants 12:3–4
The field is white!

Because "sickle" and "reap" are words not commonly used today, have a family member look them up in a dictionary and share the meanings. Explain that as a field of grain grows closer to harvest, it gradually loses its green color and turns a golden white color. Have a family member read D&C 12:3–4. Ask:

- What is the Lord trying to tell us about the people of the world?
- What do you think the Lord would like us to do about all those people who need to hear the gospel?

Share the following story:

"In 1840 Wilford Woodruff, then one of the Twelve Apostles, was serving a mission in England and felt impressed to go to a rural district near Ledbury. There he met John Benbow, who had a large farm and a small pond. John introduced him to a congregation of United Brethren who were eager to hear the gospel message. He later recorded in his journal that with no other help at hand on March 7, 1840, 'I spent most of the . . . day in clearing out a pool of water and preparing it for baptizing, as I saw that many would receive that ordinance. I afterwards baptized six hundred persons in that pool of water.'" (James E. Faust, *Ensign*, May 2001, 54.)

Ask your family if they think the "field" is still "white." Share with them the following testimony of President Gordon B. Hinckley:

"There can be no doubt concerning our responsibility to the peoples of the earth. . . .

"It was said that at one time the sun never set on the British Empire. That empire has now been diminished. But it is true that the sun never sets on this work of the Lord as it is touching the lives of people across the earth.

"And this is only the beginning. We have scarcely scratched the surface. We are engaged in a work for the souls of men and women everywhere. Our work knows no boundaries. Under

BIOGRAPHICAL SKETCH: JOSEPH KNIGHT SR.

Joseph Knight Sr. was born November 3, 1772, in Massachusetts. Sometime around 1810, he and his family established a farm in Colesville, New York, where they lived for the next nineteen years. Joseph Sr. was baptized in June 1830 and followed the Saints to Ohio and later to Missouri. As a result of persecutions, Joseph and his family, along with the rest of the Saints, were forced to leave Missouri in the winter of 1838–39 and eventually ended up in Nauvoo. In 1846 he left Nauvoo with the Saints seeking to gather in Winter Quarters, Nebraska, but died at Mt. Pisgah, Iowa, February 2, 1847. While in Nauvoo, Joseph Smith said of Joseph Knight Sr., "Behold, he is a righteous man, . . . and it shall be said of him, by the sons of Zion, while there is one of them remaining that this man was a faithful man in Israel; therefore his name shall never be forgotten." (*History of the Church*, 5:124–25.)

the providence of the Lord it will continue. Those nations now closed to us will someday be open." (Gordon B. Hinckley, *Ensign*, November 2003, 4, 7.)

Ask your family how they feel about what the prophet said concerning this work. Discuss ways your family can be more engaged in "reaping" the harvest spoken of by the Lord.

Doctrine and Covenants 12:6–9
Who can assist in this work?

Ask your family what an "assist" is in the sport of basketball (when one player passes the basketball to another player who then scores). Invite a family member to read Moses 1:39. Ask:

- What is God's work?
- In what ways can we "assist" in God's work?

Read together D&C 12:6–9 and have family members underline qualities needed to "assist" in God's work. Give each family member a blank sheet of paper. Have them write down one of the qualities mentioned in verse 8. Then have them

turn the paper over and write why this quality is needed to help in God's work. After everyone has had time to write, invite each person to show the quality he or she chose and share why it is an important attribute to assist in "bringing to pass" God's work. Challenge your family to work on the qualities they chose.

DOCTRINE AND COVENANTS 13: THE AARONIC PRIESTHOOD RESTORED

Historical background: As Joseph Smith and Oliver Cowdery worked on the translation of the Book of Mormon plates, they discovered that Nephite prophets mentioned the ordinance of baptism several times. The Lord Himself instructed the Nephite disciples concerning this important ordinance. This caused them to ponder and pray about the subject. What then occurred is described in Joseph Smith—History 1:68–74 and in a special footnote to Joseph Smith—History 1:71. Look for the three keys of the Aaronic Priesthood.

Doctrine and Covenants 13:1
The need for authority

Use several small pieces of paper to make some fake coupons for a few businesses near your home that offer products that would be appealing to family members. Examples might include: "Buy one sandwich, get ten free," "Take 90% off any item in the store," or "Buy anything on the menu for ten cents." Then announce to your family that you have some coupons to give away. Distribute the coupons to different family members and ask:

- What do you think would happen if you tried to use your coupon?
- Why wouldn't any of these businesses accept the coupons?
- What if the coupon said, "Get into heaven free!" Do you think the Lord would accept it?

Have family members find the lengthy footnote to Joseph Smith—History 1:71 (pages 58–59 of the Pearl of Great Price), which contains Oliver Cowdery's account of the history behind the restoration of the Aaronic Priesthood. Have them

read the fourth paragraph (which begins, "After writing the account . . ."). Ask them what Joseph Smith and Oliver Cowdery came to realize as they translated the Book of Mormon (authority from God was needed to perform gospel ordinances). Have one family member read aloud Joseph Smith—History 1:68 and another D&C 13:1 to see what happened next. Invite them to write the cross-reference "JS—H 1:68–74 and footnote" in the margin of their scriptures next to the section heading for section 13. Then read the section heading for D&C 13 aloud and ask:

- What authority was restored to the earth on May 15, 1829?
- Who restored it?
- How do we know that John had this authority?

If you have access to a picture showing John the Baptist conferring the Aaronic Priesthood (such as Gospel Art Picture Kit 407), show it as you bear testimony of the reality of this sacred event. You may also want to have one of the better readers in your family read aloud the last paragraph of Oliver Cowdery's testimony on page 59 of the Pearl of Great Price.

Doctrine and Covenants 13:1
The keys of the Aaronic Priesthood

Hold up a ring of keys and ask your family to name the purposes for each key (make sure that "unlocking things" and "turning on the power of some kind of machine" are noted). Have them read D&C 13:1 and find the keys given to Joseph Smith and Oliver Cowdery. Ask some or all of the following questions:

- Which keys belong to the Aaronic Priesthood?
- What things are "unlocked" by the keys of the Aaronic Priesthood?
- What power can be "turned on" in our lives because of these keys?
- What do you think it means that the Aaronic Priesthood holds "keys of the ministering of angels and of the gospel of repentance, and of baptism by immersion for the remission of sins"?

To help your family answer that question, share the following statement by Elder Dallin H. Oaks:

"The meaning is found in the ordinance of baptism and in the sacrament. Baptism is for the remission of sins, and the sacrament is a renewal of the covenants and blessings of baptism. Both should be preceded by repentance. When we keep the covenants made in these ordinances, we are promised that we will always have His Spirit to be with us. The ministering of angels is one of the manifestations of that Spirit." (*Ensign,* November 1998, 39.)

If time permits, share the following story about the Aaronic Priesthood:

"On a trip to Japan it was my privilege to attend a sacrament meeting of the Naha Branch on the island of Okinawa. I was so impressed with the quality of the sacrament service and the reverence and dignity exhibited by the Aaronic Priesthood that when I was called to speak I asked one of the young men to join me at the pulpit. I asked him, 'How do you feel knowing that you hold the priesthood of God?' Not tall enough to see over the pulpit, he raised on his toes so he could see the congregation, then with deep emotion responded: 'It's the greatest honor of my life!'" (Robert L. Backman, in *New Era,* May 2001, 45.)

Elder Reed Smoot, who served as an apostle and a United States senator, said, "If I had to take my choice of being a deacon in The Church of Jesus Christ of Latter-day Saints or being the President of the United States, I would be a deacon." (Bryant S. Hinckley, *The Faith of Our Pioneer Fathers,* 243.)

Ask your family why they think these two people would say such things about the Aaronic Priesthood. Invite them to suggest ways they can more fully feel and experience the power of the Aaronic priesthood, which has been restored to bless their lives in such important ways.

DOCTRINE AND COVENANTS 14: DAVID WHITMER'S DUTY

Historical background: Because of persecution in Harmony, Pennsylvania, Joseph Smith and Oliver Cowdery were unable to focus on the work of translating the Book of Mormon plates. Therefore, the Whitmer family invited Joseph and Emma to live with them in Fayette, New York. They sent David Whitmer to Harmony with a wagon to help with the move. The Whitmers were enthusiastic about the work and supported the Smiths (along with Oliver Cowdery) while the translation continued. During this time, David, John, and Peter Whitmer Jr. wanted to know their responsibility regarding the Lord's work. Joseph inquired of the Lord and received sections 14 through 16. Look for the similarities in the counsel the Lord gave these three men and why he repeated that counsel three times.

Doctrine and Covenants 14:1–4

How does it feel to be part of a "great and marvelous work"?

Write each of the following scripture references on a slip of paper and place them in a jar: 1 Nephi 14:7; 1 Nephi 22:8; 3 Nephi 21:9; D&C 6:1; D&C 11:1; D&C 12:1. Ask family members to draw slips of paper from the jar until it is empty. Have each person read aloud his or her scripture verses. Ask:

- What phrase is found in all of these verses? ("Marvelous work.")
- What "great and marvelous work" do you think is being foretold in these verses? (Consider sharing the following quotation from President Howard W. Hunter: "This church, . . . that had been prophesied to be a latter-day marvelous work and a wonder, has come forth from the most humble of beginnings." [*Ensign,* May 1991, 63.])
- Which of these prophecies is the oldest? (1 Nephi 14:7, about 600 B.C.)
- How does it feel to be a member of a Church that was prophesied to come forth thousands of years ago?
- What do you think the Lord expects of us because we have been given such a wonderful blessing?

Read together D&C 14:1–4 and look for (1) our responsibility as members of the Church, and (2) what the Lord has provided to help us fulfill our latter-day mission. Discuss the following questions as you read:

- What responsibility has the Lord given us? (Give heed to His word and thrust in our sickle.)
- Why should we give heed to God's word? (If we don't, we will be "divided asunder" with the Lord's two-edged sword.)
- Why is a two-edged sword more dangerous than a single-edged one?
- What tool has the Lord provided to harvest the field that is ready to harvest?
- What does it mean to thrust in the sickle and reap?
- What is the harvest that we can reap? (Souls.)

Have one family member draw a two-edged sword and another a sickle. As they display their

Sickle.

drawings, ask your family to review D&C 14:2–4 and then answer the following questions:

- Would you rather have the Lord use the sword as described in verse 2 or let you use the sickle as described in verses 3–4?
- What are some important things we can do to help with the Lord's harvest?

Doctrine and Covenants 14:5–8
Actions that bring blessings

 Write this list of blessings on a poster board or large sheet of paper so all can see it:

- You shall receive.
- Opened unto you.
- Bring forth and establish Zion.
- You shall have eternal life . . . which is the greatest of all the gifts of God.
- Receive the Holy Ghost.
- Stand as a witness of the things of which you shall both hear and see.

Tell your family that D&C 14:5–8 lists what we must do to receive the blessings listed. Read those verses together, and as each action is identified, have family members take turns writing the action on a slip of paper and taping it in front of the matching phrase. Some of the actions they should find are: "ask," "knock," "seek," "keep," "endure," "ask . . . in my name . . . in faith believing," and "declare repentance." Ask:

- Why are the listed blessings worth the actions required to get them?
- What are some of the actions we could be better at in our family?
- Why do you think you would be much happier if the Holy Ghost were a bigger influence in your life?

Doctrine and Covenants 14:7
What is the greatest gift?

Set a wrapped gift in front of your family. Ask:

BIOGRAPHICAL SKETCH: DAVID WHITMER

David Whitmer, son of Peter Whitmer Sr. and Mary Musselman, was born near Harrisburg, Pennsylvania, on January 7, 1805. He was baptized June 1, 1829, became one of the Three Witnesses to the Book of Mormon, and was one of the original six members of the Church. He became president of the High Council in Clay County, Missouri on July 13, 1834, and was later sustained as president of the Saints in Far West. Unfortunately, David eventually failed to heed the Prophet's counsel and was excommunicated April 13, 1838. Though he never returned to the Church, David never denied his witness of the Book of Mormon. He died on January 25, 1888, in Richmond, Missouri.

- What is the greatest gift you have ever received?
- What do you think is the greatest gift a person could receive from Heavenly Father?

Read D&C 14:7 to your family and ask why they think eternal life is the greatest gift. Have everyone read again verse 7 and find two things we must do to obtain this gift. Give each person a sheet of paper. Ask, "If there were an eleventh commandment about enduring to the end, how would it be written?" Have family members write their own eleventh commandment and share their ideas. Post these commandments where your family can see them. D&C 14:7 would be good to memorize as a family.

Doctrine and Covenants 14:9–11
How will the Lord bring forth His light?

Turn out your house lights, light a candle, and read D&C 14:9–11 to your family by candlelight. Ask:

- What did Jesus testify about himself? (He is the Son of God, the creator, and a light in the darkness.)
- What will this "light" bring forth? (The gospel.)
- How is that "light" or "gospel" to be brought forth?

Review with your family the section heading for D&C 14 and the historical background above. Then read D&C 14:11 and ask:

- Who is this revelation to? (David Whitmer.)

- Why was it given?
- What did the Lord want David to assist in doing? (Bringing forth the gospel.)
- What blessing was David promised if he faithfully assisted the Lord?
- How can we also be blessed both temporally and spiritually?

Share your testimony of how the Savior has brought light into your life and of the blessings that have come as you also have assisted in the work of bringing the light of the gospel into the world.

DOCTRINE AND COVENANTS 15: JOHN WHITMER DISCOVERS WHAT IS OF "MOST WORTH"

Historical background: See the historical background for section 14.

Doctrine and Covenants 15:1–6
What is of "most worth unto you"?

Have your family sit close enough to each other that they will be able to whisper into the ear of the person next to them. Tell them you are going to play the telephone game. Begin the game by whispering something that has to do with missionary work in the ear of the person to your right (for example, "The gospel will be preached to every kindred, tongue, and people"). Have that person whisper the same message to the next family member. This should continue until all have heard the message. Ask the last person to repeat out loud what he or she heard. Then share what the original message was. It is likely that the message changed. If so, ask the follow questions:

- Why did the message change?
- What might have kept the message from changing?
- Why is it important to get an important message directly from the source?
- Who is the source of all truth? (See Alma 38:9.)

Take turns reading D&C 15:1–6. Invite your family to look for the message of "most worth" that was given to John Whitmer and underline it. Ask:

- What message of most worth did John receive from the Lord?
- Why would missionary work be considered the thing of "most worth"?
- Why do you think teaching repentance is such an important message?

To help answer that question, ask someone to read the following statement from President Ezra Taft Benson:

"Missionaries are engaged in the greatest work in all the world—saving the souls of our Father in Heaven's children." (*The Teachings of Ezra Taft Benson*, 190.)

Discuss the following questions:

- What words do returned missionaries use to describe how they felt about doing missionary work? (Happy, joy, love—see D&C 18:15.)

BIOGRAPHICAL SKETCH: JOHN WHITMER

John Whitmer was the son of Peter Whitmer Sr. and Mary Musselman. He was born on August 27, 1802, in Fayette, New York. John met Joseph Smith when he and Emma and Oliver Cowdery came to live in their home. Some of his Church experience included: acted as Joseph's scribe for the inspired translation of the Bible; called as Church Historian (see D&C 47:1, John served faithfully for a short time writing ninety-six pages of early Church history); carried (with Oliver Cowdery) Joseph's written revelations to Independence, Missouri, to be printed as the Book of Commandments (the predecessor to the Doctrine and Covenants). As the Saints migrated to Missouri, John was called as an agent to purchase lands for them to settle on. He misused the Lord's money and was excommunicated on March 10, 1838. Bitter over his excommunication, John refused to return the history he had written. When the Saints fled to Far West, he bought their lands, taking advantage of the cheap prices, and remained there until his death on July 11, 1878.

- Would you like to have that kind of joy in your life?
- Can you think of anything that would be of greater "worth" than eternal happiness?
- What could we do as a family to have more of that joy?

Give a sheet of paper and pencil to each person. Invite your family to make a list of people they know who may be receptive to hearing more about the Church. Narrow the list to one family or person. As appropriate, find an opportunity to befriend that family and then, when the time is right, invite them to a family home evening or other activity where you can introduce them to the gospel. You could also give their name to the missionaries. Ask the missionaries to let you know how their visit went. Share your testimony with your family about the importance of missionary work.

DOCTRINE AND COVENANTS 16: PETER WHITMER JR. DESIRES TO KNOW THE WILL OF THE LORD FOR HIM

Historical background: See the historical background for section 14.

BIOGRAPHICAL SKETCH: PETER WHITMER JR.

Peter Whitmer Jr. cabin.

Peter Whitmer Jr. was born to Peter Whitmer Sr. and Mary Musselman on September 27, 1809, in Fayette, New York. In the summer of 1829, young Peter became acquainted with Joseph Smith when Joseph and Emma and Oliver Cowdery came to live with them in Fayette. Peter was one of the first elders ordained in the latter days, and in September 1830 he was called by revelation to preach the gospel. (See D&C 30:5–6.) One month later, Peter, along with Parley P. Pratt, Oliver Cowdery, and Ziba Peterson, went on the first mission to the Lamanites. (See D&C 32:2.) After this mission Peter stayed in Independence, Missouri, where he began a trade as a tailor. Peter and his family suffered greatly from the mobbings in Jackson County, Missouri, and were forced to flee to Clay County. As a result of this stress and exposure, Peter contracted tuberculosis and infection. He died near Liberty, Clay County, Missouri, on September 22, 1836, still true to the faith.

Doctrine and Covenants 16:1–6
What does it mean to hearken?

Invite your family to identify the first word in D&C 15 and 16. Write the word

"HEARKEN" in large letters on a sheet of paper and show it to your family. Ask them what they think it means. Cross out the first letter and fifth through seventh letters (H̶EAR̶K̶E̶N). Ask:

- How does this help explain what the word "hearken" might mean?
- What part does the ear play in hearkening to the Lord?

Explain that to hearken means so much more than simply listening. Share the following definition: "HE'ARKEN, *v. i. h'arken.* [Saxon *heorcnian, hyrcnian;* German *horchen.*]

"1. To listen; to lend the ear; to attend to what is uttered, with eagerness or curiosity. 2. To attend; to regard; to give heed to what is uttered; to observe or obey. 3. To listen; to attend; to grant or comply with." (Webster, *An American Dictionary of the English Language,* 1828 edition, s.v. "hearken.")

Ask, "According to this definition, what was the Lord expecting Peter Whitmer to do?" (Listen with eagerness and obey.) Read D&C 16:2–6 and find what the Lord wanted Peter to hearken to. Share the biographical sketch above about Peter Whitmer Jr. Then ask:

- How well would you say Peter "hearkened" to the Lord?
- What did he do to show that he listened and obeyed?
- How can we better "hearken" to the Lord's counsel?

DOCTRINE AND COVENANTS 17: THE THREE WITNESSES

Historical background: *Joseph Smith learned from translating the gold plates that three witnesses would be chosen to see the plates. He wrote, "Almost immediately after we had made this discovery, it occurred to Oliver Cowdery, David Whitmer and the aforementioned Martin Harris (who had come to inquire after our progress in the work) that they would have me inquire of the Lord to know if they might not obtain of him the privilege to be these three special witnesses; and finally they became so very solicitous, and urged me so much to inquire that at length I complied; and through the Urim and Thummim, I obtained of the Lord for them the following." (History of the Church, 1:52–53.) Look for what the Three Witnesses would be able to see.*

Doctrine and Covenants 17:1
What did the Three Witnesses see?

Write the following words or phrases on separate slips of paper: "Gold plates," "breastplate," "sword of Laban," "Urim and Thummim," "Liahona," and "angel."

Give each family member one or more slips of paper. Have them take turns describing that item to the rest of the family (without saying the word on the slip of paper) until someone guesses what the item is.

When each item has been guessed, have your family guess what these items have in common. To find out, read the section heading for D&C 17; D&C 17:1; and the "Testimony of the Three Witnesses" at the beginning of the Book of Mormon. Ask your family how they would feel if they were given an opportunity to see those sacred things.

Doctrine and Covenants 17:2–6
Why was it so important to have additional witnesses?

Read D&C 17:2–6 with your family and have them look for reasons why it would be important that additional witnesses be called to see and testify about the gold plates. Ask:

- How do witnesses besides Joseph Smith help when teaching people about the Book of Mormon?

- How would these witnesses help protect Joseph from being "destroyed"?

Share the following account by Joseph's mother:

"On coming in, Joseph threw himself down beside me, and exclaimed, 'Father, mother, you do not know how happy I am: the Lord has now caused the plates to be shown to three more besides myself. They have seen an angel, who has testified to them, and they will have to bear witness to the truth of what I have said, for now they know for themselves, that I do not go about to deceive the people, and I feel as if I was relieved of a burden which was almost too heavy for me to bear, and it rejoices my soul, that I am not any longer to be entirely alone in the world.'" (Lucy Mack Smith, *History of Joseph Smith*, 152–53.)

Explain to your family that besides these three witnesses, eight others also were allowed to view the plates. Together, read "The Testimony of Eight Witnesses" in the front of the Book of Mormon. Talk about similarities and differences between the experience of the Three Witnesses and the experience of the Eight Witnesses. Discuss some of the following questions:

- Why do you think having additional witnesses has helped further the cause of the Book of Mormon?
- Would it be possible to be a "witness" of the Book of Mormon without actually seeing the

gold plates? How? (Yes, by receiving a testimony of its truthfulness.)

- When have you heard someone share a testimony of the Book of Mormon?
- How strong is your testimony regarding that sacred book?
- What can you do to strengthen your witness?

Doctrine and Covenants 17:7–9
Did the Three Witnesses stay faithful?

Read D&C 17:7–9 and look for the blessings promised to the Three Witnesses.

Show the following chart to your family and ask the accompanying questions:

- Do you think it would have been easier or harder to remain faithful if you were able to be a witness of the gold plates? Why?
- Does the fact that the witnesses left the Church cast doubt on the fact that the gold plates actually existed? Why not?
- How does the fact that the Three Witnesses lost fellowship in the Church but never denied their testimony make their witness even stronger?

Witness	Did he ever become disaffected from the Church?	Was he ever rebaptized?	Did he ever deny his testimony of the Book of Mormon?
Oliver Cowdery	Yes, excommunicated April 12, 1838	Yes, November 1848	No
David Whitmer	Yes, excommunicated April 13, 1838	No	No
Martin Harris	Yes, disfellowshipped September 1837	Yes, September 17, 1870	No

DOCTRINE AND COVENANTS 18: THE WORTH OF SOULS

Historical background: Joseph Smith and Oliver Cowdery had previously received the Aaronic Priesthood from John the Baptist. (See D&C 13.) They were told if they remained faithful, they would receive the Melchizedek Priesthood. Joseph Fielding Smith explained, "Before the Church could be organized it was essential that there be revealed such matters as pertained to the organization of the Church. This was done between the time the witnesses viewed the plates of the ancient record and the sixth of April, 1830. The first of these (D&C Sec. 18) was given to Joseph Smith, Oliver Cowdery and David Whitmer, at Fayette." (Essentials in Church History, 84–85.) Look for what responsibilities the Twelve Apostles will have.

Doctrine and Covenants 18:1–8
What should we rely upon?

Have your family identify some activities that require complete reliance on equipment (scuba diving, rappelling, skydiving, and so on). Talk about the importance of that equipment

to the person using it. Invite a family member to read D&C 18:1–4. Ask:

- What was Oliver commanded to rely upon?
- What written words do we have "concerning the foundation of [the Lord's] Church"? (Scriptures, words of the living prophets.)

- What other spiritual "equipment" have you found useful in your life?

Read D&C 18:6–8 and discuss some of the following questions:

- What do you think the phrase "the world is ripening in iniquity" means?
- What evidences do you see that this is true today?
- What did the Lord teach we should do as the world ripens in iniquity?
- How would relying on that which is "written" help us in these days?
- What could you do to improve your daily scripture study?

Doctrine and Covenants 18:9–16
"The worth of souls is great"

Display several items, some of great value and others of little value (a diamond ring, a video camera, a piece of candy, a souvenir, and so on). Ask your family to guess how much each of these items is worth and place an appropriate "price tag" on each one. Ask:

- Who determines the value of something?
- Why would you be willing to pay more for some of these items than for others?
- What is the highest price you would pay for the most valuable of these items?

Now display a picture of your family. Talk about how "valuable" each of you are, and why Heavenly Father's children could be considered "of great worth." Read D&C 18:9–16 together and discuss the following questions:

- Who declared that "the worth of souls is great"?
- What "price" has been paid for each of us? (Jesus Christ gave His life for us.)
- How does the Atonement help prove our individual worth?
- What obligation do we have because God values His children so much? (Help bring all people into the Kingdom of God.)

- Why do you think great joy comes when you help others repent?

Share your love and appreciation for each family member. Testify of God's love for your family, and share why you hope that all of your family is saved in the kingdom of God.

Doctrine and Covenants 18:17–25; 42–47
How strong is your foundation?

Place a very light object in front of a family member (for example, a feather, a small piece of paper, or a leaf). Have that person blow the object off the table. Now place a slightly heavier object (such as a small rock or a piece of candy) in front of that person and ask him or her to blow it off the table. Finally, place a large object (such as a big rock, book, or plate) on the table. Invite the same person to blow this off, even using the help of other family members. Discuss the following questions:

- How might these objects represent our testimonies?
- Which objects would represent a stronger testimony?
- What are some examples of influences that "blow against" or try to knock down our testimonies?
- What does Helaman 5:12 teach about this idea?

Read D&C 18:5 aloud and find the rock upon which we should build our foundation. Explain to your family that section 18 teaches us ways we can strengthen our individual testimonies. Ask family members to search D&C 18:17–25, 42–47 and identify every item they think would help strengthen our testimonies. When they are all finished, have them share what items they identified and how those items would help build a person's testimony.

Doctrine and Covenants 18:26–41
The calling of the Twelve

Explain to your family that "nearly six years before the calling of the Twelve Apostles in this dispensation, and several months before the organization of the Church, the Lord indicated that a council of twelve Apostles would be chosen, and Oliver Cowdery and David Whitmer were informed that it was to be their privilege to choose out the Twelve and instruct them in the duties of their calling." (Joseph Fielding Smith, *Church History and Modern Revelation,* 1:80; see also D&C 18:26–27, 37.)

Show a picture of the current Quorum of the Twelve Apostles from the May or November *Ensign.* See if family members can name the apostles from their pictures. Talk about your feelings concerning the apostles, their talks you have heard, or your testimony of their calling. Ask family members to discuss what they think might be some of the duties of an apostle. Take turns reading D&C 18:26–39. Then ask:

- What apostolic responsibilities do you think are most interesting? Why?
- What part of their responsibilities do you think would be most difficult? Why?
- How were Oliver Cowdery and David Whitmer to know whom to call?
- What Article of Faith teaches us how apostles are called today? (Number 5.)

DOCTRINE AND COVENANTS 19: ETERNAL PUNISHMENT AND THE ATONEMENT

Historical background: Little information is given concerning the circumstances surrounding the receiving of this revelation other than that provided in the section heading. Elder B. H. Roberts wrote, "No words of the Prophet introduce this revelation in his History. Nothing is known of the circumstances which called it forth. And yet there are few revelations that have been given in the present dispensation of the Gospel more important than this one. The doctrine of the atonement of the Lord Jesus, as directly applying to the individual, and God's exposition of 'Eternal Punishment' as here set forth, give it a place of first importance in the doctrinal development of the Church." (History of the Church, 1:72 footnote.) Look for what the Lord teaches us aobut the words "eternal" and "endless."

Doctrine and Covenants 19:1–4
"Alpha and Omega"

Draw the two Greek letters shown here on a larger piece of paper and show them to your family. $A\Omega$ Ask if anyone knows what they are. If no one does, read D&C 19:1 together for help. Explain that alpha and omega are the first and last letters of the Greek alphabet. Read together D&C 19:1–4. Ask:

- Why is "Alpha and Omega" a good description of the Savior?

- What other titles are used for the Savior in these verses?
- What do these verses teach us about the powers the Savior possesses?
- What other important characteristics do these verses teach about the Savior?
- Why do you think it is important to know these characteristics of Jesus Christ?

Doctrine and Covenants 19:4–12
How long does "endless punishment" last?

Make a label for each member of your family with their name on it. Ask each

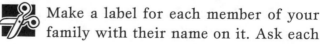

family member to quickly find an item that belongs to them, put their label on it, and bring it to show the family. After all have gathered, identify some of the items using the person's name that owns it. For example, you may say: "This is Dad's tie," or "This is Andy's ball." Explain that we often use our names to identify our things.

Think of some characteristics that are particular to members of your family (such as: happy, thoughtful, a tease, helpful, etc.). Use the following questions substituting different characteristics that fit your family members.

- "If I say (happy), which family member do you think of?
- "If I say (a tease), which family member do you think of?
- "If I say (helpful), which family member do you think of?

Explain that our names can also be used to describe our characteristics. Ask your family to keep names and characteristics in mind as you study D&C 19:4–12. Discuss the following questions after you have finished reading.

- What happens to those who do not repent? (Verses 4–5.)
- What is another name for "endless punishment" and "eternal punishment." (God's punishment—verses 11–12.)
- Why is "endless torment" not the same thing as "torment that never ends"? (Verses 6–10.)
- Why is it called "eternal damnation" if it does not last for eternity? (Verse 7.)
- How do the truths taught in these verses show God's love for His children?

Doctrine and Covenants 19:13–20
The blessings of the Atonement

Ask your family to fill in the blanks in the following statement by referring to the section heading. "Joseph Smith introduced this revelation as a (commandment) of God to (Martin Harris). Have family members read D&C

19:13–20 and mark in their scriptures each time they find the word "command." Ask:

- How many times in these verses is Martin Harris commanded to repent?
- Do you think what the Lord said here could be applied to anyone besides Martin Harris?

Show a picture of Jesus praying in Gethsemane, such as Gospel Art Picture Kit 227. Have a family member read aloud D&C 19:16–19. Ask:

- For whom did Jesus suffer in the garden of Gethsemane?
- How difficult was His suffering?
- What must we do so that His suffering will save us from suffering the same way?

Share any of the following statements from the prophets you feel would be helpful:

"Christ's agony in the garden is unfathomable by the finite mind, both as to intensity and cause. . . . He struggled and groaned under a burden such as no other being who has lived on earth might even conceive as possible. It was not physical pain, nor mental anguish alone, that caused him to suffer such torture as to produce an extrusion of blood from every pore; but a spiritual agony of soul such as only God was capable of experiencing. . . . In that hour of anguish Christ met and overcame all the horrors that Satan, 'the prince of this world,' could inflict. . . . In some manner, actual and terribly real though to man incomprehensible, the Savior took upon Himself the burden of the sins of mankind from Adam to the end of the world." (James E. Talmage, *Jesus the Christ,* 613.)

"We may never understand nor comprehend in mortality *how* He accomplished what He did, but we must not fail to understand *why* He did what He did. . . . Everything He did was prompted by His unselfish, infinite love for us." (Ezra Taft Benson, in *Ensign,* November 1983, 6.)

"This obviously means that the unrepentant transgressor must suffer for his own sins. Does it also mean that a person who repents does not need to suffer at all because the entire punishment is borne by the Savior? That cannot be the meaning because it would be inconsistent with the Savior's other teachings. What is meant is that the person who repents does not need to suffer 'even as' the Savior suffered for that sin. Sinners who are repenting will experience some suffering, but because of their repentance and the Atonement, they will not experience the full, 'exquisite' extent of eternal torment the Savior suffered. President Spencer W. Kimball, who gave such comprehensive teachings on repentance and forgiveness, said that personal suffering 'is a very important part of repentance. One has not begun to repent until he has suffered intensely for his sins. . . . If a person hasn't suffered, he hasn't repented.'" (Dallin H. Oaks, in *Ensign,* July 1992, 70.)

Allow family members to share their feelings about the Atonement and their love for Jesus Christ. Sing together "I Stand All Amazed" (*Hymns,* no. 193).

Doctrine and Covenants 19:21–41
"Find the verse"

Write each of the following words on separate slips of paper: "peace," "covet," "vocally," "debt," and "always." Put the slips of paper in a small container and have family members draw out the slips. Explain that the words they have selected are found in D&C 19:21–41 and that their task is to find the word, tell which verse it is in, and explain to the rest of the family what is being taught in that verse. ("peace"—verse 23; "covet"—verses 25–26; "vocally"—verse 28; "debt"—verse 35; "always"—verse 38.)

DOCTRINE AND COVENANTS 20: THE ARTICLES AND COVENANTS OF THE CHURCH

Historical background: Joseph Smith received many revelations concerning the governing of the Lord's Church before the Church was organized on April 6, 1830. These revelations were compiled and called the "Articles and Covenants" of the Church. They contained doctrinal statements, historical information, and Church policies. "At the first conference of the Church held in Fayette, New York, on 9 June 1830, Doctrine and Covenants 20 was read to the members and unanimously sustained as the articles and covenants of the Church of Christ, thus making it the first revelation of this dispensation to be formally presented to and sustained by its members. . . . This section served as the first priesthood manual or handbook for the Church." (Stephen E. Robinson and H. Dean Garrett, A Commentary on the Doctrine and Covenants, *1:128.) Notice what the Lord said about the purpose of the Book of Mormon.*

D&C 20:1–4
"The precise day"

Share the historical background above with your family, and then have someone read aloud the section heading to D&C 20. Ask:

- What did the Prophet say the Lord gave them as a part of this revelation?

- What was the Lord referring to when He spoke of a "precise day"?
- Have someone read D&C 20:1 to find what that "precise day" was.
- Why was April 6 the particular day the Lord chose for the organization of the Church?

To help answer that question, read the following from President Harold B. Lee:

"[April 6] is a particularly significant date because it commemorates not only the anniversary of the organization of The Church of Jesus Christ of Latter-day Saints in this dispensation, but also the anniversary of the birth of the Savior, our Lord and Master, Jesus Christ." (*Ensign,* July 1973, 2.)

Have family members read D&C 20:2–4 and look for reasons why Joseph Smith and Oliver Cowdery were chosen to organize the Church. (For example, they were commanded to, they were called of God and ordained apostles, and they received grace or help from the Savior.) How do these reasons make The Church of Jesus Christ of Latter-day Saints different from all other churches on the earth today?

Doctrine and Covenants 20:5–16
What is the purpose of the Book of Mormon?

Choose two family members to do a short role-play. Have one of them ask the other, "Why do you think the Book of Mormon is valuable? What does it teach? Why is it important to your Church?" Let the other person answer. Next, have other family members offer suggestions of what they liked about the explanation and what they would change or add to what was said.

Have your family take turns reading aloud D&C 20:8–16 and have them look for more reasons the Book of Mormon is so important. When you have finished reading, discuss any of the following questions you think would be helpful:

- How did Joseph Smith find out about the Book of Mormon? (Verses 6–8.)
- By what power was the Book of Mormon translated? (Verse 8.)
- What important information does the Book of Mormon contain? (Verse 9.)
- How did the Book of Mormon writers get that information? (Verse 10.)
- What does the Book of Mormon "prove" and "show"? (Verses 11–12.)
- What will happen to those who accept the Book of Mormon? (Verses 13–14.)

- What will happen to those who reject it? (Verse 15.)

Share with your family the following statement about the significance of the Book of Mormon in the organization of the Church:

"A second powerful testimony to the importance of the Book of Mormon is to note where the Lord placed its coming forth in the timetable of the unfolding Restoration. The only thing that preceded it was the First Vision. In that marvelous manifestation, the Prophet Joseph Smith learned the true nature of God and that God had a work for him to do. The coming forth of the Book of Mormon was the next thing to follow.

"Think of that in terms of what it implies. The coming forth of the Book of Mormon preceded the restoration of the priesthood. It was published just a few days before the Church was organized. The Saints were given the Book of Mormon to read before they were given the revelations outlining such great doctrines as the three degrees of glory, celestial marriage, or work for the dead. It came before priesthood quorums and Church organization. Doesn't this tell us something about how the Lord views this sacred work?" (Ezra Taft Benson, *Ensign,* November 1986, 4.)

Tell your family how you feel about the Book of Mormon and how the principles it teaches have blessed your life.

Doctrine and Covenants 20:17–28
The three pillars of eternity

Display a copy of the Book of Mormon. Ask your family why it is titled "Another Testament of Jesus Christ." Show your family the picture of a pillar on the next page, or display one built from stackable toys. Ask:

- What does a pillar provide to a building? (Support.)
- What would happen if a building's pillars were removed?

Share the following statement from Elder Bruce R. McConkie:

"God himself . . . ordained and established a plan of salvation whereby his spirit children might advance and progress and become like him. It is the gospel of God, the plan . . . that saves and exalts, and it consists of three things. These three are the very pillars of eternity itself. They are the most important events that ever have or will occur in all eternity." (*Sermons and Writings of Bruce R. McConkie,* 177.)

Have your family read D&C 20:17–28 and make a list of the important truths and events the Lord says are taught in the Book of Mormon. Ask someone to tell which events on the list they think are the most important "pillars" of the gospel that Elder McConkie was referring to. Ask the rest of the family if they agree with those choices and have them explain why.

To help answer that question, tell your family that Elder McConkie went on to say the following:

"Be it known, then, that salvation is in Christ and comes because of his atoning sacrifice. The atonement of the Lord Jesus Christ is the heart and core and center of revealed religion. . . . [See D&C 20:21–27.]

"But, be it remembered, the Atonement came because of the Fall. Christ paid the ransom for Adam's transgression. If there had been no Fall, there would be no Atonement with its consequent immortality and eternal life. . . . [See D&C 20:19–20.]

"And be it also remembered that the Fall was made possible because an infinite Creator, in the primeval day, made the earth and man and all forms of life in such a state that they could fall. This fall involved a change of status. All things were so created that they could fall or change, and thus was introduced the type and kind of existence needed to put into operation all the terms and conditions of the Father's eternal plan of salvation. [See D&C 20:17–18.]" (*Sermons and Writings of Bruce R. McConkie,* 178.)

Discuss the following questions to help your family understand what Elder McConkie was teaching:

- Why is it important to know that there is a God and that He created all things?
- If there was no creation, what would that mean for Adam and Eve and the Fall? (Adam and Eve would not have been created, and there would have been no Fall.)
- If there had been no Fall, what would that mean for the Savior? (If there had been no Fall, we would not need a Savior.)

Share your testimony of the truth of these three events and the blessings that are ours because of the Creation, the Fall, and the Atonement.

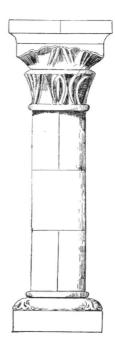

A pillar.

Doctrine and Covenants 20:29–36
What are justification and sanctification?

On a sheet of paper write "justification" and "sanctification." Cut the letters out but keep the letters that make up each word in separate piles. Divide your family in half and give each group one of the piles of letters. Tell them that each pile makes up a single word. They are to put the letters in the proper order to form that word. Let them struggle with this for a while; then ask if they would like a clue. Tell them that these words can be found in D&C 20:29–36. After each has put their letters together forming "justification" and "sanctification," explain the meaning of each using the following definitions:

Justification: "What then is the law of justification? It is simply this: 'All covenants, contracts, bonds, obligations, oaths, vows, performances, connections, associations, or expectations' (D. & C. 132:7), in which men must abide to be saved and exalted, must be entered into and performed in righteousness so that the Holy Spirit can justify the candidate for salvation in what has been done. (1 Ne. 16:2; Jac. 2:13–14; Alma 41:15; D. & C. 98; 132:1, 62.) An act that is justified by the Spirit is one that is sealed by the Holy Spirit of Promise, or in other words, ratified and approved by the Holy Ghost." (Bruce R. McConkie, *Mormon Doctrine,* 408.)

Sanctification: "To be sanctified is to become clean, pure, and spotless; to be free from the blood and sins of the world; to become a new creature of the Holy Ghost, one whose body has been renewed by the rebirth of the Spirit." (Bruce R. McConkie, *Mormon Doctrine,* 675.)

Doctrine and Covenants 20:37
What are the requirements for baptism?

Ask a family member to imagine himself or herself as a missionary interviewing someone for baptism. Using D&C 20:37 as a guide, create a list of questions to ask that would help you know if the person is ready according the instructions of the Lord. Also read Mosiah 18:8–10 together and find additional responsibilities people take upon themselves when they are baptized. Talk about ways your family can better fill those responsibilities.

Doctrine and Covenants 20:38–59
What are the duties of the different offices of the priesthood?

Ask a priesthood holder in your family to briefly explain the duties of a deacon, a teacher, a priest, and an elder to the other family members.

Tell your family that a more detailed list of duties is found in D&C 20:38–59. If possible, divide your family into four groups. Assign each group to find and make a list of the duties of one of the following priesthood offices:

1. Elders. (Verses 38–45.)
2. Priests. (Verses 46–52.)
3. Teachers. (Verses 53–57.)
4. Deacons. (Verses 58–59.)

When each group has completed their list, collect all the lists and play the game "Who am I?" Read the duties from their lists and see who can guess which priesthood office is being described. For example, you might read the following points for a teacher:

I am to watch over the church and strengthen them.

I am supposed to see that all the members do their duty.

I am to see that there is no evil speaking or backbiting in the Church.

I take the lead if no elder or priest is there.

Who am I?

Doctrine and Covenants 20:60–67
How are priesthood leaders chosen?

Ask your family if they can explain how the bishop of your ward was chosen. Tell your family that D&C 20:60–67 explains how all priesthood leaders are chosen. Ask your family the following questions and have them find the answers in the accompanying verses:

- Who calls priesthood leaders in the Church? (See verse 60 and Articles of Faith 1:5.)
- Who ordains priesthood leaders in the Church? (See verse 60 and Articles of Faith 1:5.)
- What meetings are we commanded to hold besides our weekly sacrament meetings? (See verses 61–62.)
- How many different kinds of conferences do

we hold each year? (General conference, stake conference, and ward conference.)

- What do we do in our Church meetings and conferences to be obedient to the instructions in verses 63–64? (Every priesthood holder must be sustained by the vote of his ward before he can be ordained and receive his certificate of ordination.)
- What else do we do in ward, stake, and general conferences each year that fulfills the instructions in verse 65? (We vote to sustain all our ward, stake, and general Church leaders. This is called the Law of Common Consent. [See D&C 26:2.])

Doctrine and Covenants 20:68–84
What is the counsel given to Church members on blessings and ordinances?

Tell your family that D&C 20:68–84 contains instructions from the Lord on a number of items of Church organization. Assign the following blocks of verses to your family members (D&C 20:68–69; D&C 20:70–74; D&C 20:75–77; D&C 20:78–79; D&C 20:80–84.) Have them study their assigned verses and report back to the family what the Lord taught there. After all have reported, use the questions below to help your family discuss the importance of the Lord's counsel in those verses:

D&C 20:68–69

- What are some reasons why it would be important to continue teaching the gospel to new members of the Church even after their baptism?

D&C 20:70–74

- What ordinance do we perform in the Church that fulfills the Lord's instructions in verse 70?
- What does this teach us about the importance of priesthood blessings?
- What do we learn in these verses about why we do not baptize infants? (See verse 71.)
- Why do you think the Lord mentions twice in verse 73 that baptism must be performed by one who has the proper authority?
- What lesson do you think the Lord wants us to learn by requiring that baptism be done by immersion (meaning being placed completely under the water)?

D&C 20:75–79

- What do you think are the two or three most important words or phrases in the sacrament prayers?
- What do we promise to do when we partake of the sacrament, and what does God promise us in return?
- Is it worth doing what we promise to receive what the Lord promises?
- Why do you think Elder Joseph Fielding Smith said that sacrament meeting is "the most sacred, the most holy, of all the meetings of the Church." (*Doctrines of Salvation,* 2:340)?

D&C 20:80–84

- Why do you think the Lord requires that we keep a careful record of who joins the Church and who is expelled (removed) from the Church?

DOCTRINE AND COVENANTS 21: CHURCH ORGANIZATION

Historical background: As commanded by the Lord (see D&C 20:1–4), Joseph Smith invited all who had come to believe in the Restoration to gather on April 6, 1830, and organize the Lord's church in the latter days. Although twenty to thirty people were likely in attendance at the Whitmer home in Fayette, six men who had previously been baptized were chosen to sign the legal documents required by the State of New York to officially organize a church. The meeting went as outlined in the section heading of D&C 21. Joseph Smith and Oliver Cowdery laid their hands on those who had been previously baptized to confirm them members of the Church and bestow the gift of the Holy Ghost. The Prophet said, "The Holy Ghost was poured out upon us to a very great degree—some prophesied, whilst we all praised the Lord, and rejoiced exceedingly." (History of the Church, 1:78.) In the midst of this spiritual outpouring, the Prophet received the revelation recorded in section 21. Notice the responsibilities the Lord places on the Prophet.

Doctrine and Covenants 21
Important historical details

Show the following list to your family, or write the following phrases on a paper or board where all can see:

1. Unanimous vote to organize.
2. Baptized six people.
3. Oliver Cowdery ordained Joseph Smith.
4. April 8, 1830.
5. Sacrament was administered.
6. Smith home in Palmyra, New York.
7. Joseph and Oliver sustained as presiding officers of the Church.
8. Some were confirmed and received the Holy Ghost.

Ask your family to read the section heading to D&C 21 and determine whether or not each phrase is an accurate detail of the history related to the organization of the Church and D&C 21. When they determine that a detail is inaccurate, have them change it so that it accurately describes historical detail.

To help your family visualize this important day in the restoration of the true church in the latter days, you may want to view that part of the video *Restoration of the Priesthood* (available in Church meetinghouse libraries) that depicts the events of April 6, 1830.

Doctrine and Covenants 21:1–2
What is a seer, a translator, a prophet, an apostle, and an elder?

The chart on the following page lists groups of words and phrases describing the titles the Lord gave Joseph Smith. Show each description to your family and have them find the word that matches the description from D&C 21:1. Have them use their Bible Dictionary if they need help.

Invite everyone to underline in D&C 21:1 all of the titles by which Joseph Smith is known. Then ask:

- How did Joseph Smith act in that specific role (of apostle, prophet, elder, and so on)?
- Which of those roles has the current prophet functioned in?
- Can the current prophet fulfill all those functions as the need arises?

Bear your testimony that the president of the Church holds all the keys of God's power that have been restored to the earth at this time.

Doctrine and Covenants 21:4–9
Overcoming "hell" and "darkness" in our lives

Give red pencils to your family and have them mark everything they can find in

Description	Title from D&C 21:1
God's messenger. Preserves and edits records, denounces sin, foretells punishment, and is a preacher of righteousness. (See BD, 754.)	Prophet.
Revelator and prophet. Uses the Urim and Thummim. Greater than a prophet. (See BD, 771.)	Seer.
One sent forth as a special witness of Jesus Christ. Part of an administrative body. A personal, select representative of God. (See BD, 612.)	Apostle.
Older men in a tribe entrusted with governing or ruling others. Ordained in Old Testament times. A priesthood office in New Testament times. (See BD, 662.)	Elder.
One who translates one language into another.	Translator.

verses 4–9 that describe what Joseph Smith did for the Church and the ways the Lord blessed him. (These will include "words and commandments which he shall give unto you as he receiveth them"; "inspired to move the cause of Zion in mighty power for good"; "his diligence I know"; "his prayers I have heard"; "his weeping for Zion"; "shall mourn no longer"; "his days of rejoicing are come unto the remission of his sins and the manifestations of my blessings upon his works"; "all those who labor . . . shall believe on his words"; and "words . . . given him through me by the Comforter.")

Ask a couple of family members to tell which of the things they marked impressed them most and why. Ask, "Do you think the current prophet feels the same way about the Church?"

Have your family mark (in a different color if possible) everything they can find in verses 4–9 that tells how we should regard the instructions from the president of the Church. ("Give heed unto all his words and commandments"; "walking in all holiness"; "his word ye shall receive, as if from mine own mouth in all patience and faith"; "believe on his words"; and "contrite heart.")

When they are finished, have them circle the word "all" each time it occurs in verses 4–5. Ask family members what they think they should learn from the repeated use of the word "all" in these verses—especially as it relates to following the prophet.

Finally, with a third color, have your family mark the blessings God promises us in connection with living prophets. ("The gates of hell shall not prevail against you"; "disperse the powers of darkness from before you"; "cause the heavens to shake for your good and his name's glory"; "remission of sins.")

Invite family members to tell how they are currently experiencing, or have in the past experienced, one of the blessings they underlined in association with receiving counsel from the president of the Church. Sing as a family "We Thank Thee, O God, for a Prophet." (*Hymns*, no. 19.)

Doctrine and Covenants 21:9

What is the role of the Comforter?

Read D&C 21:9 with your family. Then ask:

- What is the first thing mentioned in that verse that the Holy Ghost (or Comforter) did for Joseph Smith? (Revealed the words of Christ.)

- What else was Joseph told by the Holy Ghost? (That Jesus was crucified for the sins of the world.)
- What must we do so that Christ's sacrifice will cover our sins? (Have a contrite heart.)
- What does it mean to have a contrite heart?

(To be repentant, "broken in spirit" [*Webster's New Dictionary,* s.v. "contrite"].)

Give family members a sheet of paper and ask them to draw a broken heart. Have them write on the inside of their drawing things they can do to keep their hearts repentant. Encourage them to hang their drawings in their rooms.

DOCTRINE AND COVENANTS 22: THE NEW AND EVERLASTING COVENANT OF BAPTISM

Historical background: The first people to accept the message of the Restoration already believed in Christ. Many belonged to a Christian church and had accepted some form of baptism. In those days, as well as today, baptisms performed in one church were often accepted by another church. Orson Pratt said that shortly after the organization of the Church on April 6, 1830, a few people, who were "very moral and no doubt as good people as you could find anywhere, . . . came, saying they believed in the Book of Mormon, and that they had been baptized into [a different church], and that they wished to come into our Church [without being rebaptized]." (Journal of Discourses, 16:293.) Joseph Smith asked the Lord for understanding on the matter and received the revelation found in D&C 22.

Doctrine and Covenants 22:1–4
The need for baptism by proper authority

Tell your family that since things are so busy at the local government office that issues driver's licenses and license plates for vehicles, you have decided to help. Share your intent to start issuing licenses for drivers and vehicles at your home. Invite family members to tell their friends and neighbors about it. Point out that it will save people time and money (since you will do it more cheaply than the government). Ask:

- What problem do you see with this plan?
- Would you question my sincerity?
- Would I be addressing a real problem or need?
- Why is it still not right? (You lack the authority to represent the government.)
- What would happen if a police officer asked

to see a driver's license issued by me instead of the Department of Motor Vehicles?

Have family members read the section heading to D&C 22 and look for the circumstance that led to this revelation. Share the additional information found in the historical background above. Ask your family how the imaginary situation just considered is like the situation Joseph Smith faced in 1830.

As family members take turns reading D&C 22 aloud, one verse at a time, discuss the following:

- What word in verse 1 describes what baptism is? (Covenant.)
- How long has baptism been necessary and important? (From the beginning. Have family members write "Moses 6:52–68"— where Adam learned about and received baptism—next to D&C 22:1.)

- What does the Lord call their previous baptisms? (Dead works.)
- What makes our baptism into the restored Church of Jesus Christ a "live" work instead of a "dead" one? (See 2 Nephi 25:23–27.)
- Who baptized you, and where did he get his authority? (Invite this person to share his priesthood line of authority, if available.)

Invite family members to do one of the following:

- Share their experiences with baptism that have increased their faith and testimony.

- Offer suggestions for how baptism can continue to be an important "living work" in the lives of family members.
- Read Robert D. Hales's talk "The Covenant of Baptism: To Be in the Kingdom and of the Kingdom," *Ensign,* November 2000, 6–9.
- Since the Lord speaks of a "strait gate" in D&C 22 (which refers to specific requirements for a valid baptism), have family members search the following scriptures to find what some of those requirements are: 3 Nephi 11:18–28; Moroni 6:1–3; Moroni 8:10; D&C 20:37, 72–74; D&C 68:25.

DOCTRINE AND COVENANTS 23: GOD'S WILL TO FIVE INDIVIDUALS

Historical background: Section 23 was originally five separate sections (sections 17–21) given to five individuals within days of the organization of the Church. Each of these individuals had already played important roles in building up the kingdom of God, even though one of them, Joseph Knight, had yet to be baptized. Notice the prophetic warning given to Oliver Cowdery.

Doctrine and Covenants 23:1–7
The tragic flaw

Tell your family that in scripture study today they will get to do a little detective work. Have a family member read the historical background above and the section heading of D&C 23. Explain to your family that each of the people mentioned in this section remained faithful except one. Their assignment is to discover clues about who fell away and why.

Write the following names and verses in large letters on a sheet of paper: Oliver Cowdery (verses 1–2), Hyrum Smith (verse 3), Samuel Smith (verse 4), Joseph Smith Sr. (verse 5), and Joseph Knight (verses 6–7). Have family members choose a name and read aloud the verses listed. After the verses have been read, ask:

- What clues did you find in the verses about which one fell away from the Church?
- Which of the five men was the only one to be given a warning? (See verse 1.)
- How serious is the sin of pride?

- Who do you think left the Church?

Explain that Oliver Cowdery was the one who later left the Church. Share the following quotation from Elder George A. Smith:

"It is said, and I presume correctly, that Oliver Cowdery remarked at one time to Joseph Smith, 'If I should apostatize and leave the Church, the Church would be broken up.' The answer of the Prophet was, 'What and who are you? This is the work of God, and if you turn against it and withdraw from it, it will still roll on and you will not be missed.' It was not long until Oliver turned away, but the work continued. God raised up men from obscurity to step forth and shoulder the burdens, and it was hardly known when and where he went. In about ten years he came back again, came before a local conference at Mosquito Creek, Pottawattomie Co., Iowa, Oct., 1848, and acknowledged his faults." (*Journal of Discourses,* 13:347–48.)

BIOGRAPHICAL SKETCH: SAMUEL SMITH

Samuel Harrison Smith was the third person to be baptized in this dispensation, after Joseph Smith and Oliver Cowdery. He was also one of the Eight Witnesses of the Book of Mormon and one of the six original members of the Church. Samuel Smith is recognized as the Church's first missionary; his efforts led to the baptism of Brigham Young and Heber C. Kimball. He remained faithful all his life and died three days after the death of his brothers, Joseph and Hyrum, on July 30, 1844.

Doctrine and Covenants 23:6–7
The first miracle in this dispensation

Have your family scan D&C 23:1–7 and look for answers to the following questions:

- Which of the five men mentioned in this revelation was *not* told "Thou art under no condemnation"? (Joseph Knight—verses 6–7.)
- What do you see in verses 6–7 that might explain why the Lord left this phrase out of His instructions to Joseph Knight? (He needed to pray before the world as well as in secret and be baptized.)
- Why is it not enough to be a good person who believes in God?
- What more does God require of us? (To follow all of His commandments.)

Tell your family that Joseph Knight's son, Newel, also found it difficult to pray in front of others. Share the following story told by Joseph Smith:

"During this month of April, I went on a visit to the residence of Mr. Joseph Knight, of Colesville, Broome county, New York, with whom and his family I had been for some time acquainted, and whose name I had previously mentioned as having been so kind and thoughtful towards us while translating the Book of Mormon. . . .

"Amongst those who attended our meetings regularly was Newel Knight, son of Joseph Knight. He and I had many serious conversations on the important subject of man's eternal salvation. We had got into the habit of praying much at our meetings, and Newel had said that he would try and take up his cross, and pray vocally during meeting; but when we again met together, he rather excused himself. . . .

"Accordingly, he deferred praying until next morning, when he retired into the woods; where, according to his own account afterwards, he made several attempts to pray, but could scarcely do so, feeling that he had not done his duty, in refusing to pray in the presence of others. He began to feel uneasy, and continued to feel worse both in mind and body, until, upon reaching his own house, his appearance was such as to alarm his wife very much. He requested her to go and bring me to him. I went and found him suffering very much in his mind, and his body acted upon in a very strange manner; his visage and limbs distorted and twisted in every shape and appearance possible to imagine; and finally he was caught up off the floor of the apartment, and tossed about most fearfully. . . .

"After he had thus suffered for a time, I succeeded in getting hold of him by the hand, when almost immediately he spoke to me, and with great earnestness requested me to cast the devil out of him, saying that he knew he was in him, and that he also knew that I could cast him out.

"I replied, 'If you know that I can, it shall be done,' and then almost unconsciously I rebuked the devil, and commanded him in the name of Jesus Christ to depart from him; when immediately Newel spoke out and said that he saw the devil leave him and vanish from his sight. This was the first miracle which was done in the Church, or by any member of it; and it was done, not by man, nor by the power of man, but it was done by God, and by the power of godliness." (Joseph Smith, *History of The Church of Jesus Christ of Latter-day Saints,* 1:81–83.)

Challenge your family to make prayer, both private and public, a practice in their lives.

DOCTRINE AND COVENANTS 24: TO "STRENGTHEN, ENCOURAGE, AND INSTRUCT" THE SAINTS

Historical background: Four months after the Church was organized, the Lord revealed this section to Joseph Smith as a message of comfort and encouragement. During this time Joseph and other Church members experienced great persecution. On one occasion they had prepared a pool in a stream for baptisms only to arrive and find that enemies of the Church had destroyed it. Threats by mobs increased, and on two occasions Joseph was arrested on false charges. Fortunately, he was released in both instances. Look for the differences between Joseph's duties and Oliver's duties.

Doctrine and Covenants 24:1–9
What's your job?

Ask the father and mother of your family to share in detail what they do on an average day. As a family, make a list of duties that would be included in a "job description" for Mom and Dad. Then have your family take turns reading D&C 24:1–9 and individually make a list of things that might show Joseph Smith's "job description." Have family members share what they wrote. Ask:

- What part of Joseph's calling do you think would be the most exciting?
- What duties do you think would be the most difficult?
- To what was Joseph to devote all his strength? (Verse 7.)
- What blessings were promised if he fulfilled his calling?
- What were the Church members supposed to do to help Joseph? (Verse 3.)
- What did the Lord promise the members if they supported Joseph?

- What were they promised if they didn't? (Verse 4.)
- What was one thing Joseph was not called to do and why? (Temporal labors, meaning working at an ordinary job to earn money—verse 9.)

Invite your family to share responsibilities they have (be sure to include father, mother, children, home teacher, and visiting teacher). Ask:

- Where should we devote our strength?
- What blessings have you received for fulfilling your calling?
- What could we do to support the prophet and our other Church leaders today?

Doctrine and Covenants 24:10–19
Create a missionary pamphlet

Give family members a sheet of paper and have them roll it up like a megaphone. Use your "megaphone" or trump as you read D&C 24:10–12. Have your family answer the following questions using their megaphones:

- What did the Lord ask Oliver told to do? (Declare the gospel as with a trump.)
- In what ways are full-time missionaries asked to do the same thing today?

Have your family unroll their "megaphones" and fold their papers into thirds (as they would a letter or brochure). Then have them unfold their papers again. Each person should have a sheet of paper with three columns. At the top of each column write the following titles: Miracles (D&C 24:13–14); Cursings (D&C 24:15–17); Without Purse or Scrip (D&C 24:18–19). The papers should look like the chart below.

Divide your family into three groups and have them imagine they have been called to create a pamphlet to help mission presidents teach their missionaries about these three items. Assign each group one of the titles on their paper. Have them study the verses listed and write under their assigned heading what the Lord wants missionaries to know. Encourage them to be creative. They could even add drawings. When finished, have each group "show and tell" with their pamphlet. Discuss why this information might be helpful to a new missionary.

Modern dictionaries indicate that the word *scrip* is archaic and means "a small bag or wallet." Modern usage lists another definition as "paper currency." Thus, when a missionary is instructed to go forth without purse or scrip, he is not to be burdened by taking excessive money with him but is to rely upon the Lord and those he teaches to supply him with the necessities of life. The custom of traveling without purse or scrip was followed in New Testament times and in the early part of this dispensation. (Daniel H. Ludlow, *A Companion to Your Study of the New Testament: The Four Gospels*, 222.)

Miracles (D&C 24:13–14)	Cursings (D&C 24:15–17)	"Without Purse or Scrip" (D&C 24:18–19)

DOCTRINE AND COVENANTS 25: "AN ELECT LADY"

*Historical background: Emma Smith, Joseph Smith's wife, was baptized just a few weeks before this revelation was received. As persecution of the Church and its leaders became more intense, Emma was admonished to be a comfort and support for her husband and to develop her talents to bless the Church. President Gordon B. Hinckley said, "Insofar as I know, this is the only revelation given specifically to a woman." (*Ensign, *November 1984, 89.) Watch for the responsibilities and promises given to Emma Smith.*

Doctrine and Covenants 25:1, 16
"My voice unto all"

 Have a family member read D&C 25:1 aloud. Ask:

- To whom was this revelation given? (Emma Smith.)
- How did the Lord address Emma? (My daughter.)
- How would you feel if God addressed you as personally as He did Emma?
- According to this verse, what must we do to be considered a son or a daughter in God's kingdom? (Receive the gospel.)

Have another family member read aloud D&C 25:16 and tell who else this revelation could be for. (All.) Invite your family to look for words of counsel the Lord gave to Emma that could also apply to them.

Doctrine and Covenants 25:2–10, 13–15
"An elect lady"

Read D&C 25:3 as a family and ask:

- What two things did the Lord declare to Emma?
- What do you think was meant by "an elect lady"?

Share the following quotation from President Gordon B. Hinckley:

"Emma was called 'an elect lady.' That is, to use another line of scripture, she was a 'chosen vessel of the Lord.'" (*Ensign,* November 1984, 90.)

Invite your family to search D&C 25:2–10,

13–15. Have half of them look for what the Lord counseled Emma, "an elect lady," to do. Have the other half find the blessings she was promised. Possible answers are:

Counsel

- Be faithful and walk in paths of virtue. (Verse 2.)
- Murmur not. (Verse 4.)
- Be a comfort to your husband and use consoling words in a spirit of meekness. (Verse 5.)
- Go with your husband and serve as a scribe. (Verse 6.)
- Expound the scriptures and exhort the Church as given by the Spirit. (Verse 7.)
- Write and learn much. (Verse 8.)
- Lay aside the things of this world and seek for the things of a better. (Verse 10.)
- Rejoice and cleave unto the covenants you have made. (Verse 13.)
- Continue in meekness, beware of pride, and delight in your husband. (Verse 14.)
- Keep the commandments continually. (Verse 15.)

Blessings

- Your life will be preserved, and you will receive an inheritance in Zion. (Verse 2.)
- Your sins are forgiven. (Verse 3.)
- Receive the Holy Ghost. (Verse 8.)
- Your husband shall support thee. (Verse 9.)
- You will receive a crown of righteousness. (Verse 15.)

BIOGRAPHICAL SKETCH: EMMA SMITH

"Emma, the daughter of Isaac and Elizabeth Lewis Hale, was born on July 10, 1804, in Harmony, Susquehannah County, Pa. She grew to maturity in that rural community and there she met young Joseph Smith. At the time of their meeting Emma was 22 years old and stood about 5 feet 9 inches tall, had dark hair and brown eyes." (Susan Easton Black, *LDS Church News,* 01/04/97.) She married Joseph Smith January 18, 1827, and was privileged to accompany her husband to the Hill Cumorah the morning he obtained the plates from the angel Moroni. She also served as scribe during part of the Book of Mormon translation. Her concern was always for her family. Emma and Joseph had nine children of their own, of which only four grew to maturity. She served as the first president of the Relief Society and reached out in service to others in spite of personal trials. Lucy Mack Smith, the Prophet's mother, wrote of Emma, "I have never seen a woman in my life who would endure every species of fatigue and hardship, from month to month, and from year to year, with that unflinching courage, zeal and patience, which she has ever done." (*History of Joseph Smith,* 190–91.) Emma bore strong and continuing testimony of her husband's prophetic calling. She died in Nauvoo on April 30, 1879, at the age of seventy-four.

Ask each group to share what they found. Ask:

- What counsel given by the Lord to Emma applies to you?
- Which blessings promised to Emma would you most want in your life?

Invite one or two family members to read the following quotations:

"The world has enough women who are tough; we need women who are tender. There are enough women who are coarse; we need women who are kind. There are enough women who are rude; we need women who are refined. We have enough women of fame and fortune; we need more women of faith. We have enough greed; we need more goodness. We have enough vanity; we need more virtue. We have enough popularity; we need more purity." (Margaret D. Nadauld, former Young Women general president, in *Ensign,* November 2000, 15.)

"There is no surer way for a man to show his lack of character . . . than for him to show lack of respect for woman or to do anything that would discredit or degrade her." (President N. Eldon Tanner, in *Ensign,* January 1974, 7.)

Discuss as a family what a woman can do to become an "elect lady" and what a man can do to show honor and respect for womanhood.

Doctrine and Covenants 25:11–12
"Name that Hymn"

Invite your family to play a game called "Name that Hymn." Divide your family into teams. Have someone play or hum the first few notes of different hymns. See which team is first to name the hymn as the notes are played. You could also use songs from the *Children's Songbook.* Ask:

- What are your favorite Church hymns or songs?
- How does sacred music help you worship the Lord?

Read D&C 25:11–12 together as a family. Then ask:

- What was Emma Smith asked to do for the Church?
- What did the Lord teach about music?

Consider reading together the section on music in the *For the Strength of Youth* pamphlet or the

First Presidency Preface in the front of the LDS hymnbook. Discuss as a family what you can do to enhance the positive power of music in your lives.

Explain that the first hymnbook Emma made consisted of words only. The hymns were sung to different tunes the Saints were familiar with. The same hymn could be sung to different tunes. As

an example, the words to hymn no. 2, "The Spirit of God," can also be sung to the tune of Hymn no. 3, "Now Let Us Rejoice," and vice versa.

For fun, mix and match the words and tunes of the following hymns: no. 7, "Israel, Israel God Is Calling"; no. 26, "Joseph Smith's First Prayer"; no. 102, "Jesus, Lover of My Soul"; no. 163, "Lord, Dismiss Us with Thy Blessing."

DOCTRINE AND COVENANTS 26: THE LAW OF "COMMON CONSENT"

Historical background: D&C 26 was received at about the same time as sections 24 and 25. The Church continued to experience severe persecution that made it difficult for Joseph Smith to spend much time building up the kingdom. In this revelation the Lord told Joseph Smith, Oliver Cowdery, and John Whitmer to prepare for the second conference of the Church, at Fayette, September 26th, 1830. (*See* History of the Church, 1:110.) There the Lord promised to make "known what you shall do." (See also the historical background for D&C 24 in this book.) Notice how Church government by "common consent" is different from a dictatorship or a democracy.

Doctrine and Covenants 26:1
Can we really find answers in the scriptures?

Fill two clear glasses one-third full of water and place them on a cookie sheet in front of your family. Add a teaspoon of baking soda to each glass. Explain that the glasses of water represent individual family members and the baking soda represents scripture reading. Add vinegar (the Spirit) to one of the glasses until it overflows. Ask:

- What do you think this person might have done while reading the scriptures that caused him or her to overflow with the Spirit? (Study, pray.)
- Why is the Spirit necessary when we read the scriptures?
- How can study and prayer increase our enthusiasm for the word of God?

Have one person read the section heading for D&C 24 and then read together as a family D&C 26:1. Ask:

- What instructions did the Lord give Joseph about how to spend his time while in hiding?
- Why do you think the first thing on the Lord's list was for Joseph, during a period of persecution, to continue to study the scriptures?
- What does it mean to "preach" and "confirm" the Church? (Testify to and strengthen their testimonies.)

Share the following statement from President Harold B. Lee:

"I say that we need to teach our people to find their answers in the scriptures. . . . But the unfortunate thing is that so many of us are not reading the scriptures. We do not know what is in them, and therefore we speculate about the things that we ought to have found in the scriptures themselves. I think that therein is one of our biggest dangers of today." (*Teachings of Harold B. Lee,* 153.)

Ask:

- Why is the lack of scripture study "one of our biggest dangers today"?
- How can you solve personal problems through scripture study?
- How can scripture study help to "preach" and "confirm" the Church?
- How can it help prepare you to communicate with the Lord?

Challenge your family not just to read the scriptures but also to study them for a week. Follow up next week to see if scripture study has increased the influence of the Spirit in their lives.

Doctrine and Covenants 26:2

What is common consent and what does it have to do with faith and prayer?

Share the following two situations with your family and ask them to think about which one they would prefer:

Situation 1: You live in a country ruled by one man who favors a few of his associates. He decides what you can do and punishes you for disobedience. You lack freedom of choice and often live in fear.

Situation 2: You live in a country ruled by representatives that you voted into office. They pass laws to benefit the majority of the people. You enjoy freedom of choice and a degree of happiness.

Ask:

- Which situation would you prefer and why?
- Which of these two situations more closely resembles how the Church is governed?

Read together D&C 26:2 and find the law by which all things are done in the Church. Ask your family what they think "common consent" is. Share the following statement:

"The form of government used in the Church is based on the principle of 'common consent' (D&C 26:2; 20:65). This has been explained as follows: 'Every officer of the Priesthood or auxiliary organizations, . . . holds his position in the Church only with the consent of the people. Officers may be nominated by the Presidency of the Church, but unless the people accept them as officials, they cannot exercise the authority of the offices to which they have been called. All things in the Church must be done by common consent. This makes the people, men and women, under God, the rulers of the Church' (John A. Widtsoe, *Priesthood and Church Government*, 238–239)." (Hoyt W. Brewster, Jr., *Doctrine and Covenants Encyclopedia*, 93.)

Ask:

- How does the government of the Lord's Church differ from the two situations above?
- Why do you think "much prayer and faith" are necessary in this type of government?
- Why is the right to raise your hand to sustain your Church leaders a blessing and a protection in the Church?

DOCTRINE AND COVENANTS 27: THE SACRAMENT AND THE ARMOR OF GOD

Historical background: In the early days of the Church, people who were baptized were later confirmed members of the Church in special meetings. An important focus of those "confirmation meetings" was that these new Church members would receive the sacrament for the first time. Joseph Smith recorded that the occasion leading to the revelation found in D&C 27 was one of these meetings: "Early in the month of August Newel Knight and his wife paid us a visit at my place in Harmony, Pennsylvania; and as neither his wife nor mine had been as yet confirmed, it was proposed that we should confirm them, and partake together of the Sacrament, before he and his wife should leave us." (History of the Church, 1:106.) As is mentioned in the section heading, it was while Joseph was on his way to obtain wine for the occasion that he received the first four verses of this revelation. The rest of the revelation was given the following month. Look for why we no longer use wine in the sacrament.

Doctrine and Covenants 27:1–4
What is most important when partaking of the sacrament?

Assign one member of the family to be a scribe. Ask your family to name every part or element of the sacrament they participate in each week. (Singing the hymn, blessing the sacrament, passing the sacrament, eating the bread and drinking the water, and so on.) Once the list is made, have the scribe mark with an "E" the things on the list that are "essential to have" as part of the sacrament, and note with an "N" the things that are "nice but not essential" to have as part of the sacrament.

Have a family member read aloud the section heading to D&C 27 and then read to your family the information found in the historical background above. Assign your family to read D&C 27:1–4 to themselves and look for what the angel told Joseph Smith. When they have finished reading, discuss the following questions:

- What did the messenger say was not essential to the sacrament? (Have the scribe make sure this is on the list with an "N" next to it.)
- What did he say was essential? (Have the scribe make sure this is on the list with an "E" next to it.)
- What does it mean to partake of the sacrament with an eye "single" to the Savior's glory?
- According to verse 2, what is one way we can partake of the sacrament "with an eye single" to the Savior? (By remembering Christ's sacrifice.)
- What other things could we think about to help remember Christ during the sacrament?

To help answer that question, consider sharing the following counsel from Elder Jeffrey R. Holland:

"We could remember the Savior's premortal life and all that we know him to have done as the great Jehovah, creator of heaven and earth and all things that in them are. We could remember that even in the Grand Council of Heaven he loved us and was wonderfully strong. . . .

"We could remember the simple grandeur of his mortal birth. . . .

"We could remember Christ's miracles and his teachings, his healings and his help. . . .

"We could remember that . . . the Savior found delight in living; he enjoyed people and told his disciples to be of good cheer. . . .

"We could remember that Christ called his disciples friends, and that friends are those who stand by us in times of loneliness or potential despair. . . .

"We could—and should—remember the wonderful things that have come to us in our lives and that 'all things which are good cometh of Christ' (Moro. 7:24). . . .

"On some days we will have cause to remember the unkind treatment he received, the rejection he experienced, and the injustice—oh, the injustice—he endured. . . .

"When those difficult times come to us, we can remember that Jesus had to descend below all things before he could ascend above them, and that he suffered pains and afflictions and temptations of every kind that he might be filled with mercy and know how to succor his people in their infirmities (see D&C 88:6; Alma 7:11–12).

"[We should remember that] to those who stagger or stumble, he is there to steady and strengthen us. In the end he is there to save us, and for all this he gave his life. However dim our days may seem they have been darker for the Savior of the world." (In *Ensign,* November 1995, 68–69.)

To help some of the younger children in the family, you may want to search for pictures in Church magazines (or have them draw some of their own) that represent these ideas about the Savior spoken of by Elder Holland. Cut the pictures out and make a small book the children can look at during the sacrament to remember Him.

Doctrine and Covenants 27:5–14
A glorious sacrament meeting

Ask your family, "If you could have any three people from history over for dinner this Sunday night, who would you have and why?"

Explain that at a meal with His disciples on the night before His crucifixion, Jesus introduced the ordinance of the sacrament. At that time he said that he would not eat or drink with them again until the "kingdom of God shall come." (Luke 22:18.) Have your family take turns reading D&C 27:5–14 where Jesus restated this promise to Joseph Smith. As they read, have them mark the names of others who will be invited to this great

meeting in which Jesus will again partake of the sacrament with his disciples.

Tell your family that Elder Bruce R. McConkie said this sacrament meeting "will be a part of the grand council at Adam-ondi-Ahman." (*The Millennial Messiah*, 587.) Read also the following explanation from Elder Joseph Fielding Smith:

"All who have held keys will make their reports and deliver their stewardships, as they shall be required. Adam will direct this judgment, and then he will make his report, as the one holding the keys for this earth, to his Superior Officer, Jesus Christ. Our Lord will then assume the reins of government; directions will be given to the Priesthood; and He, whose right it is to rule, will be installed officially by the voice of the Priesthood there assembled. This grand council of Priesthood will be composed, not only of those who are faithful who now dwell on this earth, but also of the prophets and apostles of old, who have had directing authority." (*The Way to Perfection,* 291.)

For each person identified in D&C 27:5–14, have your family identify (and perhaps mark) the keys, authority, or promises they restored in preparation for the kingdom of God to be established on the earth. Ask your family to suppose they were at a dinner with the people listed. Have them choose the two they would like to sit between. Invite them to tell the rest of the family what they would hope to learn from these individuals while they ate and talked. What would you say to them in return about the way your life has been blessed because of their ministry and the keys and blessings they restored?

Encourage family members to really think about the Savior's life and sacrifice as they partake of the sacrament each week.

Doctrine and Covenants 27:15–18
Putting on the whole armor of God

Show your family a piece of protective equipment that is essential to the safety of the person wearing it, such as a football helmet.

Ask them what is likely to happen if a person tried to play a serious football game without a helmet. Have your family read D&C 76:28–29 and Ephesians 6:12 and identify what kind of serious battle we are in and who we are fighting against.

Ask your family to take turns reading D&C 27:15–18. Invite them to look for ways we can protect ourselves in our war against Satan. Assign someone to be a scribe and have the rest of the family help him or her list on a poster or paper pieces of "armor" the Lord invites us to "put on." Next to each piece of armor, list what the Lord said it represents spiritually. Your chart may look something like this:

Physical Armor	Spiritual Armor
Loins girt	Truth
Breastplate	Righteousness
Feet shod	Preparation of the gospel of peace
Shield	Faith
Helmet	Salvation
Sword	Spirit

Discuss each piece of armor with the help of the following explanations:

"Loins girt about with truth." Tell your family that to be "girt about" is to have a large belt around you, and that the "loins" are your many vital organs and the sacred procreative parts of your body. Explain that Satan shows no respect for the sacredness of our creative powers. Talk about what gospel truths can help protect us from violating the law of chastity.

"Breastplate of righteousness." Ask, "What important organ does a breastplate cover?" (The heart.) Have your family read 3 Nephi 6:15–16 and note what Satan did and how he was able to do it. In contrast, have them read the promise in 1 Nephi 22:26—noting what it says about righteousness, hearts, and Satan.

"Feet shod with the preparation of the gospel of peace." Ask your family how far they

think they could walk without shoes compared to how far they could walk with shoes. Remind them that mortal life is like a long journey to a place we can't really see at this time. (See also Hebrews 11:8–10, 13–16.) What keeps us going? Read together the first paragraph of the entry for "Gospels" in the Bible Dictionary (p. 682). Ask, "What is the meaning of the word 'gospel'?" What *is* the gospel? How does this knowledge keep us walking through the challenges of mortal life?

"Shield of faith." Have your family look again at D&C 27:17 and identify what the shield specifically does. (Stop the fiery darts of the wicked.) Ask them why they think Satan's weapon is compared to a dart rather than a large tank or cannon. Invite them to give examples of how others (including Satan) have tried to get them to doubt the truths of the gospel. How has your faith helped you to overcome? Read together 1 Nephi 11:16–17 as an example of how what we *do* know can help us stand firm, even in the midst of what we *don't* know. You may want to help your family memorize Nephi's response.

"Helmet of Salvation." Share with your family the following commentary from Elder Harold B. Lee: "Did you ever hear of that kind of helmet? The helmet of salvation. . . . Salvation is to be saved. Saved from what? Saved from death and saved from sin. . . . A helmet of salvation shall guide our thinking all through our days." (As quoted in Otten and Caldwell, *Sacred Truths of the Doctrine and Covenants,* 130–31.) Ask your family what they think we can do to more often remember Christ and the salvation He offers us. How would remembering Christ more regularly help us resist the influence the devil tries to have over us?

"Sword of my Spirit." Ask your family how the sword is different from the other pieces of armor listed. (It is a weapon rather than merely protection.) What did the Lord say about the Spirit in D&C 27:18 and Ephesians 6:17? (The Spirit is His word.) What are some ways we can receive God's word through the Spirit? How could it then be compared to a sharp sword? (For one example, see Helaman 3:29–30.)

Consider sharing the following quotation from Elder Boyd K. Packer about where we obtain this armor:

"Our Father's plan requires that, like the generation of life itself, the shield of faith is to be made and fitted in the family. No two can be exactly alike. Each must be handcrafted to individual specifications.

"The plan designed by the Father contemplates that man and woman, husband and wife, working together, fit each child individually with a shield of faith made to buckle on so firmly that it can neither be pulled off nor penetrated by those fiery darts.

"It takes the steady strength of a father to hammer out the metal of it and the tender hands of a mother to polish and fit it on. Sometimes one parent is left to do it alone. It is difficult, but it can be done.

"In the Church we can teach about the materials from which a shield of faith is made: reverence, courage, chastity, repentance, forgiveness, compassion. In church we can learn how to assemble and fit them together. But the actual making of and fitting on of the shield of faith belongs in the family circle. Otherwise it may loosen and come off in a crisis." (*Ensign*, May 1995, 8.)

Encourage your family to help each other put on the whole armor of God.

DOCTRINE AND COVENANTS 28: PROPHETS HOLD THE KEYS OF REVELATION

Historical background: *"As it was but a few months after the organization of the Church, the members had not learned that there was but one appointed of the Lord to receive revelations for the Church, and several others thought that Hiram Page or Oliver Cowdery could receive revelations just as well as Joseph Smith. Oliver Cowdery and the members of the Whitmer family were deceived by these false declarations of Hiram Page. This caused serious trouble and Oliver Cowdery took the Prophet to task for not accepting what Hiram Page had given. Finally the Prophet persuaded Oliver Cowdery that these things were wrong, and later the whole membership renounced the revelation given through this stone, but this did not come until the Lord had given to the Church the revelation known as section twenty-eight."* (Joseph Fielding Smith, Church History and Modern Revelation, *1:134–35.*) *Watch for what the Lord teaches us about how revelation for the Church is received and by whom.*

Doctrine and Covenants 28:1–7, 11–13
Who can receive revelation?

Share the following case studies with your family. After each example, ask your family if they can see any problems with the "revelations" received in these examples.

1. In fast and testimony meeting, a ward member tells of a dream commanding everyone to read the entire Doctrine and Covenants within two months.

2. A friend claims to have received a revelation indicating whom you are to marry.

3. A high priest teaches that it is acceptable to drink wine occasionally.

4. A Church member teaches that God wants the entire Church to get a three-year supply of food.

To help your family see what is wrong in those examples, read together the historical background and the biographical sketch and then read D&C 28:1–7, 11–13 and discuss the following questions:

• What difference does it make who receives a revelation? (Verse 2.)

BIOGRAPHICAL SKETCH: HIRAM PAGE

Hiram Page was born in 1800. He joined the Church five days after its organization and became one of the Eight Witnesses of the Book of Mormon. "Before the conference of 26 September 1830, Hiram found a stone five-by-three inches in length and one-half inch thick with two holes. He believed the stone possessed qualities that enabled him to be a 'revelator.'" (Susan Easton Black, *Who's Who in the Doctrine and Covenants*, 208.) After D&C 28 was given, Hiram was persuaded to renounce the stone. In later years Hiram was excommunicated from the Church, but he never denied his witness of the Book of Mormon.

- Who has the authority to receive revelation for the whole Church?
- Hiram Page was one of the Eight Witnesses to the Book of Mormon Plates. What was wrong with his receiving revelations through his stone? (Verses 11–12.)
- What problems would it cause if anybody could receive revelation on how the Church should operate?
- What is the difference between the revelations the president of the Church receives and the answers you get to your personal prayers?

To help answer these questions, share the following statements:

"I will inform you that it is contrary to the economy of God for any member of the Church, or anyone, to receive instructions for those in authority, higher than themselves; therefore, you will see the impropriety of giving heed to them; but if any person have a vision or a visitation from a heavenly messenger, it must be for his own benefit and instruction, for the fundamental principles, government, and doctrine of the Church are vested in the keys of the kingdom." (Joseph Smith, *History of the Church*, 1:388.)

"All faithful members are entitled to the inspiration of the Holy Spirit for themselves, their families, and for those over whom they are appointed and ordained to preside. But anything at discord with that which comes from God through the head of the Church is not to be received as authoritative or reliable." (*Messages of the First Presidency*, 4:255–86.)

Share your testimony of the value of following our living prophet.

Doctrine and Covenants 28:11–13
How do you tell people they are wrong?

 Ask your family to comment on the following two questions:

- Would you rather have someone correct your mistakes in public or in private? Why?
- Would you like the policies, revelations, and information in the Church known to all members, or only a select few? Why?

Read D&C 28:11–13 together as a family and look for teachings from those verses that give insight into the two questions you discussed previously. Ask:

- Why might it have helped Hiram Page to have Oliver Cowdery take him "alone" when explaining about Satan's deceptions?
- What lessons could our family learn from this counsel?
- What problems could creep into the Church if we did not do things by "common consent"? (For more information on the principle of "common consent," see the teaching idea for D&C 26:2.)
- Why do you think it is important that we listen to and participate in the sustaining of Church officers by common consent in our wards and stakes?

DOCTRINE AND COVENANTS 29: EVENTS PRECEDING THE SECOND COMING

Historical background: "In the Prophet Joseph Smith's history, he does not provide us with information about the reason for receiving Section 29 of the Doctrine and Covenants except that it was given prior to the conference beginning September 26, 1830. The Church had been organized more than five months before this. We know that at the first time the angel Moroni visited the Prophet considerable emphasis was given by that holy messenger to what would transpire in the latter days. In his second appearance during the night of September 21–22, 1823, the Prophet said:

"'. . . he informed me of great judgments which were coming upon the earth, with great desolations by famine, sword, and pestilence; and these grievous judgments would come on the earth in this generation. . . .'
(History of the Church, 1:14.)

"[D&C 29] deals, in general, with some of these judgments and events associated with them." (Roy W. Doxey, The Doctrine and Covenants Speaks, *1:164.) Look for what the Lord says about the Second Coming.*

Doctrine and Covenants 29:1–8
Jesus Christ is our "advocate"

Consider sitting behind a table, holding a gavel. Ask your family to imagine they are in a courtroom, in front of a "judge" who will determine their fate. Discuss these questions:

- What people might be in court to assist you? (Attorneys, witnesses, family.)
- What qualities would you hope those people had? (Love you, trust you, be fair.)
- According to Revelation 20:12, what will happen to each of us eventually?
- Why would it be nice to have someone pleading or speaking for you on that day?

Have your family take turns reading D&C 29:1–8 and look for who might be there for us at the Judgment. Discuss the following questions as you read:

- What must we do to be "gathered" by our Redeemer, Jesus Christ? (Verses 1–2.)
- What is an "advocate"? (One who pleads, or speaks for, another's cause—verse 5.)
- Who is our "advocate with the Father"?
- How can we be gathered with the Savior's "elect"? (Verse 7.)

- Why would you want to be gathered? (Verse 8.)
- How does it feel to know that the Savior pleads your cause before the Father?

Tell your family how you would answer the last question and share your testimony of the Savior with them.

Doctrine and Covenants 29:9–29
Events in the last days

Before scripture study, get five pieces of paper and write one of the following five references at the top of each paper: D&C 29:9–11; D&C 29:12–15; D&C 29:16–20; D&C 29:21–25; D&C 29:26–29. Have each person take a paper. Ask your family to read the verses listed and write one question someone might have that could be answered from those verses. Tell them they should become the "expert" for those verses.

Gather the five pieces of paper and read the questions one at a time. Let everyone but the "expert" try to answer the question. Then let the "experts" review and teach the message in those verses and answer the question according to what they studied. As a summary, discuss the following questions:

- Was there anything in those prophecies about the last days that worried you?
- Which prophesied events will you be glad to see happen?
- What should we do to be prepared for the troubling events?
- How can we make sure we will be worthy to be gathered with the righteous?

Doctrine and Covenants 29:30–35
Why have we been given the commandments?

Write "The Word of Wisdom" on a chart and put two columns under that title. Ask family members what blessings come from keeping the Word of Wisdom. Write down their answers as they give them, listing physical or temporal blessings in the left column and spiritual blessings in the right column. Do not tell them what each column represents. When you have finished, your chart may look something like this

Ask:

- What difference do you see between the two columns? (One contains physical blessings, the other spiritual.)
- Which blessings are more important to you, physical or spiritual? Why?

- In your opinion, is the primary purpose of commandments to provide us with physical or spiritual blessings?

To help answer that last question, read together D&C 29:30–35 and mark what the Lord said about His commandments in verses 34–35. Have your family look again at the chart you made on the Word of Wisdom. Ask, "How can the temporal or physical side of the Word of Wisdom still be considered a spiritual blessing?"

Doctrine and Covenants 29:36–39, 45
The importance of agency

Read D&C 29:36–39 with your family. Ask:

- How many were cast out of the premortal life with Satan? (A third part)
- Where were they sent? (See the quotation from Brigham Young below.)

"That is the situation of the spirits that were sent to the earth, when the revolt took place in heaven, when Lucifer, the Son of the Morning, was cast out. Where did he go? He came here, and one-third part of the spirits in heaven came with him. Do you suppose that one-third part of all the beings that existed in eternity came with him?

The Word of Wisdom

health	wisdom
marrow	hidden treasures
run	destroying angel shall pass by
walk	

No, but one-third part of the spirits that were begotten and organized and brought forth to become tenants of fleshly bodies to dwell upon this earth . . . forsook Jesus Christ, the rightful heir, and joined with Lucifer, the Son of the Morning, and came to this earth; they got here first. As soon as Mother Eve made her appearance in the garden of Eden, the devil was on hand." (*Journal of Discourses,* 3:369.)

Ask:

- What did the devil and those who followed him rebel against? (Verse 36.)
- Since God is all-powerful, why did He not stop them from rebelling so they wouldn't be cast out and lost? (See the quotation from President Howard W. Hunter below.)

"Where and when did all of this happen? Well, it happened long before man's mortal birth. It happened in a great premortal existence where we developed our identities and increased our spiritual capabilities by exercising our agency and making important choices. We developed our intelligence and learned to love the truth, and we prepared to come to earth to continue our progress.

"Our Father in Heaven wanted our growth to continue in mortality and to be enhanced by our freedom to choose and learn. He also wanted us to exercise our faith and our will, especially with a new physical body to master and control. But we know from both ancient and modern revelation that Satan wished to deny us our independence and agency in that now-forgotten moment long ago, even as he wishes to deny them this very hour. Indeed, Satan violently opposed the freedom of choice offered by the Father, so violently that John in the Revelation described 'war in heaven' (Revelation 12:7) over the matter.

Satan would have coerced us, and he would have robbed us of that most precious of gifts if he could: our freedom to choose a divine future and the exaltation we all hope to obtain." (*The Teachings of Howard W. Hunter,* 11.)

Invite your family to silently read D&C 29:45. Ask:

- What are the wages Satan offers?
- What are the wages the Lord offers?
- Who will determine whether you are paid by Satan or the Lord?

Doctrine and Covenants 29:46–50
Is it possible for children to sin?

Display a picture of each member of your family when they were less than eight years of age. Ask each person to use the scripture index or Topical Guide to find one scripture describing how the Savior feels about children. Ask family members to share the scriptures they chose.

Read D&C 29:46–50 together and discuss what else we learn from these verses about little children. Consider discussing the following questions:

- What two reasons do we see in verse 47 why little children cannot sin? (Satan is not allowed to tempt them, and they are not old enough to be accountable or understand the difference between right and wrong.)

- What do you think the "great things" are that will be "required at the hands of their fathers"?

- What does the Lord require of those who do have "knowledge" and "understanding"? (See verses 49–50.)

DOCTRINE AND COVENANTS 30: "FEAR NOT"

Historical background: The material in this section was originally published as three separate revelations given to the Whitmer brothers: David, age twenty-five, Peter, age twenty-one, and John, age twenty-seven. (See also biographical sketches for sections 14–16.) The Whitmer family played a very influential role in the early days of the Church. "Of the Book of Mormon's eleven witnesses, seven were Whitmers by blood or marriage. The Book of Mormon translation was finished at the Whitmer home in Fayette; near it the Three Witnesses saw Moroni and the plates; there the organization of the Church and early New York conferences were held; half of the revelations in the Doctrine and Covenants from the New York period—twenty—were received there, a record unequaled by any other dwelling in the state. Joseph Smith's family had carried the first burden in inquiry and persecution in the gospel's restoration, but the Whitmers were the family that nourished the Church." (Richard Lloyd Anderson, Ensign, August 1979, 35.) Look for what the Lord says that we should "fear not."

Doctrine and Covenants 30:1–11
We should not fear man more than God

Invite your family to search the section heading for D&C 30 and identify three things having to do with the number 3. (It was directed to three individuals, following a three-day conference, and was originally published as three separate revelations.) Invite your family to scan the section and mark the three individuals whose names are mentioned. (Verses 1, 5, 9.)

Read together verses 1, 5, and 11. Ask:

- What is one problem or weakness the Lord counseled each of these brothers about? (Fear of man.)
- What problems come up when we are more concerned with what other people think than what God thinks?
- How can our fears get in the way of our willingness to follow God?

Share the following statement about fear: "The proud stand more in fear of men's judgment than of God's judgment. (See D&C 3:6–7; D&C 30:1–2; D&C 60:2.) 'What will men think of me?' weighs heavier than 'What will God think of me?'" (Ezra Taft Benson, *Ensign,* May 1989, 4.)

Ask your family to find and mark the three times the word "heed" is used in this section (see Verses 2, 5, and 8.) Make a list of what the Lord asked the Whitmer's to "heed." Ask:

- Why should we heed the Spirit?
- What are some ways you have been blessed when you have followed the Spirit?
- Why should we heed the advice of a righteous family member or Church leader?
- What family advice have you received that has blessed your life?
- Why is it important to heed the prophet?
- What is the last prophetic statement you remember giving heed to?

Invite your family to have the courage to heed the prompting and instruction of the Spirit, of our families, and of the Lord. Read or sing together "Let Us All Press On." (*Hymns,* no. 243.) point out the verse that reads:

Fear not, though the enemy deride;
Courage, for the Lord is on our side.
We will heed not what the wicked
    may say,
But the Lord alone we will obey.

DOCTRINE AND COVENANTS 31: A REVELATION TO THOMAS B. MARSH

Historical background: On September 26, 1830, the second conference of the Church was held at the Peter Whitmer home in Fayette, New York. Thirty-five people had joined the Church since the first conference in June, bringing the total Church membership to sixty-two. Among the new converts was Thomas B. Marsh. Notice how well the Lord knows Thomas Marsh.

Doctrine and Covenants 31:1–13
Find the blessings, assignments, cautions, and gifts

Ask your family to read D&C 31:13 and find who is speaking to Thomas B. Marsh. Give each family member a sheet of paper, divided into four columns, with these four headings: Blessings, Assignments, Cautions, and Gifts. Ask your family to search D&C 31:1–13 and fill in the chart using information given to Thomas B. Marsh. Their finished charts should look something like the chart on the following page.

Discuss the following questions:

- Which blessings given to Thomas B. Marsh would you most desire?
- How are your assignments from the Lord similar to his? How are they different?
- Why would it be important for you to be cautious of the same things he was to be cautious of?
- Which of his spiritual gifts most impresses you? What are some of your spiritual gifts?

Read the historical background for D&C 31 and the biographical sketch of Thomas B. Marsh to your family. Discuss what Thomas B. Marsh did with the counsel and cautions given in this revelation. What can we learn from his experience?

Invite family members who have patriarchal blessings to make a chart similar to the one on the following page and go through the same exercise with their patriarchal blessing. Testify that our patriarchal blessings are the Lord's counsel to us personally. Talk about how important it is that we heed the direction and counsel found in those blessings.

BIOGRAPHICAL SKETCH: THOMAS BALDWIN MARSH

Thomas B. Marsh was baptized on September 3, 1830, in Cayuga Lake by David Whitmer. Earlier he had heard rumors of a "golden bible" and had come to Western New York from Boston to investigate. He gained the desire to be baptized after reading part of the manuscript from the Book of Mormon. A few days after his baptism, Thomas B. Marsh was ordained an elder, and the Lord called him to serve a mission. (See D&C 31:3.) Thomas B. Marsh had many talents and served in several Church callings, including being the first president of the Quorum of the Twelve Apostles. However, in August 1838, he had a disagreement with other Church leaders. He became angry over a personal conflict with the Church leaders and was excommunicated on March 17, 1839. For many years he spoke bitterly against Joseph Smith and the Church. "Later in his life, however, when he was a broken man, he returned to the Church and standing before the congregation called upon them to look upon him as an object of apostasy, and he warned the members to avoid a course which would bring them to a similar condition." (Joseph Fielding Smith, *Church History and Modern Revelation,* 1:137.)

Blessings	Assignments	Cautions	Gifts
• Family will believe and be in the Church. (Verse 2.) • Tongue loosed, declare glad tidings. (Verse 3.) • Sins forgiven, family shall live. (Verse 5.) • Place prepared for family. (Verse 6.) • People's hearts will open, they will receive you. (Verse 7.) • I am with you. (Verse 13.)	• Lift up heart, rejoice, serve mission. (Verse 3.) • Thrust in sickle with all your soul. (Verse 5.) • Go from family and declare my word. (Verse 6.) • A church will be established by your hand; strengthen and prepare them. (Verse 7–8.) • Physician unto church but not world. (Verse 10.)	• Be patient in afflictions, revile not against those that revile. (Verse 9.) • Govern your house in meekness and be steadfast. (Verse 9.) • The world will not receive you. (Verse 10.) • Go your way whithersoever I will. (Verse 11.) • Pray always, lest you enter into temptation and lose your reward. (Verse 12.) • Be faithful unto the end. (Verse 13.)	• Faith. (Verse 1.) • It shall be given you by the Comforter what you shall do and whither you shall go. (Verse 11.)

DOCTRINE AND COVENANTS 32: MISSION TO THE LAMANITES

Historical background: *Oliver Cowdery and Peter Whitmer Jr. were called to serve a mission to the Lamanites. (See D&C 28:8 and 30:5.) "Joseph Smith later stated that some time close to the September conference the elders manifested a great desire to know if additional missionaries couldn't be sent with Oliver Cowdery and Peter Whitmer Jr. . . . In consequence of their urging, Joseph inquired of the Lord and received in reply section 32, which added Parley P. Pratt and Ziba Peterson to the Lamanite Mission." (Stephen E. Robinson and H. Dean Garrett,* A Commentary on the Doctrine and Covenants, *1:219.)*

On their way to the Indian Territory the four missionaries stopped in Kirtland, Ohio, where Parley P. Pratt wanted to share his new religion with his old friend Sidney Rigdon. Sidney was a prominent minister in the area and the leader of a group of devout Christians called "Seekers" who were looking for a return of New Testament Christianity. The missionaries shared with them the message of the restoration through the Prophet Joseph Smith and baptized one hundred and twenty-seven of them. This doubled the size of the Church. After his conversion, Fredrick G. Williams joined the missionaries on their mission, making five in all. The missionaries were successful in teaching and placed copies of the Book of Mormon among many Native Americans. Notice what the Lord promises these missionaries.

BIOGRAPHICAL SKETCH: PARLEY P. PRATT

Parley P. Pratt was born April 12, 1807, in Burlington, Otsego County, New York, the son of Jared Pratt and Charity Dickinson. Even though Parley was not privileged with much formal education, he loved to read and learn, especially things of the Spirit. This love of the Lord and reading brought him in contact with the Book of Mormon while preaching in western New York. After reading all night, he was determined to find Joseph Smith and learn more. He was baptized by Oliver Cowdery in September 1830 and ordained an elder. One month later, Parley was called to be a missionary to the Lamanites.

In February 1834 he marched with Zion's Camp to deliver the Saints from the mobs in Missouri. He was ordained an apostle on February 21, 1835. Parley then served successive missions to Pennsylvania, New York, New England, Canada, and New York again before settling in Missouri in 1838. In Far West he and five other men, including Joseph Smith, were betrayed and taken captive. They suffered imprisonment in Independence and Richmond.

In the 1840s Parley served a mission in England, where he was editor and publisher of the *Millennial Star,* a newspaper for the Saints in England. He also wrote a number of hymns that are in the LDS hymnbook today. He also served missions in the Pacific and South America. His final mission was to the Southern States, where, near Van Buren, Arkansas, the fifty-year-old Parley was murdered in May 1857.

Doctrine and Covenants 32:1–5
How did the Lord fulfill prophecy?

Show your family a world map. Ask them to choose a location where they would like to serve a mission. Then discuss the following questions:

- Who determines where we serve as missionaries?
- Why are missionaries needed in all parts of the world?
- Will you be willing to serve wherever you are called? Why or why not?

Tell your family that seven months after the Church was organized, missionaries were sent to a particular place that helped fulfill a prophecy made in the Book of Mormon. Ask your family to search the following verses and see if they can identify which people the Lord revealed would one day receive the teachings of the Book of Mormon: Enos 1:13; D&C 3:16–18; Book of Mormon Title Page: paragraph 1.

Have your family read D&C 32 and the historical background for this section to find answers to the following questions:

- Which verse indicates where they were to serve this mission? (Verse 2.)
- Which five men were the first missionaries to the Lamanites in the latter days? (See heading and verses 1–3.)
- What do you think may have made that mission especially challenging?
- What specific counsel was given to Parley P. Pratt and Ziba Peterson to help them succeed on this mission?
- How is this counsel similar to counsel missionaries receive today?
- How can this story help increase our faith to be able to serve wherever we are called on our missions?

Sing together "I'll Go Where You Want Me to Go." (*Hymns,* no. 270.)

BIOGRAPHICAL SKETCH: ZIBA PETERSON

Ziba Peterson was baptized on April 18, 1830, and ordained an elder by June 1830. The following October, the Lord called him on a mission to the Lamanites. The missionaries arrived in Independence, Missouri, in December 1830. Ziba and Peter Whitmer preached to the Indians across the Missouri River on April 8, 1831. "Ziba preached with Oliver Cowdery in Lafayette County, where Ziba met and may have converted his future wife, Rebecca Hooper." (Susan Easton Black, *Who's Who in the Doctrine and Covenants,* 222.)

On June 25, 1833, Ziba was excommunicated as a result of apostasy. While the Saints were being driven from Missouri, Ziba chose to stay and make his home in Independence. In 1848 he moved to California, where he died in Placerville in 1849.

DOCTRINE AND COVENANTS 33: "OPEN YOUR MOUTHS"

Historical background: Ezra Thayre and Northrup Sweet both lived in the Palmyra, New York, area. In his later years, Ezra wrote that his conversion to the Church came as a result of hearing Hyrum Smith, the Prophet's brother, bear testimony of the Book of Mormon. Hyrum allowed Ezra to look through the book. As he did, he reported, "I received a shock with such exquisite joy that no pen can write and no tongue can express. . . . I felt as though I was truly in heaven" (Lyndon W. Cook, The Revelations of the Prophet Joseph Smith, *47–48.) Parley P. Pratt baptized both Ezra Thayre and Northrup Sweet in October 1830. Shortly after their baptism, the Prophet received instructions from the Lord for them now recorded in D&C 33. Notice how different books of scripture work together to teach truth.*

Doctrine and Covenants 33:1–18
Background and insight from the other Standard Works

Explain to your family that sometimes when the Lord gives modern revelation, He refers to things He has said elsewhere in scripture. Knowing those other scriptures can help us understand the present one. There are several examples in D&C 33.

Make sure each family member has something to mark the scriptures with (such as a red pencil). Study one or all six of the following examples of how former scriptures can help enrich our understanding of modern scriptures.

Verse 1

Have your family circle the small "b" next to "word" in verse 1 and then mark "Hel. 3:29 (29–30)" in footnote 1b. After reading together Helaman 3:29–30, ask your family what additional insight these verses provide—particularly about *whose* thoughts and intents we are better able to discern with the help of God's word. What does this sword (the word) eventually help us do?

Verse 3

Have your family circle the small "c" next to "eleventh" in verse 3 and then mark "Matt. 20:6 (1–16)" in footnote 3c. Invite someone to read Matthew 20:1–16; then ask your family how this parable helps us understand what the Lord was saying to Ezra and Northrup (and us) in D&C 33:3. What is significant about the eleventh hour? What happens at the twelfth hour?

BIOGRAPHICAL SKETCH: EZRA THAYRE

Ezra Thayer was born October 14, 1791, in Randolph, Vermont. In the 1820s he built bridges, dams, and mills in the Palmyra, New York area, where he became acquainted with the Smith family. He was baptized in 1830, and in 1831 he was called as a missionary companion to Thomas B. Marsh (see D&C 52:22) but was unable to go (see section heading to D&C 54; D&C 56:5–10). He was, however, able to serve a mission with Brother Marsh the following year. (See D&C 75:31.) (See Susan Easton Black, *Who's Who in the Doctrine and Covenants*, 320.) Ezra refused to support the Twelve Apostles after the death of Joseph and Hyrum and did not move west with the Saints. In 1860 he was baptized a member of the Reorganized Church while living in Michigan. (See Lyndon W. Cook, *The Revelations of the Prophet Joseph Smith*, 48.)

BIOGRAPHICAL SKETCH: NORTHRUP SWEET

Northrup Sweet was born in the state of New York in 1802. After joining the Church in 1830, he moved with the Saints to Ohio but left the Church before the end of 1831. Sweet helped organize a church called "The Pure Church of Christ," which soon failed. There is evidence that he lived in Michigan from 1845 to 1880. (See Lyndon W. Cook, *The Revelations of the Prophet Joseph Smith*, 48.)

Verse 4

Have your family mark the word "priestcrafts" in verse 4 and write the cross-reference "2 Nephi 26:29" in the blank space under the word in the verse. Ask, "How does 2 Nephi 26:29 define priestcrafts? Why, then, do many people 'err,' or follow ways that are not truly God's ways?"

Verse 5

Have your family circle the small "c" next to "wilderness" in verse 5 and then mark the cross-reference "Rev. 12:6 (1–6)" in footnote 5c. Take turns reading Revelation 12:1–6. Then ask your family who they think the woman is. Read the first line of the chapter summary in the LDS edition of the Bible for an explanation. (The woman is the Church, and driving it into the wilderness refers to the apostasy after New Testament times.) Have them go back to D&C 33:5 and tell in their own words what it means.

Verse 8

Have your family circle the small "b" next to "Nephi" in verse 8 and then mark the cross-reference "2 Nephi 1:27" in footnote 8b. Read together 2 Nephi 1:25–27, which contains Lehi's counsel to Laman and Lemuel about their relationship with Nephi. Ask, "According to 2 Nephi 1:27, why did Nephi 'open his mouth'? What does that teach us about what we must do to better fulfill this commandment of the Lord repeated three times in D&C 33:8–10?"

Verse 17

Have your family circle the small "b" next to "trimmed" in verse 17 and then mark the cross-reference "Matt. 25:7 (1–13)" in footnote 17b. Have them also write "D&C 45:56–57" next to "Matt. 25:7 (1–13)" in the footnotes. After reading Matthew 25:1–13 and the interpretation in D&C 45:56–57, ask your family what they think the Lord was asking us to do in D&C 33:17. Discuss what things seem to invite the Holy Spirit into your home, and what things seem to prevent the Spirit's influence from being felt. Determine a way that, as a family, you can remind yourselves to "keep your lamps trimmed and burning."

Doctrine and Covenants 33:1–18
A call to serve

If anyone in the family has previously served a full-time mission, invite that person to share some of the events related to his or her call, such as what the call said, what other instructions were given, how the person felt about the call, what the person learned in the Missionary Training Center, and what he or she recognized as most important when actually going forth to serve. (If no one in the family has had this experience, you might speak with someone in your ward or branch who has.)

Divide a piece of paper into three columns. Label these columns "What missionaries should *know*"; "What missionaries should *say*"; "What missionaries should *do*." As your family takes turns reading verses in D&C 33:1–18, stop at the end of each verse and ask, "What does this verse say we should know, say, or do as full-time or member missionaries?" Try to word each piece of counsel so it represents a principle that applies not only to Ezra Thayre and Northrup Sweet but also to all who have been called to serve—at home or as full-time missionaries.

When you finish reading the revelation and making the lists, invite each family member to do one of the following:

- Share one thing from the "Know" column that most impressed you and tell how this knowledge can help us be more effective.
- Share one thing from the "Say" or "Do" columns that you think is hard and tell what might make it easier.

Discuss as a family how to become better missionaries or how to better prepare. Make plans to follow up and improve in these areas.

DOCTRINE AND COVENANTS 34: A REVELATION TO ORSON PRATT

Historical Background: "In the fore part of November, Orson Pratt, a young man nineteen years of age, who had been baptized at the first preaching of his brother, Parley P. Pratt, September 19th (his birthday), about six weeks previous, in Canaan, New York, came to inquire of the Lord what his duty was, and received the following answer." (History of the Church, 1:127–28.) The Prophet then recorded the revelation that is now section 34. Look for the reason the Lord gives here for preaching the gospel.

Doctrine and Covenants 34:1–12
Stump or Be Stumped

Play a game with your family called Stump or Be Stumped. To play this game you will need some small treats, such as M&Ms or breakfast cereal. First read to your family the historical background above and biographical sketch below. Then give them five minutes to read the section heading and D&C 34:1–12. (Young family members may need to be paired up with better readers.) Have them study with the following two purposes in mind:

1. To know the revelation well enough to be able to answer any question about this revelation without being "stumped."

2. To think of questions about the section that might "stump" other family members.

After the five-minute study time, ask each family member, "Stump or be stumped?" If the person says "Stump," then he or she asks a question in an attempt to stump you. If the person says, "Be stumped," then you ask him or her a question about D&C 34. Once a question is asked, the other person may not look in the scriptures for the answer. Those who give correct answers or are able to stump you receive a treat. Below are some questions you may want to use to stump your family:

- To whom was this revelation directed? (See section heading.)

- On what special day was Orson Pratt baptized? (See historical background.)
- How old was Orson Pratt at the time of this revelation? (See section heading.)
- Orson Pratt was one of the first men to hold what Church position in this dispensation? (See biographical sketch.)
- Name two titles of Jesus used in this revelation. (Verse 1.)
- How did Jesus show he "loved the world"? (Verse 3.)
- In this revelation, Jesus is said to be the "light and the _____ of the world." (Verse 2.)
- Orson was blessed because he believed and more blessed for what other reason? (Verses 4–5.)
- Orson was told to preach the gospel as if playing what musical instrument? (Verse 6.)
- When Christ comes again, what will the nations do? (Verse 8.)
- What will happen to the sun when Christ returns? (Verse 9.)
- What gift of the Holy Ghost was Orson given? (Verse 10.)
- What blessing was Orson promised if he remained faithful? (Verse 11.)

Now that you have played the game, have your family look over D&C 34 again, thinking about what it might have been like for a nineteen-year-old convert of six weeks to read it for the first time. Ask which parts of the revelation they think would have most impressed, enlightened, or inspired Orson, and explain why they think so.

Doctrine and Covenants 34:10
Spare me

Ask your family, "What does it mean to spare someone?" (To to excuse them or let them off the hook from punishment or responsibility.) Read D&C 34:10 to your family and ask:

- What does it mean that Orson Pratt was to "spare not" when lifting up his voice? (He

BIOGRAPHICAL SKETCH: ORSON PRATT

Orson Pratt was born on September 19, 1811. Six weeks after his baptism, he was called by the Lord to preach the gospel. (See D&C 34:5–6.) Over the next fifty years, Orson traveled thousands of miles by foot, boat, and otherwise in response to this call—including sixteen crossings of the Atlantic Ocean to preach in the British Isles. He was the first man in the Church called as an elders' quorum president, and in 1835 he was ordained to be one of the first twelve apostles in this dispensation. In 1842 Orson temporarily fell into apostasy and was excommunicated in August. However, he quickly repented and was rebaptized by the Prophet in January of 1843 and was also reinstated into the Quorum of the Twelve. As part of Brigham Young's advance company on the trek west, Orson used scientific instruments to keep a meticulous log of the journey, and he was one of the first Saints to see the Salt Lake Valley. Orson Pratt died on October 3, 1881. Wilford Woodruff stated of Orson Pratt, "I never saw a man in my life that I know of that has spent as few moments idly as he has." (*Journal of Discourses,* 21:315.)

was not to hold back or leave anyone out from hearing the gospel message.)

- Why might a Church member or missionary choose not to share the gospel with someone?
- What promise does this verse say the Lord will give to those who fulfill His command?
- Why should we not judge who or who not to share the gospel with? (See 1 Samuel 16:7.)

As a family, discuss people you may want to share the gospel with and how to approach them.

DOCTRINE AND COVENANTS 35: "MY SERVANT SIDNEY"

Historical background: Read the section heading for background information on this section. As you study this revelation, look for how the Lord prepared Sidney Rigdon and what he was promised.

Doctrine and Covenants 35:1–6
What is God's plan for you?

Have your family divide into pairs and give them paper and pencils. Ask each person to write a brief life plan for the person he or she is paired with for the upcoming year. When all have finished, invite some family members to share the plan they wrote for their partners. Ask some of the partners what they liked or disliked about the plans written for them. Read D&C 35:1–6. Ask:

- What does "Alpha and Omega" mean? (They are the first and last letters of the Greek alphabet. See also the teaching idea for D&C 19:1–4 in this book.)
- What might the Lord mean when He says that He is "Alpha and Omega"?
- How would knowing the end from the beginning make it easier for the Lord to prepare Sidney for his future?
- How had God prepared Sidney Rigdon for service in the Church? (See the biographical sketch on the next page. Sidney had been a preacher.)
- How did this preparation allow Sidney to fulfill the Lord's plan for him?
- Even though you may not know what the Lord has in mind for your future, in what ways has He been preparing you to fulfill His plan for you?

Share your testimony with your family that God does have a plan for each of us and that as we live the best we can, we will see His hand in our lives.

Doctrine and Covenants 35:7–12
Faith precedes the miracle

Read the following story by President Thomas S. Monson to your family:

"Fifty years ago, I knew a young man—even a priest—who held the authority of the Aaronic Priesthood. As the bishop, I was his quorum president. Robert stuttered and stammered, void of control. Self-conscious, shy, fearful of himself and all others, this impediment was devastating to him. Never did he fulfill an assignment; never would he look another in the eye; always he would gaze downward. Then one day, through a set of unusual circumstances, he accepted an assignment to perform the priestly responsibility to baptize another.

"I sat next to Robert in the baptistry of the Salt Lake Tabernacle. He was dressed in immaculate white, prepared for the ordinance he was to perform. I leaned over and asked him how he felt. He gazed at the floor and stuttered almost uncontrollably that he felt terrible, terrible.

"We both prayed fervently that he would be made equal to his task. Suddenly the clerk said, 'Nancy Ann McArthur will now be baptized by Robert Williams, a priest.'

"Robert left my side, stepped into the font, took little Nancy by the hand and helped her into that water which cleanses human lives and provides a spiritual rebirth. He spoke the words, 'Nancy Ann McArthur, having been commissioned of Jesus Christ, I baptize you in the name of the Father, and of the Son, and of the Holy Ghost. Amen.' Not once did he stutter! Not once did he falter! A modern miracle had been witnessed. Robert then performed the baptismal ordinance for two or three other children in the same fashion.

"In the dressing room, as I congratulated Robert, I expected to hear this same uninterrupted flow of speech. I was wrong. He gazed downward and stammered his reply of gratitude.

"To each of you brethren this evening, I testify that when Robert acted in the authority of the

Aaronic Priesthood, he spoke with power, with conviction, and with heavenly help." (*Ensign*, November 2000, 47–48.)

Take turns reading D&C 35:7–12. Ask:

- How is this story an example of the doctrine taught in these verses?
- To whom will God show miracles, signs, and wonders?
- Why do you think faith is so important that God will not show anything without it?

Write the following sentence where all can see it: "If I have the faith, God can _____." Invite your family to write that sentence in their journals and fill in the blank with a righteous blessing they would like to receive from the Lord. Share your testimony with your family of a time when a miracle came after you exercised faith.

Doctrine and Covenants 35:13–21
Thrashing the nations

Give each family member a blank sheet of paper and ask them to fold it in half. Explain that they are going to create two lists. On one side, have them write characteristics that describe the president of a very big company. On the other side, have them write characteristics that describe a full-time missionary. Compare the two lists with your family. Read together D&C 35:13–14. Ask:

- How might young men at age nineteen be considered "weak things of the world"?
- What does the Lord want them to do? (Thrash the nations.)
- What does the word "thrash" mean? (Have someone read the definition in a dictionary.

BIOGRAPHICAL SKETCH: SIDNEY RIGDON

Sidney Rigdon was born February 19, 1793, in Allegheny County, Pennsylvania. "In the fall of 1830 Sidney Rigdon was introduced to the restored Church by his friend Parley P. Pratt. Being a former Baptist preacher and one of the founders of the Campbellite movement, he was initially skeptical of the new religious thinking. However, when he read the Book of Mormon he recognized truth and was baptized on November 14, 1830. Sidney became a key figure in the Church from 1830 to 1838. He dedicated Independence, Missouri, as the land of Zion, pronouncing 'this land consecrated and dedicated to the Lord for a possession and inheritance for the Saints' (see D&C 58:57). He was a scribe for the Prophet Joseph Smith for much of the translation of the Bible. He shared many revelations with the Prophet, including the vision of the degrees of glory (see D&C 76). He was a spokesman for Joseph and a powerful speaker, and was known as a 'defender of the truth.'" (Susan Easton Black, *Who's Who in the Doctrine and Covenants*, 244–45.)

Sidney suffered great persecutions as a member of the Church. On March 24, 1832, he was tarred and feathered and dragged by his feet behind a horse. He took years to recover. On March 18, 1833, he became a member of the First Presidency. (See D&C 90:6.) However, by 1842, he was having disagreements with the Prophet and eventually was cut off from the Church. After Joseph Smith's martyrdom, Sidney came back to the Church to stand as its "guardian," but he was rejected in favor of Brigham Young and the Twelve. Sidney parted from the Church for good and later died in New York on July 14, 1876.

To "thrash" or "thresh" means to separate seeds from the chaff by beating.)

- How is missionary work like thrashing or threshing wheat?
- By what power are they to do this?
- Why might "weak" and "unlearned" (in the ways of the world) people be more receptive to the Spirit?
- In what ways does the Lord say He will support them?

Read to your family D&C 35:15–21. While you read, discuss the following questions. Invite your family to turn their papers over and write the answers they find from the reading and the discussion.

- To whom will the gospel be preached?
- Through whom has the Lord sent the gospel? (Verse 17.)
- What keys does Joseph Smith hold? (Verse 18.)
- Where could we read the truths the Lord revealed to Joseph Smith? (The scriptures— verse 20.)
- How will these latter-day scriptures help prepare the "poor and meek" for the Lord's coming? (Verse 21.)
- What can you do to help prepare yourself and others for the Lord's coming?

Invite family members to read their answers. Discuss how a study of the Doctrine and Covenants might help your family prepare to be "weak things" that effectively share the gospel.

Doctrine and Covenants 35:24–27
How can you cause the heavens to shake for your good?

 Have your family think of a time (or use their imagination) when they were sitting in a sports stadium. Ask: "Did it ever feel like the stadium was shaking for the good of the team?"

Ask your family to keep that idea in mind as you read together D&C 35:22–24. Then ask:

- What was Sidney Rigdon commanded to do for Joseph Smith in verses 22–23? (Stay with him and prove his words from the scriptures.)
- What else was Sidney commanded to do in verse 24?
- What did the Lord promise Sidney if he stayed faithful? (Verse 24.)
- How does that remind you of the cheering of the crowd for the home team?
- Who in heaven cheers for us when we do good?
- What more do you think it means when the Lord causes the "heavens to shake for your good"?

Have your family silently read D&C 35:24–27 and look for blessings that come to those who "keep all the commandments and covenants by which [they] are bound." Ask:

- What would it be like to live in a time when Satan "trembles" and the righteous "rejoice"?
- What modern examples can you think of when God caused "the heavens to shake" for someone's good as he or she kept "the commandments and covenants"?

Invite your family to write in their journals what they will do to better keep the commandments and the covenants they have made.

DOCTRINE AND COVENANTS 36: EDWARD PARTRIDGE IS CALLED TO THE WORK

Historical background: After being taught by missionaries in Ohio, Edward Partridge traveled with Sidney Rigdon to meet Joseph Smith in New York. After hearing the Prophet preach, Edward desired baptism and was baptized by the Prophet on December 11, 1830. Edward asked the Prophet to seek the Lord's will concerning him. The revelation found in this section was received in reply. Watch for what every priesthood holder should be doing.

Doctrine and Covenants 36:1–8
Tic-Tac-Toe

Tell your family you are going to play a game of Scripture Tic-Tac-Toe. Divide your family into two teams; assign one to be the X's and the other the O's. Read the historical background above and biographical sketch on the following page to your family and then have them carefully read D&C 36. Have one team choose which square they would like to try for; then ask them one of the questions below. If a team is able to answer a question correctly, they get the square. If they give a wrong answer, the other team gets the square. Alternate between teams until one team has three squares in a row or all the squares are filled. Depending on the ages of the players, you may or may not choose to let the players refer to their books during the game.

Questions:

- To whom was D&C 36 given? (See the section heading.)
- "The Prophet said that Edward Partridge was a "pattern of _____, and one of the Lord's _____ ____." (See the section heading.)
- What did the Lord tell Edward about his sins? (Verse 1.)
- What was Edward Partridge called to do? (Verse 1.)
- Who would give Edward the Holy Ghost? (Verse 2.)
- What would the Holy Ghost teach? (Verse 2.)

- The Lord gave a command that every elder who embraced the gospel should do what? (Verse 5.)
- The message of the elders includes "crying _____." (Verse 6.)
- Where would the Lord come suddenly? (Verse 8.)

After playing the game, ask family members what they think is meant by "the peaceable things of the kingdom" in verse 2. Share this statement by Elder Marvin J. Ashton:

"Most men yearn for peace, cry for peace, pray for peace, and work for peace, but there will not be lasting peace until all mankind follow the path pointed out and walked by the living Christ. There can be no peace in sin and disobedience. If I do not have peace within me, others around me will suffer." (*Ensign,* November 1985, 69.)

Doctrine and Covenants 36:2
Acting in God's name

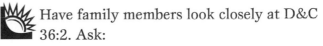 Have family members look closely at D&C 36:2. Ask:

- Who said he would lay his hands upon Edward? (The Lord.)
- Through whom would the Lord work to give the gift of the Holy Ghost? (Sidney Rigdon.)
- What does this teach about using the priesthood?

Share the following statement by Elder Gene R. Cook:

"The scriptures are literal. They really do mean

BIOGRAPHICAL SKETCH: EDWARD PARTRIDGE

Edward Partridge was born August 27, 1793, in Pittsfield, Massachusetts. He learned the hatter's trade and was living in Ohio when first contacted by Mormon missionaries in 1830. Less than two months following his baptism, Edward Partridge was called to serve as the first bishop of the Church, for, as the Lord said, "His heart is pure before me, for he is like Nathanael of old, in whom there is no guile." (D&C 41:11.) In the midst of the persecution in Missouri, Bishop Partridge was taken to the town square in Independence in July 1833 and was tarred and feathered. He was later taken prisoner in Far West and spent time in jail in Richmond before being released. Continued threats against his life forced Edward to flee to Illinois. He eventually made it to Nauvoo, where he also served as bishop. Having served valiantly, Edward died May 27, 1840, at the age of forty-six. The Lord revealed in D&C 124:19 that he had received Edward Partridge unto himself.

what they say. In D&C 36:2, for example, the Lord says to Edward Partridge, 'I will lay my hand upon you by the hand of my servant Sidney Rigdon, and you shall receive my Spirit, the Holy Ghost, even the Comforter, which shall teach you the peaceable things of the kingdom.'

"Think of what he is saying. A bishop might place his hands upon the head of a member and say, 'I now lay my hands upon you, John, as your bishop, to set you apart'—and at the same time, it would be as if Jesus Christ were saying, 'It will be as if I laid my own hands upon your head. I will do it through my servant, the bishop.'

"Does this scripture really mean that? It really means that. If you're a priesthood holder, then, and you're giving someone a blessing, you are standing in the stead of the Lord in putting your hands on his or her head. Your hands are very literally representing the hands of the Lord.

"And if you're receiving that blessing, what a great thing it is to know that the person who is officiating is standing in for the Lord." (*Searching the Scriptures*, 79.)

Discuss ways you can help priesthood holders in your family to better use their priesthood.

DOCTRINE AND COVENANTS 37: THE CHURCH MOVES WEST TOWARD ZION

Historical background: *Sidney Rigdon was acting as Joseph's scribe while the Prophet worked on the inspired translation of the Bible (see D&C 35:20) when the Lord commanded them to cease their work, leave Fayette, New York, and go to Ohio. Joseph Fielding Smith gave two reasons for this direction: (1) "The trend of the Church was ever westward; as persecution arose, and it became necessary to seek protection, the Church moved farther . . . west." (2) "The place of the City of Zion was west and it was necessary that eventually the Church be located there, although it would not be a permanent residence until Zion is redeemed." (Church History and Modern Revelation, 1:163.)*

Doctrine and Covenants 37:1
What was Joseph translating?

Invite your family to read D&C 37:1. Ask them what it was that Joseph was told to stop doing for a little while. Explain that Joseph had already translated the Book of Mormon. To find out what Joseph was now translating, invite your family to unscramble the following message using the key below: first word = [20, 18, 1, 14, 19, 12, 1, 20, 5]; second word = [20, 8, 5]; third word = [2, 9, 2, 12, 5].

To help explain what the Prophet Joseph was doing with the Bible, share the following explanation. (See also "Joseph Smith Translation" in the Bible Dictionary, 717.)

"The Prophet's inspired version of the Bible is generally referred to as the Joseph Smith Translation (JST). It is not a translation in the usual sense because no foreign-language texts were involved. The Prophet received through revelation revisions that clarified the meaning of the King James Bible, sometimes correcting errors or restoring material that had been lost. The Joseph Smith Translation is more than a commentary on biblical passages. It is a clarifying restoration of the original scriptural message, or, more strictly speaking, an inspired English translation of that original message." (Richard O. Cowan, *Answers to Your Questions About the Doctrine and Covenants,* 49.)

As an example of the important changes Joseph made to the Bible, invite your family to read Exodus 9:12 and look for something that seems wrong with the verse. (Does the Lord harden hearts?) Then have them read footnote 12a to see Joseph Smith's inspired correction. Discuss how the footnote helps teach correct doctrine. Share with your family how you have been helped by Joseph Smith's inspired translation of the Bible.

Doctrine and Covenants 37:2
The prayer of faith

Write the following references on masking tape and stick the tape to some kind of packaged treat (mints, bite size candy bars, suckers, etc.): James 5:15; Alma 31:38; D&C 5:24; 28:13; 41:3; 42:14; 43:12; 52:9; 58:44; 93:51–52; 104:79–80. Each person must read a scripture and share what was given as the reward for "the prayer of faith" before receiving a treat. After everyone has had an opportunity to share a

A	B	C	D	E	F	G	H	I	J	K	L	M
1	2	3	4	5	6	7	8	9	10	11	12	13
N	O	P	Q	R	S	T	U	V	W	X	Y	Z
14	15	16	17	18	19	20	21	22	23	24	25	26

scripture passage, invite a family member to read aloud D&C 37:2. Ask:

- Who else prayed in faith?
- What was their reward?
- What advantages can you see to praying with faith?

Read the following quotation:

"The prayer of faith is the secret of the strength of the church. There is no progress without prayer." (Hyrum M. Smith and Jane M. Sjodahl, *The Doctrine and Covenants Commentary*, 194.)

Tell about a time when you prayed in faith and your prayer was answered.

Doctrine and Covenants 37:3–4
The Church moves west toward Zion

 Ask each family member a question like one of the following:

- If you were not feeling well at school, where would you most want to go?
- If you were really sad about a score you received on a test, where would you want to be?
- If some of your classmates at school were being unkind to you, where would you want to go?

The answer to all of these questions would probably be "home." Ask your family why we always want to be home with those we love, and who love us, when things go bad. Tell your family that Heavenly Father wants His children to be safe when things go bad in the world too.

Take turns reading D&C 10:65 and 29:7–8. Ask:

- What was the Lord teaching the Saints in these verses? (The need for the gathering.)

- Why did they need to gather together? (To escape the Lord's punishment of the wicked— D&C 29:8.)
- Where does it say they were supposed to gather? (It doesn't.)

Have everyone read D&C 37:3–4. Then discuss the following questions:

- Where were the Saints to gather?
- Who would meet them there?
- Why was it "wisdom" for the Saints to gather in Ohio at this time? (Read the historical background above.)
- Why was it important that each person be able to "choose for himself" in this decision? (See D&C 88:81–82.)
- When new converts join the Church, how are they gathered even though they do not change where they live?

To help explain that question, share the following statement: "A branch of Israel is gathered when the people accept the true Messiah and become part of the true fold and church of God. (See 2 Ne. 9:2; 25:14.) That gathering is twofold: first spiritual and secondly temporal. People are gathered, first, when they join the true church and, secondly, when they gather to that appropriate location wherein the Saints of God in their area congregate." (Kent P. Jackson, ed., *Studies in Scripture, Vol. 7: 1 Nephi to Alma 29*, 77.)

Discuss reasons why you are currently "gathered" where you are. The following questions might help your discussion:

- What choices brought you here?
- How have you fulfilled the Lord's purposes here?
- What would you do if the Lord called you to gather someplace new?

DOCTRINE AND COVENANTS 38: THE SAINTS ARE COMMANDED TO BE ONE

Historical background: News that the Lord had commanded the Saints to move to Ohio (D&C 37:3) traveled quickly. During a conference of the Church in January 1831 at Peter Whitmer Sr.'s home in Fayette, New York, the gathered Saints wanted to know more about this commandment. Joseph Smith inquired of the Lord and received section 38. Notice what the Lord said we must do to obtain our land of promise.

Doctrine and Covenants 38:1–4
How does the Lord introduce himself?

Role-play the following situation with your family. Have one family member stand and introduce himself or herself as if meeting your family for the very first time. After this introduction, ask your family:

- What is the most difficult thing you experience when introducing yourself?
- What things would be the most important for others to know about you?
- How do you think the Lord would introduce himself?

Take turns reading D&C 38:1–4 with your family and invite them to mark the different ways the Lord introduces himself. Invite them to choose one of the introductions that most impressed them and share why it was impressive. If some wonder what the "seraphic hosts of heaven" are as mentioned in verse 1, see "Seraphim" on page 771 in the Bible Dictionary to discover the meaning.

Doctrine and Covenants 38:5–9
What is meant by the phrase "gird up your loins and be prepared"?

Ask your family to tell what kind of work needs to be done around the house. What do they do to prepare for physical work? (Wear old clothes, roll up their sleeves, etc.) Read together D&C 38:5–9. Ask:

- What is the "work" or task the Savior is preparing to do? (The Second Coming.)

- How does verse 9 suggest we prepare for the day of His coming?
- What does it mean to "gird up your loins and be prepared"? ("'Gird up your loins' means gather up the long robe under the belt or sash and get ready for action" [Daniel H. Ludlow, *A Companion to Your Study of the Old Testament*, 315]. In other words, girding up your loins frees your legs in preparation for physical work.)
- What can we do to "get ready for action" and prepare for the second coming of the Savior? (Consider reviewing D&C 4 and D&C 27:15–18.)

A person "girding up his loins."

Doctrine and Covenants 38:10–12, 30
When will the angels be loosed to reap the earth?

Ask your family to look at the section heading for D&C 38 and find the date that section was revealed. Invite a family member to read D&C 38:10–12. Ask:

- What do we learn about the world in January 1831?
- What were the angels "waiting" to do? ("Reap down the earth.")
- What does this mean? (Cut down the wicked and gather the righteous, in preparation for the coming of the Lord.)

Share the following quotation from an address of President Wilford Woodruff at Brigham City, Utah, in June 1894:

"God has held the angels of destruction for many years lest they reap down the wheat with the tares. But I want to tell you now, those angels have left the portals of heaven, and they stand over this people and this nation now, and are hovering over the earth waiting to pour out the judgments. And from this very day they shall be poured out. Calamities and troubles are increasing in the earth and there is a meaning to these things. Remember this and reflect upon these matters. If you do your duty, and I do my duty, we shall have protection and shall pass through the afflictions in peace and safety. Read the scriptures and revelations." (*Discourses of Wilford Woodruff,* 230.)

Ask:

- What had changed by 1894?
- What are some evidences that these angels are now reaping the earth? (World War I, World War II, etc.)
- What can we do to prepare for the trying times ahead?
- What are some things the prophets have asked us to do to prepare?

Have one family member read D&C 38:30 and

then have another share the following quotation: "Here then is the key—look to the prophets for the words of God, that will show us how to prepare for the calamities which are to come." (Ezra Taft Benson, *Ensign,* January 1974, 69.) Give family members a sheet of paper (or their journal) and have them write and finish the following sentences:

1. "If I am prepared for the coming of the Lord, then _____."
2. "I will prepare for the coming of the Lord by _____."

Doctrine and Covenants 38:16–27
What must I do to obtain the "land of promise"?

In one hand have a sack labeled "lots of money"; in the other hand have a spoon. Show your family what you have in your hands and ask them which they would rather have and why. Replace the spoon with a picture of your family and ask the same question. Hold up the money and ask, "Is it wrong to seek for riches?" Turn to and read Jacob 2:18–19. Ask:

- What should we seek before we seek for riches? (Verse 18.)
- Why is the kingdom of God more valuable than earthly wealth?
- If the Lord blesses us with riches, what should we do with them? (Verse 19.)
- What other kinds of riches can the Lord bless us with?

Take turns reading D&C 38:16–27 and discuss the following questions as you read:

- What are the greater "riches" mentioned here?
- What sort of "land of promise" were the Saints hoping for? (It is also called Zion or the New Jerusalem, where Christ will come to be with His people at his second coming.)
- How can we receive this "promised land" for our inheritance? (Verse 19.)

- How can we possess the promised land even in eternity? (Verse 20. See also D&C 88:17–20. This earth will become a celestial kingdom.)
- According to verses 21–23, what else must we do to be worthy of the promised land?
- What does it mean to "esteem his brother as himself" (verses 24–25), and why do you think it is said twice?
- What phrase in verses 26–27 best summarizes what the Lord requires of us in those verses?

Share your testimony of the greater joy that comes from the Lord's eternal blessings compared to temporary, earthly blessings.

Doctrine and Covenants 38:31–42
Why did the Lord want the Church members in the East to move to Ohio?

Remind your family of your most recent move, or have them imagine having moved, and ask:

- What makes moving so difficult?
- Are there times when it is the best thing to do? When?
- Would you want to move again? Why?

Tell your family that the Saints in 1831 were facing a move from New York to Ohio. Work through the chart below as a family and determine why it was "best" for the Saints to move. Read each verse listed and find the purposes for the move to Ohio. Also discuss possible ways each of these prophecies was fulfilled. Review the column "Some Possible Ways These Prophecies Were Fulfilled" and the accompanying scriptures to aid your discussion.

Have your family read D&C 38:39 and look for the warning the Lord gave to the Saints as they prepared for the move to Ohio. Testify that as Church members obey, they will always receive the promised blessings.

Verse	Purpose for the Move to Ohio	Some Possible Ways These Prophecies Were Fulfilled
31	Escape the power of enemies.	The Saints experienced a time of peace when they arrived in Ohio.
31	Gather a righteous people.	D&C 42:1–3. Ohio did become the gathering place for the Saints
32	To be given the Lord's law.	D&C 42. The law of consecration. ("The law of the Church")
32	To be endowed with power from on high.	D&C 109:22. An endowment of power is given in the temple.
35	To look to the poor and the needy.	D&C 42: 30–31. The establishment of the law of consecration.
39	To have the riches of eternity.	D&C 109. The dedication of the temple.
42	To go out from among the wicked.	D&C 38, historical background. The gathering to establish Zion.

DOCTRINE AND COVENANTS 39: A MESSAGE TO JAMES COVILL

Historical background: This revelation was given shortly after the Church conference in Fayette, New York, in early January 1831. There is no other historical information known about this revelation other than that given in the section heading. Notice what the Lord promises to all who receive the gospel.

Doctrine and Covenants 39:1–6
Learning about the Lord

In preparation for studying these verses, show the following objects to your family:

- A light bulb.
- A card with the symbol for infinity written on it (∞).
- An electrical cord.

Ask your family to suggest ways these things can remind us of Jesus Christ. Have them read D&C 39:1–6 to find descriptions of Him that are symbolized by what you showed them. (For example, the infinity symbol could relate to the description that He is "from all eternity to all eternity" in verse 1, or an electric cord could remind us that He is our source of power to become His "sons" in verse 4.)

Assign one member of your family be a scribe. Have the rest of your family review D&C 39:1–6 and find the things those verses teach us about the Lord. After your scribe completes the list of the things your family found, discuss each item by asking:

- Why would it be important to know this particular truth about the Savior?
- What difference should it make in our lives if we believe this truth?

The following ideas, while not addressing everything that could be listed in these verses, may help as you discuss these verses as a family:

- "The Great I AM": This is the name by which the Lord identified Himself to Moses at the time Moses was called to lead the children of Israel out of Egypt. (See Exodus 3:11–16.) The same God who led the children of Israel out of Egypt is here promising to lead James Covill out of the life he has been leading to a better one. He promises the same to us.
- "The light and life of the world": Everything that has life, shows movement, grows, or otherwise exists in this dynamic world does so by power that comes from the Lord. With that kind of power, wouldn't we want to "hearken and listen" (see D&C 39:1) when He gives commands—no matter how hard, strange, or simple they seem to us?
- "Power to become my sons": Although we are all children of God, the Fall cuts us off from the blessings of receiving the full inheritance of sons and daughters (all that the Father has). Those who receive Christ by fully receiving his gospel (see D&C 39:5–6) are given power to become like Him—and thus become sons and daughters unto God and heirs of all He has. Only Christ can do this for us, but we must be willing to receive it. He will not force these blessings upon us

BIOGRAPHICAL SKETCH: JAMES COVILL

Almost nothing is known of James Covill—either before or after the revelations found in D&C 39 and 40. Efforts by scholars to uncover his history have ended in uncertain results. (For example, see Lyndon W. Cook, *The Revelations of the Prophet Joseph Smith*, 56–57; Susan Easton Black, *Who's Who in the Doctrine and Covenants*, 72.) All we really know about James Covill is found in D&C sections 39–40.

(as is seen in the end of the story of James Covill).

Ask your family to name some of the other "voices" we are tempted to listen to and follow besides the Lord's. Ask, "What are some reasons we may follow these other voices instead of His? What can we do to more fully remember the truths we learned about Him in this revelation and hearken to His voice?"

Doctrine and Covenants 39:7–24
Blessings and promises for James Covill

Have a family member who has received his or her patriarchal blessing share what it has taught them about God and how it has influenced his or her life. Share with your family the following quotation from President James E. Faust:

"Heavenly Father knows His children. He knows their strengths and weaknesses. He knows their capabilities and potential. Our patriarchal blessings indicate what He expects of us and what our potential can be." He also said that patriarchal blessings contain "blessings, spiritual gifts, promises, advice, admonition, and warnings" from God. (*Ensign*, November 1995, 62–63.)

Tell your family that although there were not yet patriarchs in the Church at the time, this revelation for James Covill was much like a patriarchal blessing in that it came from God, who knew his "strengths and weaknesses" as well as his "capabilities and potential" and offered him "blessings, spiritual gifts, promises, advice, admonition, and warnings."

Assign each family member one or more of the following categories:

- Strengths and weaknesses.
- Capabilities and potential.
- Spiritual gifts.
- Promises.
- Advice and "warnings."

Tell family members that they are in charge of identifying things belonging to the category (or categories) they were assigned as your family takes turns reading verses in D&C 39:7–24. Stop after each verse to let family members tell what they identified. Ask family members who identify something to tell how they would feel if the Lord said that same thing to them. What would they do as a result? Of the things the Lord said to James Covill, which ones do you think the Lord is also saying to us?

Tell your family that, as they will read in D&C 40, receiving the blessings God would give us depends on our willingness to be obedient to His counsel. Share with them this analogy from Elder Carlos E. Asay:

"When a stake patriarch places his hand upon your head, gives you a blessing, and inspires you with pronounced prophecies and promises, an exciting beginning has been made. It is left to you to keep those prophecies and promises riveted in your mind—regarding them as attainable goals—and proceed forward with righteous living and faithful service so that you might draw claim upon the related blessings.

"By way of illustration, the patriarch stands with you at the starter's gate. He envisions for you the race that lies ahead. With the aid of his special gifts, he outlines the rules of the contest, he describes the challenges that will be faced, and he cites the laurels that may be won. However, you, the runner, must stay in the marked lane, abide the rules, cover the course, and cross the finish line if you expect to receive the victor's prize." ("Write Your Own Blessing," *New Era*, October 1981, 4.)

Encourage family members who have patriarchal blessings to read them again, noting strengths and weaknesses, capabilities and potential, spiritual gifts, promises, advice, admonitions, and warnings.

DOCTRINE AND COVENANTS 40: JAMES COVILL REJECTS THE WORD

Historical background: This revelation was given as a result of James Covill's rejection of the Lord's instructions received earlier the same month. See the section heading for D&C 39 and the historical background for section 39 in this book.

Doctrine and Covenants 40:1–3
What could cause a person to break covenants?

Read the following statements to a family member (inserting the person's name in the blank) and ask which one he or she most prefers and why:

1. _____ is a righteous person.
2. _____ was a righteous person.
3. _____ will become a righteous person.
4. _____ may become a righteous person.

Ask your family to silently read the section heading for D&C 40 and identify whom the Lord was speaking about in this revelation. (Note that James Covill was also the man to whom section 39 was given.) Read D&C 40:1, 3 and determine which of the statements you read previously would best describe James Covill. How would you feel if the Lord said these things about you? Why?

Read D&C 40:2 and discuss these questions:

- What were some reasons James Covill broke his covenant?
- What does this teach you about his heart?
- What soil described in Mark 4:14–20 is most like James's heart?
- How can we help make sure we will never reject the word of the Lord?

Share the following statement from Joseph Fielding Smith:

"When [James Covill] withdrew from the influence of the Spirit of the Lord and had time to consider the fact that he would lose the fellowship of the world, and his place and position among his associates, he failed and rejected the promises and blessings which the Lord offered him. . . . How many others there have been, and now are, who have rejected the word of the Lord because of the love of the world and the fear of men, to mortals may never be made known." (*Church History and Modern Revelation,* 1:159–60.)

DOCTRINE AND COVENANTS 41: THE RESPONSIBILITY OF DISCIPLESHIP

Historical background: Section 41 is the first revelation in the Doctrine and Covenants received in Ohio after Joseph Smith and his wife arrived in Kirtland around February 1, 1831. Many people in Kirtland belonged to a group called "seekers" who were trying to the live the gospel as described in the New Testament. Many of them enthusiastically received the message of the Restoration when it was preached to them. Nearly 200 people had joined the Church by the time Joseph Smith came to Kirtland. Although these new converts were sincere, they needed the guidance of the Lord's prophet. This revelation, along with sections 42 and 43, provided instruction, correction, and direction to the rapidly growing Church. Watch for what the Lord considers true discipleship.

Doctrine and Covenants 41:4–6
Listen and obey!

Before scripture study, arrange with a family member to act out a brief situation like the following: Ask the person kindly to do something, such as put away some laundry or put an item back in its place somewhere else in the house. The person looks at you and says, "Okay" but then does nothing about it. Go on to something else briefly; then come back and say, "Did you hear what I said about [whatever you asked them to do]?" The person will then say, "Yes, I heard you" but then continue to do nothing about it. You respond by saying, "I mean I want you to do it right now." The person should say, "Okay" and still do nothing. After a short time, when it's obvious that this family member is not moving, say, "I don't think you are really listening to me." Stop the role-play and tell your family that the two of you were demonstrating an idea found in D&C 41.

Read D&C 41:1–2 together. Ask:

- How do these verses apply to the situation we just acted out?
- Do you think the one family member was really "hearing" me?
- Why do you think the Lord used the words "hearken" and "hear" in verse 1?
- Do you think this is really about just listening? Why or why not?
- What does the Lord promise about those who hear and those who don't hear?

Have family members read to themselves D&C 41:3–5, looking for a word that means "a follower." ("Disciple.") Have them highlight the word in their scriptures. Ask:

- What does the Lord want the Saints to receive from Him?
- How does He define what it means to be a disciple?

Share with your family the following teachings of Elder Dallin H. Oaks. He helps us see that while listening to and knowing the truth is important, there is more if we want to be true disciples:

"Jesus' challenge shows that the conversion He required for those who would enter the kingdom of heaven (see Matt. 18:3) was far more than just being converted to testify to the truthfulness of the gospel. To testify is to *know* and to *declare*. The

gospel challenges us to be 'converted,' which requires us to *do* and to *become*. If any of us relies solely upon our knowledge and testimony of the gospel, we are in the same position as the blessed but still unfinished Apostles whom Jesus challenged to be 'converted.' We all know someone who has a strong testimony but does not act upon it so as to be converted. For example, returned missionaries, are you still seeking to be converted, or are you caught up in the ways of the world?" (*Ensign*, November 2000, 32.)

Ask your family:

- What did Elder Oaks say the gospel challenges us to do to become converted?
- What is the difference between "testify" and "converted?"
- What did you learned from Elder Oaks's statement about being a true disciple?

Testify to your family of the importance of not only hearing the gospel but also living it.

Doctrine and Covenants 41:7–12
The first bishop

Ask your family to think about your bishop. Ask each family member to name one quality they admire in him. After everyone shares, read D&C 41:7–12 aloud and ask:

- Who was named as the first bishop?
- In what way was his calling different from your bishop's calling today? (He would be more like the presiding bishop among the General Authorities today—verse 9.)
- What two qualities did the Lord say Edward Partridge possessed in verse 11?
- How do you think these qualities would help him be a good bishop?

Have your family think of a service they could do to show your bishop how your family appreciates his service. Make a plan to carry out this service project during the week.

DOCTRINE AND COVENANTS 42: "THE LAW"

Historical background: In December 1830, the Church was commanded to assemble in Ohio. (See D&C 37:3.) On January 2, 1831, the Lord declared that part of the reason for the move was to receive the Lord's law and be endowed with power from on high. (See D&C 38:32.) Section 42 was received February 9, 1831, answering the Prophet's concern about how to care for the poor and needy saints who were arriving in great numbers. The Lord revealed the law of consecration in addition to other laws by which the Church should be governed. "Altogether this was a most important revelation. It threw a flood of light upon a great variety of subjects and settled many important questions." (George Q. Cannon, Life of Joseph Smith the Prophet, 87.) Notice how many different "laws" are explained in this revelation.

Doctrine and Covenants 42:1–3
Obedience and flying a kite

Have a family member read aloud the section heading. Ask, "What is another name for section 42?" (The Law.) Read together D&C 42:1–3. Ask:

- What three things are faithful members of the Church to do when they receive the law? (Hearken, hear, and obey.)
- What is the purpose of laws?
- Do you think laws restrict us or give us more freedom?

Share the following story:

"The boy was very young. It was his first experience with kite flying. His father helped him, and after several attempts the kite was in the air. The boy ran and let out more string, and soon the kite was flying high. The little boy was so excited; the kite was beautiful. Eventually there was no more string left to allow the kite to go higher. The boy said to his father, 'Daddy, let's cut the string and let the kite go; I want to see it go higher and higher.'

"His father said, 'Son, the kite won't go higher if we cut the string.'

"'Yes, it will,' responded the little boy. 'The string is holding the kite down; I can feel it.' The father handed a pocketknife to his son. The boy cut the string. In a matter of seconds the kite was out of control. It darted here and there and finally landed in a broken heap. That was difficult for the boy to understand. He felt certain the string was holding the kite down." (Patricia P. Pinegar, *Ensign*, November 1999, 67.)

Discuss as a family the following questions:

- How are God's laws like the kite string?
- Why do some people, like the little boy in the story, resist the direction the Lord gives us through His commandments?
- If disregarding the laws of God gave you more freedom, who would be the freest person? (Satan.)
- God is perfectly obedient to His laws. How does His power and freedom compare to Satan's?

Write the following statement where all can see it, leaving out the words in parentheses, and have your family fill in the blanks: "When I (obey) the commandments, I am the most (free)."

Doctrine and Covenants 42:4–17
The law of preaching the gospel

Explain to your family that D&C 42 contains important laws for preaching the gospel. Read together verses 4–17 and look for answers to the following questions as you read:

- What is the first commandment given to the missionaries? (Verse 4.)
- In what groupings are the missionaries to go forth? (Verse 6.)

- Why do you suppose the Lord wants missionaries to go "two by two"?
- They are to build up the Church in every region in preparation for the establishment of what city? (Verse 8–9.)
- Which Article of Faith goes along with verse 11? (Fifth. See if someone can recite it from memory. If no one can recite it, turn to the back of the Pearl of Great Price and read it.)
- What are we to teach? (Verse 12.)

Point out that when this revelation was received, the Bible and the Book of Mormon were the only scriptures available. We now have the Doctrine and Covenants and the Pearl of Great Price. Have family members mark footnote 12b, the reference to D&C 52:9. Have a family member read D&C 52:9 aloud. Ask:

- According to this verse, what other writings should we teach from? (The words of the living prophets.)
- According to D&C 42:13, what else must we do besides teach from the scriptures? (Keep the covenants and commandments.)
- According to D&C 42:14, what must a person have to effectively teach? (The Spirit.)
- How do you get the Spirit? (Verse 14.)
- According to verses 16–17, why is it so important to have the Spirit, called the Comforter in these verses, when we teach? (The Comforter will bear testimony to the truths we teach.)

Share this insight from Elder Hartman Rector Jr.:

"On the surface it appears that all that is necessary to receive the Spirit is to ask for it, but it is not quite so easy a question! What is the difference between just ordinary prayer and a 'prayer of faith'? As we consider that question, the difference is immediately apparent. The difference is *faith,* and what *is* faith? Of course, there are many definitions of faith, but one definition is 'a strong belief plus *action.*' . . . The Lord's formula for receiving the Spirit, then, is to get on our knees

and communicate with him. Tell him what we are going to do—make commitments with him—outline our program—and then get up off our knees and go and *do* precisely what we have told him we would do. In the *doing,* the Spirit comes." (*Ensign,* January 1974, 106–7.)

Doctrine and Covenants 42:18–29
"Thou shalt not!"

Have family members read D&C 42:18–29 and mark in their scriptures each time the phrase "thou shalt" occurs. Ask:

- How many times is the word "not" added to the "thou shalt"? (All but three.)
- What other list of commandments is similar to the one we just read? (The Ten Commandments. See Exodus 20:3–17 if no one can answer the question.)
- What does the list in D&C 42 teach us about the importance of the Ten Commandments today?

You might share the following quotation: "Strange as it may seem, there are some people who believe that the Ten Commandments pertained to the Law of Moses, and therefore when Christ came, these laws . . . were done away. Nothing could be farther from the truth. There is not a single commandment in the [Ten Commandments] that was not accepted by the people of God as a commandment from the very beginning. . . . In this Dispensation of the Fulness of Times, the Lord restated these fundamental laws and commanded us to observe them with the strictest obedience." (Joseph Fielding Smith, *Church History and Modern Revelation,* 1:185.)

Have a family member read D&C 42:29 and tell what we can do to demonstrate our love for God. Share this insight:

"I believe this is the greatest lesson that can be learned by the youth of Zion—to do the right thing because you love the Lord. It is so vitally important that, I feel, if you do anything in righteousness for any other reason than you love the

Lord, you are wrong—at least you are on very shaky ground. And, somewhere your reasons for acting in righteousness will not be strong enough to see you through. You will give way to expediency, or peer group pressure, or honor, or fame, or applause, or the thrill of the moment, or some other worldly reason. Unless your motives are built upon the firm foundation of love of the Lord, you will not be able to stand. . . .

"I pray that we may walk in righteousness because we love the Lord, for surely this *is* the right reason." (Hartman Rector Jr., *Ensign,* January 1973, 130.)

Discuss as a family ways you can increase your love for the Lord and better keep the commandments.

Doctrine and Covenants 42:22
What does it mean to "cleave unto"?

Show your family a wedding picture (your own or one of a family member) and ask:

- Why do people always take pictures of their wedding day?
- How important do you think this day was to these people?
- How important should it be to them today?

Read together D&C 42:22. Ask what "cleave unto" means in this context. ("To unite or be united closely in interest or affection; to adhere with strong attachment; to be faithful." [*Webster's New Twentieth Century Dictionary.*])

Tell your family that President Spencer W. Kimball spoke of this verse and noted that it does not say "cleave unto her and *no one* else" but "*none else.*" He taught: "The words *none else* eliminate everyone and everything. The spouse then becomes preeminent in the life of the husband or wife, and neither social life nor occupational life nor political life nor any other interest nor person nor thing shall ever take precedence over the companion spouse." (*Faith Precedes the Miracle,* 143.) Ask, "Why do you think the Lord places such high priority on the marriage relationship?"

Doctrine and Covenants 42:30–42, 53–55, 71–73
What is the law of consecration?

Write the words *food, clothing, shelter, money,* and *books and games* on separate pieces of paper, and put the papers in a bowl or other container in front of your family. Play the game "I Don't Need It—Would You Like It?" Give each family member a sheet of paper and a pencil and have them list *food, clothing, shelter, money,* and *books and games* on their papers. The object of the game is for each family member to obtain all the items on this list by either picking the items from the container or receiving them from another family member.

Pass the container of papers to a family member and have him or her choose a paper, read it, and put it back into the container. Have that family member circle the named item on his or her list. Then pass the container to the next family member. When each person has had a turn, begin again with the first family member and have him or her pick another paper.

If a family member picks an item that is already circled on his or her list, he or she turns to the family member on the left and says, "I don't need it—would you like it?" Then the family member sitting to the left can circle that item on his or her list. If that family member already has the item circled, he or she asks the question of the next family member to the left. Play the game until each family member has circled every item on the list. (Adapted from Primary Manual Course 5, "The Lord Reveals the Law of Consecration," 91.)

Explain that the game shows some principles involved in living the law of consecration that was introduced to the Saints in section 42. (See historical background above.) Tell your family that many of the recent converts in the Kirtland area were already familiar with the idea of consecration. They had belonged to a group called the Disciples and had been trying to develop a society where they all shared their possessions based on some New Testament scriptures. (See Acts 2:44–45; 4:32.) Share the following quotation:

"The practice had begun on the farm owned by Isaac Morley, but discord arose among members over the way the system operated. They considered that what belonged to one brother belonged to any of the brethren in the society. 'Therefore,' wrote John Whitmer, 'they would take each other's clothes and other property and use it without leave, which brought on confusion and disappointment.'" (Ivan J. Barrett, *Joseph Smith and the Restoration,* 166.)

Have a family member read D&C 42:54 aloud, which seems to have been given in direct response to this confusion. As you read together D&C 42:30–42, 53–55, and 71–73, discuss the following questions:

- Who should we be concerned with that we sometimes forget? (Verses 30–31.)
- What were the Saints to do with their properties or substance? (Verses 30–31.)
- What does "consecrate" mean? (To dedicate or devote for a sacred purpose.)
- Who would be responsible for these consecrations? (Verses 31–33.)

Explain that the bishop together with the head of each family decided what property and possessions that family needed, and they received that as their stewardship. Families would then work hard to provide for themselves using the things they had been given. After providing for the family's own needs and wants, the unused portion was then given back to the bishop. Have family members read D&C 42:34–36 and find what happened to the unused portion. Ask:

- What four purposes are mentioned for which the excess was to be used?
- How might the law of consecration have been a blessing to the Saints in those days?
- What laws do we live today that are like the law of consecration? (You might show your family a donation slip that shows tithing, fast offerings, and other voluntary Church contributions.)

If time permits, you might find the following quotation from Elder David B. Haight useful:

"We hear that some young men not only request a pair of new shoes for school, but another for sports, and another for church. But not just any athletic shoe will do. They must have special designer label or be a special advertised brand. . . . Have *you* fallen into a trap of peer pressure that requires a certain look for you to be included in the 'in' crowd, whether or not your parents can afford such demands? Do others set *your* standards—what you will wear and what you will do—and not do? Believing young men and women with standards and values make these decisions for themselves and let others follow. Why aren't we, as Latter-day Saints—with our high ideals—the examples, the peer leaders setting the standards and criteria that others follow? The brand of clothes and the shoes you wear, and the gadgetry, probably not affordable by your parents, has absolutely no bearing on what you will eventually become. Our actions, our personal behavior, and our attitude determine our character and future." (*Ensign,* November 1991, 38.)

Doctrine and Covenants 42:43–52
What is the law of sickness and death?

Give family members something bitter to eat such as parsley or a radish. Have them describe the taste. If you do not have something for them to actually eat, just ask them if they can remember eating something bitter like parsley and have them describe the taste. Then give them something sweet to eat, such as a marshmallow or a piece of candy. Ask them to describe the taste. Tell your family that bitter and sweet are used to describe something in D&C 42:46–47. Invite them to read those verses to discover what it is.

Ask:

- Which word would you like to describe your death?

- What will determine whether your death is bitter or sweet?
- What do you think it means to "die in me" or "not die in me"?
- What can you do to make sure when you die, you die in the Lord?

Have your family search D&C 42:43–52 to find answers to the following questions:

- Who can be called to help the sick? (Verse 44.)
- Why is it all right to weep when someone dies? (Verse 45.)
- Why might we feel worse for some than for others when they die? (Verse 45.)
- What can you assume when a faithful person has been administered to and still dies? (Verse 48.)

Doctrine and Covenants 42:74–92
What is the law concerning sinners?

Take turns reading D&C 42:74–92 and make a list of the different sins that are mentioned and how the transgressors are to be dealt with. Determine which require Church discipline and which are to be delivered up to the law of the land. Ask:

- If someone offends you, or if you offend someone, how should the problem be resolved?
- How is the situation different if one is offended secretly or openly?

DOCTRINE AND COVENANTS 43: RECEIVING REVELATION AND MISSIONARY WORK

Historical background: Approximately five months before D&C 43 was received, a revelation to Joseph Smith said, "No one shall be appointed to receive commandments and revelations in this church excepting my servant Joseph Smith, Jun." (D&C 28:2.) Many claimed to receive revelations that would affect the entire Church. In February 1831 a woman named Mrs. Hubble arrived in Kirtland. "She professed to be a prophetess of the Lord, and professed to have many revelations, and knew the Book of Mormon was true, and that she should become a teacher in the church of Christ. She appeared to be very sanctimonious and deceived some who were not able to detect her in her hypocrisy; others, however, had the spirit of discernment and her follies and abominations were manifest." (History of the Church, 1:154.) In consequence of Mrs. Hubble, the Prophet inquired of the Lord and received section 43. Notice the several different ways the Lord calls on people to repent.

Doctrine and Covenants 43:1–7
How to detect true revelation

Have a woman or daughter in your family come to scripture study with a name tag identifying her as "Mrs. Hubble." Have her describe herself by reading the historical background information about Mrs. Hubble to your family. Also ask her to share a "revelation" with your family. (This supposed revelation could be strange or silly.) When she has finished, discuss some of these questions:

- Why might some people pretend to receive revelation?
- Can you think of an example of someone like Mrs. Hubble giving false revelations in our day?

- How were some of the people in Kirtland able to detect her lies? (They had the spirit of discernment.)
- Have you ever heard anyone contradict or make fun of the teachings of our prophets?
- How is that like claiming to receive revelation?
- How can we tell true revelation from lies and deception?

To help answer that last question, ask family members to do some "detective" work by studying D&C 43:1–7. Have them find and mark the passages that help clarify the process of receiving revelation for the Church. Talk about what they find, making sure the following points are identified:

1. Only the prophet is appointed to receive commandments and revelations for the Church. (See verses 2–3.)

2. The prophet can appoint others to this gift. (See verse 4.)

3. We are commanded not to receive the teachings of any other person as revelations or commandments. (See verse 5.)

4. These teachings help protect us from being deceived. (See verse 6.)

5. The Lord's prophet will always "come in at the gate," or in other words, be called and ordained in the established pattern of the Church. (See verse 7.)

Summarize this instruction from the Lord by sharing the following statement from Joseph Smith:

"It is against the laws of God for any member of the Church, or anyone, to receive instruction for those in authority, higher than themselves." (*Teachings of the Prophet Joseph Smith,* 21.)

Doctrine and Covenants 43:8–22
Instructions from the Lord to help us avoid deception

 Read the following statement to your family:

"After the Lord had explained and given His law of revelation to His church in order to prevent deception amongst the membership [D&C 43:1–7], He gave, by way of commandment, several instructions for the Saints to follow. Those who follow these instructions are not deceived. The Lord gave direction in at least three important areas." (Otten and Caldwell, *Sacred Truths of the Doctrine and Covenants,* 211.)

Assign each family member to one of the following three groups. Have them study the accompanying verses, looking for how those teachings can protect us from deception and keep us on the Lord's path. When each group has finished, invite them to give a brief report of (1) what their verses taught about our duties, (2) why they think it would be important to follow those teachings, and (3) how carrying out those duties will help protect us from Satan's deceptions.

Group 1: D&C 43:8–11. (As we gather together, we should instruct and edify one another.)

Group 2: D&C 43:12–14. (We should uphold, pray for, and help provide for our prophet.)

Group 3: D&C 43:15–22. (We should share gospel truths with the people of the earth.)

Share your feelings about the joys of understanding the Lord's truths and the dangers of being deceived.

Doctrine and Covenants 43:17–35
What does it mean to hearken to the voice of the Lord?

Have your family read D&C 43:17, 23, 34 and find a word that is repeated in all three verses. ("Hearken.") Ask, "What do you think the word 'hearken' means?" Have someone look the word up in a dictionary and share what it means. (To listen or pay attention to; to heed.)

- How is hearkening different from just hearing? (It means doing something, hearing and obeying.)
- According to D&C 43:17–18, what is one reason for us to hearken to (hear and obey)

the Lord? (To be prepared for the Second Coming.)

Take turns reading D&C 43:17–35. As you read, have family members notice each time a particular voice or sound (see below) is mentioned, the verse it is mentioned in, and what the accompanying message is. Compile a chart similar to the one below as you study.

After you have completed your chart, ask:

- What seems to be a recurring theme throughout these verses? (Repent.)

- Have you seen any of the promised calamities happening in our day?
- How much closer are we to the Second Coming than we were when this revelation was given?
- According to verses 29–32, what will happen to the righteous at the last day?
- According to verse 33, what will happen to the wicked?
- According to verses 34–35, what can we do to be among the righteous and not the wicked?

Voice or Sound	Verse	Message	What I can do to hearken to this command
The Lord's voice.	18	Saints arise and live, sinners stay and sleep.	Live to be worthy of rising in the first resurrection.
Church members' voices.	20	Call upon all people to repent, and prepare for the Lord's coming.	Live the teachings of the Church and share the gospel with others.
Thunders.	21	Repent.	Repent of any sins that are keeping me from being ready for the Second Coming.
And so on . . .			

DOCTRINE AND COVENANTS 44: A FOURTH CHURCH CONFERENCE

Historical background: The first three conferences of the Church were held in Fayette, New York. Joseph Smith was directed in late February of 1831 to call the missionaries to Kirtland for the Church's fourth general conference, to be held on June 3, 1831. Look for how the Lord cares about the poor and the needy.

Doctrine and Covenants 44:1–5
Why do we hold conferences?

Read the historical background above to your family. Ask family members to share some favorite things they enjoy about general conference. Read the following statement describing some purposes of general conference:

"To worship . . . the Lord . . . ; to build up in faith, testimony, and desires of righteousness; to transact the business of the Church; to sustain the officers whom the Lord has appointed to administer the affairs of his kingdom; and to receive, from those appointed so to serve, the counsel, inspiration, and revelations needed in both temporal and spiritual fields. . . . They consist of a series of meetings at which the mind and will of the Lord is manifest to the people by the mouth of his servants." (Bruce R. McConkie, *Mormon Doctrine*, 155–56.)

Read D&C 44:1–5 together and find reasons why this fourth Church conference was called. Ask:

- According to verse 2, what blessing would the elders receive by assembling together?
- What requirements does verse 2 mention before the Lord's Spirit would be poured out upon the people?
- Following the conference, where were the missionaries to focus their efforts? (See verse 3.)
- What blessings would come to the Church as they were obedient? (See verses 4–5.)
- How have we seen the fulfillment of those promises in the Church today?

Doctrine and Covenants 44:6
What are our duties concerning the poor?

Plan a family service project for a needy family. When your plans are completed, read D&C 44:6 aloud and ask:

- What did you think of our idea to do a family service project?
- Why would it be important for each of us to contribute to this project?

- How do you think the Lord feels about this project? (See also Mosiah 2:17.)
- After reading D&C 44:6, are there additional things you think we should do for this family?
- What does "my law" have reference to in this verse? (The law of consecration; see D&C 42:32–33, 105:29.)

Share the following about Joseph Smith:

"At no time during the Prophet's career did the care of the poor escape his attention or become a matter of indifference to him. He was a man of large benevolence, and his sympathies were quickly aroused by any tale of sorrow or appeal for relief. In the most busy and trying periods of his life those who went to him for counsel in their troubles, always found him willing to listen, and they were sure to receive encouragement and assistance. To extend comfort to the bruised spirit, and to help the needy and distressed appeared a constant pleasure to him. His hospitality, also, was a marked feature in his character. His house was always open to entertain the stranger. One of the most cherished recollections of many of the old members of the Church is the kindness with which they were treated by 'Brother Joseph,' and the warm welcome he gave them to his house upon their arrival at Kirtland and other places where he lived." (George Q. Cannon, *The Life of Joseph Smith, the Prophet*, 109–10.)

Discuss what else your family might do to follow the example of the Prophet Joseph.

DOCTRINE AND COVENANTS 45: THE SECOND COMING: "STAND IN HOLY PLACES"

Historical background: Within six months of the first missionaries arriving in Kirtland, Ohio, hundreds had joined the Church, the Prophet Joseph had moved to the area, and Church members from other places were commanded to gather to Ohio. (See D&C 37.) This flurry of activity drew the attention of many in northeast Ohio. As often happens, the success of the Church was met with opposition, and some people spread false stories about the Church and its members. As the Prophet pondered how the Saints "had to struggle against every thing that prejudice and wickedness could invent," he received the revelation found in D&C 45. This revelation not only teaches about the destruction of the wicked at the time of the Second Coming but also reminds the Saints that the Lord will be with and bless his gathered followers in preparation for that great day. Furthermore, "in 1831, as now, the exact circumstances and details of the second coming of Christ generated a lot of speculation among the Saints—the type of speculation that is not particularly healthy. . . . Section 45 may have been given in part to answer some of the questions of the members and to quiet down the extreme speculations and doctrinal hysteria [panic] that some were indulging in." (Stephen E. Robinson and H. Dean Garrett, A Commentary on the Doctrine and Covenants, *2:48–49.) Look for how we are supposed to prepare for the Second Coming.*

Doctrine and Covenants 45:1–15
Why would we listen to the Lord?

Share with your family the information found in the historical background above and have them identify what subjects they will read about in this revelation. Have someone read aloud the section heading for D&C 45 and find the phrase that describes how the Saints felt about this revelation. (Joy.)

Read D&C 45:1–15 together as a family and make a list of things that brought joy to the Saints in Kirtland. The following are some ideas that may help draw attention to important ideas along the way:

- Stop the person who reads verse 1 as soon as he or she reads the first word. Ask someone to define "hearken." (To listen *and* follow.) Have the person continue reading the verse, noting the descriptions of Him who is inviting them to "hearken." Ask, "How do these things affect our desire and willingness to listen to the Lord?"

- Stop the person who reads verse 3 as soon as he or she reads the first word. Note what is being asked of us again. Let the reader read through verse 6. As the person reads, remind your family to pay attention again to the description of Him who invites them to listen. Ask, "How does it make you feel to know this is what Jesus says about us as we stand before the Father?" Share with your family the following story, as told by President Gordon B. Hinckley, that illustrates a small part of the feeling evoked by D&C 45:3–6:

"Years ago there was a little one-room schoolhouse in the mountains of Virginia where the boys were so rough that no teacher had been able to handle them. . . .

"The first day of school came, and the teacher appeared for duty. One big fellow named Tom whispered: 'I won't need any help with this one. I can lick him myself.'

"The teacher said, 'Good morning, boys, we have come to conduct school.' They yelled and made fun at the top of their voices. 'Now, I want a good school, but I confess that I do not know how unless you help me. Suppose we have a few rules. You tell me, and I will write them on the blackboard.'

"One fellow yelled, 'No stealing!' Another yelled, 'On time.' Finally ten rules appeared on the blackboard.

"'Now,' said the teacher, 'a law is not good unless there is a penalty attached. What shall we do with the one who breaks the rules?'

"'Beat him across the back ten times without his coat on,' came the response from the class.

"'That is pretty severe, boys. Are you sure that you are ready to stand by it?' Another yelled, 'I second the motion,' and the teacher said, 'All right, we will live by them! Class, come to order!'

"'In a day or so, 'Big Tom' found that his lunch had been stolen. The thief was located—a little hungry fellow, about ten years old. 'We have found the thief and he must be punished according to your rule—ten stripes across the back. Jim, come up here!' the teacher said.

"'The little fellow, trembling, came up slowly with a big coat fastened up to his neck and pleaded, 'Teacher, you can lick me as hard as you like, but please, don't take my coat off!'

"'Take your coat off,' the teacher said. 'You helped make the rules!'

"'Oh, teacher, don't make me!' He began to unbutton, and what did the teacher see? The boy had no shirt on, and revealed a bony little crippled body.

"'How can I whip this child?' he thought. 'But I must, I must do something if I am to keep this school.' Everything was quiet as death.

"'How come you aren't wearing a shirt, Jim?'

"He replied, 'My father died and my mother is very poor. I have only one shirt and she is washing it today, and I wore my brother's big coat to keep me warm.'

"The teacher, with rod in hand, hesitated. Just then 'Big Tom' jumped to his feet and said,

'Teacher, if you don't object, I will take Jim's licking for him.'

"'Very well, there is a certain law that one can become a substitute for another. Are you all agreed?'

"Off came Tom's coat, and after five strokes the rod broke! The teacher bowed his head in his hands and thought, 'How can I finish this awful task?' Then he heard the class sobbing, and what did he see? Little Jim had reached up and caught Tom with both arms around his neck. 'Tom, I'm sorry that I stole your lunch, but I was awful hungry. Tom, I will love you till I die for taking my licking for me! Yes, I will love your forever!'

"To lift a phrase from this simple story, Jesus, my Redeemer, had taken 'my licking for me' and yours for you." (*Ensign,* December 2000, 2–3.)

After sharing this story, ask your family how they think it relates to verses 3–6, and how they think they will feel at that day.

- As someone reads verses 8–9, note the things it says Jesus has done. Ask, "Why do you think He has done these things? How has your life been blessed as a result?"
- After reading all fifteen verses, have family members look at their list of things they think brought joy to the Saints and choose one that most impresses them. Invite them to share why, and in what ways it will encourage them to "hearken" or "listen" more carefully to the Lord.

Doctrine and Covenants 45:16–59
Jesus speaks of His second coming

(Note: Because of its length, you may choose to present this material over two or more sessions.)

Show your family a picture representing the second coming of Jesus Christ (such as picture 238 in the Gospel Art Picture Kit). Ask them what first comes to their minds when they think of the Second Coming. Is it positive or negative? Have someone read aloud D&C 45:16–17. Ask:

- What did Jesus' apostles think of when they thought of the Second Coming? (The fulfillment of promises made to the fathers, the resurrection, and the restoration of scattered Israel.)
- Would you categorize those thoughts as positive or negative? Why?

Invite your family to pay close attention as they read the verses in D&C 45 that are related to the Second Coming. Have them look for things that will help them look forward to this event as Jesus' apostles did.

Explain to your family that in D&C 45:16–59 the Lord retells some of things he said to his apostles the week before he was crucified. (See Matthew 24–25 for the biblical account.) In these verses the Lord explains things that apply specifically to our time.

Read together D&C 45:18–24. Ask, "What clues tell us the time period Jesus was speaking of in these verses?" (Note "this temple . . . in Jerusalem" in verse 18, "this generation of Jews" in verse 21, and "this I have told you concerning Jerusalem" in verse 24.) Tell your family that all these things occurred—just as Jesus said they would—at about A.D. 70 when the Romans put down a Jewish rebellion, resulting in the destruction of the temple, the death of many Jews, and the scattering of many others. Ask, "How does knowing that the events Jesus prophesied for the times of the apostles all came true affect the way we look at the rest of the prophecies in this section?"

Read together D&C 45:24–33 and discuss the following:

- Have someone define "remnant." (Look in a dictionary if necessary.) Who is the remnant Jesus is speaking of in verse 24? (The scattered Jews.)
- What should we know when we see the remnant begin to be gathered? (The times of the Gentiles is being fulfilled—verse 25.)
- Explain that from the time of Abraham,

Isaac, and Jacob (Israel) until the time of Jesus, the gospel was always given first to the family of Israel. The New Testament tells us that changed after the time of Jesus. Because the Jews rejected Jesus, the Gentiles became the focus of preaching the gospel. (Note: The Gentiles are nations who are not, or who think they are not, of the house of Israel. The "times of the Gentiles" refers to the time when the gospel is offered to all other nations before it is again primarily offered to those who acknowledge themselves to be of the house of Israel.)

- As a family, list the things these verses say will occur during the times of the Gentiles. Ask, "Which of these things is great or exciting? Which is troubling to you? Which is comforting?"
- Tell your family that, in reference to D&C 45:32, President Ezra Taft Benson said, "Holy men and women stand in holy places, and these holy places consist of our temples, our chapels, our homes, and stakes of Zion." (*The Teachings of Ezra Taft Benson*, 106.) Invite your family to write that statement in the margin of their scriptures next to verse 32. Then ask, "How can we make our home a more holy place in the midst of the negative and troubling things that are occurring in the last days?"

Have a family member read D&C 45:34. Ask, "What was the response of the apostles to these prophecies?" Then read together D&C 45:35–47. As you do, identify and mark in your scriptures why the apostles (and we) have reason to "be not troubled." These reasons may include:

- Jesus said to be not troubled.
- The fulfillment of the signs help us know that God will fulfill all His promises.
- We will be able to see the signs and know the time is close.
- Israel will be gathered.
- Those who are faithful will not be cut off.

- Those who have died that are faithful will be caught up to meet the Savior.

Prior to reading D&C 45:48, tell your family that "this mount" in that verse refers to the Mount of Olives just east of Jerusalem. Read together D&C 45:48–55. Ask, "In the midst of these judgments, what examples do these verses give of the merciful nature of God?"

Invite a family member to briefly tell the parable of the ten virgins. (See Matthew 25:1–13 if you need help.) Ask:

- What do you think the oil and the lamps represent in that parable?
- According to D&C 45:56–57, what does the oil in the lamps represent?

Finally, have someone read D&C 45:58–59. Ask:

- What do you think it would be like to live in that day?
- What do you think the people would say about the things they went through to be there?

Remind your family that this experience is not limited to those who live during the Millennium, for all who obtain the celestial kingdom will "dwell in the presence of our God and his Christ forever and ever." Ask your family what it would be worth to obtain that blessing. Share with them the following thoughts from President Brigham Young:

"We talk about our trials and troubles here in this life: but suppose that you could see yourselves thousands and millions of years after you have proved faithful to your religion during the few short years in this time, and have obtained eternal salvation and a crown of glory in the presence of God; then look back upon your lives here, and see the losses, crosses, and disappointments, the sorrows . . . you would be constrained [forced] to exclaim, 'But what of all that? Those things were but for a moment, and we are now here. We have been faithful during a few moments in our mor-

tality, and now we enjoy eternal life and glory, with power to progress in all the boundless knowledge and through the countless stages of progression, enjoying the smiles and approbation [approval] of our Father and God, and of Jesus Christ our elder brother.'" (*Journal of Discourses,* 7:275.)

Reflect on these teachings concerning the Second Coming by asking your family which part of Jesus' coming most thrills them.

Doctrine and Covenants 45:62–71
Peace, refuge, and safety in Zion

 Assign family members to one or more of the following roles:

1. A person called to gather people to Zion.
2. A person who lives in Zion.
3. A person who chooses not to be in Zion.
4. A person who is gathering to Zion.

Have family members carefully read D&C 45:62–71 and be prepared to answer questions as if they were the assigned person. Assign one family member to serve as the "interviewer." He or she should also read the verses and be prepared to evaluate the answers given. Use the following questions:

Person 1

- What are you trying to do?
- Why are you trying to do it?
- How do you do it?
- What do you say to people about why they would want to gather to Zion?

Person 2

- In what ways has your life been blessed by living in Zion?
- What would you like to say to others who are considering gathering to Zion?

Person 3

- What is your life like?
- What do you think about Zion?

Person 4

- Why did you decide to gather to Zion?

Share with your family the following statement by President Ezra Taft Benson:

"The prophets likened latter-day Zion to a great tent encompassing the earth. That tent was supported by cords fastened to stakes. Those stakes, of course, are various geographical organizations spread out over the earth. Presently, Israel is being gathered to the various stakes of Zion.

" . . . [Stakes] are organized to assist parents who have 'children in Zion' to teach them the gospel of Jesus Christ and administer the ordinances of salvation. Stakes are formed to perfect the Saints, and that development begins in the home with effective gospel instruction. . . .

"Stakes in Zion are strengthened and Zion's borders enlarged as members reflect the standard of holiness that the Lord expects of His chosen people. . . .

"The Lord then reveals that the stakes of Zion are . . . a defense for the Saints from enemies both seen and unseen. The defense is direction provided through priesthood channels that strengthens testimony and promotes family solidarity and individual righteousness." (*Ensign,* January 1991, 2.)

Based on the counsel of President Benson and what you read in D&C 45, ask your family:

- How much like the Zion described in D&C 45:62–71 is our ward and stake?

Zion can be compared to a tent with stakes.

- In what ways is our home like the Zion described in D&C 45:62–71?
- What could we do in our family to better "gather to Zion"?
- What do you think will make our home a "land of peace," a place of "refuge" and "safety," and a place where "the glory of the Lord shall be"?

In conclusion, share the following counsel from President Spencer W. Kimball:

"Our success, individually and as a Church, will largely be determined by how faithfully we focus on living the gospel in the home." (*Ensign,* May 1978, 101.)

DOCTRINE AND COVENANTS 46: THE GIFTS OF THE SPIRIT

Historical background: *John Whitmer, the first Church historian (see D&C 47), wrote of D&C 46, "In the beginning of the Church, while yet in her infancy, the disciples used to exclude unbelievers which caused some to marvel and converse on this matter because of the things written in the Book of Mormon. (3 Nephi 18:22–24.) Therefore, the Lord deigned to speak on this subject, that his people might come to an understanding, and he said that he had always given to his elders to conduct all meetings as they were led by the Spirit." (The Book of John Whitmer, typescript.) Look for who is given spiritual gifts and why.*

Doctrine and Covenants 46:1–7
Excluding and including

Ask your family to visualize the sign on the front of your chapel. Tell them that a similar sign appears on every chapel throughout the world. Ask, "In addition to the name of our Church, what other familiar sentence appears on this sign?" ("Visitors welcome.") Why do you think that is an important sentence to have on our Church buildings?

Explain to your family that you are going to give them a quiz on D&C 46:1–7. Have one family member read the section heading for D&C 46 and another read the historical background above. Then read together D&C 46:1–7. Give the following quiz:

- According to the section heading for D&C 46, what was one of the main reasons the Lord gave this revelation? (To give a "unified pattern" for conducting Church meetings.)
- What is the main idea taught in verses 1–2 and 7? (Church services are to be directed and guided by the Spirit.)
- Why are we often afraid to invite those not of our faith to Church? (We may be afraid of what they might think.)
- What benefit would come from allowing our nonmember friends to attend our meetings when they are directed by the Spirit? (The meetings are inspiring and can lead to conversion.)
- Are there other ways we exclude people from attending Church? (Neglecting to invite or fellowship with them.)
- What would help the people you know feel welcome to attend Church services or activities with you?
- When was the last time you invited someone to attend Church services or activities with you?

Challenge each family member to invite someone not of our faith, or a less-active member, to a Church meeting or activity. Have family members write on a piece of paper:

Who will you invite?

What are you going to invite them to?

When will you invite them?

Why it is important to invite them?

Doctrine and Covenants 46:8–33
What are your gifts from the Spirit?

(Note: This teaching idea has two parts. Because of its length, you may choose to present the material over two or more sessions.)

Part One

Gift-wrap a box in solid-color wrapping paper. Label the box "Gifts of the Spirit." Read together as a family D&C 46:8–12 and discuss the following questions:

- In verse 8, what does the Lord say we should seek for?
- What do we need to remember as we seek for gifts of the Spirit?

- Why does God give us these spiritual gifts? (Verse 9, 12.)
- Does a person need to be perfect in order to receive, or be blessed by, a spiritual gift? (Verse 9.)
- What would be a wrong reason to want a gift of the Spirit? (Verse 9.)
- What problems could come from someone seeking or receiving spiritual gifts for the wrong reason? (Jealousy, pride, and so on.)
- Does everyone get a gift of the Spirit? (Verse 11.)
- How can you discover your gifts? (Personal prayer, patriarchal blessing, accepting Church callings, and so on.)
- How can you develop your gifts? (Verse 9.)

Part Two

Read together as a family D&C 46:12–26. Each time a gift of the Spirit is mentioned, have family members mark it in their scriptures and take turns writing the name of the gift on the box. As you read about each gift, discuss the following questions and consider using the quotations below to help your family better understand spiritual gifts:

- Knowing that Jesus is the Christ and believing on the testimony of one who knows are both gifts of the Spirit. What do we learn from that?
- What do you think the differences are between the gift of wisdom and the gift of knowledge?
- What examples do we have of the gift of tongues in the Church today?
- What can we learn from the fact that the bishop is given the gift of discernment?
- Are there other spiritual gifts not listed here?

The Gift of Knowing and The Gift of Believing

"Spiritual gifts come by the power of the Holy Ghost, that all the faithful may be benefited. One of these gifts is 'to know that Jesus Christ is the Son of God, and that he was crucified for the sins of the world.' (D&C 46:13.) Those who receive that gift have the duty to testify of it. We know this because immediately after describing the gift of knowing that Jesus Christ is the Son of God, the Lord says: 'To others it is given to believe on their words, that they also might have eternal life if they continue faithful.' (D&C 46:14; see also 3 Ne. 19:28.) Those who have the gift to know must give their witness so that those who have the gift to believe on their words can enjoy the benefit of that gift." (Dallin H. Oaks, *Ensign,* November 1990, 30.)

The Gift of Tongues

"According to the Prophet Joseph Smith, the purpose of the gift of tongues is to preach the gospel 'among those whose language is not understood' (*Teachings of the Prophet Joseph Smith,* sel. Joseph Fielding Smith [1976], 148–49.)

"Elder Bruce R. McConkie of the Quorum of the Twelve explained: 'In their more dramatic manifestations [the gift of tongues and their interpretation] consist in speaking or interpreting, by the power of the Spirit, a tongue which is completely unknown to the speaker or interpreter.' More frequently, 'these gifts are manifest where the ordinary languages of the day are concerned in that the Lord's missionaries learn to speak and interpret foreign languages with ease, thus furthering the spread of the message of the restoration' (*Mormon Doctrine,* 2nd ed. [1966], 800).

"Sister Rhonda Patten Grow experienced the gift of tongues in a way familiar to many missionaries. When her husband was called from the United States to be a mission president in Uruguay, she was afraid she couldn't learn to speak Spanish. But gradually, with the help of members, she finally learned to bear her testimony in Spanish. She was amazed, however, at how much more she could say when under the influence of the Spirit. 'In fact, the Spirit helped me so much when I spoke in meetings that the members usually assumed my Spanish was much better than it actually was.'

"At one meeting, Sister Grow noticed a young

woman signing for a hearing-impaired sister. When Sister Grow stood to speak, 'It seemed as if the Spirit was lifting me up and giving me utterance beyond my own abilities. I was filled with tender feelings of love for the people, and I especially noticed the smiling face of the young hearing-impaired woman looking up at me.'

"Sister Grow learned later that when she had begun to speak, the woman communicated she no longer needed signing interpretation. She could understand Sister Grow's message without it." (*Ensign,* October 1997, 71.)

The Gift of Discernment

"The gift of discernment is essential to the leadership of the Church. I never ordain a bishop or set apart a president of a stake without invoking upon him this divine blessing, that he may read the lives and hearts of his people and call forth the best within them. The gift and power of discernment in this world of contention between the forces of good and the power of evil is essential equipment for every son and daughter of God." (Stephen L Richards, Conference Report, April 1950, 163.)

Other Spiritual Gifts

"Taken at random, let me mention a few gifts that are not always evident or noteworthy but that are very important. Among these may be your gifts—gifts not so evident but nevertheless real and valuable.

"Some of these less-conspicuous gifts are the gift of asking; the gift of listening; the gift of hearing and using a still, small voice; the gift of being able to weep; the gift of avoiding contention; the gift of being agreeable; the gift of avoiding vain repetition; the gift of seeking that which is righteous; the gift of not passing judgment; the gift of looking to God for guidance; the gift of being a disciple; the gift of caring for others; the gift of being able to ponder; the gift of offering prayer; the gift of bearing a mighty testimony; and the gift of receiving the Holy Ghost.

"We must remember that to every person is given a gift by the Spirit of God. It is our right and responsibility to accept our gifts and to share them. God's gifts and powers are available to all." (Marvin J. Ashton, *The Measure of Our Hearts,* 16.)

DOCTRINE AND COVENANTS 47: KEEPING A HISTORY

Historical background: Read the section heading for background information on this section.

D&C 47:1–4
Keeping a history

Before family scripture study, gather as many journals as you can (your own, a grandparent's, an ancestor's, and so on). Invite your family to bring their journals also.

Invite a family member to read aloud the section heading for D&C 47. Invite a family member to read D&C 47. Ask:

- Who was called as the new Church historian? (For more information on John Whitmer, refer to the biographical sketch for Doctrine and Covenants 15 in this book.)
- What two words describe how John Whitmer should keep a record? (See verse 1, "regular"; and verse 3, "continually.")
- What guidelines do these verses suggest we should follow as we keep our own personal histories?
- Why do you think that "regularly" and "continually" keeping a personal history is important?
- What blessings have come to the Church because some kept a Church history?
- What blessings can come to us for keeping a "regular" personal history?

Hold up one of the journals you gathered earlier and ask your family to tell about things they have gained from reading about the lives of those who have lived before us. What have you gained from keeping your own journal? After some discussion, read the following statements from President Spencer W. Kimball:

1. "Those who keep a book of remembrance are more likely to keep the Lord in remembrance in their daily lives." (*Teachings of Spencer W. Kimball,* 349.)

2. "I promise you that if you will keep your journals and records they will indeed be a source of great inspiration to you, each other, your grandchildren, and others throughout the generations." (*Teachings of Spencer W. Kimball,* 349–50.)

3. "Do not suppose life changes so much that your experiences will not be interesting to your posterity. . . . Your journal should contain your true self rather than a picture of you when you are 'made up' for a public performance. . . . Begin today and write in it your goings and comings, your deepest thoughts, your achievements and your failures, your associations and your triumphs, your impressions and your testimonies." (*Teachings of Spencer W. Kimball,* 350.)

Ask:

- How does a journal help us keep the Lord more in our lives?
- What should we write in our journals?
- According to D&C 47:4, what influence can be a source of inspiration as we write in our journals?

Share some lines from your own journal or an ancestor's journal. Share your testimony of keeping a history with your family and invite everyone to either begin writing or continue writing in their journals.

DOCTRINE AND COVENANTS 48: CARING FOR THE GATHERING SAINTS

Historical background: *Church members had been commanded to gather in Ohio (D&C 37:3, 38:32, 39:15, 45:64), where the Lord promised they would be "endowed with power from on high." Joseph Smith arrived in Kirtland in February 1831. Most of the Saints from New York followed as soon as they could. Members who were already in Kirtland had questions about where the gathering Saints would live and work. They wondered if this was the beginning of the gathering and Kirtland was to be the city of Zion. Questions on these subjects led the Prophet to inquire of the Lord. He received this revelation in March 1831. Notice how the Lord continues to teach the Saints about the process of revelation.*

Doctrine and Covenants 48:1–6
How does the Lord reveal things to the Church?

 Have a family member quote or read the ninth Article of Faith. Ask:

- Why do you think it is important that we believe all that God *has* revealed?
- Why is it equally important to believe all that He reveals *now,* and all that He *will yet* reveal?
- Why do you think God didn't simply reveal everything about His kingdom right in the beginning?

As an illustration, invite your family to share examples of things that cannot be learned all at once but have to be learned one step at a time. (For example, reading, musical instruments, or the times tables.) Ask what would happen if a teacher presented all of the information required for a high school diploma to those in second or third grade.

Read the historical background above and then have a family member read the section heading for D&C 48. Explain that D&C 48 is an example of how the Lord gives revelation *now* to answer questions from His prophet. Read together D&C 48:1–6 and have your family look for how the Lord answered these questions. Also look for clues that show God *will yet* reveal important things about His kingdom. Ask:

- What phrase (repeated three times in verses 1–3) helps us know that this revelation would be followed by future instructions?
- What things were the Saints in Kirtland to do immediately? (Share their lands with those who are gathering and save all the money they can.)
- What were the Saints to do later? (Purchase lands for "the city" yet to be revealed; send men to the place to be revealed and begin "the city"; gather under the direction of Church leaders.)

Read the following story and ask your family to listen for how it relates to D&C 48 and the principle of ongoing revelation:

"There is a story that has oft been told by President [David O.] McKay, particularly during the early days of the welfare program, that I should like to repeat. It is the story of an engineer who pulled his train into a station one dark and stormy night, and while the engineer was going calmly about oiling his engine, getting ready for the next run, a timid passenger from the coach came up to him and asked him if he were not afraid of going out into the dark. Without looking up the engineer said, 'I'm not pulling my train out into the dark tonight.' 'Oh, I beg your pardon, I thought you were going to be our engineer,' said the man. 'I am, but I won't be in the dark tonight.' He said, 'Why, I should think you would be very nervous with the lives of all these men and women on this train depending upon you.' For an answer the engineer pointed up to the headlight that threw an intense white light several hundred yards ahead on the track and said, 'When I pull out of this station tonight I am going to run just to the edge of that light, and when I get there, that light will be extended several hundred yards ahead, and I shall run to the end of that light and so on throughout the night. I'll be running in the light all the way.'" (Henry D. Moyle, Conference Report, April 1956, 59–60.)

Ask your family how the train's headlight is like ongoing revelation. Discuss how receiving revelation "line upon line and precept upon precept" applies to your family.

Doctrine and Covenants 48:2
To share or not to share?

Think about each family member and identify a personal belonging you think they would rather not share. Without telling them why, ask them to go to their rooms and bring back the item you previously identified. When they return, ask them how they would feel about sharing their prized possession with another family member. Then tell the following story:

"The teacher of a group of three-year-old Primary children . . . laid newspapers on the floor and gave each child a ball of clay. She observed that her ball of clay was much smaller than anyone else's and invited each child . . . to share with her. At first the children were reluctant, but when they saw her willingness to share with them, they began to enjoy sharing—not only with their teacher, but with each other." (Janelle Lysenko, *Ensign*, March 1987, 71.)

Discuss as a family why this teacher was successful in teaching her class the joy of sharing. What would have happened if she had just demanded that they share? Invite someone to read aloud D&C 48:2. Ask:

- What were Church members in Kirtland asked to "impart" (give) to Saints arriving from the east?
- How do you think they felt about sharing so much with strangers? (You may want to relate this to how your children felt about sharing their favorite items.)
- How would you feel about sharing our yard and home with people you do not know?
- What do you think the people in Kirtland did and why?
- What are some ways we have the opportunity to do what the early Kirtland Saints did?

DOCTRINE AND COVENANTS 49: REVELATION TO THE SHAKING QUAKERS

Historical background: As a religion, the United Society of Believers in Christ's Second Appearing began in England in 1774. They were also known as Shakers or Shaking Quakers because of their dress (they looked like Quakers) and their enthusiastic dancing during worship (shaking, twirling, shouting, and singing in tongues). Early Church historian John Whitmer wrote, "Leman Copley, one of the disciples who was formerly a Shaker Quaker, was anxious that some of the elders should go to his former brethren and preach the gospel. He also feared to be ordained to preach himself, and desired that the Lord should direct in this and all matters." (The Book of John Whitmer, typescript.) Notice how the Lord specifically corrects the false beliefs of the Shakers.

Doctrine and Covenants 49:1–4
Who were the Shaking Quakers?

Have your family read D&C 49:1–4 and look for answers to the following questions:

- Who was being called to preach the gospel?

- To what group of people were they sent?

Read the historical background above to your family and then have someone read the section heading to D&C 49. Then read the following statement from John Whitmer:

"The above-named brethren went and proclaimed [the Gospel] according to the revelation given them, but the Shakers hearkened not to their words and received not the Gospel at that time, for they are bound in tradition and priestcraft." (*History of the Church*, Ms., 20.)

Ask:

- Now that you know how the mission turned out, can you see any clues in verse 2 as to why their message was rejected?
- Can you see any clues in verse 4 as to why Leman had a hard time staying faithful?
- How is this experience similar to what missionaries experience today?
- What traditions do some believe in today that make it hard for them to accept the restored gospel?

Share your testimony that the Lord has called missionaries to share the message of truth but that all Heavenly Father's children have their agency to accept it or reject it.

Doctrine and Covenants 49:5–25
What was the Lord's message to the Shaking Quakers?

Divide a sheet of paper in half. On one side write "Beliefs of the Shaking Quakers." On the other side write "The Lord's Doctrine." Read as a family the section heading for D&C 49 and find at least five beliefs of the Shaking Quakers. Write these beliefs on your sheet of paper under the heading "Beliefs of the Shaking Quakers." Some of the beliefs you may want to identify are:

- The second coming of Jesus Christ has already occurred.
- Jesus came the second time in the form of a woman (Ann Lee).
- Baptism by water is not necessary.
- Eating pork is forbidden.
- Celibacy (living singly without marriage) was "higher" than marriage.

Then take turns reading D&C 49:5–25 and find

Leman Copley was born in Connecticut in 1781. He was a member of the Shakers religion (United Society of Believers in Christ's Second Appearing), but when he heard the message of the Restoration, he was baptized in March 1831. Shortly after serving a brief mission among his friends of his former religion, Leman consecrated 759 acres of his farm in Thompson, Ohio, as a place for the Saints from Colesville, New York, to gather in Ohio. Unfortunately, he broke his covenant in June 1831 and ordered Saints from his land. The Lord rebuked Leman in D&C 54. He was disfellowshipped in the summer of 1831. Though reinstated in October 1832, Leman struggled with his testimony. He remained in Ohio after the Saints left and eventually died a wealthy landlord in December 1862.

how the Lord corrected these doctrines. List the true doctrines under the heading "The Lord's Doctrine." After you have completed the list, you may want to share some or all of the following insights:

D&C 49:13–14: "Baptism is essential for entering the kingdom of heaven." (Joseph Fielding Smith, *Answers to Gospel Questions,* 1:45; see also 2 Nephi 31:17; John 3:5.)

D&C 49:15–16: "Marriage between man and woman is essential to [God's] eternal plan. Children are entitled to birth within the bonds of matrimony, and to be reared by a father and mother who honor marital vows with complete fidelity [faithfulness]. Happiness in family life is most likely to be achieved when founded upon the teachings of the Lord Jesus Christ." ("The Family: A Proclamation to the World"; see also D&C 131:1–4.)

D&C 49:18–21: In a later revelation the Lord said, "Every herb in the season thereof, and every fruit in the season thereof; all these to be used with prudence and thanksgiving. Yea, flesh also of beasts and of the fowls of the air, I, the Lord, have ordained for the use of man with thanksgiving; nevertheless they are to be used sparingly; and it is pleasing unto me that they should not be used, only in times of winter, or of cold, or famine." (D&C 89:11–13.)

D&C 49:22–25: "The physical gathering here alluded [referred] to is the assembling of the Latter-day Saints in the tops of the mountains in western America. It is there that Zion shall flourish upon the hills and rejoice upon the mountains. The wilderness referred to is the then uninhabited areas that were colonized by Brigham Young less than a score of years later. And as to the day when the Lamanites shall blossom as the rose, it has scarcely commenced. They are not yet, except in a beginning degree, the pure and delightsome people of whom the scriptures speak." (Bruce R. McConkie, *The Millennial Messiah,* 210.)

Doctrine and Covenants 49:26–28
What does the Lord mean by "I will . . . be your rearward"?

Invite your family to imagine that they are taking a dangerous journey through a land filled with your enemies. Ask:

- What kinds of things would you do to protect yourself?
- How important would it be to have someone leading who knew the way?
- Where else, besides in front of you, would it be helpful to have someone providing safety?

Read together D&C 49:26–28 and ask:

- What promises did the Lord give to Sidney Rigdon, Parley P. Pratt, and Leman Copely in these verses?
- How might knowing that the Lord would be with them give them confidence?
- What is a "rearward"?

Point out footnote 27a to your family and have them read Isaiah 52:12. Ask them if that verse helps explain what a "rearward" might be. Have them look at the footnotes for verse 12 and find another similar word. Ask:

- What might a "rearguard" do? (Provide protection from an enemy.)
- In what ways does the Lord lead us, dwell among us, and provide protection for us today?

DOCTRINE AND COVENANTS 50: RECOGNIZING SPIRITUAL MANIFESTATIONS

Historical background: *"Soon after the Gospel was established in Kirtland, and during the absence of the authorities of the Church, many false spirits were introduced, many strange visions were seen, and wild, enthusiastic notions were entertained [believed]."* (History of the Church, 4:580.)

Concerning the situation, Parley P. Pratt stated, "As I went forth among the different branches, some very strange spiritual operations were manifested, which were disgusting, rather than edifying. Some persons would seem to swoon away, and make unseemly gestures, and be drawn or disfigured in their countenances. Others would fall into ecstasies and be drawn into contortions, cramps, fits, etc. Others would seem to have visions and revelations which were not edifying, and which were not congenial to the doctrine and spirit of the gospel. In short, a false and lying spirit seemed to be creeping into the Church.

"All these things were new and strange to me, and had originated in the Church during the absence, and previous to the arrival of President Joseph Smith from New York.

"Feeling our weakness and inexperience, and lest we should err in judgment concerning the spiritual phenomena, myself, John Murdock, and several other Elders, went to Joseph Smith, and asked him to inquire of the Lord concerning these spirits or manifestations.

"After we had joined in prayer in his translating room, he dictated in our presence the following revelation: each sentence was uttered slowly and very distinctly, and with a pause between each, sufficiently long for it to be recorded by an ordinary writer in long hand." (Autobiography of Parley P. Pratt, 61–62.) *Look for the relationship between light and truth.*

Doctrine and Covenants 50:1–9
What does the Spirit of the Lord feel like?

To prepare for this teaching idea, bring a thick blanket or comforter to scripture study.

Introduce this section by having different family members do the following for thirty seconds each: have one jump up and down, another spin, and another hold his or her breath. After they are finished, ask each one:

- How did that activity make you feel?
- How does that feeling compare to feeling the Holy Ghost?
- How can you know if something you feel is from the Spirit or not?

Assign a family member to read aloud the section heading for D&C 50 and the historical background above. Ask:

- What do you think it might have been like to watch people do the unusual actions Parley P. Pratt mentioned?
- How was that different from the experience Parley P. Pratt had watching the Prophet Joseph receive this revelation?
- How would you explain those differences?

Take turns reading D&C 50:1–9. Ask:

- Who might be the deceiving spirits mentioned in verse two? (See also D&C 29:36–37.)
- Why might Satan want there to be "abominations [wickedness] in the church?"
- What words did the Lord use to describe those who had introduced these false manifestations of the Spirit into the church?
- Why is it important to be able to tell the difference between the Lord's Spirit and evil spirits?

Share the following teaching from Joseph Smith:

"Nothing is a greater injury to the children of men than to be under the influence of a false spirit when they think they have the Spirit of God." (*Teachings of the Prophet Joseph Smith,* 205.)

Wrap one family member in the blanket or comforter. Read D&C 50:14 aloud and ask that family member what the title "Comforter" teaches about how the Holy Ghost makes us feel. Discuss ways that the feelings of being in a blanket or comforter are similar to the feelings we receive from the Holy Ghost. (Both make us feel safe, warm, comfortable, and secure.)

Ask family members to silently scan D&C 50:10–25, Galatians 5:22, and Moroni 7:16–19 and look for ways we can identify the Spirit of the Lord. Have family members share what they have found. Share your experiences of feeling the true influence of the Holy Ghost in your life.

Doctrine and Covenants 50:10–23
Preaching "by the Spirit of Truth"

Give two family members identical piles of materials that could be stacked together. (These could be wooden building blocks, Lego toys, or game pieces.) Have the two family members sit back to back. Ask one to be a "builder." He or she is to construct a small structure, and while doing so, explain to the other person how to build an identical structure. Ask the other person to be a "listener." He or she is to follow the building instructions but without talking, communicating, looking at the builder's building, or asking any questions. When both the "builder" and "listener" have finished, compare the two structures and talk about why it was so difficult to build an exact replica without being able to talk, see, or ask questions.

Ask a family member to read D&C 50:10–12. Ask:

- What did the Lord suggest we do in these verses that might have helped in this activity?

- Why do you think it is more effective to "reason together" and ask questions rather than just being preached to?
- Why would it be important to participate and ask questions during family scripture study, Church classes, or seminary?
- How would that increase your understanding and reduce misunderstanding?

Now have two people do the same activity with the blocks, but this time let them converse together while they are building the structure. Compare the structures using this method.

Have your family scan verses 13 through 23 and count every question mark. Read verses 13 through 23 with your family. After each question, discuss what the answer might be. As you read the verses indicated below, share the following questions and insights:

Verses 13–14: What is our most important responsibility? Joseph Smith stated, "After all that has been said, the greatest and most important duty is to preach the Gospel." (*Teachings of the Prophet Joseph Smith,* 113.) Challenge your family to find a way to share the gospel with someone they know.

Verses 17–18: What is the most important thing to remember when teaching the gospel? Ezra Taft Benson taught, "I have said so many times to my Brethren that the Spirit is the most important single element in this work. With the Spirit, and by magnifying your call, you can do miracles for the Lord in the mission field. Without the Spirit you will never succeed regardless of your talent and ability." (*The Teachings of Ezra Taft Benson,* 205.)

Verses 22–23: What will happen when we teach by the Spirit? What does the word "edify" mean? (It means to build.) Have family members share a time when they felt built up after hearing someone speak by the power of the Holy Ghost or after a lesson where the Spirit was present.

Doctrine and Covenants 50:23–25
Receiving more light in your life

These verses could be effectively taught in a room having a light that could be made brighter or dimmer.

Bring to scripture study a recent newspaper that reports some of the bad things people are doing in the world today and also the latest conference edition of the *Ensign* magazine.

Ask a family member to read aloud D&C 50:23–24. Ask someone to answer these questions:

- What does the word "edify" mean in verse 23? (To build or improve.)
- What examples do you see in the world today of ideas or practices that are not edifying? (You might show your family newspaper reports of greed, worldliness, immorality, violence, or dishonesty.)
- Why is "darkness" a good description of ideas and practices that are not of God?
- What are some of the edifying truths we have received from God? (You might show your family the index of the conference talk subjects, such as charity, love, scriptures, kindness, truth, priesthood, service, and families.)
- Why is "light" a good description of these truths?

Draw a diagram like the one below and show it to your family.

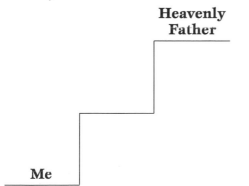

Heavenly Father

Me

Have another family member read aloud verse 24 again and add verse 25. Ask:

- According to verse 24, what must we do to receive more of God's light?
- What do you think we must do to "continue in God"?
- How is receiving light from God like the stairway in this diagram?
- What phrases in verse 24 indicate that we do not get all of God's light at once?
- According to verse 25, why does God want us to receive the light and truth He offers?

Have family members take turns reading D&C 50:26–46. As they read, have them look for truths in those verses that help us, step-by-step, come closer to our Heavenly Father and grow "brighter and brighter until the perfect day?"

Share the following statement:

"It is comforting to know that we need not become holy in a day. Our quest for sainthood is gradual, and the climb is steep. Enoch's Zion was established 'in process of time' (Moses 7:21), and with but few exceptions, the pure in heart become so in the same manner. Nor need we traverse [travel] the stony path to perfection alone. Indeed, we cannot. C. S. Lewis has observed that in a marvelous manner 'this Helper,' the Lord Jesus Christ, 'who will, in the long run, be satisfied with nothing less than absolute perfection, will also be delighted with the first feeble, stumbling effort you make tomorrow to do the simplest duty. As a great Christian writer (George McDonald) pointed out, every father is pleased at the baby's first attempt to walk [though] no father would be satisfied with anything less than a firm, manly walk in a grown-up son. In the same way, he said, 'God is easy to please, but hard to satisfy.' The process may take time." (Robert L. Millet, *An Eye Single to the Glory of God: Reflections on the Cost of Discipleship,* 11.)

DOCTRINE AND COVENANTS 51: ORGANIZE THE SAINTS

Historical background: *"Shortly after the Revelation recorded in Section 50 had been received, the Saints from Colesville, N. Y., began to arrive in Ohio. They had been directed to gather in that locality (Sec. 37:3) and they had been promised that there they would receive The Law (Sec. 38:32). The Saints in Ohio had been instructed to divide their land with their Eastern brethren (Sec. 48:2), and it was the duty of Edward Partridge, who had been appointed Bishop (Sec. 36) to take care of the newcomers, as far as possible. Under the circumstances, Bishop Partridge asked for divine guidance. The Prophet inquired of the Lord for him, and received this answer to his prayers." (Hyrum M. Smith and Janne M. Sjodahl,* Doctrine and Covenants Commentary, *296.)* Look for the qualities the Lord requires of those who live the law of consecration.

Doctrine and Covenants 51:1–19
Organize the Saints—honestly

Before family scripture study write the following titles on separate pieces of paper, and distribute these titles to members of your family:

- Bishop Edward Partridge. (D&C 51:1–8, 12–13.)
- Family of Saints migrating from the East. (D&C 51:4 and section heading.)
- Family of Saints that transgresses. (D&C 51:4–5.)
- Storehouse. (D&C 51:13–15.)
- Every man. (D&C 51:9–12, 19.)

Invite your family to read the historical background above and the section heading for section 51 to discover what was happening during this time. Also have family members locate the city Thompson in the map section of their Doctrine and Covenants. (See the map of the New York–Ohio area.)

Ask each family member to search the verses assigned to them and write down the roles and responsibilities of their assigned title. Help those who need it as they complete their assignment. Ask the following:

- Bishop Partridge: How are you to distribute the portions to the new families coming in? (See verse 3.)
- Family of Saints migrating from the east: What will you receive to show that your portion (part) is really yours? (See verse 4.)
- Family of Saints that transgresses: When you transgress and leave the Church, what part will you get back? (See verse 5.)
- Storehouse: What do you store? (See verses 13–14.)
- Bishop Partridge: What is to be done with the money that is extra? (See verse 8.)
- Every man: How are we to "deal" with others? (See verse 9.) Who will enter into the joy of the Lord and have eternal life? (See verse 19.) What problems might arise from dealing dishonestly?

Explain to your family that the Lord desires to unify His people. (See Moses 7:18; John 17:20–21.) They should strive for unity in earthly as well as spiritual things. Share your testimony that unity among the Saints can exist only as we are completely honest with our fellowmen. Encourage your family to be honest in all their dealings.

Doctrine and Covenants 51:16–17
Prepare for tomorrow by living today

Ask your family to compare how a committed person might react and an uncommitted person might react under the following circumstances:

- There is less than a week left in school, and your teacher gives you an assignment.
- You have only a few days left on your mission, and your companion wants to go tracting.
- You begin a new job next week, but your current employer wants you to do some extra tasks.
- You are moving out of your home next month, but there is some needed repair work on the plumbing.

Read to your family D&C 51:16–17. Ask:

- How long will the Saints gather in Ohio?
- Despite the fact that they will be in Ohio just a little while, how does the Lord want them to live? (See verse 17.)

Share the following statements:
"The location of the Saints at Thompson was only temporary. Those who came there did not generally accept the order revealed to them. . . . They were, however, to perform their temporal duties, as if they were to remain at Thompson for years. That is always a good rule, 'Whatsoever thy hand findeth to do, do it with thy might' (Ecclesiastes 9:10)." (Hyrum M. Smith and Janne M. Sjodahl, *Doctrine and Covenants Commentary*, 300.)

"Sometimes we let our thoughts of tomorrow take up too much of today. Daydreaming of the past and longing for the future may provide comfort but will not take the place of living in the present. This is the day of our opportunity, and we must grasp it." (Thomas S. Monson, *Ensign,* May 2003, 19.)

Discuss the following questions:

- Why do you think the Lord would want us to live this way?
- How could this principle be important in our Church callings?
- How would believing this principle affect your reactions in the first four situations discussed above?

Testify to your family of the importance of always doing our best.

DOCTRINE AND COVENANTS 52: MISSIONS TO MISSOURI

Historical background: In section 44, the Lord commanded "the elders of [His] Church" to gather in Kirtland and hold a conference, where He promised to pour out His Spirit upon them. (See D&C 44:1–2.) Of that conference the Prophet recorded, "The Lord displayed His power to the most perfect satisfaction of the Saints" and "The Lord gave us power in proportion to the work to be done, and strength according to the race set before us, and grace and help as our needs required." (History of the Church, 1:175–77.) The adversary also made his presence known at this conference. John Whitmer, Church historian at the time, recorded that "the devil took a notion to make known his power. He bound Harvey Whitlock and John Murdock so that they could not speak, and others were affected but the Lord showed to Joseph, the seer, the design of the thing; he commanded the devil in the name of Christ, and he departed, to our joy and comfort." (History of the Church, 1:175.) The day after the conference, Joseph Smith received the revelation recorded in section 52. (See History of the Church, 1:177.) Watch for what the Lord commanded these missionaries to teach.

Doctrine and Covenants 52:1–11
Mission calls and responsibilities

If someone in your family has a copy of his or her call to serve a mission, have the person show it to the family and read it. (If no one has a mission call, make an imaginary one for a family member.) Talk about the excitement of receiving a mission call.

Have your family scan D&C 52:1–11 for the names of men called on missions. Let them choose one for whom they will write a "mission call." As they prepare to write the mission call to their chosen person, have them carefully read D&C 52:1–11 and note all the important information, including where he will serve, whom he will serve with, responsibilities, instructions, promises, and anything else they believe to be important. More than one family member could work together as needed.

Let each family member who wrote a call read it to the rest of the family. Then ask:

- How do you think these men felt about their calls? Why?
- What do we learn about the importance of faithfulness as a missionary? (See verses 4–6.)
- What were the men asked to do that would require courage?
- What were they asked to do that would require advance preparation? (See verse 9.)
- What would help them be more successful?

Remind your family that not only are we invited by the Lord to prepare to serve full-time missions, but we should also be prepared to be missionaries even now. Ask your family what counsel given to the missionaries in D&C 52 applies to them right now.

Doctrine and Covenants 52:12–21
A pattern to avoid deception

Have one family member read the section heading to D&C 52 and another the historical background above. Ask:

- What do you think the people who attended the conference thought about the experiences of Harvey Whitlock, John Murdock, and others who were affected by the power of Satan?
- What questions do you think they had after those experiences?
- What do you think Lyman Wight thought about the warning in D&C 52:12?
- In what ways do you worry about being influenced or deceived by the adversary?

Have a family member read the promise of the Lord in D&C 52:13. Then share the following quotation from President James E. Faust:

"Satan is our greatest enemy and works night and day to destroy us. But we need not become paralyzed with fear of Satan's power. He can have no power over us unless we permit it. He is really a coward, and if we stand firm he will retreat." (*Ensign,* October 2002, 3.)

Write the following statement where your family can see it (be sure to leave off the words in parentheses) and ask them to complete the statement from what they learned from D&C 52:13 and President Faust:

"If I want to have power over Satan then I must be (faithful) and stand (firm)."

Read together D&C 52:14 and identify what the Lord is about to reveal in the next few verses. ("A pattern . . . that ye may not be deceived.") Assign a family member to be a scribe as you take turns reading D&C 52:15–21, looking for "the pattern" that helps us avoid being deceived by Satan. Have the scribe make two lists: one of things the Lord said we must *do,* and another of things we must *be* to avoid deception. As you talk about the things recorded on your list, do the following:

- Note repeated ideas, words, or phrases.
- Look up "contrite" (Verses 15–16) in a dictionary and define it.
- Ask, "What does language that is 'meek and edifieth' sound like?"

- Note any promises or warnings the Lord makes.

Invite family members to share which of the things on this list most impressed them as something they could work on to be protected from Satan's deception.

Doctrine and Covenants 52:22–40
Who are these missionaries? What should they do?

Read together D&C 52:22–38 and have your family circle the names they are familiar with of those called by the Lord to serve a special mission to Missouri. Divide the names among family members and have them use the index in the back of the Triple Combination or the biographical sketches in this book to report something about one or more of the individuals mentioned.

After each family member has reported, ask:

- What do we learn from the idea that the Lord mentioned each individual one by one? (Share the following testimony of Sister Sydney S. Reynolds in a talk in General Conference: "I believe the Lord knows my name and your name as well. . . . The Lord not only knows who we are, He knows where we are, and He leads us to do good." [*Ensign,* November 2003, 76.])
- What "good things" was the Lord leading these men to do? (See D&C 52:25–27, 36.)
- According to D&C 52:39–40, what must those who remain at home do to be considered disciples of Jesus?

Invite family members to tell about ways the Lord shows that He personally knows each individual. If time permits, show your family that not everyone is receptive to this important message by sharing the following story about Simonds Ryder mentioned in D&C 52:37:

"Simonds Ryder is mentioned but once in the Doctrine and Covenants (D&C 52:37), an occasion on which he was promised a blessing forfeited by another. His experience is a classic example that signs and wonders are not the means to lasting conversion. Ryder came into the Church as a result of an earthquake in China that some papers burlesqued as 'Mormonism in China' (HC, 1:158). When Ryder read of the account in the newspaper, 'he remembered that six weeks before, a young "Mormon girl" had predicted the destruction.'

"His departure from the Church came on just as shaky ground. Sometime after his baptism, he was informed in a written communication from Joseph Smith and Sidney Rigdon that it was the will of the Lord that he should preach the gospel. However, inasmuch as his name was spelled 'R-i-d-e-r' instead of 'R-y-d-e-r,' he apostatized, stating that if the Spirit of God did not know how to spell his name, it must have been the wrong spirit (HC, 1:260–61, footnote).

"Ryder's venom surfaced when on one occasion he led a mob that attacked the Prophet Joseph, leaving him tarred, feathered, and beaten (HC 1:264)." (Hoyt W. Brewster Jr., *Doctrine and Covenants Encyclopedia,* 481.)

DOCTRINE AND COVENANTS 53: INSTRUCTION TO A. SIDNEY GILBERT

Historical background: *Numerous men received priesthood callings on June 7, 1831, following a Church Conference in Kirtland. (See D&C 52.) Later that same month, Algernon Sidney Gilbert wanted to know the Lord's will concerning his life. Joseph received this revelation as a result of Brother Gilbert's request. Notice what the Lord told Sidney Gilbert he must do to be saved.*

Doctrine and Covenants 53:1–2
Are some commandments difficult for you to obey?

Read the following list to your family. As you do, ask each person to rank each task (on a scale from 1–10, with 1 being very easy and 10 being very hard) according to how difficult it would be for them to accomplish that task:

- Do ten pushups.
- Run one mile.
- Eat a bowlful of food you do not like.
- Share your testimony in church.
- Teach a Sunday School class.
- Serve a mission.

Read D&C 53:1–2 and then the biographical sketch for Algernon Sidney Gilbert to your family. Ask them to identify what command he thought was especially difficult. Ask:

- Even if something is difficult, do you think the Lord still expects us to obey? Why?
- What did the Lord remind Brother Gilbert about before asking him to preach the gospel? (That the Lord was crucified for the world—see D&C 19:18.)
- How could remembering the sacrifice of Jesus Christ help us keep His commandments?

Doctrine and Covenants 53:3–7
The Lord reveals His will concerning His Saints

Ask family members to briefly tell about some of the Church callings they have had. Ask them to discuss such questions as these:

BIOGRAPHICAL SKETCH: ALGERNON SIDNEY GILBERT

Algernon Sidney Gilbert was raised in Connecticut and later became a successful businessman in Ohio. He was a man of great practical sense, and he entered into a partnership with Newel K. Whitney. Together they opened a small store in Kirtland, Ohio. Brother Gilbert joined the Church in 1830 but lived only four years following his baptism. During those four years, he was ordained an elder (see D&C 53:3); accepted a call from the Prophet to establish a store in Jackson County, Missouri (see D&C 57:8–10); and served as one of the seven presiding high priests in Missouri.

B. H. Roberts remarked that "the Lord has had few more devoted servants in this dispensation than Algernon Sidney Gilbert. . . . In the persecutions that came upon the Saints in Jackson County he sacrificed all his goods. He was one of the six who offered their lives for their friends. . . . But, nevertheless, he shrank from speaking publicly, and it appears that, when called to go on a mission to preach the gospel, he said he would rather die. Not long afterwards he was attacked by cholera, and the disease proved fatal." (*History of the Church,* 2:118–19.)

- What did you enjoy most about your callings?
- Was there anything required in that calling that was particularly difficult for you?
- What were some blessings you received as you served?
- What are some important lessons you learn from serving in the Church?

Have family members read the section heading for D&C 53 and identify for whom this revelation was received. Read together D&C 53:3–7 and mark everything the Lord asked Sidney Gilbert to do. Take turns allowing family members to identify something they marked until you find everything. Ask:

- Which of Sidney Gilbert's responsibilities would you have most liked to do?
- How are his responsibilities similar to those we receive in the Church today?
- Do you believe we receive Church callings from the Lord, just as Brother Gilbert did? Why? (See Article of Faith 1:5.)
- Why do you think the Lord reminded Brother Gilbert to endure "unto the end" in this revelation? (See biographical sketch.)
- Why is enduring important for us as we serve the Lord?

DOCTRINE AND COVENANTS 54: IN CONSEQUENCE OF BROKEN COVENANTS

Historical background: After joining the Church, Leman Copley agreed to consecrate his farm of more than 700 acres to the Church. Saints from the Colesville, New York, branch had recently arrived in Kirtland in response to the Lord's call to gather to Ohio and were commanded to settled on this land. (See D&C 51.) When Copley returned from what he believed to be an unsuccessful mission to the Shakers (see D&C 49), he backed out of his previous agreement to consecrate this property and demanded that the Colesville Branch leave his land. Furthermore, he charged the poor Saints sixty dollars for the time they had spent on his farm, even though they had built fences and planted crops. D&C 54 was received when Newel Knight and other Saints asked the prophet what they should do as a result of Leman's actions. (See Lyndon W. Cook, The Revelations of the Prophet Joseph Smith, 85.) Notice what the Lord said we should do to escape our enemies.

Doctrine and Covenants 54:1–10
What should we do when hurt by the choices of others?

Share with your family the historical background above, and have a family member read aloud the section heading for D&C 54 to give them an idea of what occurred prior to this revelation. Invite your family to imagine the feelings of the Colesville Saints who gave up their lands in New York for little or nothing to follow the Lord's command to gather to Ohio, spend a few weeks improving what they thought would be their land, and then be told they were to be homeless (and with outstanding rent of sixty dollars). Ask:

- How do you think they felt about Leman Copley?
- What questions do you think they had for the Lord?
- What do you suppose they hoped the Lord would say through Joseph Smith in this revelation?

Read together D&C 54:1–10. As you read, have your family look for answers to the following questions:

BIOGRAPHICAL SKETCH: NEWEL KNIGHT

Newel Knight was born on September 13, 1800, in Marlborough, Vermont. Newel became acquainted with Joseph Smith in 1826 when Joseph came to board with the Knight family in Colesville, New York. In April 1830 the Prophet cast the devil out of Newel. This experience is often referred to as the first miracle in the Church in this dispensation. (See *History of the Church,* 1:82–83.) He was baptized shortly after this in May 1830.

In January 1831 he and his family gathered to Ohio with the rest of the Colesville Saints. He served as branch president in Ohio; a bishop's counselor in Jackson County, Missouri; and on the High Council at Far West, Missouri. Newel gathered with the Saints at Nauvoo after they were forced out of Missouri, and he headed west with the Saints when they were forced out of Nauvoo. He did not make it to Utah, however. He died on January 11, 1847, in Nebraska. (See Susan Easton Black, *Who's Who in the Doctrine and Covenants,* 168–71.)

- What were the members of the Colesville (now Thompson) Branch supposed to do now?
- What did the Lord say about their situation?
- What promises were made to them?

After answering the above questions from the reading, ask:

- Which parts of this revelation do you think the Colesville Saints found comforting? Why?
- Which parts of this revelation do you think they might have found challenging in their affliction? Why?

As you consider why the Lord asked those who had been taken advantage of to "repent" and "become more truly humble" (verse 3), you may want to share the following counsel from Elder Richard G. Scott:

"Oh, how we all need the healing the Redeemer can provide. Mine is a message of hope for you who yearn for relief from heavy burdens that have come through no conscious act of your own while you have lived a worthy life. It is based on principles embodied in the teachings of the Savior. . . .

" . . . The Lord will give relief with divine power when you seek deliverance in humility and *faith in Jesus Christ.* . . .

"When anguish comes from evil acts of others, there should be punishment and corrective action taken, but the offended is not the one to initiate that action. Leave it to others who have that responsibility. Learn to forgive; though terribly hard, it will release you and open the way to a newness of life. Time devoted by one injured to ensure the offended is punished is time wasted in the healing process." (*Ensign,* May 1994, 7–9.)

Have your family again identify the things in D&C 54 that can strengthen our faith that in the end all will work for our good.

DOCTRINE AND COVENANTS 55: INSTRUCTIONS TO W. W. PHELPS

Historical background: "*About the middle of June, while we were preparing for our journey to Missouri, William W. Phelps and his family arrived among us—'to do the will of the Lord,' he said: so I enquired of the Lord concerning him and received the following: [D&C 55].*" (*Joseph Smith,* History of the Church, *1:184–85.) Notice what the Lord said about the education of children.*

Doctrine and Covenants 55:1–6
What is the Lord's will concerning me?

As a family, sing or read the first verse of the following hymns: "The Spirit of God" (no. 2), "Now Let Us Rejoice" (no. 3), "Redeemer of Israel" (no. 6), and "Praise to the Man" (no. 27). Ask your family what all four hymns have in common. If no one knows, give them the hint to look for the author of the hymns. (Each of these hymns was written by W. W. Phelps. For a listing of additional hymns written by him, see "Authors and Composers" list, *Hymns,* 390.)

Ask one family member to read the biographical sketch of W. W. Phelps, and one to read the historical background for section 55. Then read together D&C 55:1–6 while someone makes a list of the things W. W. Phelps was called to do. Ask the following questions:

- What requirements are given for receiving the Holy Spirit? (See verses 1, 3.)
- What are the requirements for confirming another or giving someone the gift of the Holy Ghost? (Verses 2–3.)
- In verse 4, what does the Lord say is pleasing to him?
- Why do you think it is important for little children to receive proper instruction?
- What books or magazines does the Church have today to teach children?
- What organizations are set up in the Church today to help parents teach their children?

BIOGRAPHICAL SKETCH: WILLIAM W. PHELPS

"William W. Phelps was first introduced to the Church when he purchased a Book of Mormon on 9 April 1830 from Parley P. Pratt. He 'sat up all night to compare the Book of Mormon with the Bible.' The following morning William exclaimed, 'I am going to join that church; I am convinced that it is true.'" (Susan Easton Black, *Who's Who in the Doctrine and Covenants,* 223.)

A short time later, William was appointed as printer for the Church and printed the Book of Commandments as well as the first newspaper of the Church, *The Evening and the Morning Star.* During the early persecution in Missouri, he offered himself as ransom if the mob would stop their destruction. William helped prepare the first Church hymnbook and is the author of a number of well-known hymns, including "The Spirit of God," "Praise to the Man," "Now Let Us Rejoice," and "Redeemer of Israel." He also served as a scribe to Joseph Smith for the writings of the book of Abraham. In 1838 William became embittered against the Church and testified against its leaders. He was excommunicated in 1839 but later repented and was received back into full fellowship in 1841. He moved west with the Saints and helped draft the constitution for the State of Deseret. He served as an ordinance worker in the Endowment House and died March 6, 1872, at the age of eighty. (See Susan Easton Black, *Who's Who in the Doctrine and Covenants,* 224–26.)

DOCTRINE AND COVENANTS 56: THE LORD'S WORD TO THE REBELLIOUS

Historical background: *Ezra Thayre, who had been called on a mission, refused to leave at the time appointed. "Thayer's investment in a piece of real estate lay at the heart of the matter. The property was being shared by at least three parties, and apparently Thayer was requesting a division be made to secure his interests. . . . The essentials of the problem were later recorded by Elder [Thomas B.] Marsh: 'In June 1831 I was ordained a High Priest at a Conference held in Kirtland, where I received an appointment to go to Missouri with Ezra Thayer and preach by the way. In consequence of Ezra Thayer delaying so long, I went to Joseph who received the word of the Lord' ("History of Thomas B. Marsh, Written by Himself," [November 1857], Church Archives)"* (Lyndon W. Cook, The Revelations of the Prophet Joseph Smith, 88; see D&C 54 section heading and the historical background for section 54 in this book.) *The Lord revealed section 56 as an answer. Watch for the Lord's counsel to the rich and the poor.*

Doctrine and Covenants 56:1–11
Am I rebellious to God?

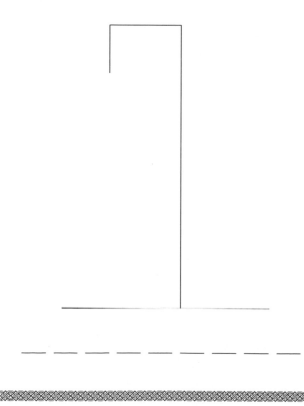 Play the game Hangman. Draw the hangman gallows on a piece of paper and provide ten blank spaces for the word "rebellious." Show the paper to your family. Add a part of the body each time a wrong letter is guessed. Once the word "rebellious" is guessed, have your family silently read D&C 56:1–4 and mark each time the word is used. Ask:

- What will happen to the rebellious?
- What is the difference between making a mistake and being rebellious?

Have your family write 3 Nephi 6:18 next to D&C 56:1; then turn to 3 Nephi 6:18 and read it together. Ask:

- According to this verse how is a person rebellious?
- What often causes a person to be rebellious to God and His commandments?

To help answer this last question, have your family search D&C 56:5–11 looking for the answer. Invite your family to write in their journals how they may be acting in a rebellious way toward God. Then have them write what will happen if they continue to do it. Testify to your family of the importance of being humble and keeping God's commandments.

Doctrine and Covenants 56:14–20
"It's New To Me"

Tell your family they are going to do an activity called "It's New To Me." Divide your family into pairs. Have them silently read D&C 56:14–20 and find something they didn't know before. Have each pair tell each other what was "new" to them. Then ask each person to share what his or her partner said with the rest of the family. After everyone has finished, ask:

- What does it mean to "counsel in your own ways"? (To do what you want rather than what God has commanded.)
- Why do we sometimes do what we want rather than what God wants?
- Why does the Lord chasten the rich in verse 16?
- What is a "canker sore" and how does it feel?
- How can riches cause spiritual "canker sores" on our souls? (Verse 16.)
- Why do you think some rich people refuse to help the poor?
- What are some reasons the Lord chastens the poor in verse 17?
- Why do people steal?
- What does verse 18 say the poor need to do to receive the Lord's blessings?
- What are ways we as a family can help those

in need? (Fast offerings, humanitarian aid, Perpetual Education Fund, local charities.)

Andrew Workman, an acquaintance of Joseph Smith, shared the following story:

"I was at Joseph's house; he was there, and several men were sitting on the fence. Joseph came out and spoke to us all. Pretty soon a man came up and said that a poor brother who lived out some distance from town had had his house burned down the night before. Nearly all of the men said they felt sorry for the man. Joseph put his hand in his pocket, took out five dollars and said, 'I feel sorry for this brother to the amount of five dollars; how much do you all feel sorry?' (*Juvenile Instructor* 27:641)." (Jack M. Lyon, Linda Ririe Gundry, and Jay A. Parry, eds., *Best-Loved Stories of the LDS People*, 405–6.)

Ask your family:

- How was Joseph Smith an example of what is taught in D&C 56:14–20?
- What did you learn from this story?

DOCTRINE AND COVENANTS 57: ZION–JACKSON COUNTY MISSOURI

Historical background: "In the Book of Mormon the Saints were told (Ether 13:1–12), that the New Jerusalem and [temple] of the Lord should be located in America (compare 3 Nephi 20:22; 21:23), and they were anxious to know where the site for the City was. In September 1830, the Lord gave them to understand that the City should be erected 'on the borders by the Lamanites' (Sec. 28:9). In February 1831, they were promised that a Revelation should be given on that subject, if they would pray for it (Sec. 42:62). On the 7th of March, the same year, they were given to understand that the gathering from the eastern States and the sending out of Elders on the mission to the West were preparatory steps to the establishment of that City, wherefore the Saints should gather up their riches and purchase an inheritance in the place to be indicated, which should be a place of refuge for the Saints of the most High God (Sec. 45:64–66). The time had now come . . . and this Revelation was received." (Hyrum M. Smith and Janne M. Sjodahl, Doctrine and Covenants Commentary, 327–28.) Notice that the temple is the first building mentioned in the building of Zion.

Doctrine and Covenants 57:1–16
Zion—Jackson County, Missouri

Tell your family that you are going to play a game using the following questions.

Divide your family into two teams. Explain that each of the questions can be answered from the section heading for D&C 57 and verses 1–16. A point will be scored for each correct answer.

When a team misses a question, the other team can win the point with a correct answer. Continue to play until each question has been asked. You can read the section first with your family or have your family search the section as you ask the questions.

- What was Joseph Smith thinking about just before this revelation was given? (See section heading.)
- What land has God appointed for the gathering of the Saints? (See verse 1.)
- What city is the center place? (See verse 2.)
- Will the temple be to the east or west of the place called Independence? (See verse 3.)
- What are the Saints to do with the land? (See verse 4.)
- What does "between Jew and Gentile" refer to in verse 4? (See footnote 4b.)
- Who is to receive money and be an agent to the Church? (See verse 6.)
- Who is to divide the inheritances (lands) to the Saints? (See verse 7.)
- Who is to establish a store to buy and sell goods? (See verse 8.)
- Why does God want to provide for His Saints? (See verse 10.)
- Who is to build a printing shop? (See verse 11.)
- Who is to help do copying and correcting at the print shop? (See verse 13.)
- When will the rest of the Saints come to Zion? (See verses 15–16.)

Ask your family to ponder what is remarkable about this revelation. You might ask:

- Which of the questions that Joseph Smith asked in the section heading did the Lord answer?
- What did the Lord tell Joseph that was more than what he asked?

- What does that tell us about receiving revelation from the Lord?

Doctrine and Covenants 57:1–3
Zion

Read to your family D&C 57:1–3 and the following statement by Joseph Smith:

"I received, by a heavenly vision, a commandment in June [1831] . . . , to take my journey to the western boundaries of the State of Missouri, and there designate the very spot which was to be the central place for . . . the gathering together of those who embrace the fullness of the everlasting Gospel. . . . After viewing the country, seeking diligently at the hand of God, He manifested Himself unto us, and designated, to me and others, the very spot upon which He designed to commence the work of the gathering, and the upbuilding of an 'holy city,' which should be called Zion—Zion, because it is a place of righteousness, and all who build thereon are to worship the true and living God, and all believe in one doctrine, even the doctrine of our Lord and Savior Jesus Christ." (*History of the Church*, 2:254).

Ask:

- How did Joseph Smith know to go to Missouri?
- How did Joseph and others know the very spot the gathering was to take place?
- What do you think it was like for Joseph to see for the first time the very land he had seen in a vision?

Invite your family to imagine that they were present in Joseph's room while he received D&C 57:1–3. Read these verses and discuss with your family what they think it might have been like for Joseph when he received this important revelation.

DOCTRINE AND COVENANTS 58: DILIGENCE, REPENTANCE, AND ZION

Historical background: "On their first Sunday in Jackson County ... W. W. Phelps preached to a [mixed] audience on the western frontier composed according to the Prophet, 'of all the families of the earth'—Lamanites or Indians, a large number of Negroes and citizens of the surrounding country. When the meeting closed, two, who had previously believed the gospel, were baptized. On July 25 the Colesville Saints arrived in the land of Zion.... This was the first branch of the Church to emigrate to Zion." (Ivan J. Barrett, Joseph Smith and the Restoration, 188.) Watch for what the Lord teaches about tribulation, agency, and repentance.

Doctrine and Covenants 58:1–12
Natural eyes versus spiritual eyes

Draw two eyes on a piece of paper and show them to your family. Have your family read D&C 58:1–5 and look for what "eyes" have to do with these verses. After giving them time to read, ask:

- What does the Lord warn is coming? (Tribulation—verse 3.)
- What can't "natural eyes" see? (The glory that will follow tribulation—verses 3–4.)
- Why does the Lord want them to "remember" the glory that they are promised? (So they can "receive" or endure the trouble that is coming—verse 5.)
- How can knowing God's plan for us help us be faithful even during hard times?

Have a family member read *just* the first two lines of D&C 58:6 aloud. Tell your family to look for reasons the Lord sent the Saints to Missouri as you read together verses 6–12. After reading, make a list of reasons, which could include:

- To learn obedience.
- That their hearts might be prepared to bear testimony.
- To lay the foundation of Zion.
- That a feast of fat things might be prepared for the poor.

You might explain that the "the 'fat things' and 'wine on the lees' were to the ancient Hebrews a representation of prosperity. 'Wine on the lees' is wine matured by resting on the lees or dregs at the bottom of the wine cask, hence 'well refined.' The 'fat things' and 'wine on the lees' at the feast are therefore a representation of the offering of the rich things of the Gospel at the Lord's table." (Hoyt W. Brewster Jr., *Doctrine and Covenants Encyclopedia,* 641.)

As a family, list some of the trials you have passed through. Discuss ways your family can better endure trials in the future.

Doctrine and Covenants 58:19–23
Laws of God vs. laws of the land

As you take turns reading D&C 58:19–23, ask your family to think of an Article of Faith that is similar to these verses. Once the twelfth Article of Faith is mentioned, ask if anyone can quote it. If not, turn to Articles of Faith 1:12 in the Pearl of Great Price and have someone read it. Ask:

- Why is it important to obey the laws of the land?
- How can obeying the laws of God help us obey the laws of the land?

Doctrine and Covenants 58:26–29
Should we be commanded in all things?

Show the accompanying picture to your family and ask if anyone knows what the animal is. Share the following story from A. Theodore Tuttle, a former member of the First Quorum of Seventy:

Sloth.

"One day in South America we had the interesting experience of seeing in a hot jungle area a small brownish gray animal hanging upside down in a tree. It had rather long front paws and short back legs. Its movements were so slow that it was hard to know whether it was alive or dead. We were told that it was a sloth. I was intrigued because reference to the sloth appears in scripture." (*Ensign,* May 1978, 87.)

Read D&C 58:26–29 together as a family and ask how the Lord feels about "slothfulness." Tell your family that in reference to "sloth," Elder Tuttle continued:

"The Lord used it [the word] with disdain, referring to those who were slow to act. . . . The word sloth or slothfulness appears in scripture twenty-five times, generally to condemn those who were slow to act. As we watched that sloth hanging in the tree, it reached out ever so slowly to pull off a leaf, then slower still brought it back and put it into its mouth. As we watched it we could understand the words *impatient, irritated, exasperated.* The Savior's reference to the sloth and slothfulness illustrates His displeasure and impatience with the person who is slow to act, who is slothful." (*Ensign,* May 1978, 87–88.)

Ask:

- What does the Lord say is not "meet" or necessary?
- Instead of being commanded or compelled in all things, what is our responsibility?

Ask a family member to summarize the message of these verses in their own words. Then ask your family to list in their personal journals ways they can be "anxiously engaged" at home, at church, at work, or at school. Invite family members to choose one goal in each category to work on in the coming week.

Doctrine and Covenants 58:34–43
What must we do to repent?

Display an empty backpack and have a family member put it on. Slowly fill the backpack with heavy items like rocks or books. Periodically have the person wearing the backpack step up onto a chair or bench several times in succession. Add more weight to the backpack and then have the person step again. Continue this process until the stepping becomes difficult. Ask the person how it feels to carry such weight. Read together D&C 58:38–39 and discuss how sin not repented of could be like the weight in the backpack.

Share the following statement by President Harold B. Lee:

"If I were to ask you what is the heaviest burden one may have to bear in this life, what would you answer? The heaviest burden that one has to bear in this life is the burden of sin." (*Ensign,* July 1973, 122.)

Read together D&C 58:42–43. Ask:

- How can one get rid of the burden of sin?
- What does the Lord do after we repent?
- According to verse 43, what are two steps of repentance?
- To whom should we confess our sins? (The Lord, the persons we have offended, and the Lord's authorized servant when necessary.)

- What does it mean to forsake our sins? (Turn away from, give up, abandon.)

Take the weights out of the backpack and have the person step up again and describe the difference. Ask your family how much easier it will be to step into the presence of Heavenly Father without the burden of sin.

Doctrine and Covenants 58:44–48, 64–65
When shall the Saints gather in Zion?

Show your family a map of the state of Missouri and also a map of the United States or the world. Have someone point out on the map of Missouri where the Saints would one day gather and build the city of Zion. (See D&C 57:3; see also the maps at the end of your Doctrine and Covenants, if necessary.) Ask your family why we haven't yet gathered there. Take turns reading D&C 58:44–48, 64–65 to find an answer. Ask:

- What did the elders of the Church need to do before they could gather in Zion?
- What does it mean to "push the people together from the ends of the earth"? (To gather them.)
- How is this "pushing" still being done today?

Now look at the world map, noting where Missouri is located. Ask:

- How many countries can you identify where missionaries are now preaching the gospel?
- Do you know of any countries where missionaries are not yet allowed?
- How can our family help the gospel be preached "unto the uttermost parts of the earth"?

Doctrine and Covenants 58:50, 57
Dedicating the land of Zion

Have family members read D&C 58:50, 57 and find what assignments were given to Sidney Rigdon. Tell your family that the dedication took place the day after this revelation was received. Oliver Cowdery reported the events of that meeting:

"On the second day of August, 1831, Rigdon stood up and asked, saying,

"'Do you receive this land for the land of your inheritance with thankful hearts from the Lord?'

"Answer from all: 'We do.'

"'Do you pledge yourselves to keep the law of God in this land which you never have kept in your own lands?'

"'We do.'

"'Do you pledge yourselves to see that others of your brethren who shall come hither do keep the laws of God?'

"'We do.'

"After prayer, he arose and said: 'I now pronounce this land consecrated and dedicated unto the Lord for a possession and inheritance for the Saints, and for all the faithful servants of the Lord to the remotest ages of time. In the name of Jesus Christ, having authority from Him. Amen.'" (*History of the Church*, 1:196.)

Discuss as a family the responsibilities Elder Rigdon put upon the Saints to keep the land of Zion consecrated to God. How might this help us know how to keep church buildings, and even our homes, dedicated to the Lord?

DOCTRINE AND COVENANTS 59: COMMANDMENTS FOR THE PEOPLE OF ZION

Historical background: Among the first families to arrive in Jackson County, Missouri, from Ohio were the Knights. "Polly Knight's health had been failing for some time, according to . . . her son, Newel. She was very ill during her journey from Kirtland to Missouri. 'Yet,' says her son, 'she would not consent to stop traveling; her . . . greatest desire was to set her feet upon the land of Zion, and to have her body interred in that land. . . . The Lord gave her the desire of her heart, and she lived to stand upon that land.'" (Scraps of Biography, 70.)

On August 1, the temple site was dedicated; on August 4 a conference of the Church was held. On August 7 the funeral for Polly Knight, wife of Joseph Knight Sr. was held. Joseph Smith wrote, "This was the first death in the Church in this land, and I can say, a worthy member sleeps in Jesus till the resurrection." (History of the Church, 1:199.) That very day, the Lord revealed to the Prophet section 59, declaring, "Those that die shall rest from all their labors" and "shall receive a crown in the mansions of my Father." (D&C 59:2.) Notice what the Lord teaches about this earth he created for us.

Doctrine and Covenants 59:1–4, 23–24
Why would you want to "stand upon the land of Zion"?

Ask your family to name some blessings they enjoy because of membership in the Church. Ask if those blessings are important enough to them that they would move to another place if the Lord asked them to. Read aloud the historical background above and ask:

- What blessing did Polly Knight desire?
- In what ways do you think she suffered to obtain this blessing?
- Why do you think she was so determined to stand in Zion?

Choose one member of your family to read D&C 59:1–4 while the rest of the family mark the blessings that come to those who are obedient to the Lord. Ask:

- How many of these blessings could Polly Knight have received?
- How might receiving more commandments be considered a blessing? (Verse 4.)
- In what ways can we "stand upon the land of Zion"? (We can make our homes a Zion—see Bible Dictionary, "Zion," 792–93.)

- How can we be worthy of the same blessings Polly Knight received?

Read D&C 59:23–24 to your family and ask what is promised to those who do the "works of righteousness." Point out footnote 23d and have everyone turn to and read that verse. (D&C14:7.) Ask:

- What are two requirements for obtaining eternal life?
- How does this help you understand why Polly Knight was so adamant about obeying the Lord's command to gather to Zion?
- What would you be willing to do to get to Zion?

Doctrine and Covenants 59:5–8
What are the commandments for those who live in Zion?

Write each of the Ten Commandments on separate word strips without numbering them. (See Exodus 20:3–17.) Randomly tape the word strips where your family can see them, and have family members work together to arrange them in the proper order. Next give everyone a blank word strip and assign each person a different verse from D&C 59:5–8. Have your family write a commandment they find in their assigned verse on their word strip. Tape these new word strips next to the corresponding commandment already listed. Ask:

- Which of the Ten Commandments are missing from the new list?
- Which commandments are new in the second list?
- In what ways might each of the Ten Commandments be included in the second list?
- Why do you think a commandment about gratitude is added?
- What sacrifice does the Lord require of His Saints?

Give all family members a piece of white paper and a red crayon or marker. Ask them to draw what they think a broken heart looks like. Ask:

- What do you think it means to have a "broken heart"? (To be brokenhearted is to be truly and deeply sorry for our sins.)
- What do you think it means to have a contrite spirit? (To be humble, teachable, and willing to change.)
- How can we become more truly sorry for our sins?
- How can we keep our spirits contrite?
- What will the Savior do to fix our broken hearts? (See Jacob 2:8.)

Consider having family members write a definition next to their pictures of a broken heart. Invite them to write in their journal a commandment upon which they wish to improve.

Doctrine and Covenants 59:9–19
How can we stay "unspotted from the world"?

Have your family make a list of things that are spotted. (Dalmatian dogs, leopards, dirty cars, children with chicken pox, and so on.)

Ask your family if they feel it would be better to be spotted or unspotted. You could have fun with this by talking about measles, chicken pox,

warts, freckles, and moles. Read D&C 59:9 to your family and ask:

- What are some spots that wouldn't be "fun" to have?
- What can we do to get rid of those spots?
- What can we do to keep them off?

Give each family member a sheet of paper that has been folded in half. Group your family into pairs and have each group read D&C 59:9–19, listing on the left side of their paper things that would help them remain "unspotted" from the world and on the right side blessings that come from keeping the Sabbath holy. Discuss the following questions:

- How can keeping the Sabbath Day holy help us become spotless?
- Why shouldn't Sunday be the only day we use to keep ourselves "unspotted"? (Verse 11.)
- How can fasting help us keep "unspotted"? (Verses 13–14.)
- How many blessings are offered to those who strive to keep themselves unspotted from the world?
- Which blessings could you use in your life right now?

You may want to take time to memorize D&C 59:9–10.

Doctrine and Covenants 59:20–22
Thanksgiving and gratitude

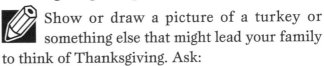 Show or draw a picture of a turkey or something else that might lead your family to think of Thanksgiving. Ask:

- What day does this picture remind you of?
- What does our family do on Thanksgiving?
- What is there to be thankful about?
- In what ways do we show our "thanksgiving"?

Have your family quickly scan D&C 59:9–19 and identify some of the blessings God gives to

His children. Then read together D&C 59:20–22. Ask:

- What pleases God?
- How is He offended?
- Why might Heavenly Father be "offended" if we express our gratitude to Him only one day each year?

- How can we "confess His hand in all things" on Thanksgiving Day and on all other days of the year?

Have family members make a journal entry about something for which they feel especially grateful. If it involves another person, suggest that they write a thank-you note to that individual.

DOCTRINE AND COVENANTS 60: "LIFT UP YOUR VOICE"

Historical background: The missionaries called in D&C 52:20–35 made their way to Independence, Missouri, from Kirtland, Ohio, teaching the gospel as they had been directed. After their arrival, they helped establish a bishop's storehouse and a bishopric. On Monday, August 8, 1831, the elders asked Joseph Smith how they should return to Ohio. Section 60 was given in response. Among the elders were Joseph Smith, Oliver Cowdery, Sidney Rigdon, Samuel H. Smith, Reynolds Cahoon, Sidney Gilbert, W. W. Phelps, Ezra Booth, Fredrick G. Williams, Peter Whitmer Jr., and Joseph Coe. Look for what would make the Lord not pleased with a missionary.

Doctrine and Covenants 60:1–4
We must open our mouths

 Have each member of your family open their mouths as wide as they can. Ask:

- What does it mean when someone says, "Shut your mouth"?
- Can you think of a time when you had your mouth open when you should have kept it closed?
- Can you think of a time when you should have opened your mouth and said something but kept your mouth closed instead?
- What are some examples of times when we should remain quiet?
- What are some examples of times when we should speak up?

Read together D&C 60:1–4 and ask:

- In what situation does the Lord say we need to open our mouths?
- Why are some afraid to open their mouths in sharing the gospel? (Verse 2.)

- What could we do to be more comfortable in sharing the gospel?
- According to verse 3, what will be taken away if we are not more faithful?
- In what ways can our family do better in opening our mouths to share the gospel?

Doctrine and Covenants 60:5–9
Missionaries should "preach the word"

Divide your family into two groups and give each paper and pencils. Assign one group to read D&C 60:5–7 and the other D&C 60:8–9. As each group reads their assigned verses, have them report on the following:

- Which missionaries are being instructed? (Also see the historical background above.)
- What are they to do?
- How can the information given help us prepare to be better missionaries?

After each group has reported, invite each family member to underline in their scriptures one word or phrase that impressed them the most.

Doctrine and Covenants 60:13–16
What is dusting of feet?

Tell your family that during this time in Church history there were two Church centers: one in Kirtland, Ohio, and the other in Independence, Missouri. Missionaries were frequently called to travel between these two places. Have family members take turns reading D&C 60:13–16. Ask:

- As missionaries traveled between Kirtland and Independence, what were they supposed to do?
- What "talent" were they not to bury? (See verse 13.)
- What special instructions were they given in verse 15?

- What does it mean for a missionary to "shake off the dust" of his feet?

Share the following insight:

"The custom of having missionaries cleanse their feet, either by washing or wiping off the dust, as a testimony against the wicked who refused to accept the gospel, was practiced in New Testament times and was reinstituted by the Lord in this dispensation. Because of the serious obligation associated with this act, Church leaders have counseled that it should be done only under the direction of the Spirit. The act appears to be associated with the commandment that the missionaries (and members) are to make certain they are clean from the sins of the wicked." (Daniel H. Ludlow, *A Companion to Your Study of the New Testament: The Four Gospels*, 91.)

DOCTRINE AND COVENANTS 61: DANGER UPON THE WATERS

Historical background: After receiving the revelation instructing them to return home to Ohio (see D&C 60), ten of the missionaries who had come to Missouri—including Joseph Smith—immediately began their journey. On the third day traveling down the Missouri River, the Joseph Smith and Sidney Rigdon had a canoe accident. Others also experienced troubles. Concerned about conditions on the river, they made an early stop at a place called McIlwaine's Bend. (See Stephen E. Robinson and H. Dean Garrett, A Commentary on the Doctrine and Covenants, 2:174–75). The Prophet noted, "after we had encamped . . . Brother [William W.] Phelps . . . saw the destroyer in his most horrible power, ride upon the face of the waters; others heard the noise, but saw not the vision." (History of the Church, 1:203.) The next morning, after prayer, Joseph received the revelation in D&C 61 as a helpful explanation of these events. Notice that, in spite of the devil's power, the Lord is really in control.

Doctrine and Covenants 61:1–6
Bearing record of dangers

Invite your family to think about times they were in danger and worried about what would happen to them. Have family members share their experiences. Read aloud the section heading for D&C 61 and share with your family the historical background above. Discuss how the dangers those missionaries faced compare to the dangers family members described earlier.

Read together D&C 61:1–2. Ask:

- What comfort do you think these missionaries found in verse 1 regarding the dangers they had and would face?
- According to verse 2, what other type of danger does the Lord seem more concerned about? (Unrepented sin.)

- How could being forgiven help you as you experience physical or spiritual danger?

Have your family look back at the previous revelation (D&C 60:12–13) and identify what the Lord had commanded the missionaries to do as part of their journey home. (Missionary work.) Read aloud D&C 61:3 and ask what these missionaries had been doing instead. Have someone else read D&C 61:4–5 and look for reasons why the Lord may have allowed them to experience the fearful dangers the previous day. Finally, have someone read D&C 61:6 and discuss why we can trust in the Lord when we face difficulties or dangers.

Point out to your family that these missionaries were supposed to be warning the people but had not done so. As a result, the Lord gave *them* a warning. This warning helped them recognize their duty. Share the following counsel from Elder Henry B. Eyring:

"The Lord would not use the word *warn* if there is no danger. Yet not many people we know sense it. They have learned to ignore the increasing evidence that society is unraveling and that their lives and family lack the peace they once thought was possible. That willingness to ignore the signs of danger can make it easy for you to think: *Why should I speak to anyone about the gospel who seems content? What danger is there to them or to me if I do or say nothing?*

"Well, the danger may be hard to see, but it is real, both for them and for us. For instance, at some moment in the world to come, everyone you will ever meet will know what you know now. They will know that the only way to live forever in association with our families and in the presence of our Heavenly Father and His Son, Jesus Christ, was to choose to enter into the gate by baptism at the hands of those with authority from God. They will know that the only way families can be together forever is to accept and keep sacred covenants offered in the temples of God on this earth. And they will know that you knew. And they will remember whether you offered them what someone had offered you." (*Ensign,* November 1998, 33.)

Discuss with your family some of the dangers facing individuals and families in today's world. How might D&C 61:3–4 be likened to these dangers today? Discuss some appropriate ways your family could warn others of the dangers facing individuals and families in our day.

Doctrine and Covenants 61:7–39
Evidence of God's love

Ask each family member to think of some evidences showing that God loves him or her. Invite all to share their thoughts. Have a family member read D&C 61:13. Then ask your family what it says about how God shows His love. Share with your family the following statement from Elder Robert D. Hales:

"These commandments are loving instructions provided by God our Father for our physical and spiritual well-being and happiness while in mortality. Commandments allow us to know the mind and will of God regarding our eternal progression. And they test our willingness to be obedient to His will.

"The commandments are not a burden or a restriction. Every commandment of the Lord is given for our development, progress, and growth. The Prophet Joseph Smith taught: 'God has designed our happiness. . . . He never will institute an ordinance or give a commandment to His people that is not calculated in its nature to promote that happiness which He has designed' (*Teachings of the Prophet Joseph Smith,* sel. Joseph Fielding Smith [1976], 256)." (*Ensign,* May 1996, 35.)

Explain to your family that God also shows His love for us by promising blessings. Divide family members into two groups. Have both groups read D&C 61:7–39. Ask one group to notice all the commandments God gives in these verses, and ask the other group to notice the promises that are mentioned. Once they have finished, have each group share what they found and explain how those items are an expression of God's love. Ask your family to put a check mark in their scriptures next to each commandment or promise that they think applies to people today. Have several family members share two or three check-marked items they think are significant.

(Note: Your family may have questions about the cursing of the waters or the implications of restrictions the Lord gave about the waters. If they do, you might point out that although the Lord said some negative things about the waters, He also told Sidney Gilbert and William W. Phelps that they could travel by water if they chose. [See D&C 61:22.]) Consider this commentary:

"There is little indication in the historical record that the Saints understood Doctrine and Covenants 61 as a blanket prohibition against water travel, though they were clearly advised to travel up to Zion by land. For example, Parley P. Pratt and his wife traveled to Missouri by water in the summer of 1832. Rather, section 61 was seen as an expression of the Lord's preference that those called to settle permanently in Zion travel by land, perhaps because of the physical dangers of going by boat, but also because of the missionary opportunities that would otherwise be lost." (Stephen E. Robinson and H. Dean Garrett, *A Commentary on the Doctrine and Covenants*, 2:180–81.)

This section is not the reason missionaries today are prohibited from swimming. The rule about swimming is comparable to this revelation, however. In both instances, the Lord gives counsel that helps prevent dangers and accidents.

DOCTRINE AND COVENANTS 62: BLESSINGS TO FAITHFUL MISSIONARIES

Historical background: Concerning the context of Section 62, George Q. Cannon stated, "After three days of rowing down the Missouri, Joseph and Sidney and Oliver were directed to journey by land speedily to Kirtland, while the others were instructed to proceed with the canoes. [See the heading of section 61.]

"On the day following this division, the 13th of August, [1831] Joseph met several elders who were on their way to Independence. A meeting was held in which joy abounded. [Section 62, received on the bank of the Missouri River.] After this the elders parted, the Prophet and his two companions continuing their journey and the other advancing toward the land of Zion." (Life of Joseph Smith, 123–24.) Watch for the blessings that come as we share our testimonies with others.

Doctrine and Covenants 62:1
What help does the Lord offer in our trials, sufferings, and temptations?

Ask your family what feelings they have when they see news stories of people suffering (such as accidents, sickness, or war)? Ask if their feelings are different when they see someone they love suffering. (Consider having a mother in your family talk about seeing her child suffer.)

Ask a family member to read D&C 62:1 aloud. Ask:

- How do you think Jesus feels when He sees us suffering because of sin?
- Do you think Jesus knows what we are feeling?

For a scriptural answer, have them highlight footnote b next to the word "succor" in D&C 62:1 and the cross-reference to Alma 7:12. Read Alma 7:11–13 together and discuss what these verses teach about Jesus' understanding of our weaknesses, pains, afflictions, and so forth.

Point out the word "succor" in both Alma 7

and D&C 62. Share with your family the following definition from *Webster's 1828 Dictionary:*

"Succor: Literally, to run to, or run to support; hence, to help or relieve when in difficulty, want or distress; to assist and deliver from suffering."

With a better understanding of the meaning of this word, have your family re-read D&C 62:1 to themselves. Discuss new insights they have gained about what the Savior is teaching in this verse. Share your testimony, and invite family members to share experiences when they have felt the Savior's succor.

Doctrine and Covenants 62:2–3
What are some blessings that come as we bear our testimonies?

Have a family member read the section heading for D&C 62. Add to this information by sharing the historical background above. Ask your family to identify the people to whom this revelation was directed. (Missionaries.) Read D&C 62:2–3 together as a family. Discuss the following questions:

- What reason did the Lord give for why these missionaries were blessed?
- How do you suppose that made them feel?
- Who else rejoiced over the testimony those missionaries bore?
- What specific blessing did these missionaries receive for bearing testimony? (Their sins were forgiven.)
- Why do you suppose the Lord is willing to forgive your sins as you testify of the truth of the gospel to others? (See D&C 18:10–16.)
- Where do you think might be the most important place to bear testimony of the truth of the gospel?

To help answer that last question, share the following statement from Elder Henry B. Eyring:

"There is a caution I would give and a promise I would offer about such choices of how to use family time. For a person not yet a member of the Church, to fail to provide such moments of love

and faith is simply a lost opportunity. But for those under covenant, it is much more. There are few places where the covenant to love and to bear witness is more easily kept than in the home. And there are few places where it can matter more for those for whom we are accountable. For members of the Church, my caution is that to neglect those opportunities is a choice not to keep sacred covenants.

"Because God always honors covenants, I can make a promise to those who in faith keep the covenant to create experiences of giving love and bearing testimony with their families. They will reap a harvest of hearts touched, faith in Jesus Christ exercised unto repentance, and the desire and the power to keep covenants strengthened." (*Ensign,* November 1996, 32.)

Explain to your family that there are ways to bear testimony other than formally standing in a meeting, or beginning with the sentence "I'd like to bear my testimony." Talk about other ways you can show that you believe in the gospel message and in the Savior Jesus Christ. Challenge your family to live in such a way that others recognize their testimony.

Tell your family how much you love them, and share with them your testimony of the gospel.

Doctrine and Covenants 62:4–9
When do we need a revelation from God?

Share the following case studies with your family. After you read each case study, ask your family if they think it is necessary to pray for guidance in this situation:

- Your family is going to repaint the trim on your home. Someone suggests you pray about what color of paint you should purchase.
- You are choosing a counselor to serve with you in the deacons quorum presidency. Your bishop suggests that you pray for direction.
- Your parents ask you to fix dinner. You have many options and are not sure what to choose.

- You have just finished reading the Book of Mormon and want to know if it is true.
- A friend at school asks you a question about the Church, and you are not sure what to say.

Talk about why prayer is appropriate in some situations and not always necessary in others.

Read D&C 62:4–9 together. Ask your family to note which things the Lord specifically commands these missionaries to do and the things he leaves to their choice. Ask:

- What does this teach us about receiving guidance from the Lord?
- Why doesn't God give a revelation about every decision?
- On the other hand, how can we make sure we will have God's Spirit to direct us when we need it? (See verse 9.)

Share the following counsel from Elder Dallin H. Oaks:

"The Spirit of the Lord is not likely to give us revelations on matters that are trivial. I once heard a young woman in a testimony meeting praise the spirituality of her husband, indicating that he submitted every question to the Lord. She told how he accompanied her shopping and would not even choose between different brands of canned vegetables without making his selection a matter of prayer. I think that is improper. I believe the Lord expects us to make most of our decisions by using the intelligence and experience he has given us. When someone asked the Prophet Joseph Smith for advice on a particular matter, the Prophet stated: 'It is a great thing to inquire at the hands of God, or to come into His presence: and we feel fearful to approach Him on subjects that are of little or no consequence.'" (*The Lord's Way*, 37.)

DOCTRINE AND COVENANTS 63: A WARNING TO THE WICKED

Historical background: "*When the report spread among the members of the Church that the Lord had revealed definitely where the city New Jerusalem was to be built, naturally there was rejoicing and many expressed the desire to know what they were to do in order to obtain inheritances. The Lord has given instruction repeatedly that all who go to Zion shall obey His law—the celestial law on which Zion was to be built. Those who were weak in the faith, or indifferent to the commandments, were warned that they would not be made welcome in that land unless they repented. 'Hearken, O ye people, and open your hearts and give ear from afar; and listen, you that call yourselves the people of the Lord, and hear the word of the Lord and his will concerning you.' These are the words by which this revelation is introduced.*" (Joseph Fielding Smith, Church History and Modern Revelation, 1:229.) *Notice what the difference is between sign-seeking and receiving signs of faith.*

Doctrine and Covenants 63:1–6, 12–18, 32–37

"A day of wrath shall come upon the wicked"

 Read the historical background to your family and ask:

- What topic most occupied the Saints' minds in 1831?
- What requirements did the Lord have for those wanting to move to Zion?

Give several paper strips to each family member. Divide the verses from D&C 63:1–2, 12–14, 17 among family members and ask them to study their assigned verses. As they do, have them write words or phrases on individual pieces of paper describing the characteristics or activities of a wicked person.

Ask your family to place their word strips where all can see them and then talk about each characteristic or activity one by one. Discuss why that word or phrase is associated with wickedness and contrary to the building up of Zion. Finally, give an example of how that wickedness exists today.

Read D&C 63:6, 18, 32–35 aloud and ask family members to identify what the Lord warns will come upon the wicked. Talk about ways we may avoid wickedness and avoid these curses. Testify of the importance of keeping God's commandments.

Contrast the Lord's message to the wicked with His message to the righteous by reading aloud verses 23–24, 36–37. Point out the important part righteousness plays in the establishment of Zion. Read Moses 7:18 together and talk about how your family can better apply the phrase they "dwelt in righteousness" in your home.

Doctrine and Covenants 63:7–12
What is the relationship between "signs" and "faith"?

Write the words "signs" and "faith" on two separate papers. Hold both words up and ask your family which of these should come first. Ask them to explain why they think the Lord expects us to have faith before we are given signs or miracles.

Explain that another word for signs is "miracles." Ask your family to think of some examples of miracles they have witnessed or read about in scripture. Read together the discussion under "Miracles" in the Bible Dictionary (see pages 732–33). Ask your family to identify and then discuss one teaching about miracles they did not understand before they read the Bible Dictionary definition.

Explain that you want to create a "family test."

Have each family member silently read D&C 63:7–12 and write three questions about signs and faith that these verses answer. When all are finished, give all family members an opportunity to ask one of their questions. Have the others give correct answers after each question. Testify that as we exercise faith, the Lord can perform miracles, according to His will, in our behalf.

Doctrine and Covenants 63:13–20
What are some consequences of breaking the law of chastity?

Invite your family to read silently D&C 63:13–20 and mark the teachings they think are most important. Allow them to share what they marked and why. Ask:

- What does it mean to lust after a woman?
- According to verse 16, what happens when people lust and commit adultery in their hearts?
- What do you think it means to commit adultery in your heart?
- What can we do to help keep appropriate thoughts?
- What does *For the Strength of Youth* teach about this principle?

Read the following statement from President Gordon B. Hinckley:

"Run from the tide of sleaze that would overcome you. Flee the evils of the world. Be loyal to your better self. Be loyal to the best that is in you. . . . I have witnessed much of the best and much of the worst in marriage. Every week I have the responsibility of acting on requests for cancellation of temple sealings. Divorce has become a very common phenomenon throughout the world. Even where it is not legal, men and women simply step over the line and live together. I am grateful to be able to say that divorce is much less frequent with those married in the temple. But even among these there is far more divorce than there should be. . . . Be loyal to your companion." (*Ensign,* May 2003, 58.)

Discuss with your family how we can be more committed to the law of chastity in our actions and our thoughts.

Doctrine and Covenants 63:37–58
Raise a warning voice

Ask one family member to say the word "stop" three times, using the tone of voice he or she would use under the following three circumstances:

1. You wanted a family member to not change a television channel you are watching.

2. You saw a man taking a woman's purse and running away down the street.

3. You saw a younger family member dashing into the street after a ball, not realizing a car was approaching.

Talk about these questions:

- In which of these circumstances is a warning voice needed?
- How does a warning voice compare to a teaching or asking voice?

Read D&C 63:37 and ask family members to mark the phrase "lift a warning voice." Ask:

- To whom are the righteous to lift a warning voice?
- Why is it important to warn the inhabitants of the earth?
- What tone should we use when we give this warning?
- What is a kind and loving way we can warn our neighbors and friends?

Explain that verses 38–48 contain instructions to particular individuals regarding their duties and their desires to go to Zion. Also explain that verses 49–54 talk about some of the blessings that will come to the righteous at the Second Coming. Have your family scan through those verses and highlight some instructions that stand out to them. Ask:

- Why would messages of Zion and the Second Coming be worth warning others about?
- Why are members of the Church in the best position to warn others about these two subjects?

Read D&C 63:57 aloud and ask who is to warn sinners. Talk about why your family should be "meek" and why "desire" is important when it comes to raising a warning voice. Testify that "this is a day of warning." Encourage your family to share the gospel with their friends and neighbors. Talk about ways you can further the cause of Zion in preparation for the Lord's coming.

Doctrine and Covenants 63:59–63
How do you use the name of Christ?

Ask your family if they can think of a time when they heard someone make fun of their name or the name of another person. Talk about how it might feel to have your name mocked or ridiculed. Read D&C 63:59–63 together as a family. Ask:

- What did the Lord say about those who misuse His name?
- What are some examples of how a person might misuse the name of the Lord?

Share the following quotation from Elder Lynn A. Mickleson:

"Prepare your children to take upon themselves the name of Christ through the covenant of baptism. When we make this covenant, we become known as His children and promise to keep His commandments. When we break the promises and covenants we make to Him and do not repent, we take His name in vain." (*Ensign,* November 1995, 78.)

Share your feelings about the importance of the Savior's name and why we should take His name upon us. Encourage family members to always respect the Lord so they can remain free from condemnation.

Doctrine and Covenants 63:64–66
How are we to treat sacred things?

Show your family a valuable or delicate item. (Fine china, jewelry, or a family heirloom). Ask your family to explain how these items should be cared for or protected. Why should they be handled differently than other household items?

Read D&C 63:64 and ask:

- What did the Lord identify as sacred? (That coming from above.)
- What things come from above? (answers to prayer, revelation, blessings from God, and so on.)
- Why do you think those things should be treated with special care?
- What does the teaching found in Matthew 7:6 have to do with this principle?

Share the following statement with your family:

"The increase of profanity and vulgarity in music, books, television, and movies serves as a commentary on our times. It seems likely that people's inhumanity to people is related to their neglect of sacred matters, that the growing harshness, crudeness, and insensitivity in society are correlated directly with denying, defying, or ignoring God. When we love the Lord, cherish his word, and humbly bow beneath his rod, we seek always to act and speak with deferential reverence toward Deity. On the other hand, one who knows not God and finds no personal value in worship or devotion cannot understand the true, deep meaning of *holy* and *holiness*. Such a person may have no sense of restraint in regard to speech, no hesitation to drag the sacred out of its context and thrust it into the profane." (Robert L. Millet, *Ensign*, March 1994, 7.)

DOCTRINE AND COVENANTS 64: "FORGIVENESS AND SACRIFICE"

Historical background: "*Because of interference and because he needed a quiet place in which to work, the Prophet on September 12, 1831, moved to the home of John Johnson in the township of Hiram. This was in Portage County, Ohio, about thirty miles southeast of Kirtland. From the time he moved until early in October, the Prophet spent most of his spare time preparing for the continuation of the translation of the Bible. By translation is meant a revision of the Bible by inspiration or revelation as the Lord had commanded him, and which was commenced as early as June 1830. (HC 1:215.) Sidney Rigdon continued to write for the Prophet in the work of revision. The day before the Prophet moved from Kirtland he received an important revelation, Section 64, as it now appears in the Doctrine and Covenants. This revelation contained a wealth of information, counsel and warning, for the guidance of the members of the Church.*" (Joseph Fielding Smith, Church History and Modern Revelation, *1:234–35.) Look especially for what the Lord said about the importance of forgiving others.*

Doctrine and Covenants 64:1–7
What does it mean to overcome the world?

Read together as a family D&C 64:1–2 and ask what it means to "overcome the world." Tell your family that Elder Quentin L. Cook of the Quorum of the Seventy suggested three questions for all to consider. Invite your family to write yes or no in response to each question in their journals and write down one suggestion for improvement in each area.

"First, is the way we live consistent with what we believe, and would our friends and associates recognize . . . that we have separated ourselves from worldly evils?

"Second, are worldly pleasures, profits, and similar pursuits distracting us from following, worshiping, and serving the Savior in our daily lives?

"Third, in order to serve God and be holy, are we making sacrifices consistent with our covenants?" (*Ensign*, November 2003, 95.)

When your family has finished writing, take turns reading D&C 64:3–7 and discuss the following questions:

- Does the Lord know we are going to make mistakes as we try to overcome the world?
- What phrase do you like most from those verses?
- What does the Lord require of us so we can be forgiven for our mistakes?
- How does it make you feel to know that the Lord is so willing to forgive us when we repent?

Doctrine and Covenants 64:8–13
What would you do?

Before beginning this activity, give each family member a small pebble to hold.

Share one of the following case studies with your family, or create some of your own. Ask family members to think about how they would feel and what they would do if this happened to them.

- You have worked hard drawing a beautiful picture. You leave the room for just a few minutes, and when you return, you discover that your little sister came in and scribbled all over it. What would you do?
- You are carrying an armful of things down the hall at school. Some kids are goofing around, and one of them bumps into you,

scattering your things all over the floor. The person who bumped into you laughs and runs off. What would you do?
- You tell a friend something very personal, and the friend promises not to tell anyone. Later you find out that your friend broke the promise and even told other things about you that are not true. What would you do?

Allow family members to respond and discuss the answers. Read D&C 64:8 aloud and ask:

- Why did Jesus chastise his disciples?
- What does "sought occasion against one another" mean? (Looked for reasons to criticize each other.)
- What is significant about the phrase "in their hearts"?

Ask your family to put the pebbles they are holding into one of their shoes. Have each person walk around and describe about how uncomfortable it is. Ask, "How can a little pebble be compared to feelings we have when we don't forgive a person who has offended us?" (Adapted from Jane McBride Choate, "Pebble of Forgiveness," *Friend*, February 2003, 42.)

Take turns having family members read D&C 64:9–13. Ask the following questions and discuss the accompanying quotations:

- Whom does the Lord say we must forgive? (Verse 10.)
- What does the Lord say about those who will not forgive others? (Verse 9.)
- How can we gain strength to forgive others? (Put judgment into God's hands—verse 11.)
- If someone who has offended us does not repent or seek our forgiveness, are we still required to forgive that person?

President Spencer W. Kimball said, "A common error is the idea that the offender must apologize and humble himself to the dust before forgiveness is required. Certainly, the one who does the injury should totally make his adjustment, but as for the offended one, he must forgive the offender regardless of the attitude of the other. . . . Yes, to be in the right we must forgive, and we must do so without regard to whether or not our [enemy] repents, or how sincere is his transformation, or whether or not he asks our forgiveness." (*The Miracle of Forgiveness,* 282–83.)

- Why would the greater sin remain in those who do not forgive?

"When we take the position of withholding forgiveness from our fellow men, we are attempting to block his progress towards salvation. This position is satanical and our motive is not Christlike. We are endeavoring to impede the progress of a living soul and deny him the forgiving blessings of the atonement. This philosophy is saturated with impure motives that are designed to destroy the soul. What greater sin is there than this?" (Leaun G. Otten and C. Max Caldwell, *Sacred Truths of the Doctrine and Covenants,* 1:314.)

- How do you feel when you do not forgive others?

William W. Phelps was a close friend of Joseph Smith. He was appointed printer for the Church. William sacrificed much for the gospel. He moved to Missouri and was called to other leadership positions. Later, because of some faults he thought he saw in the Prophet, William left the Church. He became a bitter man and an enemy of the Prophet. His false testimony in 1838 helped put the Prophet and other Church leaders in jail, where they suffered terribly for many months.

Two years later, William Phelps realized that what he had done was wrong. "I am as the prodigal son," he wrote in a letter to the Prophet. "I know my situation, you know it, and God knows it, and I want to be saved if my friends will help me. . . . I have done wrong and I am sorry."

He begged for Joseph's forgiveness and asked to be received again as a member of the Church.

Joseph answered immediately with love and forgiveness. He wrote, "Believing your confession to be real, and your repentance genuine, I shall be happy once again to give you the right hand of

fellowship, and rejoice over the returning prodigal. . . . 'Come on, dear brother, since the war is past, for friends at first, are friends again at last.'" (See *History of the Church,* 4:141–42, 163–64.)

In spite of the terrible things William did to hurt the Prophet, Joseph forgave his friend, and William became a valiant servant of the Lord once more. He wrote the words to fifteen hymns; many of them were included in the first LDS hymnbook. One of them, "Praise to the Man," was written especially about his forgiving friend, the Prophet Joseph. (Adapted from "Sharing Time: The Prophet's Example," *Friend,* November 2000, 8.)

Ask family members to think of someone who has hurt or offended them or against whom they hold a grudge, and invite them to seek to forgive this person.

Doctrine and Covenants 64:23–25
"A day of sacrifice"

Ask your family to answer the following two questions:

- How long is a day?
- What is going to happen tomorrow?

Have family members read D&C 64:23–25 and then respond to those same two questions in light of what they read. ("Today" is the period of time before the Second Coming of Christ. "Tomorrow" the proud and the wicked will be destroyed.) Discuss these questions:

- If today is a "day of sacrifice," what are some things the Lord asks us to sacrifice? (Tithing, fast offerings, missionary service, temple service, and so on.)
- How does it make you feel when you make sacrifices to the Lord?
- What blessings have you received by making sacrifices?
- According to verse 23, what is a blessing that comes to those who sacrifice and pay an honest tithe?
- What do you think the phrase "shall not be burned at his coming" means?

Share the following commentary on these verses with your family:

"Does that mean that if a man will not pay his tithing, that the Lord is going to send a ball of fire down from heaven and burn him up? No; the Lord does not do it that way. The Lord works on natural principles. This is what it means, if I read correctly: a man who ignores the express command of the Lord, by failing to pay his tithing, it means that the Spirit of the Lord will withdraw from him, it means that the power of the priesthood will withdraw from that man, if he continues in the spirit of neglect to do his duty. He will drift into darkness, gradually but surely, until finally (mark you) he will lift up his eyes among the wicked. That is where he will finally land; and then when the destruction comes and when the burning comes, he will be among the wicked, and will be destroyed; while those who observe the law will be found among the righteous, and they will be preserved. There is a God in heaven, and He has promised to shield and protect them. I tell you there is a day of burning, a day of destruction coming upon the wicked. And where will we be? Will we be with the wicked, or with the righteous?" (Rudger Clawson, Conference Report, October 1913, 59.)

Doctrine and Covenants 64:27
"The bondage of debt"

Show your family a simple budget form and discuss what it means to have a budget. Ask your family if they can describe the difference between *income* and *expenses*. Ask:

- What do we call it when our expenses exceed our income? (Debt.)
- What problems come when a person or family is in debt?
- How can a person or a family get out of debt? (Increase their income or decrease their expenses.)
- What counsel does D&C 64:27 have about debt?

Share the following counsel from President Gordon B. Hinckley:

"President Heber J. Grant spoke repeatedly on this matter from this pulpit. He said: 'If there is any one thing that will bring peace and contentment into the human heart, and into the family, it is to live within our means. And if there is any one thing that is grinding and discouraging and disheartening, it is to have debts and obligations that one cannot meet.' . . . What a wonderful feeling it is to be free of debt, to have a little money against a day of emergency put away where it can be retrieved when necessary. . . . I urge you . . . to look to the condition of your finances. I urge you to be modest in your expenditures; discipline yourselves in your purchases to avoid debt to the extent possible. Pay off debt as quickly as you can, and free yourselves from bondage." (*Ensign*, November 1998, 51.)

You may want to set some family goals concerning your budget. Ask family members to help make efforts to follow and stay within the budget.

Doctrine and Covenants 64:33–43
What is a small or simple thing I can do?

Before beginning scripture study, find a seed and the fruit or vegetable it came from (or a picture of them). A watermelon seed would work well for this illustration. Also prepare a piece of paper for each family member with the following written on it, but do not give it to them until later.

A Small or Simple Thing I Can Do For . . .

My family:

My friend or neighbor:

My church or community:

Show the seed and ask:

- What sort of plant does this seed come from?
- What does the seed have to do with D&C 64:33?

• Can you tell about a time when someone did a small and simple thing that lifted your spirits and brightened your day?

Share this statement from Elder M. Russell Ballard:

"We observe vast, sweeping world events; however, we must remember that the purposes of the Lord in our personal lives generally are fulfilled through the small and simple things, and not the momentous and spectacular." (*Ensign,* May 1990, 6.)

Give family members the previously prepared pieces of paper and some pencils and invite them to write down, privately, one simple thing they can do to make someone's life better in each of the categories.

Read together D&C 64:22, 34. Ask:

• What does the Lord say He requires of us?
• What is meant by the phrase "the heart and a willing mind"?
• Why is it not enough just to be obedient; why does the Lord require that we do things for the right reason?

Take turns reading D&C 64:37–43. As you do, ask family members to look for some "great" things that will come to the earth because the Lord has restored His Church. Highlight the things you discover and discuss them together. Share your testimony of your family doing your small part in the kingdom so the Church can fill the earth and Zion can flourish.

DOCTRINE AND COVENANTS 65: THE KINGDOM OF GOD ROLLS FORTH

Historical background: "*[Joseph Smith] was now living in Hiram, about thirty miles south-east of Kirtland. He had gone there, on invitation of Father Johnson, in order to devote himself to his work on the Bible revision. From September 12, 1831, until the first of October, he did little more than prepare to re-commence the translation of the Bible. (HC, Vol. 1., p. 215.) What the preparations consisted in is not stated, but this revelation, which is an inspired prayer, indicates that an important part of such preparation was communion with God in prayer.*

"At Hiram, several important conferences were held. There thirteen Revelations were received, including the memorable vision recorded in Section 76. There a mob, excited by the agitation of Ezra Booth, who had denied the faith and become an enemy, tried to take the life of the prophet and Sidney Rigdon. No doubt, this Revelation, came to strengthen them for the work and experiences before them." (Hyrum M. Smith and Janne M. Sjodahl, Doctrine and Covenants Commentary, 397). *Look for what we can learn here about the Second Coming of the Savior.*

Doctrine and Covenants 65:1, 3–5
How can we prepare for the coming of the Lord?

Ask each family member to think about the following question: "If you knew that the Second Coming of Jesus Christ would be in two days, what is one important thing you could do to prepare?" Have them share their ideas.

Ask your family to compare their ideas to the counsel given by the Lord in D&C 65:1, 3–5. Read those verses together and mark the word

"prepare" each time you find it. Also, look for and discuss what preparations are called for there.

Do the following activities for each of the instructions given in this section:

"Make his paths straight." (Verse 1.)

Look in the Topical Guide under the word "path." Select and read several passages, looking for insights about the straight path. Ask, "What do you think it means to 'make his paths straight?' Why would it be important to be on the straight path?"

"Prepare ye the supper of the Lamb." (Verse 3.)

Read and discuss the following statement (you could also read about the supper of the Lamb from Revelation 19:9–16):

"This prophecy of the marriage of the Lamb is a figure of speech, having reference to the second coming of our Savior and the feast, or supper, that the righteous shall receive at his coming. When teaching the Jews, and more especially his disciples, the Savior spoke of the Bridegroom when referring to himself." (Joseph Fielding Smith, *Doctrines of Salvation,* 3:61.)

Ask:

• Why would you like to attend that supper?
• What should you do to prepare to feast with the Lord?

"Pray unto the Lord . . . make known his wonderful works among the people." (Verse 4.)

Ask:

• Why is prayer such a valuable tool of preparation?
• How can we improve our prayers?
• Why do you think it is important to share our knowledge with others?
• What is a missionary activity we could participate in this upcoming week?

Doctrine and Covenants 65:2
The rolling stone

Show your family a key and ask them what keys are for. Read together D&C 65:2 and Matthew 16:19 footnote a. Ask what the keys mentioned there represent. Share the following with your family:

"Keys signify authority to administer the ordinances, teach the doctrines, and take part in the government of the Church. . . . The 'key' is a symbol of authority." (Hyrum M. Smith and Janne M. Sjodahl, *Doctrine and Covenants Commentary,* 398.)

Ask your family to quickly scan D&C 65:2, 5–6. Ask:

• Once the keys are given to man on earth, what did the Lord say could then transpire? (The gospel could spread throughout the earth.)
• Why is holding the proper authority an essential part of spreading the gospel throughout the earth?
• What are some evidences that the keys of authority are held in The Church of Jesus Christ of Latter-day Saints?

Show a round stone to your family. Read aloud D&C 65:2 and ask family members to cross-reference it with Daniel 2:31–45. Read that prophecy from Daniel and ask:

• What does the stone represent?
• Who will set up this kingdom? (See Daniel 2:44.)
• What will happen to the other kingdoms of the earth? (See Daniel 2:44.)
• What testimony does Daniel give about the dream? (See Daniel 2:45.)

If you have family members who served missions, have them share what they did to help the "stone roll forth." Set some family goals to help the gospel increase in the earth. Share this statement from Joseph Smith, and bear your testimony about how wonderful it is to be part of this great latter-day work:

"Our missionaries are going forth to different nations. . . . The Standard of Truth has been erected; no unhallowed hand can stop the work from progressing; persecutions may rage, mobs may combine, armies may assemble, calumny may defame, but the truth of God will go forth boldly, nobly, and independent, till it has penetrated every continent, visited every clime, swept every country, and sounded in every ear, till the purposes of God shall be accomplished, and the Great Jehovah shall say the work is done." (*History of the Church,* 4:540.)

DOCTRINE AND COVENANTS 66: GOD ANSWERS OUR QUESTIONS

Historical background: *Shortly after William E. McLellin joined the Church, he traveled to Ohio, where he found Joseph Smith in the community of Orange, where a conference of the Church was underway. William tells what happened next, "On Saturday, the 29th, I received through him, and wrote from his mouth a revelation concerning myself. I had expected and believed that when I saw Bro. Joseph, I should receive one: and I went before the Lord in secret, and on my knees asked him to reveal the answer to five questions through his prophet, and that too without his having any knowledge of my having made such a request. I now testify in the fear of God, that every question, which I had thus lodged in the ears of the Lord of Sabbaoth, were answered to my full and entire satisfaction. I desired it for a testimony of Joseph's inspiration. And I this day consider it to be an evidence which I cannot refute." (*Ensign of Liberty, of the Church of Christ, *61). "The fact that William wrote this account ten years after his excommunication from the Church lends credibility to its truth." (Stephen E. Robinson and H. Dean Garrett,* A Commentary on the Doctrine and Covenants, *2:226–27.)*

The revelation that William received is now canonized as Doctrine and Covenants 66. As you study this revelation, look for a special blessing that is promised to the Lord's faithful servants.

Doctrine and Covenants 66:1–3
How well does Heavenly Father know us?

Have your family think of someone they know who was converted to the Church. Then discuss these questions:

- What changes did you see come into that person's life?
- What helped the person make the decision to be baptized?
- Do you think it would be easy or difficult to join The Church of Jesus Christ of Latter-day Saints? Why?
- What are some requirements that would be expected of a person who decided to join the Church of Jesus Christ?

Read D&C 66:1–3 aloud and have your family look for the blessings promised to the new convert, William E. McLellin. Compare his list of blessings to the blessings new converts receive today.

Explain that Heavenly Father gives counsel and warning to all worthy Church members to help them in their journey through life. Have them re-read verse 3 and discuss the following questions:

- What was the warning William E. McLellin was given?
- Why would that warning be important to follow?
- How is this warning a demonstration of Heavenly Father's love for William?
- In what ways could this warning apply to each of us?
- According to the biographical sketch of William E. McLellin, how well did he heed this warning?

Doctrine and Covenants 66:3
Can I become perfectly clean?

Show your family three sheets of white paper: one perfectly white, with no marks on it; a second one with a few pencil marks or other dark marks; and a third that is almost completely covered with pencil or other messy markings.

Have your family imagine that these papers represent a person's spiritual life. Ask, "Which paper would you want your life to be like and why?

Ask family members to silently read D&C 66:3 and identify which paper best exemplifies the life of William E. McLellin. Ask:

- What might it mean to be "clean, but not all?"
- According to Isaiah 1:18, is it possible to become completely clean?
- How do we become clean? (Through repentance and the Atonement.)

Ask family members to use the Topical Guide to find one scripture reference about repentance that they feel is important. Allow them to share what they found and tell how they feel about the power of repentance. Invite your family to think about the sins they need to remove from their lives and encourage them to do so.

Doctrine and Covenants 66:1–13
What questions would you like to ask the Lord?

Ask your family to think about this question: "If you could ask the Lord any five questions, what would they be and why?" Discuss some of their answers; then read the historical background for this section. Look for the reasons William E. McLellin asked five questions of the Lord, and why this revelation may have helped him know that Joseph Smith was a true prophet.

Explain that even though William's questions are not outlined in D&C 66, the answers he received are listed. Read D&C 66:1–13 together as a family and make a list of some of the answers the Lord gave to Brother McLellin. When you have finished, ask your family to think about and imagine what questions William McLellin may have asked to get the answers he did. See if your family can come up with at least five possible questions. Then ask:

BIOGRAPHICAL SKETCH: WILLIAM E. MCLELLIN

William E. McLellin (sometimes spelled M'Lellin) was born on January 18, 1806, in Smith County, Tennessee. He first heard the preaching of the gospel in the summer of 1831 from David Whitmer and Harvey Wheelock and was later baptized by Hyrum Smith. William served as a missionary with Parley P. Pratt in Missouri and Illinois. On February 15, 1835, he was called to the Quorum of the Twelve Apostles.

In 1835 he began to criticize the First Presidency, and by 1836 he had apostatized.

William was excommunicated in 1838 for "unbelief and apostasy." (Andrew Jenson, *Latter-day Saint Biographical Encyclopedia,* 1:83.) He died on April 24, 1883, at the age of seventy-seven, in Independence, Jackson County, Missouri.

- Do you think it is important to ask the Lord questions?
- Can you think of other questions people in the scriptures have asked the Lord?
- What are some ways the Lord may give us answers to our questions?
- How would receiving the Lord's answers bless our lives?

Read James 1:5 aloud. Share your feelings about answers to prayers and encourage your family members to seek answers from the Lord regularly.

DOCTRINE AND COVENANTS 67: A TESTIMONY OF THE REVELATIONS

Historical background: By the fall of 1831, Joseph Smith had received many revelations. Some of these revelations were given to individuals, others to the Church, and some to the whole world. Church members wanted to study these revelations and share them with others. So a special conference was called for November 1, 1831, to make decisions about publishing these revelations. Not only did the Lord approve of publishing the revelations, but He also revealed a preface for the book (the Book of Commandments). This preface is now section 1 of the Doctrine and Covenants. (See historical background for D&C 1.)

"It was the intention of the Prophet Joseph Smith that the elders present at this conference should bear written testimony to the world of the truth of these revelations in the same manner that the Three Witnesses and the Eight Witnesses had testified to the truth of the Book of Mormon." (Stephen E. Robinson and H. Dean Garrett, A Commentary on the Doctrine and Covenants, 2:232–33). After the Prophet recorded what is now section 1, some of the elders present were critical of the language in the revelation. It was in this setting that the Prophet received the revelation contained in Section 67. Notice in this revelation how the Lord supports and defends His prophet.

Doctrine and Covenants 67:1–2
Learning about the Lord

Tell your family that Joseph Smith once told the Saints that a person could not have real faith in God without "a correct idea of [God's] character, perfections, and attributes." (*Lectures on Faith*, 3:4.) Ask:

- How does knowing these things about God help us exercise faith in Him?
- Where could we go to learn more about the nature of God so we might exercise more faith in Him? (The scriptures, prayer, Church, and so on.)

Have family members read D&C 67:1–2 and look for six things we ought to know about the Lord. Invite them to write on a sheet of paper or in a scripture-study journal the six things they find. (If some family members need help, you might give the following hints: prayers, hearts, desires, God's eyes, God's hands, and the riches of eternity.) Ask:

- How would you live differently today and tomorrow if you really believed and understood these things?
- How might you keep them in the forefront of your mind?

Share the following teaching from Elder Boyd K. Packer: "True doctrine, understood, changes attitudes and behavior." (*Ensign,* November 1986, 17.) To help family members think more deeply about God's nature and character, tell them they are going to write the six things they learned about the Lord in the form of principles or statements of truth. Have them write the six statements using the example below as a pattern:

1. "Because the Lord (knows my heart) I will (be honest and open with Him in my prayers).

2. "Because I know the Lord's (eyes are upon me), I will (ask for His help every day to guide my life)."

Invite family members to share what they wrote. Encourage them to keep these truths where they will see and remember them often. (They might post them in their room or on a mirror in the bathroom.). Challenge them to think about what they will do because of them.

Doctrine and Covenants 67:3–9
A challenge from the Lord

Invite one person to read aloud the section heading to D&C 67 and another to read the historical background above. Have family members keep this information in mind as they silently read D&C 67:3. Then discuss the following:

- Why did these brethren miss out on a blessing from the Lord?
- What do you suppose they were afraid of?
- What "fears" do people have about the Prophet's words today that might keep them from receiving blessings?
- How might being critical of the Prophet's words influence whether a person receives blessings?

Take turns reading D&C 67:4–8 and look for the challenge the Lord gave to the elders involved. Then share with your family what happened on that occasion:

"William E. M'Lellin [or McLellin, see the biographical sketch for D&C 66 in this book], as the wisest man, in his own estimation, having more learning than sense, endeavored to write a commandment like unto one of the least of the Lord's, but failed." (History of the Church, 1:226.) Ask:

- How would you feel if you were William E. McLellin?
- Why would it be difficult to write a revelation in the name of the Lord?

Share with your family the following quotation from Elder Orson F. Whitney:

"[William E. McLellin] could utter, of course, certain words, and roll out a mass of rhetoric [intelligent ideas]; but the divine spirit was lacking, and he had to acknowledge himself beaten.

"It is not so easy to put the spirit of life into things. Man can make the body, but God alone can create the spirit. You have heard . . . of the scientist who took a grain of wheat and endeavored to make one just like it? First he separated the grain of wheat into its component parts, and

found that it contained so much lime, so much silica, so much of this element and that; and then he took other parts corresponding thereto, brought them together by means of his chemical skill, and produced a grain of wheat so exactly similar to the other that the natural eye could not detect any difference between them. But there was a difference, a vast difference, and it was demonstrated when he planted the two grains. The one that God made sprang up, and the one that man made stayed down. Why? Because the manmade grain of wheat had no spirit—only a body, and the body without the spirit is dead. Man cannot breathe into the body of things the breath of life; that is a function and prerogative of Deity It is not so easy to frame revelations from God." (Conference Report, April 1917, 42.)

Ask:

- How did Elder Whitney apply what happened with William E. McLellin to more than just rewriting God's revelations?
- What was missing from the grain of wheat that was also missing from William McLellin's words?
- According to D&C 67:9, what is an additional test to determine the value of the revelations?

Testify that only God can give the Prophet's words the spirit and power Elder Whitney spoke of. Then share again from the History of the Church the conclusion to this incident:

"The Elders and all present that witnessed this vain attempt of a man [William E. McLellin] to imitate the language of Jesus Christ, renewed their faith in the fullness of the Gospel, and in the truth of the commandments and revelations which the Lord had given to the Church through my instrumentality." (History of the Church, 1:226.)

Challenge your family to show greater faith in the revelations given through Joseph Smith by studying and applying them in their lives.

Doctrine and Covenants 67:10–14
Coming to know God

Ask your family to list people who have achieved much in science, technology, medicine, music, or some other field that requires years of disciplined effort. Invite them to figure out how many years of schooling, practice, and study it took to reach such a high level of achievement. Ask, "What do you suppose were some of the significant steps these people took along the way that led to where they now are?"

Share the following quotation from Elder John A. Widtsoe:

"Men will gladly devote time every day for many years to learn a science or an art; yet will expect to win a knowledge of the gospel, which comprehends [encompasses] all sciences and arts, through perfunctory [casual] glances at books or occasional listening to sermons." (*Evidences and Reconciliations*, 16.)

Ask:

- If you were to list the steps that lead to a greater understanding of God, what would they be?
- How might these explain why some do not put forth the same effort they give for schoolwork?

Read together D&C 67:10–14 and look for:

1. Things that teach us what we must do to draw closer to and know God.

2. Things that keep us from coming to know Him.

Assign one person to be a scribe to record what is found. As you complete your lists, the following will help you discuss these things:

- Pay attention to footnote 12a and the cross-reference to Mosiah 3:19. Look up this scripture as a family and add to your list some more specific counsel about how we put off "the natural man" and thus qualify to "abide the presence of God."
- Point out that the items on your lists cannot be learned by study and memorization but describe who we are or what we have become. Ask, "If you cannot study to learn them, how can we 'learn' and acquire these things?"
- Ask your family what comfort they find in verses 13–14.
- Encourage your family to more fully experience the closeness of God in their lives by eliminating pride, jealousy, and selfishness from their lives.

DOCTRINE AND COVENANTS 68: GUIDANCE FOR OFFICERS AND MEMBERS OF THE CHURCH

Historical background: Joseph Fielding Smith wrote, "At the close of the conference of November 1–2, 1831, Elders Orson Hyde, Luke Johnson, Lyman E. Johnson, and William E. McLellin, came to the Prophet and sought the will of the Lord concerning themselves, and their ministry. The Prophet made inquiry and received the revelation which appears as section sixty-eight. Surely the Lord in his wisdom poured out knowledge, line upon line, precept upon precept as the members of the Church were prepared to receive it. While this revelation was given at the request of these brethren it was not intended for them alone, but for the guidance of all officers and members of the Church." (Church History and Modern Revelation, 2:29.) Look for what the Lord has commanded parents to do for their families.

Doctrine and Covenants 68:1–11
Counsel to missionaries

Divide your family into two groups and have both groups read D&C 68:1–11. Assign one group to look for the Lord's counsel to missionaries. Have the other group look for the blessings the Lord gives to those who serve as missionaries. Have both groups share what they find.

Ask your family to give the name of the main person mentioned in verses 1–11. (Orson Hyde.) Read to your family the historical background above and biographical sketch below, inviting them to listen carefully and tell what interested them the most. Have a family member read D&C 68:3–4. Ask:

- How do missionaries know what they should say to investigators? (The Holy Ghost "moves upon" them.)
- If a missionary's inspired words are considered scripture, can missionaries receive revelation for the whole Church? Why or why not?

Share the following quotation from J. Reuben Clark:

"Some of the General Authorities [apostles] have had assigned to them a special calling; they possess a special gift; they are sustained as prophets, seers, and revelators, which gives them a special spiritual endowment in connection with their teaching of the people. They have the right, the power, and authority to declare the mind and will of God to his people, subject to the over-all power and authority of the President of the Church. Others . . . are not given this special spiritual endowment and authority covering their teaching; . . . and the resulting limitation . . . applies to every other officer and member of the Church, for none of them is spiritually endowed as a prophet, seer, and revelator. . . .

"Here we must have in mind—must know— that only the President of the Church, the Presiding High Priest, is sustained as prophet, seer, and revelator for the Church, and he alone has the right to receive revelations for the Church. . . . He is God's sole mouthpiece on earth for The Church of Jesus Christ of Latter-day Saints, the only true Church. He alone may declare the mind and will of God to his people." (*Address to Seminary and Institute Faculty,* BYU, July 7, 1954.)

Doctrine and Covenants 68:13–35
What would you say?

The case studies below are to help your family study many of the verses in D&C 68:13–35. Choose one, two, or all three case studies as time allows. For each case study, have a

BIOGRAPHICAL SKETCH: ORSON HYDE

Orson Hyde was born on January 8, 1805, in Connecticut. Later in life Orson migrated to Ohio and served as a Campbellite pastor. While preaching against the Book of Mormon, impressions came that told him he was doing something wrong. After investigating the book further, he was convinced of its truthfulness and was soon baptized by Sidney Rigdon. He was called on a mission in 1831 (see D&C 68:1), marched with Zion's Camp in the summer of 1834, was called as an apostle in 1835, and served a valiant mission in the British Isles. Unfortunately, Orson faltered for a time and was removed from Church fellowship, but shortly thereafter he repented and was reinstated in the Quorum of the Twelve. In 1841 Orson traveled to the Holy Land and dedicated it for the return of the Jews and the building of the temple. He traveled west with the Saints to Utah and there served in numerous capacities until his death on November 8, 1878. (See Susan Easton Black, *Who's Who in the Doctrine and Covenants*, 141–45.)

family member read the case study aloud; then, as a family, read the assigned verses to find answers and insights that help solve the problem. Ask any additional questions or read other information that is included. After discussing each case study, you might enjoy role-playing the case by having one family member be the person in the case study and another family member pretend to be the friend who is giving the inspired counsel.

Case 1. "My name is Aaron Bishop. I am the oldest in my family, and my patriarchal blessing says I am a literal descendent of Aaron. After reading D&C 68:15–16, I decided I have a legal right to the bishopric and am going to write a letter to the prophet to let him know I should be the presiding bishop of the Church."

Read D&C 68:13–21 and look for things you could use to tell him not to take this course of action. After your family has shared what they found, ask the following questions:

- According to verses 20–21, who is to "designate" or identify a literal descendant of Aaron for the office of presiding bishop?
- What other condition must exist in order for a literal descendant to be called? (He must be worthy.)

Case 2. "My name is Sister Ira Sponcible. My husband and I have decided not to 'force' our beliefs on our children by teaching them to pray or by giving spiritual guidance in our home. Besides, there are good Church leaders and teachers who have been called to teach, and our children can learn from them."

Read D&C 68:25–28 as a family and look for things that you would share with Sister Ira Sponcible. After your family has shared what they find, ask:

- Who will be held accountable if children are not taught the gospel properly?
- According to verse 25, what four doctrines are parents to emphasize?
- What is the age of baptism for children?
- What might be the best way parents can teach their children the two things listed in verse 28?

Share the following insight from President Heber J. Grant:

"It is folly to imagine that our children will grow up with a knowledge of the Gospel without teaching. Some men and women argue 'Well, I am a Latter-day Saint and we were married in the Temple and were sealed over the altar by one having the Priesthood of God, according to the new and everlasting covenant, and our children are bound to grow up and be good Latter-day Saints; they cannot help it; it is born in them.'

"I have learned the multiplication table, and so has my wife, but do you think I am a big enough fool to believe that our children will be born with a knowledge of the multiplication table?

"I may know the Gospel is true, and so may my wife, but I want to tell you that our children will not know the Gospel is true unless they study it and gain a testimony for themselves. Parents are deceiving themselves in imagining that their children will be born with a knowledge of the Gospel." (*Gospel Standards,* 155.)

Share your testimony about how important it will be for your children to teach their children properly.

Case 3. "My name is Brother Dolittle. I've been out of work for the past few months. I've been offered several other jobs, but they weren't in my field of choice. I also am enjoying the freedom of not going to work. I'm going to ask the bishop for Church assistance to pay the bills.

Read D&C 68:30–31 as a family and look for things you could share with Brother Dolittle. After your family has shared what they found, ask:

- How will the Lord take care of one who is idle? (Verse 30.)
- What is being taught to the children by idle parents?

DOCTRINE AND COVENANTS 69: ONE WHO IS TRUE AND FAITHFUL

Historical background: Read the section heading for background information on this section. One additional note: John Whitmer (who was called in D&C 47) was serving as Church historian when this revelation was given.

Doctrine and Covenants 69:1–2
Could you have been chosen?

Invite a family member to read aloud the section heading for D&C 69. Then have your family turn to the map section of the Doctrine and Covenants and try to figure out how long Oliver Cowdery's journey would have been. Ask, "When you consider the value of what Oliver was carrying and the distance he had to travel, what kind of companion do you think was needed?"

Read together D&C 69:1–2. Ask:

- Who was selected to go with Oliver?
- What words did the Lord use to describe John Whitmer?
- How would these qualities be a blessing to Oliver Cowdery and the Church?

Invite family members to imagine that they were given the same assignment as Oliver Cowdery—except in current times. Ask who they would want to go with them that would meet the needs of the task and the description given by the Lord. After family members share some of their choices (and explain why), give them about thirty seconds to consider privately if *they* would have been chosen.

Discuss opportunities each person has to show the degree of their faithfulness. Invite family members to suggest ways they can improve their faithfulness. Testify of the importance of being true and faithful.

Doctrine and Covenants 69:3–8
John Whitmer's responsibilities

Ask family members to tell about the duties required in their current callings in the Church. Then have your family read D&C 69:3–8 and list John Whitmer's responsibilities. Ask:

- What was John Whitmer's calling in the Church? (See D&C 47 and the historical background above.)

- In what ways are we responsible for some of the same things the Lord asked John Whitmer to do?

As a family, list what you consider to be the "important things" (verse 3) your family should select, write, and copy for the good of your family and the "rising generations" (verse 8). After making a list, schedule a family home evening or a Sunday when these "important things" can be written and put into a special family book.

DOCTRINE AND COVENANTS 70: IMPORTANT STEWARDSHIPS

Historical background: This revelation was received near the end of several conferences held between November 1 and 12, 1831, in Kirtland, Ohio. As the last conference drew to a close, priesthood leaders considered "a proposal to provide compensation [payment] to the Prophet Joseph Smith and to his scribes . . . for their labors and sacrifices in receiving, writing, copying, and preparing the revelations of God for the Church in the latter days. This compensation would come out of any proceeds from the sale of the revelations. The conference voted to sustain this proposal." (Stephen E. Robinson and H. Dean Garrett, A Commentary on the Doctrine and Covenants, *2:255–56.) The Prophet then took the matter to the Lord and noted, "In answer . . . I received the following: [Section 70]." (*History of the Church, *1:235–36.) Notice what the Lord teaches here about the importance of equality.*

Doctrine and Covenants 70:1–18
What does the Lord expect of us?

On a large piece of paper make eleven blanks similar to the following:

—— —— —— —— —— —— —— —— —— —— ——

Show the paper to your family and tell them that a word from section 70 fits in the blanks—one letter per blank. (The word is "stewardship.") Their object is to discover the word that matches the blanks, and your object is to help them, one letter at a time. Tell them you will ask them some questions about D&C 70. When they answer a question correctly, you will give them the letter to the blank of their choice—until they can guess what the word is. Give your family a few minutes to silently read D&C 70 and be prepared for your questions. Here are some questions and references where the answers can be found:

1. How many special conferences were held the first two weeks of November 1831? (Section heading.)

2. What did Joseph Smith refer to as "the foundation of the Church in these last days, and a benefit to the world"? (Section heading.)

3. What were Joseph Smith, Martin Harris, Oliver Cowdery, John Whitmer, Sidney Rigdon, and William W. Phelps appointed and ordained to be? (Verse 3.)

4. What did the Lord say he would require of these men "in the day of judgment"? (Verse 4.)

5. What was to be done with the surplus from the sale of the Book of Commandments? (Verses 6–8.)

6. Who is "worthy of his hire"? (Verse 12.)

7. What does the Lord say will be withheld if we are not equal in temporal things "and this not grudgingly"? (Verse 14.)

When someone correctly guesses the word, ask, "What is a stewardship"? Tell them President Spencer W. Kimball defined a stewardship in the Church as "a sacred spiritual or temporal trust for which there is accountability." (*Ensign,* November 1977, 78.) Ask:

- What stewardship was given in D&C 70 to the men listed in verse 1? (See verse 3.)
- In what ways do you think we have a "stewardship" with regard to the revelations?
- How can we apply D&C 70:4 to ourselves?

DOCTRINE AND COVENANTS 71: UNFRIENDLY FEELINGS TOWARD THE CHURCH

Historical background: "In September 1831, Joseph Smith took his family to Hiram, Portage County, Ohio, about thirty miles southeast of Kirtland. . . . This move was imperative to the safety of the Prophet. Apostates had joined the enemies of the church and threatened him with violence." (Ivan J. Barrett, Joseph Smith and the Restoration, 198.) Look for what the Lord said in this revelation about how to change the feelings of those deceived by enemies of the Church.

Doctrine and Covenants 71:1–4
What is so important?

List the following directions given to Joseph Smith and Sydney Rigdon on separate 3-by-5 cards or small pieces of paper:

- "open your mouths in proclaiming my gospel"
- "expounding the mysteries thereof out of the scriptures"
- "proclaim unto the world in the regions round about, and in the church also, for the space of a season"
- "labor ye in my vineyard"
- "call upon the inhabitants of the earth"
- "bear record"
- "prepare the way for the commandments and revelations which are to come"

Scatter the statements in front of your family and place a bowl nearby. Ask family members to search D&C 71:1–4 and identify the verse where the instruction on each card is given. As each instruction is identified, write the reference on the card and put it into the bowl. Invite a family member to read the following statement:

"Nephi recognized that scripture will help only those who can personally relate to its message. As he read prophetic passages to his people, he also likened the scriptures to them in their unique circumstances 'that it might be for our profit and learning' (1 Ne. 19:23)." (Victor L. Ludlow, *Ensign*, October 1990, 62.)

With that statement in mind, have family members take turns drawing a card out of the bowl and share a way they can "liken" the scripture to their own life. Continue until the bowl is empty.

Doctrine and Covenants 71:5–6
A "wisdom" warning

Share the following story with your family: "I had family members who would ask for a receipt every time I gave them a gift. Not once did they ever receive my gift without asking for a receipt to return or exchange it. Before long, I stopped caring about my purchases for them. I stopped selecting gifts with care—anything would do. Many times I considered just forgetting about special days for these family members."

Read aloud D&C 71:5–6 to your family and ask what they learned from the story that might apply to these verses. You might discuss the following questions:

- Why do you think the Lord gives "more abundantly" when we "receive" what He has already offered?
- When we "receive" from the Lord, what besides "more abundance" does He promise?
- In what ways could you use the Lord's "power" in your life?
- What can we do to "receive" these blessings? (Express gratitude, keep the commandments, and so on.)

BIOGRAPHICAL SKETCH: EZRA BOOTH

Ezra Booth was "a man who had been a Methodist priest and had become suddenly converted to the gospel by seeing a miracle performed. . . . His conversion had been by a sign, and he sought to minister by means of signs. He wanted to go forth with the power to bless in one hand and the power to curse in the other, and save souls after a fashion he thought would be successful, and entirely different from the way ordained by the Lord." (George Q. Cannon, *Life of Joseph Smith the Prophet*, 125.)

"Later in the year 1831 Ezra Booth apostatized and wrote nine letters against the Church to the *Ohio Star.* . . . Booth is generally considered to be the first apostate to write against the Church. Many people believed Booth's reports about the Prophet, and the spirit of opposition spread until a mob collected which tarred and feathered Joseph Smith." (Ivan J. Barrett, *Joseph Smith and the Restoration*, 179.)

Doctrine and Covenants 71:7–11
What shall we do with our enemies?

Ask family members to share an experience when they saw someone being picked on. Ask:

- Did you defend the person?
- Did you ignore the situation?
- Did you join in with the persecutors?

Now ask your family if they have ever been the target of persecution or false accusations. Ask:

- Did anyone come to your defense?
- How did you feel about this person?

- How would you feel about someone who could have helped you but instead joined the persecutors?
- What do you think Jesus would have us do when we see others being picked on or falsely accused?

Have one family member read the historical background above, and another the biographical sketch. Then read together the section heading for D&C 71. Ask the following questions:

- What were Joseph Smith and Sidney Rigdon working on at this time?
- What was their mission to be "for a season" instead of translating the Bible?
- Why do you think the Lord had the Prophet and his scribe set aside such an important work to deal with the false accusations and persecutions begun by Ezra Booth?

Divide your family into two teams and have each team do the assignments listed in the table on the next page:

Then ask:

- What will the Lord do about our enemies if we keep His commandments? (D&C 98:32–48.)
- Why do you think the Lord does not want us to become involved in contention?

Share the following insight from President Joseph Fielding Smith:

"Quite generally the Lord counsels his servants not to engage in debates and arguments, but to preach in power the fundamental principles of the Gospel. This was a condition that required some action of this kind, and the Spirit of the Lord directed these brethren to go forth and confound their enemies which they proceeded immediately to do, as their enemies were unable to substantiate their falsehoods and were surprised by this sudden challenge so boldly given. Much of the prejudice was allayed and some friends made through this action." (Joseph Fielding Smith,

Church History and Modern Revelation, 1:269.) Discuss the following questions:

- How did Joseph Smith and Sidney Rigdon know they were to go out and "confound their enemies"? (Verse 7.)

- How would you apply this principle in our day?
- Why do you think this is good advice? (See also 3 Nephi 11:29–30.)

TEAM 1

Write the Lord's instructions to those who are persecuted. (D&C 71:7, 11; 100:5–6.)	Write promised blessings. (D&C 71:9; 3 Nephi 22:17.)

TEAM 2

Write the Lord's instructions to false accusers and persecutors. (D&C 71:8.)	Write consequences for false accusers and persecutors. (D&C 71:7, 10; 3 Nephi 12:20.)

DOCTRINE AND COVENANTS 72: RESPONSIBILITY OF THE BISHOP

Historical background: In D&C 68:14 the Lord had made known that other bishops besides Edward Partridge would be called. This section is a fulfillment of that revelation. Newel K. Whitney was called to serve as bishop in the Kirtland area. Pay special attention to how much the Lord expects of a bishop.

Doctrine and Covenants 72:1–8
How are bishops called?

Ask your family how a bishop is called today. If no one knows, review the following:

- The person being considered must be a worthy Melchizedek Priesthood holder.
- The stake presidency recommends the person and sends his name to the First Presidency for their approval.
- After the First Presidency approves the person, they can authorize the stake president to issue the call.
- The man is presented to his ward members for a sustaining vote.
- With the First Presidency's approval, the stake president ordains and sets him apart.

Ask your family who the first bishop of the Church was. (See D&C 41:9.) Tell your family that in D&C 72:1–8 the Lord called a second bishop to serve in the Church. Invite your family to quickly search D&C 72:1–8 for the name of the new bishop. Then read the biographical sketch of Newel K. Whitney on the next page. Ask:

- In what way can you tell that Newel K. Whitney was prepared to serve as a bishop?
- What part did the Lord play in Newel's call?
- What part do you think the Lord plays in calling bishops today?

Explain to your family that Newel's assignment, like that of most bishops, was for a specific geographic location. Read the following to your family:

"During this period of time Bishop Partridge handled . . . affairs in Missouri and Bishop Newell K. Whitney served in Ohio. . . . They were among several new priesthood officers appointed in the 1830s to govern the growing Church." (Glen M. Leonard, "In Search of Zion, 1830–1835," *Tambuli,* December 1978, 33.)

Take turns reading D&C 72:1–7 and discuss the following questions:

- What was one reason the Lord called a bishop in Ohio? (So Church members could be accountable to someone for their stewardships—verse 5.)
- What is a stewardship? (A duty or responsibility.)
- What "stewardships" do we have?
- What "stewardships" do we have to see our bishop about? (Tithing, callings, and so on.)
- What reward will come to those who are faithful and wise in their stewardships on earth?

Share your testimony with your family that one day we will all give an account of our stewardships to the Lord.

Doctrine and Covenants 72:9–19
What are the responsibilities of a bishop?

Ask your family to name the bishop of your ward. Invite them to tell what they think some of his responsibilities are. Divide your family into teams of two or three. Have each team search D&C 72:9–19, identifying and marking responsibilities that were given to Bishop Newel K. Whitney. These may include the following:

- "Keep the Lord's store house." (Verse 10.)
- "Receive the funds of the church." (Verse 10.)

- "Take an account of the elders." (Verse 11.)
- "Administer to their wants." (Verse 11.)
- Take care of the "poor and needy." (Verse 12.)
- "Labor in spiritual things." (Verse 14.)
- Provide a "certificate from the judge or bishop in this part of the vineyard unto the bishop in Zion." (Verse 17.)
- Receive "an account unto the bishop" from ward members. (Verse 19.)

After each team shares what they find, ask if they can list other things a bishop might be responsible for. It might help to read together the following explanation from President Gordon B. Hinckley:

"Bishops, . . . there are many teachers in each ward. But you must be the chief teacher among them. You must see that there is no false doctrine creeping in among the people. You must see that they grow in faith and testimony, in integrity and righteousness and a sense of service. You must see that their love for the Lord strengthens and manifests itself in greater love for one another.

"You must be their confessor, privy to their deepest secrets, holding absolutely inviolate the confidences placed in you. Yours is a privileged communication that must be guarded and respected against all intruders. There may be temptations to tell. You cannot succumb. . . .

"You as an individual preside over the Aaronic Priesthood of the ward. You are their leader, their teacher, their example, whether you wish to be or not. You are the presiding high priest, the father to the ward family, to be called upon as arbiter in disagreements, as defender of the accused.

"You preside in meetings where the doctrine is taught. You are accountable for the spiritual nature of those meetings and for the administration of the sacrament to the members, that all may be reminded of sacred covenants and obligations incumbent upon those who have taken upon them the name of the Lord.

BIOGRAPHICAL SKETCH: NEWEL K. WHITNEY

Newel K. Whitney was born in Vermont on February 5, 1795. Being a religious family, the Whitney's often prayed. During a marvelous manifestation in answer to one prayer, they heard a voice declare, "Prepare to receive the word of the Lord, for it is coming." (Andrew Jenson, comp., *Latter-day Saint Biographical Encyclopedia*, 1:223.)

A short time later, missionaries came to Kirtland (see D&C 32), and in November 1830 Newel and Elizabeth were baptized. Newel longed to meet the Prophet and pled with the Lord for the opportunity. In February 1831, Joseph and Emma arrived in Kirtland in a sleigh and went straight to the Whitney store. "He sprang out, went into the store, walked up to the junior partner, and said: 'Newel K. Whitney, thou art the man.' . . . [Newel] answered: 'Stranger, you have the advantage of me; I could not call you by name, as you have me.' And the stranger then said: 'I am Joseph, the Prophet. You have prayed me here. Now, what do you want of me?'" (Jack M. Lyon, Linda Ririe Gundry, and Jay A. Parry, eds., *Best-Loved Stories of the LDS People*, 131.)

Shortly after Joseph was killed, Newel was called as presiding bishop of the Church. He and his family moved with the Saints to the Salt Lake Valley in 1848. He died September 21, 1850.

"You must stand as the strong friend of the widow and the orphan, the weak and the beleaguered, the attacked and the helpless.

"The sound of your trumpet must be certain and unequivocal [clear]. In your ward you stand as the head of the army of the Lord, leading them on to victory in the conquest against sin, indifference, and apostasy." (*Ensign,* November 2003, 62.)

As a family, compose a letter of gratitude to your bishop, thanking him for all that he does for you. Assign a family member to deliver it to the bishop.

Doctrine and Covenants 72:20–26
The Lord directs the publishing of the revelations

Explain to your family that you are going to create a scripture chain. You chain scriptures together by writing a cross-reference next to a passage of scripture. Start your chain by reading D&C 72:20–23. In the margin next to D&C 72:20–23, write "D&C 70:1–3." Turn to the next reference as a family and read it together. Ask:

- Who were called to be stewards over the "literary concerns" (publishing and printing) of the Church?

- What literary project were they to work on? (Publishing the revelations and commandments that later became the Doctrine and Covenants.)

Next to D&C 70:1–3, write "D&C 69:1–3." Turn to that reference as a family and read it along with the section heading for D&C 69. (These brethren were to take the revelations to Missouri for printing.) Next to D&C 69:1–3, write "D&C 72:20–23." This will complete the scripture chain.

- How does this scripture chain show the Lord's care for latter-day revelation?
- How can we show our gratitude to those who worked so hard to make sure revelations received by Joseph Smith were printed?

Share your testimony about the importance of the revelations and commandments known as the Doctrine and Covenants.

DOCTRINE AND COVENANTS 73: CONTINUE WITH THE BIBLE TRANSLATION

Historical background: On December 1, 1831, the Lord commanded Joseph Smith and Sidney Rigdon to preach the gospel in the regions surrounding Kirtland, addressing negative things enemies of the Church had said and written. (See D&C 71.) They returned from this brief mission the second week of January and awaited a conference that had been planned for January 25 in Amherst, Ohio (about fifty miles west of Kirtland). As the Prophet considered how to best spend his time prior to the conference, he received the revelation recorded in D&C 73.

Doctrine and Covenants 73:1–6
The best use of your time

Give each family member a clock or watch to hold. On your signal, ask them to watch their clock tick for one minute. Point out how everyone's clock runs at the same pace. Explain that each of us has twenty-four hours each day, but some people seem to accomplish more than others. Talk about what some people do differently that seems to give them more time.

Ask, "If you were given the next three days to do whatever you wanted—with no obligations or restrictions—how would you spend your time?" After talking about their ideas for a few minutes, remind family members that although we seldom have such an opportunity, we *do* have much freedom in choosing how we spend our time. Ask, "When you think about how to spend your time, what most affects your decisions?"

Have a family member read the section heading

for D&C 73. Then read aloud the historical background above. Ask:

- Based on this background, what appears to be one way Joseph Smith decided how to best use his time? (Seeking the Lord in prayer.)
- In response to the Prophet's request, what did the Lord counsel him in D&C 73:1–6 about how to spend the next two weeks?
- What could this instruction teach you about important ways to spend your time?

Encourage your family to regularly seek the counsel of the Lord and His prophets as they decide how to best use their time—always being sure to make time for things of greatest value.

Share the following statements from Elder Neal A. Maxwell:

"How we spend our time is at least as good a measure of us as how we spend our money. An inventory of how we spend our disposable time will tell us where our treasure is." (*Notwithstanding My Weakness,* 116–17.)

"Time, unlike some material things, cannot be recycled." (*A Time to Choose,* 13.)

DOCTRINE AND COVENANTS 74: THE LORD'S EXPLANATION OF 1 CORINTHIANS 7:14

Historical background: "It was while studying these teachings of Paul that the elders were led to inquire of the Prophet as to Paul's meanings in 1 Cor 7.14. The Prophet asked the Lord and got the answer. In this saying: [Sec. 74:1, quoted], Paul spoke not by commandment, but of himself. His intent, as explained in Section 74, being that where there were mixed families in the Church, the teachings of the Law of Moses and the doctrines which were fulfilled, should not be maintained. Male children in such families were not to be circumcised, and they would be holy. It was the doctrine of the Jews that unless this were done children were unholy. This Paul wished to correct. It was very difficult for the Jewish members of the Church to forsake all of their traditions and turn from the Law of Moses, and from circumcision which were fulfilled." (Joseph Fielding Smith, Church History and Modern Revelation, *2:44–45.) Watch for what we can learn from this revelation about the importance of eternal families.*

Doctrine and Covenants 74:1–5

What problems could come from marrying outside of the covenant?

Have everyone in your family read 1 Corinthians 7:14 and raise their hands if they are not sure what that verse means. Discuss some helps the Lord provides to help us understand difficult passages of scripture. (Footnotes, the Joseph Smith Translation, revelations, and prophetic commentary.) Ask family members to read the section heading for D&C 74 and look for reasons why this section would help with our understanding of 1 Corinthians.

Take turns reading D&C 74:1–5 and look for the Lord's explanation concerning 1 Corinthians 7:14. (See the historical background.) Discuss the following questions:

- What religious practice of the law of Moses were the unbelieving Jews performing that Church members had discontinued?
- What caused the "great contention" mentioned in verse 3?

- What did Church members know about the Law of Moses? (The "law was fulfilled" by Jesus Christ and did not need to be practiced any longer.)
- Why would this contention increase if one spouse in the family belonged to a different religion?
- Why do you think religious differences can put strain on a marriage?
- What other religious differences could exist in a family where the parents belong to different churches?
- How could those differences affect the children?

Ask a family member to choose a number between 1 and 6. Get a die and roll it to see if it lands on the number that was chosen. Repeat the process for each family member. Ask:

- What is the probability that the number you chose will be rolled? (One in six.)
- Would you gamble an important life decision or event on a "one in six" probability? Why or why not?
- Would you risk the possibility of having an eternal family unit on those odds?

Explain that there are wonderful people who are not members of the Church. However, marrying outside the temple could be compared to the dice game. While sometimes the spouse who is not a member may later join the Church, most often that does not happen. Testify of the importance of temple marriage and talk about ways we can help make sure we marry someone who belongs to The Church of Jesus Christ of Latter-day Saints.

Doctrine and Covenants 74:5
Is everything a prophet says God's word?

 Ask your family their opinion about the following two questions:

- Is everything a prophet says the word of the Lord?

- Can a prophet ever express his personal opinion?

Read D&C 74:5 and have your family find anything in the verse that helps answer the questions. Also read and discuss D&C 68:3–4. Then share the following statement from Joseph Smith:

"This morning, I read German, and visited with a brother and sister from Michigan, who thought that 'a prophet is always a prophet;' but I told them that a prophet was a prophet only when he was acting as such. . . . At four in the afternoon, I went out with my little Frederick, to exercise myself by sliding on the ice." (*History of the Church,* 5:265.)

Doctrine and Covenants 74:6–7
What happens to little children when they die?

Explain to your family that some people believe that little children are born into a sinful state and need to be baptized when they are infants. Others believe that baptism is required to protect little children in case they die before they have the chance to be baptized as adults. Ask:

- What do you believe happens to children who die before the age of eight?
- Do you think little children need to be baptized before death in order to go to the celestial kingdom? Why or why not?

Read D&C 74:6 and have your family look for what the Jews used to do to children so they could be considered "holy." According to D&C 74:7, Moroni 8:8–15, and D&C 29:46–48, what does the Lord teach about little children? Share the following story from Elder Melvin J. Ballard:

"I remember a shocking incident that occurred in that first missionary experience. Coming one morning to the home of a woman in mourning, I learned that during the night her little girl, not yet a year old, had died. . . . She had neglected to have her child christened or baptized, as she called it, and had sent for the priest, but he came too late. It was her intention to have this ordinance performed before the death of the child, but he had arrived too late, and now burial in her own church, by the minister of her church, was denied, and burial in the Christian cemetery was denied because this was an unbaptized one. She was in great distress and wanted to know, since I was a minister, if I could throw any light upon her problem and give her any comfort. I showed her the plan of Christ that contemplated the salvation of little children without the ordinance of baptism, for it was for the remission of sin, and this innocent child was without sin, for of such was the kingdom of heaven. I explained that it was a mockery, a thing abominable in the sight of God, to baptize little children. She was much comforted through our long conversation and explanation, and asked me if I would conduct the funeral. I cheerfully consented; I remember that afternoon, by a little open grave under a cedar tree, outside of the cemetery, with the rain pouring down, my companion held the umbrella over me while I conducted the services, and again tried to comfort the heart of this sorrow-stricken mother.

"The thing that shocked me was that two weeks afterwards the same minister was called to the cell of a condemned man who had never been a Christian at all, but who had debauched himself, had lived a riotous life, and now had taken the life of a fellow man and had been condemned to death. His execution was to take place in a few days, and he wanted now to set himself right with God and sent for the priest who heard his confession, administered the sacrament of baptism by sprinkling of a few drops of water upon him, pronounced him a Christian, and allowed his remains to come into the church denied to the little, innocent child, and he was buried in the cemetery denied to her also. It deeply stirred me, as I am sure it would any other honest-thinking man or woman. I said to the people of that community, on another occasion, referring to this incident, that if the innocent child by any means had to be condemned to hell, it would be heaven wherever innocent children are, for the Master himself, said 'Of such are the kingdom of heaven.' And if this criminal who was condemned had been suddenly brought into the presence of God, it would be hell to him to have to look upon the face of the pure and the innocent, and he would be uncomfortable and would like to get away from that situation as soon as possible." (*Sermons and Missionary Services of Melvin J. Ballard,* 212–13.)

DOCTRINE AND COVENANTS 75: RESPONSIBILITIES AND BLESSINGS OF MISSIONARY WORK

Historical background: *"On January 10, 1832, the Lord gave a revelation to several elders in response to their concern as to how they should effectively use their time until the convening of the conference of Jan. 25, 1832. (See D&C Section 73) At that time, the Lord told the elders:*

"'For, verily, thus saith the Lord, it is expedient in me that they should continue preaching the gospel, and in exhortation to the churches in the regions round about, until conference;

"'And then, behold, it shall be made known unto them, by the voice of the conference, their several missions.' (D&C 73:1–2).

"During the conference, the revelation contained in D&C section 75 was given in fulfillment of the Lord's promise." (Leaun G. Otten and C. Max Caldwell, Sacred Truths of the Doctrine and Covenants, *2:20.) As you study this section, notice all the promises the Lord makes to faithful missionaries.*

Doctrine and Covenants 75:1–5
What blessings come to those serving honorable missions?

Begin scripture study by singing hymn no. 249, "Called to Serve." Ask your family to share qualities they have seen in faithful returned missionaries. Also discuss some blessings that come to faithful missionaries. Ask family members to read D&C 75:1–5. Have them look for, mark, and then discuss:

- Expectations the Lord has for His missionaries.
- Blessings that come to faithful missionaries.

Share your testimony of the blessings that come from sharing the gospel.

Doctrine and Covenants 75:6–22
Essential characteristics for missionaries

Assign each family member one of the following roles: firefighter, policeman, attorney, doctor, or teacher. Ask each person to quickly and briefly discuss the following about their assigned role:

- What is your main responsibility?

- What are five personal characteristics that would help you in your duties?
- What would be the best part of your job?

Now ask your family to discuss those same questions as if their assignment was as a full-time missionary. Talk about essential characteristics needed to serve in that capacity.

Assign each family member to be one of the following missionaries mentioned in D&C 75:6–22: William E. McLellin, Luke Johnson, Orson Hyde, Samuel H. Smith, Lyman Johnson, Orson Pratt, Asa Dodds, Calves Wilson, Major N. Ashley, and Burr Riggs. Use 3-by-5 cards and have your family create missionary name tags for "their missionary" that they can wear. Ask family members to read those verses, focusing especially on the message and counsel given to their missionary. Have each family member tell where they were called to serve. Also allow each family member to give a brief report on a lesson, characteristic, or message from their missionary's verses that a missionary today could benefit from.

Share your testimony of missionary work. Talk about how it feels to help another person discover or better understand the gospel of Jesus Christ. Invite family members to carry their name tags throughout the day as a reminder to prepare for a full-time mission or to have missionary experiences.

Doctrine and Covenants 75:23–26
Who is to provide for missionary service?

Ask your family what the cost is each month for a missionary serving around the world. (Currently it is $375.) Have your family figure the total cost for twenty-four months, including some estimates for clothes and other necessary items. Talk about who should pay these costs for the missionaries who have or will serve from your family, and read the following statement from Franklin D. Richards:

"When a young man goes on a mission or to school and pays some of the cost, he generally works harder and is happier and more successful." (*Ensign*, May 1979, 39.)

Invite a family member to read D&C 75:28–29. Ask, "What would happen if the missionary or family can't afford to pay for a mission?" Read D&C 75:23–27 with your family to find the answer. Share the following story with your family:

"I learned from a mission president recently that one of his young sister missionaries, nearing the end of her very faithful and successful mission, said through her tears that she must return home immediately. When he inquired as to the problem, she told him money had become so difficult for her family that to continue her support, the family had rented their home and were using the rental proceeds to pay her mission expenses. For living accommodations, they had moved into a storage locker. For water, they used a neighbor's outdoor tap and hose; and for a bathroom they went to a nearby gasoline station. This family, in which the father had recently passed away, was so proud of their missionary and so independent in spirit that they had managed to keep this recent turn of events from most of their friends and virtually all of their Church leaders.

"When this situation was discovered, the family was restored to their home immediately. Long-term solutions to their economic circumstances were put in place, and the complete amount of remaining missionary support for their missionary daughter was secured overnight. With her tears dried and fears allayed, this faithful, hardworking young sister finished her mission triumphantly and was recently married in the temple to a wonderful young man." (Jeffrey R. Holland, *Ensign*, May 2001, 16.)

Make a savings plan for each family member so they can help support themselves during their mission. Periodically follow up on each person's plan to make it realistic and successful.

DOCTRINE AND COVENANTS 76: "THE VISION"

Historical background: *While Joseph Smith and Sidney Rigdon worked on translating the Bible, they pondered the words of the Savior about the resurrection in John 5. They received a marvelous vision now recorded as section 76. (See section heading.) Philo Dibble was present during the vision and later wrote, "During the time that Joseph and Sidney were in the spirit and saw the heavens open, there were other men in the room, perhaps twelve, among whom I was one. . . . I saw the glory and felt the power, but did not see the vision. . . . Joseph sat firmly and calmly all the time in the midst of a magnificent glory, but Sidney sat limp and pale, apparently as limber as a rag, observing which Joseph remarked, smilingly, 'Sidney is not used to it as I am.'" (*Juvenile Instructor, *May 15, 1892, 303–4.)*

*When the vision was over, Sidney stayed up the entire night writing it. The Prophet said, "Nothing could be more pleasing to the Saints upon the order of the kingdom of the Lord, than the light which burst upon the world through the foregoing vision [section 76]." (*History of the Church, *1:252.)*

*President Joseph Fielding Smith said, "Section 76 . . . should be treasured by all members of the Church as a priceless heritage. It should strengthen their faith and be to them an incentive to seek the exaltation promised to all who are just and true." (*Church History and Modern Revelation, *1:279.) As you study this revelation, notice the promises to those who prepare themselves for the celestial kingdom.*

Doctrine and Covenants 76:1–10
What is the Lord's delight?

 Draw a "D" and a simple light bulb similar to the following on a piece of paper.

Show your family the drawing and have them search D&C 76:1–5 for answers to the following questions:

- What does this drawing have to do with D&C 76:1–5?
- What does the Lord "delight" to do? (Verse 5.)

Now have your family search D&C 76:6–10 and look for twelve things the Lord promises to those who serve Him in truth and righteousness to the end. Encourage them to mark and number them in their scriptures. They should find the following:

1. "Great shall be their reward."
2. "Eternal shall be their glory."
3. "To them will I reveal all mysteries."
4. "Make known unto them the good pleasure of my will."
5. "The wonders of eternity shall they know."
6. "Things to come will I show them."
7. "Their wisdom shall be great."

8. "Their understanding [shall] reach to heaven."

9. "Before them the wisdom of the wise shall perish."

10. "The understanding of the prudent shall come to naught."

11. "By my Spirit will I enlighten them."

12. "By my power will I make known unto them the secrets of my will."

Ask family members why they think the Lord is willing to make such promises.

Doctrine and Covenants 76:11–19
What brought about "The Vision"?

Read aloud the historical background above and have a family member read the section heading for D&C 76. Then take turns reading D&C 76:11–19. Ask:

- To whom was "The Vision" given? (Verse 11.)
- What were Joseph Smith and Sidney Rigdon working on at the time?
- What word in verse 19 describes what Joseph and Sidney were doing? (Meditating.)

Invite family members to mark footnote 19a in their scriptures. Have one family member read 1 Nephi 11:1 and another read D&C 138:1, 11. Ask:

- What was Nephi doing just before he received the vision of the tree of life?
- What was President Joseph F. Smith doing just before he received a vision of the spirit world?
- What does this teach you about the importance of pondering or meditating upon the things of God?

Invite family members to share experiences when pondering resulted in answers to prayers.

Doctrine and Covenants 76:20–24
The vision of the Son

Explain to your family that even though section 76 is often referred to as "The Vision," it is actually an account of six different visions. The first one is found in verses 20–24. Ask a parent to slowly read those verses aloud. Ask:

- What rarely used punctuation mark is used in verse 22? (Exclamation point!)
- Why do you think an exclamation point is used there?
- Who did Joseph Smith and Sidney Rigdon see?
- What do you think it would be like to see angels and two members of the Godhead?
- What testimony did Joseph and Sidney bear?
- What things can we learn about the Savior from these verses?
- Is it necessary to see Jesus to know that He lives? Why not?

Invite a family member to bear testimony of the Savior. You might also share a portion of "The Living Christ," the testimony of the First Presidency and Twelve Apostles.

Doctrine and Covenants 76:25–29
What has Satan been doing since his fall from heaven?

A good way to introduce this idea would be to give your family something sweet to taste and then right afterward give them something sour or bitter. Invite one of them to describe the experience. Ask why the sour or bitter taste was more of a shock after tasting the sweet than it would have been by itself.

Invite one family member to read D&C 76:20 and another to read D&C 76:25. Then have your family tell how the second vision Joseph and Sidney saw was like the taste test above. Ask:

- What did they see in verse 20?
- Whom did they see in verse 25?
- Which vision would have brought joy?

- What feelings do you think the vision of Satan's fall brought? (Verses 26–27.)
- Why do you think they were shown the vision of Satan right after the vision of the Lord?

Now have family members read D&C 76:25–28 and list the different titles given for Satan (Perdition, Lucifer, son of the morning, Satan, serpent, devil). Assign a family member to read the listing for "Lucifer" in the Bible Dictionary (page 726) and another the first paragraph of the listing for "Devil" (page 656). Ask:

- What is the literal meaning of "Lucifer"?
- How does the word "devil" differ in meaning from the word "Lucifer"?
- According to verse 25, what led to Lucifer's fall from heaven? (Rebellion.)

Read D&C 76:29 to your family and ask:

- What is Satan doing now?
- What do you think we can do to win a war against Satan?
- According to D&C 10:5, what might help us in this war?

Share this statement from Joseph Smith:
"All beings who have bodies have power over those who have not. . . . The devil has no power over us only as we permit him. The moment we revolt at anything which comes from God, the devil takes power." (*Teachings of the Prophet Joseph Smith,* 181.)

Discuss as a family ways you can keep Satan from having power in your home.

Doctrine and Covenants 76:30–39
What happens to those who follow Satan?

If you have a magazine or newspaper with war pictures from somewhere in the world, show the pictures to your family and ask:

- What do you think it would be like to live through a war?
- Can you think of anything that would be worse?

Read together D&C 76:29 and ask what kind of war it refers to. Which war would be more dangerous to live through, a spiritual war or a physical war? Read D&C 76:30 to your family and have them identify what Joseph Smith and Sidney Rigdon will see in the next vision. (The sufferings of those who lose the war with Satan.) Ask the following questions as your family searches D&C 76:31–38:

- How did they lose the war with Satan? ("Suffered themselves" means "allowed themselves"—Verse 31.)
- What will they be called? (Verse 32.)
- What will they suffer? (Verses 33–38, 44–49.)
- How would you describe their feelings for Jesus Christ? (Verse 35.)

Share the following quotation from Spencer W. Kimball:
"Those who followed Lucifer in his rebellion in the premortal life and those who in mortality sin against the Holy Ghost are sons of perdition. . . .

"In the realms of perdition or the kingdom of darkness, where there is no light, Satan and the unembodied spirits of the pre-existence shall dwell together with those of mortality who retrogress [fall] to the level of perdition. . . . They have sunk so low as to have lost the inclinations and ability to repent, consequently the gospel plan is useless to them as an agent of growth and development. . . .

"These deny the Son and the gospel of repentance, and thus lose the power to repent." (*The Miracle of Forgiveness,* 125–26.)

Discuss as a family the role repentance plays in helping us win the war with Satan

Doctrine and Covenants 76:39–43
What is Christ's mission?

Have someone tell what a "job description" is and describe some of what they do at work. Then ask your family what they think would be part of the "Savior of the world" job description? Read together D&C 76:39–43 and create a job description for "Savior of the world." Invite family members to share their feelings about how Jesus Christ fulfilled His role as "Savior of the world."

Doctrine and Covenants 76:50–113
The three degrees of glory

Note: This activity is designed to prepare your family for the three teaching ideas that follow, although you can do any of the following ideas without this one if you choose.

Draw a star, the moon, and the sun on separate pieces of paper. Make word strips for "Telestial Kingdom," "Terrestrial Kingdom," "Celestial Kingdom," and the following phrases (without the answers):

- Receive not the gospel and the testimony of Jesus. (Telestial—verse 82.)
- Liars, sorcerers, adulterers, and whoremongers. (Telestial—verse 103.)
- Receive not the gospel in this life but receive it in the spirit world. (Terrestrial—verse 74.)
- Honorable people but blinded by the craftiness of men. (Terrestrial—verse 75.)
- Not valiant in the testimony of Jesus. (Terrestrial—verse 79.)
- Receive the testimony of Jesus. (Celestial—verse 51.)
- Baptized and receive the Holy Ghost. (Celestial—verses 51–52.)
- Have faith and keep the commandments. (Celestial—verses 52–53.)
- Made perfect through the atonement of Christ. (Celestial—verse 69.)

Put all the word strips into a bowl. Place the pictures of the sun, moon, and star on a table or the floor and have family members put them in order of least light to most light. Ask your family to search D&C 76:70, 78, and 81 and match the word strips for "Celestial Kingdom," "Terrestrial Kingdom," and "Telestial Kingdom" with the proper symbol (sun, moon, or star). Then take

turns drawing the other strips out of the bowl and placing them under the kingdom to which they belong.

Explain that the last three visions in D&C 76 are of the celestial, terrestrial, and telestial kingdoms, and that each vision can be divided into two parts: (1) who will inherit the kingdom, and (2) what their blessings or limitations will be. Have them look for those two parts of the three visions that follow.

Doctrine and Covenants 76:50–70, 92–96
The celestial kingdom

Read together D&C 76:50–53, 68–69 and have family members identify and mark phrases describing those who will inherit the celestial kingdom. To help them understand what it means to be sealed by the Holy Spirit of Promise, share the following from President Joseph Fielding Smith:

"The Holy Spirit of Promise is the Holy Ghost, who places the stamp of approval upon every ordinance: baptism, confirmation, ordination, marriage. The promise is that the blessings will be received through faithfulness. If a person violates a covenant, whether it be of baptism, ordination, marriage, or anything else, the Spirit withdraws the stamp of approval, and the blessings will not be received." (*Doctrines of Salvation,* 1:45.)

Ask your family why it is important to faithfully keep the covenants we make. Have family members look for the blessings promised to those who will inherit celestial glory as you read together D&C 76:54–67, 94–95. Ask which of the great blessings promised they desire most and why.

Doctrine and Covenants 76:71–80, 91, 97
The terrestrial kingdom

Read together D&C 76:71–75 and have family members identify and mark phrases describing those who will inherit the terrestrial kingdom. To help them understand these verses, you may want to read the following quotations from Elder Bruce R. McConkie:

"Those destined to inherit the terrestrial kingdom are: (1) those who died 'without law'—those heathen and pagan people who do not hear the gospel in this life, and who would not accept it with all their hearts should they hear it; (2) those who hear and reject the gospel in this life and then accept it in the spirit world; (3) those who are 'honorable men of the earth, who [are] blinded by the craftiness of men'; and (4) those who are lukewarm members of the true church and who have testimonies, but who are not true and faithful in all things." (*A New Witness for the Articles of Faith,* 146.)

Have someone read D&C 76:79. Ask your family what they think it means to be "valiant in the testimony of Jesus." Take turns reading and discussing each paragraph of the following quotation from Elder Bruce R. McConkie:

"To be valiant in the testimony of Jesus is to 'come unto Christ, and be perfected in him'; it is to deny ourselves 'of all ungodliness,' and 'love God' with all our 'might, mind and strength.' (Moro. 10:32.)

"To be valiant in the testimony of Jesus is to believe in Christ and his gospel with unshakable conviction. It is to know of the verity and divinity of the Lord's work on earth. But this is not all. It is more than believing and knowing. We must be doers of the word and not hearers only. . . .

"To be valiant in the testimony of Jesus is to bridle our passions, control our appetites, and rise above carnal and evil things. It is to overcome the world as did he who is our prototype and who himself was the most valiant of all our Father's children. It is to be morally clean, to pay our tithes and offerings, to honor the Sabbath day, to pray with full purpose of heart, to lay our all upon the altar if called upon to do so.

"To be valiant in the testimony of Jesus is to take the Lord's side on every issue. It is to vote as he would vote. It is to think what he thinks, to believe what he believes, to say what he would say and do what he would do in the same situation. It is to have the mind of Christ and be one with him as he is one with his Father. . . .

"Am I valiant in the testimony of Jesus if my chief interest and concern in life is laying up in store the treasures of the earth, rather than the building up of the kingdom?

"Am I valiant if I have more of this world's goods than my just needs and wants require and I do not draw from my surplus to support missionary work, build temples, and care for the needy?

"Am I valiant if I engage in gambling, play cards, go to pornographic movies, shop on Sunday, wear immodest clothes, or do any of the things that are the accepted way of life among worldly people?

"If we are to gain salvation, we must put first in our lives the things of God's kingdom. With us it must be the kingdom of God or nothing. We have come out of darkness; ours is the marvelous light of Christ. We must walk in the light." (*Ensign,* November 1974, 35.)

Read D&C 76:76–78 to your family and ask what limitations those who obtain terrestrial glory will have.

Doctrine and Covenants 76:81–90, 98–112

The telestial kingdom

Read together D&C 76:81–83, 98–101, 103 and have family members identify and mark phrases describing those who will inherit the telestial kingdom. Then read together D&C 76:84–86, 102, 104–6, 112 and discover what will be the fate of those in the telestial kingdom.

Have someone read D&C 76:89. Ask, "What does the Lord say about the telestial kingdom, even though it is the lowest of the three degrees of glory?"

Doctrine and Covenants 76:113–19
Is it worth it?

 Share these two statements from Joseph Smith:

"Could you gaze into heaven five minutes, you would know more than you would by reading all that was ever written on the subject." (*History of the Church,* 6:50.)

"I could explain a hundred fold more than I ever have of the glories of the kingdoms manifested to me in the vision, were I permitted, and were the people prepared to receive them." (*History of the Church,* 5:402.)

Read together D&C 76:113–19. Ask:

- Why do you think that the things Joseph and Sidney saw "are not lawful for man to utter"? (Verses 115–16.)
- How would your life be different if you could see what Joseph saw?
- How can we have the "power of the Holy Spirit in our lives" to know the things of God? (Verses 116–17.)

Tell your family that Elder Mark E. Peterson, who was a member of the Quorum of the Twelve Apostles, posed some questions that would be good for us to answer:

"In modern revelation we are told that only those who are devoted to God and his way of life will reach the celestial glory. Only those who go there may become like him.

"All others, going to the lesser glories, will be restricted in that they may not become like him.

"I ask you here today—where do you want to spend eternity? Where would you like your family to spend eternity?

"If you knew that by living the gospel you may have celestial glory rather than a lesser one, would it not be worth the effort to obtain it?

"Who would be satisfied with the subdued twinkle of a star if he could enjoy the brilliance of the sun?

"Who would be content with the reflected light of the moon if he could have the radiance of the sun?

"Who would exchange the privilege of becoming like God for the very questionable and temporary advantages of this world?

"Who in his right mind would prefer the corruptions of the flesh, the sensual pleasures, and the false excitement of sin, rather than the opportunity of becoming like God; rather than having inspired intelligence, or of some day wielding some of the powers that God uses as he walks in his majesty?

"Which of us would sell his birthright for a mess of pottage?

"Isn't it advisable that we direct to our own selves the question raised by the Savior: ' . . . what shall a man give in exchange for his soul?'

"Whether we realize it or not, we answer that question every day of our lives by what we think and say and do. Our actions demonstrate whether we are working toward becoming like God or the world." (*Ensign,* January 1974, 110.)

Share your feelings concerning the great truths taught in section 76 and the importance of striving together as a family to be worthy of the celestial kingdom. Then invite family members to write in their journals what they would be willing to do to inherit the celestial kingdom.

DOCTRINE AND COVENANTS 77: ANSWERS TO QUESTIONS ABOUT JOHN'S REVELATION

Historical background: *"After the return of the Prophet from [the conference in Amherst (see D&C 75)], he resumed his translation of the Scriptures. About the first of March, while engaged in this work, questions arose in regard to the meaning of some of the figurative and symbolic writings of John in the book of Revelation. There are many things therein which the brethren did not understand; therefore the Prophet inquired of the Lord and received answer to his question."* *(Joseph Fielding Smith,* Church History and Modern Revelation, *2:62–63.) The things "which the brethren did not understand" may have led to specific questions posed to the Prophet and could be the reason why this section is written in a question-and-answer format (see Stephen E. Robinson and H. Dean Garrett,* A Commentary on the Doctrine and Covenants, *2:336–37). As you study this revelation, notice how modern revelation can help us understand ancient scriptures.*

Doctrine and Covenants 77
Understanding "The Revelation of John"

To help your family understand what D&C 77 is about, read together the section heading and share the historical background above. Have your family find the book of Revelation in the New Testament. As an example of what that book contains, have them silently read Revelation 6:1–8, and see if they understand or have questions about it. Talk about how this example helps us see why there were many things "which the brethren did not understand."

Share the following statement by Joseph Smith about understanding and interpreting Revelation (and other similar books in scripture):

"I make this broad declaration, that whenever God gives a vision of an image, or beast, or figure of any kind, He always holds Himself responsible to give a revelation or interpretation of the meaning thereof, otherwise we are not responsible or accountable for our belief in it. Don't be afraid . . . not knowing the meaning of a vision or figure, if God has not given a revelation or interpretation of the subject." (*Teachings of the Prophet Joseph Smith,* 291.)

Set a key in front of your family and ask them

how a key could help us get into a car or a house. Ask if they would be interested in a key that could help them get into and understand the book of Revelation. Share with them the following:

"The Book of Revelation is one of the grandest books in sacred literature, and the Lord clearly designs that the Saints should become familiar with it. Else, why this Revelation in the Doctrine and Covenants?

"But this Revelation [D&C 77] is not a complete interpretation of the book. It is a *key.* A key is a very small part of the house. It unlocks the door through which an entrance may be gained, but after the key has been turned, the searcher for treasure must find it for himself. It is like entering a museum in which the students must find out for themselves what they desire to know. The sources of information are there." (Hyrum M. Smith and Janne M. Sjodahl, *Doctrine and Covenants Commentary,* 478.)

Encourage your family to use the keys in D&C 77 to help them when they study the book of Revelation by looking back and forth between the two books and by making notes in the margins of Revelation with the things they learn from D&C 77.

Doctrine and Covenants 77:1–15
"Scriptionary"

Prepare to teach this section by marking each of the questions (the "Q." part) in D&C 77 in your scriptures. When your family gathers, tell them you are going to play a game called Scriptionary. Divide family members into two teams and tell them you will be playing this game using fifteen questions (the fifteen "Q." verses from D&C 77). As you play, go through each of the questions (or verses) in order.

Explain that in each round you will ask a question. If someone gives the correct answer without any assistance, that person's team receives three points. If someone gives the correct answer after consulting the book of Revelation, the team receives two points. If no one can offer the correct answer after looking at the corresponding verses in Revelation, then one person from each team will be selected to "draw" for the team.

Those who are selected to "draw" will first look at the answer in D&C 77 (the "A." part of the verse) and then have thirty seconds to draw something to help their team guess the correct answer.

Whichever team guesses the answer first, using the clues in the drawing, gets one point for their team. (Note: Whether a team gets three, two, one, or zero points, read the "A." part of each verse to your family. Invite them to look at the corresponding part of the book of Revelation and encourage them to make notes in the margins of their scriptures for future reference.)

Your family may still have questions. Encourage them to follow the counsel from Joseph Smith:

"Oh, ye elders of Israel, hearken to my voice; and when you are sent into the world to preach, tell those things you are sent to tell; preach and cry aloud, 'Repent, for the kingdom of heaven is at hand; repent and believe the Gospel.' Declare the first principles, and let mysteries alone, lest ye be overthrown. Never meddle with the visions of beasts and subjects you do not understand. Elder Brown, when you go to Palmyra, say nothing about the four beasts, but preach those things the Lord has told you to preach about—repentance and baptism for the remission of sins." (*Teachings of the Prophet Joseph Smith,* 292.)

DOCTRINE AND COVENANTS 78: THE BISHOP'S STOREHOUSE

Historical background: In February 1831, the revelation now found in D&C 42 was received explaining the law of consecration. As part of that revelation, the Lord designated that the "residue" or excess of donated funds were to be kept in His "storehouse" to "administer to the poor and the needy." (See D&C 42:33–34.) In May of the same year the Lord told the Saints that a storehouse was to be built to help administer that law. (See D&C 51:13.) In March 1832 a storehouse had not been constructed; however, on that date the Lord declared, "The time has come, and is now at hand." (D&C 78:3.) The Lord organized the "united firm" or the "united order" for the construction of the bishop's storehouse. Those who sat on this committee were Joseph Smith, Sidney Rigdon, and Newel K. Whitney. Within three months of this revelation, a bishop's storehouse was operating. It was Bishop Whitney's Mercantile. (See a picture of this store in the "Church History, Chronology, Maps, and Photographs" section at the end of the Doctrine and Covenants index.)

"This united firm operated like a church owned corporation with the managers Joseph Smith, Sidney Rigdon, and Newel K. Whitney taking out salary sufficient for their needs while the corporate profits went toward providing for 'the poor of my people' (D&C 78:3). In Kirtland the united firm also purchased building lots,

businesses, and the eventual site of the Kirtland temple." (Stephen E. Robinson and H. Dean Garrett, A Commentary on the Doctrine and Covenants, 2:351.) Notice how important it is to the Lord that we are willing to share our blessings with those in need.

Doctrine and Covenants 78:1–7, 14
Why is a bishop's storehouse important?

Ask each family member to draw a temple or a chapel. Ask them to show their picture and also tell how that building is used to help build the kingdom of God. Read aloud D&C 78:3 and have them identify the building mentioned in that verse. Ask them how a bishop's storehouse is different from a temple. If they don't know, share with them the information in the historical background above and the following explanation:

"The Lord's storehouse receives, holds in trust, and dispenses consecrated offerings of the Saints. The storehouse may be as simple or sophisticated as circumstances require. It may be a list of available services, money in an account, food in a pantry, or commodities in a building. A storehouse is established when faithful members consecrate to the bishop their time, talents, skills, compassion, materials, and financial means in caring for the poor and in building up the kingdom of God on the earth.

"The Lord's storehouse, therefore, exists in each ward. The bishop is the agent of the storehouse. Guided by inspiration from the Lord, he distributes the Saints' offerings to the poor and needy. He is assisted by priesthood quorums and the Relief Society. He is instructed and supported in his responsibilities by stake and area leaders." (*Church Handbook of Instructions, Book 2: Priesthood and Auxiliary Leaders* [1998], 256.)

"An important part of the Lord's storehouse is maintained as a year's supply, stored, where possible, in the homes of faithful families of the Church. . . .

"As individual members of the Church, you and I participate in the Lord's 'own way.' At least once a month, we fast and pray and contribute generous offerings to funds that enable bishops to disperse aid. This is part of the law of the gospel.

Each of us truly can help the poor and the needy, now, and wherever they are. And we, too, will be blessed and protected from apostasy by so doing." (Russell M. Nelson, *Ensign,* May 1986, 25.)

Take turns reading D&C 78:1–7 and identify how the storehouse was to be used and why. Make sure the following items are pointed out and discussed:

- Storehouse items are to help care for the poor. (See verse 3; see also Moses 7:18.)
- Storehouses help "advance the cause . . . to the salvation of man" by allowing us to contribute our means and resources to serve others. (See verse 4; see also Mosiah 2:17.)
- The storehouse system gives us the chance to have equal access to earthly items (see verse 5; see also D&C 82:17), thus allowing us to become equal in obtaining heavenly things.
- Contributing to the storehouse prepares us to obtain celestial glory. (See verse 7.)

Talk about and explain some of the resources the Church has today to care for the needs of members. Ask family members to list as many as they can think of before you share the following list:

- Fast offering money.
- Food orders from a bishop's storehouse.
- Deseret Industries items.
- Ward, stake, and regional employment specialists and centers.
- LDS Family Services.
- Service from ward and stake members.
- The Perpetual Education Fund.
- Canneries, orchards, farms, and other welfare properties.
- Humanitarian funds and aid.

Doctrine and Covenants 78:8–22
The blessings of keeping covenants

Pass out a slip of paper to each member of your family. Have them write a code name (secret name) for themselves and put the slips of paper with the names in a pile. Mix them up and read one name at a time. Have the rest of the family guess whom they think the code name represents. Ask why a person might use a code name.

Tell your family that you are going to read D&C 78:9, and invite your family to follow along. Read from the passage below, verse 9 as it was published in the first edition of the Doctrine and Covenants in Kirtland, Ohio, in 1835:

"Let my servant Ahasdah, and my servant Gazelam, or Enoch, and my servant Pelagoram, sit in council with the saints."

Have your family identify the differences in the two versions and then ask someone to read the section heading to discover why the early brethren used code names. Have someone read D&C 78:8 to see what the three men in verse 9 were supposed to do. (Join the United Order. For help with this idea, refer to the historical background above.) Ask a different family member to read D&C 78:10–12 and look for the things that would happen if Joseph, Sidney, and Newel did not sit in council. Ask each family member to silently read verses 13–22, looking for the benefits the Lord promised if these brethren kept the covenants He had established. When all have finished reading, ask them to take turns sharing what they found and discuss how these blessings could apply to your family today.

Also ask family members to find a favorite phrase from D&C 78:13–22 (such as "Be of good cheer" or "Do the things which I have commanded you.") Ask them to share the phrase they picked and why they like it. Talk about how the Lord's words can give us strength and peace.

Doctrine and Covenants 78:19
How important is it to be thankful?

As a family, make a list of things you are thankful for. Read D&C 78:19 aloud and ask what this verse has to do with the list you compiled. Ask:

- Why do you think it is important to show gratitude?
- What do Alma 34:38 and D&C 46:7 teach about this principle?
- What are some ways you could better show gratitude for your blessings?
- What could our family do to show appropriate gratitude more often?

Doctrine and Covenants 78:20
What's another name for Jesus Christ?

Read D&C 78:20 to your family and ask them what "Son Ahman" refers to. Ask, "Have you seen the word 'Ahman' used anywhere else in the section so far?" (Verse 15.) Use footnote 20a to identify who "Son Ahman" refers to. Share the following insight from Orson Pratt:

"'What is the name of God in the pure language?' The answer says 'Ahman.' 'What is the name of the Son of God?' Answer, 'Son Ahman—the greatest of all the parts of God excepting Ahman.' 'What is the name of men?' 'Sons Ahman,' is the answer." (*Journal of Discourses*, 2:342–43.)

Explain that the "pure language" is the language that Adam spoke, commonly referred to as the Adamic language. (See Moses 6:5–6.) Share your testimony of Heavenly Father and Jesus Christ.

DOCTRINE AND COVENANTS 79: JARED CARTER CALLED TO PREACH

Historical background: This revelation, calling Jared Carter to a mission in the "eastern countries," came a little more than a year after he had joined the Church in New York. Brother Carter had gathered to Thompson, Ohio, with the Colesville Saints. While there, the Lord named him as one who should be ordained a priest. (See D&C 52:38.) When Leman Copley decided the Colesville Saints could no longer stay on his farm (see D&C 54; 56), Carter decided to move to Amherst near his brother Simeon, where he lived until the time of the revelation found in D&C 79. Although nothing is mentioned in available records, Carter apparently was ordained to the Melchizedek Priesthood sometime in 1831. (See Susan Easton Black, Who's Who in the Doctrine and Covenants, *51–52; Stephen E. Robinson and H. Dean Garrett,* A Commentary on the Doctrine and Covenants, *2:360.) Look for how the Lord helps and blesses His missionaries.*

Doctrine and Covenants 79:1–4
Counsel and promises for a missionary

As you read D&C 79:1–4 together, ask a family member to act as scribe and keep a list for each of the following:

- What the Lord told Jared Carter to do in D&C 79.
- What the Lord promised Jared Carter in D&C 79.

After reading the section and making the lists, assign one or more items from these two lists to each member of the family. After giving them a minute or two of preparation, have them tell how they think either that promise or that counsel would have made a difference to Elder Carter on his mission. Discuss ways that the counsel or promises apply to your family as you seek to do the Lord's work. The following questions might encourage thoughtful discussion:

- What should be the difference between someone who simply shares the gospel and someone who goes forth "in the power of [his] ordination" to the priesthood?
- What does it really mean to hold the priesthood and function in it?
- When we share the gospel, do you think others perceive that we are sharing "glad tidings of great joy"? Why or why not?
- How can we convince others that the gospel is "glad tidings" to us?
- What experiences have you had that show one of the two functions of the Comforter (the Holy Ghost) mentioned in verse 2?

Share the following account from Jared Carter's journal:

"Now while I make this record, I remember the goodness of the Lord to me in the mission that I have lately been to the East. I have enjoyed my health continually and the Lord, notwithstanding the great opposition to this glorious work, he has blessed me. . . . I have been gone 6 months and 2 days. The Lord permitted me to administer the gospel to 79 souls, and many others by my instrumentality have been convinced of this most glorious work. All that have been baptized while I have been in the regions where I have been in this mission is 98, and many others have been convinced of the work that sooner or later I think will obey the work." (In Lyndon W. Cook, *The Revelations of the Prophet Joseph Smith,* 169–70.)

Encourage your family to follow the example of Jared Carter and write in their journals the fulfillment of the Lord's counsel and promises to them as they do the Lord's work.

DOCTRINE AND COVENANTS 80: A CALL TO SERVE

Historical background: In January 1832, Stephen Burnett had been called to serve a mission with a man named Ruggles Eames. (See D&C 75:35.) For some reason that mission was not completed, "for in March 1832 Stephen was called to be a missionary companion to Eden Smith." (Susan Easton Black, Who's Who in the Doctrine and Covenants, *39.) Section 80 contains Stephen Burnett's mission call and instructions. Look for what the Lord asked these missionaries to teach.*

Doctrine and Covenants 80:1–3, 5
Where would be the best place to serve a mission?

 Get out a world globe and blindfold a member of your family. Spin the globe and have the blindfolded person move a finger up and down the globe while it is spinning until it comes to a stop. If there is no land where the person's finger stops, spin again until the person stops on land. Let everyone in the family do the same activity. If you do not have a globe, adapt the activity by using a world map. Similarly blindfold family members and have them "pin their mission on the map" in a "pin the tail on the donkey" manner. In either activity, ask family members how they would feel if they were called to serve a future mission to that country. Ask:

- How receptive do you think the people of that land would be to the gospel message?
- Why are some people more receptive to the gospel than others?
- Do you think we should send missionaries only to the most receptive places of the world? Why or why not?

Invite someone to read D&C 80:1 aloud. Ask:

- What do you see in what the Lord said to Stephen Burnett that answers that last question above?
- What principle is the Lord trying to teach? (Everyone needs to hear the gospel.)

Read together D&C 80:2–5. Ask:

- Was there a place where Elder Burnett was not supposed to go?
- When a person receives a mission call, who is giving the call? (See verse 1 and Articles of Faith 1:5.)
- What would be more important to the success of your mission than where you are called to serve? (Have family members write in their scriptures next to verse 3, "It is not where you serve, but how you serve.")
- According to verse 5, whose will are we following when we accept a mission call?

Challenge your family to be willing to serve when and where the Lord calls.

Doctrine and Covenants 80:4
What do you need to know to serve a mission?

Read D&C 80:4 to your family and ask:

- What will a missionary teach others on his mission according to verse 4?
- What kinds of things do missionaries need to "believe and know to be true"?

As a family, list on a sheet of paper those things a missionary should have "heard" and have a testimony of. Your list might include the following:

- The Atonement of Jesus Christ.
- The Book of Mormon.
- Joseph Smith was a true prophet.
- Modern prophets.
- Repentance.
- Resurrection.

- Eternal families.
- Tithing.
- The Word of Wisdom.

Have a family member read the following statement by Elder Bruce R. McConkie. Ask your family to listen for three main elements of a testimony.

"A testimony in our day consists of three things: It consists of the knowledge that Jesus is the Lord, that he is the Son of the living God who was crucified for the sins of the world; it consists of the fact that Joseph Smith was a prophet of God called to restore the gospel truths and be the revealer of the knowledge of Christ for our day; and it consists of knowing that The Church of Jesus Christ of Latter-day Saints is the only true and living Church upon the face of the whole earth, the one place where salvation is found, the organization which administers the gospel and therefore administers salvation to the sons of men." (*Ensign,* December 1980, 15.)

If necessary, complete your list with the three things Elder McConkie spoke about. Ask your family how a person could obtain a testimony about each of the items listed. Invite your family to personally ask the Lord for a testimony of each of those truths.

DOCTRINE AND COVENANTS 81: THE FIRST PRESIDENCY

Historical background: See the section heading for D&C 81 for the historical background to this revelation.

Doctrine and Covenants 81: Section Heading
What happens if we don't fulfill our callings?

Ask your family if they can guess what the following people have in common: Thomas S. Monson, James E. Faust, Jesse Gause, and Frederick G. Williams. (They have all served in the First Presidency.)

Assign one family member to read the section heading for D&C 81 and another to read the biographical sketch for Jesse Gause to find out why Frederick G. Williams replaced Jesse Gause. Ask your family what wonderful blessings Jesse Gause lost because he wasn't faithful in his calling. Testify to your family of the importance of being faithful in our callings.

Doctrine and Covenants 81:1–2
Who holds the keys?

Show your family a set of keys. Ask them to tell what each key opens. Invite a family

BIOGRAPHICAL SKETCH: JESSE GAUSE

"The name of Jesse Gause does not appear in pre-1981 editions of the Doctrine and Covenants and only appears in the introduction to section 81 in the 1981 edition. Under the date of March 8, 1832, Joseph Smith wrote: 'Chose this day and ordained brother Jesse Gause and Brother Sidney [Rigdon] to be my counselors of the ministry of the high Priesthood.'" (Kirtland Revelation Book, 10; see also *BYU Studies* 15:362–64.)

"Gause evidently failed to fulfill his assignment, and the appointment and promised blessings were transferred to Frederick G. Williams, whose name appears in the revelation, and to whom the revelation was then addressed." (Hoyt W. Brewster Jr., *Doctrine and Covenants Encyclopedia*, 203.)

member to read D&C 81:1–2. Then ask the family what keys the First Presidency holds. Share the following statement from Elder Merrill J. Bateman:

"The priesthood is the power and authority of God delegated to man. Priesthood keys are the right to direct the use of that power. The president of the Church holds the keys necessary for governing the entire Church. His counselors in the First Presidency and the Quorum of the Twelve Apostles also hold the keys of the kingdom and operate under the President's direction." (*Ensign*, November 2003, 50.)

Discuss the following questions, allowing all family members to share:

- Who directs the use of priesthood power in the Church? The stake? The ward?
- Why do you think it is important to have priesthood keys on the earth?
- What blessings have come into your life because of priesthood keys?

Doctrine and Covenants 81:3–7
How can we do "the greatest good"?

 Ask your family if they can remember visiting a cemetery. Ask:

- Did you notice some of the things that were written on the headstones?
- Do you remember any of the headstones that included information about things a person had done in his or her life?
- If you could choose, what would be the greatest thing you would like written on your headstone?

Read together D&C 81:3–4 and mark what the Lord said was "the greatest good" Frederick G. Williams could do. Next to verse 4, have your family write Alma 29:1–3, 6. Then take turns reading those verses aloud with your family. Ask:

- What did Alma want to do? (Verses 1–2.)
- Why was this wrong? (Verse 3.)
- Why do you think the Lord wants us to be

BIOGRAPHICAL SKETCH: FREDERICK G. WILLIAMS

 Frederick G. Williams was born on October 28, 1787, in Suffield, Hartford County, Connecticut. Frederick married and moved to Kirtland, Ohio, where he met the missionaries. His wife accepted the truth quickly, but he studied it out for some time and was eventually baptized on October 30, 1830. Almost two years later he was called to replace Jesse Gause as a counselor to Joseph Smith. The Prophet trusted him with many responsibilities; he became a member of Zion's camp, a personal scribe, organizer of the printing firm, and an editor of the *Northern Times*. However, for reasons not given, Frederick G. Williams lost his membership but later was rebaptized. (See Joseph Smith, *History of the Church,* 3:55). Frederick died in October 1842 in Quincy, Illinois.

Joseph Smith wrote of him:

"Brother Frederick G. Williams is one of those men in whom I place the greatest confidence and trust, for I have found him ever full of love and brotherly kindness. . . . He shall ever have place in my heart. . . . God grant that he may overcome all evil. Blessed be Brother Frederick, for he shall never want a friend; and his generation after him shall flourish." (Susan Easton Black, *Who's Who in the Doctrine and Covenants,* 347.)

content with what He has allotted (given us)?

- What are some of the things He has allotted?
- How might serving the best we can in whatever calling we have be considered doing "the greatest good"?

Invite a family member to read D&C 81:5–7. Ask:

- What are you to do "in the office which [God has] appointed [to you]"? (Verse 5.)
- Can you share an example of someone who has served faithfully?

- What blessings come as we are faithful in our callings?

Share an experience with your family of a time when you have helped or been helped by someone faithfully serving in a calling and how you felt about it.

DOCTRINE AND COVENANTS 82: "A NEW COMMANDMENT"

Historical background: On April 1, 1832, Joseph Smith began a journey to Zion (Jackson County, Missouri) along with Bishop Newel K. Whitney, Peter Whitmer, and Jesse Gause. They were later joined by Sidney Rigdon, arriving on April 24 of that year. Joseph Smith wrote, "We found the brethren in Zion, generally enjoying health and faith; and they were extremely glad to welcome us among them." (History of the Church, 1:266.)

On April 26 the Prophet called a general conference of Church leaders and members and was "acknowledged as the President of the High Priesthood" as he had been in a similar conference in Amherst, Ohio, on January 25, 1832. "During the intermission, a difficulty of hardness which had existed between Bishop Partridge and Elder Rigdon, was amicably [kindly] settled, and when we came together in the afternoon, all hearts seemed to rejoice and I received the following [revelation]." (Joseph Smith, History of the Church, 1:265–67.) Look for some significant blessings the Lord promises the faithful in this revelation.

Doctrine and Covenants 82:1
The magnificent promise!

Read to your family the historical background above. Ask your family if they have ever experienced hard feelings with another person. Ask:

- How would you describe your feelings toward this person?
- How do you think the person felt whenever he or she saw you?
- How do you think Bishop Partridge and Sidney Rigdon changed their feelings?

Invite your family to silently read D&C 82:1 and look for an answer. Ask:

- What was the secret to settling hard feelings between these two brethren?
- What can we learn from them?
- What magnificent promise did the Lord give them?

- What do you think the Lord would do if they did not forgive one another?

Challenge your family to rethink their feelings toward others and write in their journals what they will do to be more forgiving so they can obtain the Lord's magnificent promise.

Doctrine and Covenants 82:2–7
When much is given, much is required

To introduce this idea, use the following situation or one like it. Invite the oldest and youngest members of your family to stand up next to each other. Tell your family to imagine that both family members are guilty of the same crime: they ate all of the chocolate chip cookies Mom had made for a mutual activity. Who should be held more responsible?

To help answer that question, have someone read aloud D&C 82:3 and tell how that verse answers the question above.

Explain that D&C 82 teaches us about the Lord's law of sin and punishment. Pair older family members with younger ones and have them search D&C 82:2–7. As they read, have them make a list of principles found in this law. Have each pair share their ideas. The following questions might help you discuss the Lord's law:

- What happens if we don't refrain from sinning? (Verse 2.)
- Why must those who have received greater light especially keep from committing sin? (Verses 3–4.)
- Why does the Lord say we need to "watch"? (Verse 5.)
- Who has sinned? (Verse 6.)
- What happens to those who repent, are forgiven, and then fall into sin again? (Verse 7.)

Doctrine and Covenants 82:8–20
How do you create Zion?

Read as a family Moses 7:18 and look for four ways the Lord describes Zion. (One heart, one mind, dwelt in righteousness, no poor among them.) List these four things on a sheet of paper (or poster board), leaving plenty of room between each item to write more information. Have your family search D&C 82:8–20 for verses that match the four items listed. Write these verses next to the appropriate item as they are found. When they are finished, your sheet of paper may look like the following chart:

Creating Zion	
One heart:	14–15, 19.
One mind:	14–15, 19.
Dwelt in righteousness:	10–11, 14–15.
No poor:	12–13, 17–19.

Discuss the following questions:

- Which of these principles do you think is most important and why?
- How would you describe what living in Zion would be like?
- What do you think would be the best part of living in Zion?
- What can we do to create Zion in our home?
- What could we do to help our own ward and stake become more Zion-like?

Doctrine and Covenants 82:23–24
There are some things we don't have to do

Have your family make a list of the many demands placed upon them from day to day. Ask them to share how they manage all of these demands. Ask them which of the demands they would like to eliminate and why. Have them read D&C 82:23–24 and look for a demand they can eliminate from their lives. Ask:

- Who will judge and make everything fair for us?
- How might no longer worrying about judging others be a blessing to us?
- If we let the Lord worry about "judging" and "repaying," what kind of a life can we enjoy? (Peaceful.)
- What personal characteristic will help us obtain this blessing? (Verse 24.)

Have your family write in their journals what they can do to be less judgmental and more steadfast in gospel living.

DOCTRINE AND COVENANTS 83: CARING FOR WOMEN AND CHILDREN

Historical background: *In the spring of 1832 a small group of Church leaders traveled to Independence, Missouri, to help establish the law of consecration among the Saints in Zion. This law was revealed to provide for the needs of the Saints. Joseph Smith recorded:*

"On the 27th, we transacted [performed] considerable business for the salvation of the Saints, who were settling among a ferocious set of mobbers, like lambs among wolves. It was my endeavor to so organize the Church, that the brethren might eventually be independent of every incumbrance [troublesome burden] beneath the celestial kingdom, by bonds and covenants of mutual friendship, and mutual love.

"On the 28th and 29th, I visited the brethren above Big Blue river, in Kaw township, a few miles west of Independence, and received a welcome only known by brethren and sisters united as one in the same faith. . . . The Colesville branch, in particular, rejoiced as the ancient Saints did with Paul. It is good to rejoice with the people of God. On the 30th, I returned to Independence, and again sat in council with the brethren, and received the following: [D&C 83]." (History of the Church, 1:269.) Look for what the Lord teaches here about family duties.

Doctrine and Covenants 83:1–6
Duties of fathers and the Church

Invite a family member to tell how the law of consecration works. (For help, have the person see the lesson for D&C 42:30–34 in this book.) Ask your family, "How might this law work for our family?" It might help to discuss some or all of the following questions:

- What are the stewardships, or responsibilities, of each family member?
- How would the parents' contributions differ from those made by the children?
- In what ways do some draw from "the storehouse" more than they put in? Why?
- How does the storehouse become "filled"?
- What would happen if some family members quit doing their responsibilities?
- What would happen if for some reason a family member was unable to do his or her responsibility?
- How would these situations affect the rest of the family?

Share with your family the historical background above. Then read together D&C 83:1–6, looking for answers to the following questions:

- What is the responsibility of husbands and fathers to their wives and children?
- What is the responsibility of wives and mothers?
- What if a wife has lost her husband, or children have lost their fathers?
- What responsibilities do your think children should have? (Note the word "if" in verse 5.)
- What might be the Church's responsibility?

You might find the following quotations helpful as you study these principles:

To fathers: "You who hold the priesthood have the responsibility, unless disabled, to provide temporal support for your wife and children. No man can shift the burden of responsibility to another, not even to his wife. The Lord has commanded that women and children have claim on their husbands and fathers for their maintenance (see D&C 83; 1 Tim. 5:8). . . .

"We urge you to do all in your power to allow your wife to remain in the home, caring for the children while you provide for the family the best you can. . . .

"Take seriously your responsibility to teach the gospel to your family through regular family home evening, family prayer, devotional and scripture-reading time, and other teaching moments. . . . Next to your own salvation, brethren, there is nothing so important to you as the salvation of your wife and children." (Howard W. Hunter, *Ensign,* November 1994, 51.)

To mothers: "For you young widows with ever-increasing family responsibilities, know that God is aware of your needs and that He will provide. Continue to exercise faith and good works. Faithful family and Church members will assist. Be willing to receive assistance from others as necessary. Your children will know that you provide them with a double measure of love. It is my testimony that our Heavenly Father will abundantly compensate your family with eternal blessings because of the goodness of your hearts." (Earl C. Tingey, *Ensign,* May 2003, 63.)

To children: "The responsibility for each person's social, emotional, spiritual, physical, or economic well-being rests first upon himself.

"No true Latter-day Saint, while physically or emotionally able, will voluntarily shift the burden of his own . . . well-being to someone else. So long as he can, under the inspiration of the Lord and with his own labors, he will supply himself . . . with the spiritual and temporal necessities of life." (Spencer W. Kimball, *Ensign,* November 1977, 77–78.)

To the Church: "I hope that every woman who finds herself in the kind of circumstances in which [she is a single mother because of abandonment, divorce, or death] is . . . blessed with an understanding and helpful bishop, with a Relief Society president who knows how to assist her, with home teachers who know where their duty lies and how to fulfill it, and with a host of ward members who are helpful without being intrusive." (Gordon B. Hinckley, *Ensign,* November 1996, 68.)

"When a child is fatherless and motherless the Church becomes the parent of that child, and it is obligatory upon the Church to take care of it, and to see that it has opportunities equal with the other children in the Church. This is a great responsibility." (Joseph F. Smith, in Conference Report, October 1899, 134.)

Ask your family to consider the following questions:

- How can we more fully practice these principles in our home?
- What might be the effect on the Church—even the whole community, nation, and world—if more families practiced these principles?
- Share your testimony of the principles of the Lord's law of consecration. Express your feelings aobut helping others.

DOCTRINE AND COVENANTS 84: A REVELATION ON PRIESTHOOD

Historical background: Early in 1832, the Lord called several missionaries to labor in the eastern United States (see D&C 75). The trials and challenges experienced in full-time missionary service often lead people to seek the Lord. This was apparently true in September 1832 as the missionaries called earlier in the year began to return to Kirtland. As six of these elders united in prayer with Joseph Smith (see D&C 84:1), the Prophet received the revelations found in Doctrine and Covenants 84.

Doctrine and Covenants 84:1–5
What is the relationship between the Church, the temple, and Zion?

Divide your family into two groups. Give each group a blank sheet of paper. Tell them to read D&C 84:1–5 and draw a picture or diagram that represents important ideas in these verses. Have them write an explanation of their picture or diagram on the back of the paper using the following words: "The Church," "Gathering," "City of New Jerusalem (or Zion)," and "Temple." Take time to share and explain your diagrams to each other.

Read again D&C 84:2 and look for the word "restoration." Ask:

- What is usually referred to when using the word "restoration" in a gospel or Church context?
- What does this verse say will be restored in the last days? (The Lord's people.)
- In what way are they restored? (Restored to God's presence.)
- How might the gathering of the Saints help bring this about?

Share with your family the following statement from Joseph Smith:

"What was the object of gathering the Jews, or the people of God in any age of the world? . . .

"The main object was to build unto the Lord a house whereby He could reveal unto His people the ordinances of His house and the glories of His kingdom, and teach the people the way of salvation; for there are certain ordinances and principles that, when they are taught and practiced, must be done in a place or house built for that purpose.

"It was the design of the councils of heaven before the world was, that the principles and laws of the priesthood should be predicated upon the gathering of the people in every age of the world." (*Teachings of the Prophet Joseph Smith,* 307.)

If you have time, you may find it helpful to study the following scriptures and explanations:

- Moses 7:18–21: An important meaning of "Zion" is that only righteous people can dwell in the presence of the Lord.
- D&C 97:15–16: Temples help people prepare to enter the presence of the Lord.
- President Gordon B. Hinckley: "No member of the Church has received the ultimate which this Church has to give until he or she has received his or her temple blessings in the house of the Lord." (*Ensign,* November 1997, 49.)

Doctrine and Covenants 84:6–30
Learning about two orders of the priesthood

Prior to scripture study, write each of the following words and phrases on separate index cards (or pieces of paper) big enough for your family to see what it says: Moses; Aaron; Jethro; Abraham; Noah; Enoch; Aaron's seed; Key of the knowledge of God; Power of godliness; See the face of God and live; Ministering of angels; Preparatory gospel; Repentance; Baptism; Carnal commandments; Prepare people; Coming of the Lord; Elder; Bishop; Teacher; Deacon; Lesser; Greater. Lay out the cards or pieces of paper on the floor or table where everyone can see them. On a poster or paper on the floor, label two categories, "Aaronic" and "Melchizedek."

Take turns reading D&C 84:6–30 as a family. When you find a word or phrase listed on an index card, have your family decide if it relates to the Aaronic or the Melchizedek Priesthood; then put the card under that heading.

After each card has been placed, invite your family to share ways their life has been blessed by either of these orders of the priesthood. Ask, "How have the teachings in these verses increased your knowledge or appreciation of the priesthood?"

Explain that most of the ordinances relating to the Melchizedek Priesthood are received in the temple, but both priesthoods are important in preparing people to go the temple. If you have a family member who holds the Aaronic Priesthood, have him tell how the ordinances of the Aaronic Priesthood help prepare Church members for the temple. Have one who holds the Melchizedek Priesthood tell how the ordinances of the Melchizedek Priesthood help Church members prepare for the temple.

Doctrine and Covenants 84:19–21
Does everyone need to hold the priesthood?

Before scripture study, get a key of some kind and draw a picture of a door labeled "The Knowledge of God."

Show your family the key and ask:

- What is a key for? (To unlock a door.)
- If I unlock the front door to our home, who would be able to enter? (Anyone.)

Have someone read D&C 84:19–21 aloud. Show the picture of the door and ask:

- What "key" does the Melchizedek Priesthood hold? (The key to the knowledge of God.)
- How does a Melchizedek Priesthood holder unlock that door and help us learn about

God? (Through priesthood ordinances—verses 20–21.)

- Once a Melchizedek Priesthood holder is available to unlock the door (provide the ordinances), who can receive those ordinances and learn about God? (Anyone who is worthy.)

Explain that Heavenly Father has commanded that all worthy male members prepare themselves to become priesthood holders so they can provide sacred ordinances to teach their families and others about God. While the sisters in the Church do not hold the priesthood, the door to all the blessings of the kingdom of God is open to all who are worthy.

Doctrine and Covenants 84:31–39
How do we receive all that the Father hath?

Separate your scripture study room into four distinct sections (use an adjoining room if needed). Have your whole family sit in the first section. Label the fourth (or farthest section from you) with a sign that says, "Eternal Life = All That the Father Hath." As you begin your study, point out to your family that the section where the sign is posted represents your family goal and that D&C 84 tells how to get there. Invite someone to read aloud D&C 84:31–34. Ask:

- Who are the two groups of people spoken of that will make an offering in the house of the Lord? ("Sons of Moses" and "sons of Aaron"—verses 31–32.)
- Who are these sons? (Those who obtain the two priesthoods, Aaronic [sons of Aaron] and Melchizedek [sons of Moses]—verses 33–34.)
- What kind of offering and sacrifice will they offer? (An acceptable one—verse 31.)
- According to 3 Nephi 9:20, what offering will the Lord accept?
- What similar blessing does the Lord promise to both the Nephites and the sons of Aaron

and Moses? (To be filled with or sanctified by the Holy Ghost—see 3 Nephi 9:20; D&C 84:33.)

Draw your family's attention to the sign on the other end of the room. ("Eternal Life = All that the Father Hath.") Read together D&C 84:35–39. Ask, "What is the first step toward that goal?" (Receiving the Lord's servants—verse 36.) Discuss who the Lord's servants are and how your family follows them. Then move your whole family into the second section of the room.

Ask, "According to D&C 84:35–36, if you receive the Lord's servants, what do you receive next?" (The Lord.) Invite a family member to describe how a person can receive the Lord. Then move your whole family into the third section of the room.

Ask, "According to D&C 84:37–38, what does someone receive who has received the Lord?" (The Father.) Have a parent explain what it means to receive the Father. Then move your whole family into the fourth and final section of the room. Ask:

- What does this move represent? (We receive all that the Father has.)
- What would your world be like if you became like your Father in Heaven?
- According to D&C 84:39, what makes these promises possible? (God makes an oath.)
- Why is it important to faithfully respect and hold the priesthood?

Share ways your family can show more respect for the priesthood. Tell your family that Elder Neal A. Maxwell said the oath, in its simplest form, is that if we give our all, God will give us His all. Elder Maxwell commented, "What an exchange rate!" (*Ensign,* May 2002, 38). Bear testimony of our generous and patient Heavenly Father who keeps all His promises.

Doctrine and Covenants 84:43–59
Light, spirit, truth and the word of the Lord

If possible, choose to read in a place that will get fairly dark when you turn off the lights. Invite someone to begin reading D&C 84:43–53; then turn off the lights. Have the person continue to read aloud. As the person struggles, turn on a flashlight, only a little away from the reader. Have the person continue reading, if possible. Turn all the lights on. Ask:

- Why is it easier to read now?
- What does this teach us about light?

Write the following words or phrases on four separate strips of paper: "The word of the Lord," "Truth," "Light," "The Spirit of Christ." Show the papers to your family and invite them to silently read D&C 84:43–53 and be prepared to do the following:

1. Select one of the four things written on the strips of paper and share what they learned about it.

2. Explain how two (or more) of these things relate to each other.

Give your family a short time to finish their assignment; then invite them to share what they learned. Ask your family what we commonly call the Spirit of Christ. (Our conscience.) Invite family members to think about a time when they recognized their conscience working. Ask:

1. How could this experience be compared to light?

2. What does D&C 84:47–51 say happens when we don't follow the Spirit of Christ? (It is sin, and we grow in darkness.)

3. How helpful are our decisions likely to be when we make them in this darkness?

Read together D&C 84:54–59. Ask:

- What did the Lord say was keeping the Church members from the full light they could have? (Treating lightly the things they had received—specifically the Book of Mormon and other scriptures.)

- What blessings are promised in D&C 84:58 as we take the scriptures more seriously?

Share with your family the following blessing given by President Ezra Taft Benson in a general conference of the Church. Invite them to note how it applies to D&C 84:

"Now, in the authority of the sacred priesthood in me vested, I invoke my blessing upon the Latter-day Saints and upon good people everywhere.

"I bless you with increased discernment to judge between Christ and anti-Christ. I bless you with increased power to do good and to resist evil. I bless you with increased understanding of the Book of Mormon. I promise you that from this moment forward, if we will daily sup from its pages and abide by its precepts, God will pour out upon each child of Zion and the Church a blessing hitherto unknown—and we will plead to the Lord that He will begin to lift the condemnation—the scourge and judgment. Of this I bear solemn witness." (*Ensign,* May 1986, 78.)

Encourage your family to receive the promises of this blessing by making time for the Book of Mormon in their personal scripture study.

Doctrine and Covenants 84:60–98
Preaching the gospel: what, how, and why?

Share with your family the historical background above. Explain that the missionaries referred to there are the same people the Lord speaks to in D&C 84:60–98. Here the Lord counsels them about missionary responsibilities.

Assign a family member to be the scribe. Have him or her divide a piece of paper into four columns labeled "What they are to preach," "How they are to preach," "Why they are to preach," and "Promised Blessings." Divide among family members as evenly as possible the verses in D&C 84:60–98. As they scan their verses, have them look for things that can be listed in each of the four columns. As they find answers, have them

report to the scribe what they found and if it tells them *what* missionaries are to preach or do, *how* they are to preach, *why* they are to preach, or a *promised blessing.* Note that many verses contain answers for more than one column.

As you finish making your lists, discuss the following questions:

- What things have changed in missionary work from that day to ours?
- What blessings listed are most applicable to our family at this time?
- What counsel most impressed you?
- What difference would the truth in verse 88 make in the way we serve in God's kindgom?

Assure your family that this is the Lord's work and that He will help us be successful as we exercise faith in Him.

Doctrine and Covenants 84:98–102
Expressing great spiritual truths in song

Share an experience, or invite a family member to share an experience, where music seemed to have power to express testimony beyond what words alone could do. Have someone read aloud D&C 84:98 and identify what the Lord says people will "lift up their voice" and sing about. (Their knowledge of the Lord.) Take turns reading the song in D&C 84:99–102 that will be sung at the Lord's coming. Ask:

- What truths in this song are most important to you?
- What hymns and songs do we have today that contain similar truths?

Consider singing some verses from hymns identified by family members. Share the following commentary from Joseph Fielding Smith on this song in D&C 84:

"The new song which they shall sing at this great day will be concerning the redemption of Zion and the restoration of Israel. Even now there are those who have set to music these beautiful words (vs. 99–102), but we may believe that no music has yet been produced that will compare with the music for this song when Zion is redeemed." (*Church History and Modern Revelation*, 1:346.)

Doctrine and Covenants 84:106–10
The need for each of us to do our duties and fulfill our callings

Challenge a family member to tie his or her shoes using only fingers and no thumbs. Point out that while the thumb cannot do everything, it makes certain jobs much easier. Ask your family who the most important person is on a football team. The quarterback? The running back? Explain that these players usually get the most attention—mostly because they score the points. Ask, "But what would happen if there was no one on the offensive line to block the defense and keep them from tackling the quarterback or running back?"

Have family members read D&C 84:106–10. Ask:

- Who does the Lord say is the most important person in His work? (See verses 109–10.)
- How does the Lord want us to be organized so that all are benefited in his work? (See verses 106, 110.)

Share with your family the following testimony given by President Gordon B. Hinckley when he was sustained as president of the Church:

"This church does not belong to its President. Its head is the Lord Jesus Christ, whose name each of us has taken upon ourselves. We are all in this great endeavor together. We are here to assist our Father in His work and His glory, 'to bring to pass the immortality and eternal life of man' (Moses 1:39). Your obligation is as serious in your sphere [area] of responsibility as is my obligation in my sphere. No calling in this church is small or of little consequence. All of us in the pursuit of our duty touch the lives of others. . . .

"All of us in this great cause are of one mind, of one belief, of one faith.

"You have as great an opportunity for satisfaction in the performance of your duty as I do in mine. The progress of this work will be determined by our joint efforts. Whatever your calling, it is as fraught with the same kind of opportunity to accomplish good as is mine. What is really important is that this is the work of the Master. Our work is to go about doing good as did He." (*Ensign*, May 1995, 71.)

DOCTRINE AND COVENANTS 85: A LETTER OF COUNSEL TO ZION

Historical background: "The background for this revelation was a problem developing among the brethren in Missouri. Some who had gone were refusing to consecrate their property according to the Lord's commandment. (See D&C 58:35–36; 72:15; etc.) The Lord warned that the names of the guilty would not be found among the genealogies or records of the Church or, in other words, that these people would lose their blessings as members of the Church. They would suffer the same fate as the transgressors mentioned in Ezra 2:61–62 who forfeited the birthright through which their children would have received the priesthood. Apparently Bishop Edward Partridge had been lax in dealing with these offenders; it was to him that the Lord said he would send one mighty and strong to set in order the affairs in Zion. (See verses 7–8.)" (Richard O. Cowan, The Doctrine and Covenants, Our Modern Scripture, *128.) Notice what the Lord says about the importance of doing the work of the Lord's Church in the Lord's way.*

Doctrine and Covenants 85:1–5, 11–12
What are the duties of clerks in the Church?

Ask your family to give the names of some of the clerks in your ward or branch. Ask if they understand what the clerks do. Then invite your family to search D&C 85:1–2 and list some clerical duties the Lord outlined. Why would it be important that our records contain accurate information? (See Revelation 20:12.)

Explain to family members that in the Church today, clerks use computers to keep accurate records of all Church members. If people are excommunicated from the Church, their names are removed from Church records. (See D&C 85:3–5, 11; see also verse 11 footnote c.)

Read D&C 85:12 aloud to your family and identify what verses of scripture give instructions about those whose names are removed from Church records. Have your family read Ezra 2:62. Ask:

- What happened to the men who did not have a record of their priesthood authority?
- Why would it be a tragedy for a man to lose the opportunity to exercise priesthood authority?

Challenge your family to always live faithfully and obtain the full blessings of the gospel.

Doctrine and Covenants 85:6
"The still small voice"

Before scripture study, place some objects in a bag that you could use to make sounds (such as scissors, bell, or coins). Ask your family to close their eyes while you make some sounds with the objects in the bag. Have them guess the objects by listening to the sounds. Then ask them to open their eyes. Ask:

- Why are some objects easier to identify than others?
- How is this demonstration like learning to identify the Spirit?
- According to D&C 85:6, what description is used for the Holy Ghost?

- Why might the Lord use a "still, small voice" to communicate with us?
- How can a person become more sensitive to the whisperings of the Spirit?

Invite your family to write down an experience they have had, when they listened to the Spirit. Ask if any family members would like to share their experience, and share your testimony of the importance of listening to the Lord's voice.

Doctrine and Covenants 85:7–8
Who is the mighty and strong one?

 Read the historical background to your family and ask:

- What was Bishop Partridge doing wrong?
- Why is it important to follow those in authority over us?
- Why do you think we should fulfill our Church callings with exactness?

Read together D&C 85:6–7. Then ask the following questions:

- What will the "one mighty and strong" do? (Assign to the Saints their inheritances in the proper way.)
- Who was "that man" who was supposed to be doing that work? (Bishop Partridge—see the historical background above.)
- What does the Lord say He will do with those who "steady the ark of God"? (Verse 80.)

Share the following statement with your family:

"In 1905, the First Presidency issued a lengthy statement in which they explained that in light of D&C 85, if 'one mighty and strong' were sent, he would assume the functions of the bishop in Missouri, thus disqualifying the many apostate claims. Bishop Partridge repented, however; so this warning never had to be carried out. (The First Presidency's statement is quoted in James R. Clark, comp., *Messages of the First Presidency,* [Salt

Lake City; Bookcraft, 1970], 4:108–120.)" (Richard O. Cowan, *The Doctrine and Covenants, Our Modern Scripture*, 128.)

Doctrine and Covenants 85:8
Would you steady the ark?

Share the following case studies with your family:

- Your bishop asks you to speak in Church on the subject of faith. You, however, think the ward members really need to hear about charity. You decide to give a talk on charity instead.

- Your young men's president asks you to plan your weekly activities to help fulfill your Duty to God requirements. You, however, think the young men in your quorum would rather just play basketball. You decide to calendar only basketball on your youth nights this month.

- Your mother feels impressed to begin having daily scripture study in the mornings. You have a hard time waking up in the morning, so you refuse to participate.

As a family, read the story of Uzzah in 2 Samuel 6:3–7 together. Ask:

- Why did Uzzah put his hand on the ark of God? (To keep the ark from falling over.)

- Why did God strike Uzzah dead? (Uzzah was not a Levite, and God had commanded that the ark was never to be touched by those not authorized—see Numbers 4:15.)

- Do you believe God could have cared for the ark of the covenant without Uzzah's help? Why or why not?

- How does the Uzzah story relate to the three case studies we talked about?

- Why is it important to follow the instructions of our leaders?

Read D&C 85:8 and explain to your family that "that man" refers to the bishop—Edward Partridge. Ask:

- Why is the story of Uzzah being used as a comparison to Edward Partridge? (Bishop Partridge was out of place in making modifications to the United Order, contrary to the Prophet's instructions. If he continued, he would be spiritually struck down as Uzzah was.)

- Why might some people want to do things their own way rather than following instructions from Church leaders?

- According to the fifth Article of Faith, why can we trust in our leaders?

Testify to your family of the importance of following our Church leaders.

DOCTRINE AND COVENANTS 86: PARABLE AND PRIESTHOOD

Historical background: *"In this revelation the Lord has given a more complete interpretation [of the parable of the wheat and the tares] than he gave to his apostles as recorded by Matthew. The reason for this may be accounted for in the fact that it is to be in these last days that the harvest is gathered and the tares are to be burned." (Joseph Fielding Smith,* Church History and Modern Revelation, *1:353.) Notice the additional information the Lord gives about His second coming.*

Doctrine and Covenants 86:1–7
The meaning of the parable: The Wheat and the Tares

Before scripture study, prepare a handout for each family member like the following. However, leave out the information in parentheses so your family can fill in the answers as they study.

Characters/Elements	What each represents
(Field)	(World)
(Sowers of good seed)	(Savior, apostles)
(Good seed, wheat)	(gospel, the righteous)
(Enemy)	(Satan)
(Tares)	(False doctrines, the wicked)
(Harvest)	(Second Coming)
(Reapers)	(Angels)

Give each family member the handout and read together Matthew 13:24–30. As you read, fill in the column under "Characters/Elements."

Ask your family to search Matthew 13:36–43 and D&C 86:1–7 to find out what each item in this parable represents. Have them complete their charts as they study. Share the following insight about the "sower of the good seed":

"In Matthew's account the Lord declares that he is the sower of the good seed, and in the Doctrine and Covenants it is stated that the apostles were the sowers of the seed. There is no contradiction here. Christ is the author of our salvation and he it was who instructed the apostles, and under him they were sent to preach the Gospel unto all the world, or to sow the seed, and as the seed is his and it is sown under his command, he states but the fact in this revelation and also in the parable." (Joseph Fielding Smith, *Church History and Modern Revelation,* 1:353.)

Discuss the following questions with your family:

- Why weren't the servants allowed to pull up the tares? (See Matthew 13:29–30; D&C 86:6.)
- According to D&C 86:3, why does Satan sow tares among the wheat?
- Who is gathered first, the wheat or the tares? (See Matthew 13:30 footnote b and D&C 86:7.)
- What will eventually happen to the tares? (See Matthew 13:40; D&C 86:7.)

Read the following to your family:

"God has held the angels of destruction for many years, lest they should reap down the wheat with the tares. But I want to tell you now, that those angels have left the portals of heaven, and they stand over this people, and this nation now, and are hovering over the earth waiting to pour out judgments. And from this very day they shall be poured out. Calamities and troubles are increasing in the earth, and there is a meaning to these things." (Wilford Woodruff, *Young Women's Journal,* 5:512–13.)

Invite a family member to give the parable in

his or her own words. Invite a different family member to give the meaning of the parable in his or her own words. Share your testimony with your family that the Lord is allowing the righteous and the wicked to grow together but that the righteous are beginning to be gathered in preparation for the time when the wicked will be burned.

Doctrine and Covenants 86:8–10
"Ye are lawful heirs"

Set a chair in the middle of the room and make it up to be a "king's throne." Use objects for a crown and a staff (such as a hat and broom). Sit in the "king's throne" and have your family imagine you are a king. Ask, "What is an heir"? (One who has the right to inherit or receive a possession from an ancestor or other predecessor.)

Ask your family to list some possible inheritances they could gain.

Invite your family to read D&C 86: 8–10. Ask:

- What was the inheritance the Lord spoke of in these verses?
- What blessings come to heirs of the priesthood?
- What are some spiritual blessings that come through the power of the priesthood?

Share the following:

"During the ages in which we dwelt in the premortal state we not only developed our various characteristics and showed our worthiness and ability, or the lack of it, but we were also where such progress could be observed. It is reasonable to believe that there was a Church organization there. The heavenly beings were living in a perfectly arranged society. Every person knew his place. Priesthood, without any question, had been conferred [given] and the leaders were chosen to officiate. Ordinances pertaining to that

pre-existence were required and the love of God prevailed. Under such conditions it was natural for our Father to discern and choose those who were most worthy and evaluate the talents of each individual. He knew not only what each of us could do, but what each of us would do when put to the test and when responsibility was given us. Then, when the time came for our habitation on mortal earth, all things were prepared and the servants of the Lord chosen and ordained to their respective missions." (Joseph Fielding Smith, *The Way to Perfection*, 50–51.)

Ask your family:

- According to Joseph Fielding Smith, when was priesthood first conferred?
- What did God know about you in premortal life?
- How might this help in deciding where and when to send you into mortality?

Doctrine and Covenants 86:11
"A Savior unto my people"

Have your family think of a time when they saw (or witnessed on television) a true experience of someone being rescued from dying. Talk about that experience and ask how it might feel to be the "rescued" or the "rescuer." How might the rescued person feel toward the rescuer? Invite your family to read D&C 86:11. Ask:

- Who was the Lord referring to as "savior unto my people"? (Faithful priesthood holders.)
- How was the Prophet a "savior" to the people?
- What part does the priesthood play in helping save others?
- How might we participate in helping to save Heavenly Father's children, both the living and the dead?

DOCTRINE AND COVENANTS 87: PROPHECY ON WAR

Historical background: As mentioned in the section heading, this revelation is a prophecy on war and was received December 25, 1832. It is interesting that a prophecy on war would be received on Christmas Day, the day we celebrate the birth of the Prince of Peace. Joseph Smith said he was praying earnestly about slavery when a voice declared this revelation to him. (See D&C 130:12–13.) Pay particular attention to what the Lord says we should do about the difficulties we will face before the Second Coming.

Doctrine and Covenants 87:1–5
"War will be poured out on all nations"

Divide your family into two groups. Inform them that one group will be slaves for the other group as determined by a coin toss. Whichever group wins the toss gets their choice. After it is determined which group is "free" and which group is "slave," ask the "free" group what they intend to do with the "slaves." Ask the "slaves" how they feel about this. After some discussion on slavery, have one person read the section heading for D&C 87 and another person read the historical background. Talk about why the Lord may have given a revelation on war if the Prophet Joseph's question was about slavery. (Consider how often war is fought either to free people from oppression and slavery or to conquer and gain power over others.)

Read together D&C 87:1–5. Ask:

- What war did Joseph Smith foretell twenty-eight years before it began? (The Civil War.)
- What are some of the details he gave concerning the Civil War?

Share the following:

"Every student of United States history is acquainted with the facts establishing a complete fulfilment of this astounding prophecy. In 1861, more than twenty-eight years after the foregoing prediction was recorded, and ten years after its publication in England, the Civil War broke out, beginning in South Carolina. The ghastly records of that fratricidal [brother against brother] strife sadly support the prediction concerning 'the death and misery of many souls,' though this constituted but a partial fulfilment. It is known that slaves deserted the South and were marshaled in the armies of the North, and that the Confederate States solicited aid of Great Britain. While no open alliance between the Southern States and the English government was effected, British influence gave indirect assistance and substantial encouragement to the South, and this in such a way as to produce serious international complications." (James E. Talmage, *Articles of Faith,* 23.)

Discuss the following questions:

- How many wars are predicted in this section? (More than one—verse 1.)
- According to verse 2, how far-reaching would the wars become?
- How many wars can you name that have taken place since the Civil War?
- What do we learn about Joseph Smith from the fact that he was able to prophesy with such detail, not only about the Civil War but also about World Wars, many years before they occurred? (He was a true prophet.)

Share your testimony that Joseph Smith was indeed a true prophet of God.

Doctrine and Covenants 87:6–8
"Stand ye in holy places"

Read together D&C 87:6–7 and have family members look for and mark things the Lord will use, in addition to war, to chasten his children (famine, plague, earthquake, thunder of heaven, vivid lightning). For help with the phrase "Lord of Sabaoth" in verse 7, share the following:

"The word *sabaoth* . . . means 'armies.' Jesus Christ is the Lord of Sabaoth, or Lord of Armies, also translated as Lord of Hosts." (Daniel H. Ludlow, *A Companion to Your Study of the Doctrine and Covenants,* 2:240.)

Show several items used for protection, such as a bike helmet, gloves, and goggles. (If you don't have such items, just name some your family would be familiar with.) Ask:

- What do these items have in common? (Protection.)
- How valuable do you think these items would be in protecting us from the calamities we just read about?
- What do you think would be better protection from the troubles that are coming?

Have someone read D&C 87:8 aloud. Ask:

- What instructions does the Lord give for our safety? (Stand ye in holy places and be not moved.)
- What places do you consider holy?

Share the following:

"I have learned something of what the Spirit has taught, and I know now that the place of safety in this world is not in any given place; it doesn't make so much difference where we live; but the all important thing is how we live, and I have found that security can come to Israel only when we keep the commandments, when they live so they can enjoy the companionship, the direction, the comfort, and the guidance of the Holy Spirit of the Lord, when they are willing to listen to these men whom God has set here to preside as His mouthpieces, and when we obey the counsels of the Church." (Harold B. Lee, Conference Report, April 1943, 128–29.)

- According to Elder Harold B. Lee, what is the "all important" thing?
- What things does Elder Lee outline for us to do for our security?
- As we do those things, how can that make our home a holy place?
- What can we do to make the chapel a holy place?
- What can we do to make the temple a holy place?

DOCTRINE AND COVENANTS 88: "THE OLIVE LEAF"

Historical background: On January 14, 1833, Joseph Smith sent a copy of this revelation to W. W. Phelps, editor of the Evening and Morning Star. *"At that time some of the Saints in Zion did not strictly obey the commandments of the Lord, and their feelings towards the Prophet Joseph were not those of perfect harmony. But the Prophet had only one desire, that the Saints . . . would merit the approbation [approval] of God. . . . He wrote: 'For if Zion will not purify herself, so as to be approved in all things, in His sight, He will seek another people; for His work will go on until Israel is gathered, and they who will not hear His voice, must expect to feel His wrath.' A copy of the Revelation was sent . . . as a message of peace . . . ; hence, it was called the 'Olive Leaf.'" (Hyrum M. Smith and Janne M. Sjodahl,* Doctrine and Covenants Commentary, *539–540.) As you study this revelation with your family, look for the parts that give you the most peace.*

Doctrine and Covenants 88:1–5
Who is the Comforter?

 Have a family member read the historical background. Ask:

- When Joseph Smith called this revelation an "Olive Leaf," what does that mean? (An olive leaf symbolizes peace—see Genesis 8:8–11.)
- Why do you think a message of peace was needed?

Read D&C 88:1–5 with your family and have them circle the word "Comforter" each time they find it. Have them share what the scriptures teach about the Comforter. Ask:

- Where does the Comforter dwell? (In our hearts.)
- What promised blessing does the Comforter bring? (Eternal life in the celestial kingdom.)
- To whom else did the Lord promise the Comforter? (Jesus' disciples in the New Testament.)
- What is another name for the Comforter? (The Holy Ghost—see John 14:26.)
- As you think about these verses, why do you think the Holy Ghost can be considered the greatest gift God gives us in this life?

Share your testimony of the power of the Holy Ghost in your life. Invite your family to do whatever is necessary to be worthy to have the Holy Ghost as their constant companion.

Doctrine and Covenants 88:6–13
The light of Christ

Give some modeling clay or salt dough to each family member. Assign one to shape a sun; another, a moon; one, the earth; and the rest, stars. Place the creations where all can see them. Then read aloud D&C 88:6–13, 49–50. Ask:

- Who is the light of the sun, the moon, and the stars?

- Who is the power by which these planets and stars were made?
- Who "enlighteneth your eyes [and] . . . quickeneth your understanding"? (Verse 11.)
- Who gives "life to all things"? (Verse 13.)
- Where does this light come from and how far does it travel? (Verse 12.)

Turn on a bright lamp and shine it on the clay creations. Bear your testimony about the power of the Savior's light. Challenge your family to look for evidence of the Savior in the world around them each day.

Doctrine and Covenants 88:14–21, 25–26
What on earth should we be doing?

Display a picture of the earth and also a picture of a family member. Ask your family what common destiny this family member has with the earth. After allowing some time, have them silently read D&C 88:14–21, 25–26 looking for clues. The following questions might help them discover answers:

- How do the scriptures describe _____ (the family member's) soul? (Spirit and body.)
- What happens to him or her sometime after death? (Resurrected and redeemed.)
- How is this similar to what the earth goes through?
- What will the earth become? (A celestial kingdom.)
- Who will live there? (The righteous.)
- What law must this person and the earth live to dwell in celestial glory? (The law of Christ.)

Read together D&C 88:26 and look for what the earth shall be and do. Testify that the earth will become a celestial kingdom. The only thing left to be determined is whether we will live the law of Christ and be privileged to live on the celestial earth.

Doctrine and Covenants 88:22–24, 28–33
Three kingdoms

Relate *The Parable of the Driver's License* to your family: There once was a family named Soul. Their triplet girls, Telest, Terrest, and Celest, were sixteen. All three girls enrolled in driver's education at Kingdom High. Telest was very uninterested in classwork and found excuses not to attend. She failed the examinations. Consequently, she did not pass the course and was never allowed to drive, which restricted her freedom. Terrest attended all of her classes and did well on her written examinations. She was able to obtain a learner's permit and drive with the instructor. However, the 5:30 A.M. driving practice was too much; she could not drag herself out of bed that early. Consequently, Terrest remained the rest of her life with only a learner's permit. A licensed driver always had to be in the car with her. Her freedom was limited. Celest passed her driving examinations with A's, showed up every morning for driving practice, and obtained a driver's license. Consequently, her father was so pleased with her accomplishments that he presented her with keys, a new car, and full freedom to drive. Ask:

- Which of these three consequences would you rather have?
- How did each triplet earn the consequence she received?
- How does this relate to the gospel?

Write the words "abide" and "quicken" on a sheet of paper. Give a dictionary to a family member and have him or her find the definitions of these words. Add the definitions to the sheet of paper as they are read. (Note: You'll need two definitions for *abide,* such as: 1. To remain, and, 2. To behave in accordance with; and one for *quicken,* such as: 1. To revive; come to life.) Take turns reading D&C 88:22–24, 28–32. Ask:

- How does the behavior of Telest, Terrest, and Celest relate to abiding a celestial, terrestrial, and telestial glory?

- What do you learn about bodies being quickened or resurrected, and how does that relate to the kingdoms people go to?
- If people do not inherit a particular kingdom, whom can they blame?
- What must we abide in order to abide in the celestial kingdom? (A celestial law.)
- How does living the gospel today affect your eternal reward?

Doctrine and Covenants 88:34–50
All kingdoms are governed by law

Ask your family to name some laws they like and some they don't like. Invite someone to explain why laws are important. Give each family member a sheet of paper that has been folded in half. Have them write "D&C 88:34" and "D&C 130:20–21" at the top of one half of the paper, and "D&C 88:35" at the top of the other. Have them search the verses and list the blessings for obeying the law given in the first references and then list the consequences for breaking the law given in the second reference.

Sing or read verse 3 of "As Sisters in Zion" (*Hymns,* no. 309) with your family. Ask a family member what they think their "vast purpose" and "broad mission" is. Take your family outside and have them gaze up at the sky. If it is nighttime, ask them to guess how many stars there are. If it is daytime, ask them to imagine how big the universe is. Help them to understand the "vast purpose" and "broad mission" of Jesus Christ and Heavenly Father. Read aloud Moses 1:4 and D&C 88:36–45. Ask:

- With so many kingdoms to govern, why do you think law is important to our Father in Heaven? (Verses 42–45.)
- Why is it important for us to abide Heavenly Father's laws? (Verses 39–40.)
- Whom must we become like in order to live with Heavenly Father once again?

Ask your family to explain the meaning of the following phrase: "Birds of a feather flock together." Invite them to search verse 40, underlining all the phrases they can find that are related to this phrase. Ask them if they would like to "flock together" with their Father in Heaven. Read D&C 88:50 and testify that they can as they faithfully live God's law.

Doctrine and Covenants 88:51–65
A parable

Take turns reading the parable found in D&C 88:51–61. Then discuss the following questions:

- What is the Lord "likening" this parable to? (The kingdoms He has created.)
- When will He visit these creations? (In the appropriate time and season.)
- What might this mean for our own planet?

Share the following quotations:

"The Lord wanted to represent these kingdoms so that we could understand. . . . Do we not expect that the Lord will . . . come and visit us . . . and stay about a thousand years. Yes . . . Then what? He withdraws. What for? To fulfill other purposes; for he has other worlds or creations and other sons and daughters . . . and they will be visited. . . . Thus he will go, in the time and in the season thereof, from . . . world to world." (Orson Pratt, in *Journal of Discourses*, 17:331–32.)

"Each kingdom, or planet, and the inhabitants thereof, were blessed with the visits and presence of their Creator, in their several times and seasons." (John Taylor, *The Mediation and Atonement*, 77.)

Ask:

- How do these statements help us better understand the parable?
- What does this teach you about the vastness of God's creations?

Invite a family member to read D&C 88:62–65. Ask:

- Even though God has many creations and vast numbers of sons and daughters, what do these verses say about His relationship with each one of us?
- What does He call His children who "call upon [Him]"? (Friends.)
- What invitation does He give us in verse 63?
- According to verses 64–65, what kind of prayers will keep us from "drawing near unto [God]"?

Explain that *expedient* means "appropriate or necessary." Discuss ways your family can make sure they "do not ask for that we ought not." (D&C 8:10; see 3 Nephi 19:24.)

Doctrine and Covenants 88:66–69
You can see God!

Ask your family if they know what a solarium is. If they do not, tell them it is a room enclosed in glass and exposed to the sun. If you have a clear glass bowl or cookie jar, turn it upside down to demonstrate what a solarium looks like. Set it by a bright lamp and label it *soul*arium. Ask your family to read D&C 88:66–69 silently to themselves. Then ask:

- How can our bodies, our *soul*arium, be like a solarium?
- What does the Lord say you need to do to have your whole body filled with light? (Verses 67–69.)
- How would your life differ as a *soul*arium from the life of someone in whom there is less light from God?
- What is the reward for being a *soul*arium? (Verses 67–68.)

Sing or read "Jesus Wants Me For a Sunbeam" (*Children's Songbook*, 60) with your family and invite everyone to write in their journals one thing they will do to be a *soul*arium.

Doctrine and Covenants 88:70–86
An assignment for "the first laborers in this last kingdom"

Draw a line down the center of a poster board, chalkboard, or piece of paper. Title the left-hand column "Instructions for missionaries in 1833," and the right-hand column "Instructions for missionaries today." Ask someone to act as scribe while other family members scan D&C 88:70–86 finding things that "laborers in this last kingdom" (or missionaries in 1833) were to do. Have the scribe write these things in the left-hand column. When that list is complete, ask family members to share things that missionaries are asked to do today that are similar to those listed under the first column. Have the scribe write these insights in the right-hand column. When you have completed the list, discuss these questions:

- What do you think it means to be "clean from the blood of this wicked generation"? (See verse 75. Read also the following words from Wilford Woodruff: "I realize that we have a testimony to bear, and that we shall be held responsible for the manner in which we perform our duties. . . . If we do our duty, then our skirts will be clean. We are watchmen upon the walls of Zion. It is our duty to warn the inhabitants of the earth of the things that are to come, and if they reject our testimony, then their blood will be upon their own heads. When the judgments of God overtake the wicked they cannot say they have not been warned. . . . I do not want, when I go into the spirit world, to have this generation rise up and condemn me, and say I have not done my duty." [*Journal of Discourses*, 21:283–84].)
- What are we to learn so that we can fulfill our mission? (Verses 78–79.)
- In what ways can you "warn [your] neighbor"? (Verse 81.)

Doctrine and Covenants 88:87–116
Signs of the times

If you have a trumpet, this would be a great time to sound a call. Ask members of your family to name all of the signs they can think

of that will precede the Second Coming. Take six sheets of paper, and on each one write one of the following scripture references and title:

D&C 88:87–91: Signs in the earth.

D&C 88:92–98: Angels and trumpets.

D&C 88:99–106: Seven trumps shall sound.

D&C 88:107–9: Men's thoughts will be revealed.

D&C 88:110–11, 113–14: Satan comes to battle.

D&C 88:112–16: Michael shall overcome.

Give family members crayons or markers and one of the six sheets of paper. Invite them to make an illustration of their assigned verses and title. Then have each person teach the rest of the family about the signs they have drawn. Ask:

- Which sign causes you the most concern?
- Which of the signs brings you the most comfort?
- What can you do to prepare for the day when the "secret acts" and the "thoughts and intents" of our hearts will be revealed? (Verses 109.)
- How does it make you feel to know that God's army will be victorious? (Verse 115.)
- How do the things we think and the ways we act show whose side we are on?

Doctrine and Covenants 88:118–26
What is your "house" like?

Sing together or read the hymn "Home Can Be a Heaven on Earth" (*Hymns,* no. 298.) Ask your family if they would like their home to be a heaven on earth. Tell them that the Lord revealed some excellent ideas about this to Joseph Smith. Take turns reading D&C 88:118–26 and make a list of those instructions that would help your home become a heaven on earth. Encourage family members to mark the things they find. Your completed list might look like this:

Verse	Instructions from the Lord	What I will do
118	Seek ye diligently and teach one another.	Hold family home evening.
118	Seek ye out of the best books words of wisdom.	Read with family members.
118	Seek learning, even by study and also by faith.	
119	Organize yourselves.	
119	Prepare every needful thing.	
119	Establish a house of prayer.	
119	Establish a house of fasting.	
119	Establish a house of faith.	
119	Establish a house of learning.	
119	Establish a house of glory.	
119	Establish a house of order.	
119	Establish a house of God.	
121	Cease from light speeches.	
121	Cease from lustful desires.	
121	Cease from pride.	
121	Cease from light-mindedness.	
121	Cease wicked doings.	
122	Appoint a teacher.	
122	Let not all speak at once "but let one speak at time and let all listen to his sayings."	
123	See that ye love one another.	
123	Cease to be covetous.	
123	Impart one to another as the gospel requires.	
124	Cease to be idle.	
124	Cease to be unclean.	
124	Cease to find fault one with another.	
124	Cease to sleep longer than is needful.	
124	Retire to thy bed early.	
124	Arise early.	
125	Clothe yourselves with the bonds of charity.	
126	Pray always.	

When they are finished, discuss the following questions:

- In your opinion, which of the Lord's instructions are most important for our family?

- What can we do to make these instructions more a part of our home? (Write their answers on your list in the "What I will do" column.)

Invite each person to choose an instruction they are weak in and set a goal to improve upon it.

Doctrine and Covenants 88:127–41
The School of the Prophets

Read the following to your family: "There were two schools conducted in Kirtland. One was a school of the Elders where they . . . [sought] knowledge of countries and kingdoms and languages (see D&C 88:77–79). . . .

"The other was the 'School of the Prophets,' and a very good description of this school and its purpose is given in [verses 127–41]. In a letter written by the Prophet Joseph to William W. Phelps in Zion, January 14, 1833, the following appears: 'You will see that the Lord commanded us, in Kirtland, to build a house of God, and establish a school for the prophets, this is the word of the Lord to us, and we must, yea, the Lord helping us, we will obey: as on conditions of our obedience he has promised us great things.'" (Joseph Fielding Smith, *Church History and Modern Revelation*, 2:136.)

Ask:

- What does this tell you about how the Lord feels about school and an education?
- How would you like to have attended a "School of the Prophets"? Why?

Copy the questions below on separate strips of paper and divide them among family members:

- What was the purpose of the School of Prophets, and who was to participate? (Verse 127.)
- Who was to greet the participants, and how was he to greet them? (Verses 128–33.)
- Who was not allowed to participate in the School of the Prophets and why? (Verse 134.)
- How were the participants to greet the president? (Verse 135.)
- Where were participants of the school to meet? (The temple—see verses 136–37.)

Have your family search D&C 88:127–41 for answers to their questions and write them down. When they are finished, review each question with your family. It might be helpful to share the following: "The object for which this school was organized is plainly stated in the revelation. None could join except he was clean from the blood of this generation. The only way he could be clean was to be obedient to the covenants of the Gospel and labor in behalf of his fellows for the salvation of their souls. Thus the preaching of the Gospel was a requirement made of those who desired to join this school." (Joseph Fielding Smith, *Church History and Modern Revelation*, 2:137.)

Discuss the kinds of feelings one might experience in the School of the Prophets (such as reverence, the Spirit, and joy).

DOCTRINE AND COVENANTS 89: A WORD OF WISDOM

Historical background: Although Brigham Young was not present when this revelation was received, he was aware of how it came about. He noted, "The first school of the prophets was held in a small room situated over the Prophet Joseph's kitchen, in a house which belonged to Bishop Whitney, and which was attached to his store. . . . When they assembled together in this room after breakfast, the first thing they did was to light their pipes, and, while smoking, talk about the great things of the kingdom, and spit all over the room, and as soon as the pipe was out of their mouths a large chew of tobacco would then be taken. Often when the Prophet entered the room to give the school instructions he would find himself in a cloud of tobacco smoke. This, and the complaints of his wife at having to clean so filthy a floor, made the Prophet think upon the matter, and he inquired of the Lord relating to the conduct of the Elders in using tobacco, and the revelation known as the Word of Wisdom was the result of his inquiry." (Journal of Discourses, *12:158.) Notice the promises the Lord makes to those who live the Word of Wisdom.*

Doctrine and Covenants 89:1–4
Does the phrase "not by commandment" in verse 2 mean the Word of Wisdom isn't really a commandment?

Tell a family member to lift the refrigerator or your family car off the ground. When it becomes obvious that this task is impossible, ask:

- Why shouldn't you be expected to really lift the refrigerator or car?
- According to 1 Nephi 3:7 and 1 Corinthians 10:13, does Heavenly Father give us commandments that we cannot really obey?

Take turns reading D&C 89:1–4, especially focusing on the phrase "not by commandment or constraint." Ask the following questions:

- Why did the Lord say he needed to warn us and give us the Word of Wisdom?
- Who was this principle "adapted to"?
- Why do you think the Lord may have said it was to be "sent greeting"?

Share the following: "The reason undoubtedly why the Word of Wisdom was given as not by 'commandment or restraint' was that at that time, at least, if it had been given as a commandment it would have brought every man, addicted to the use of these noxious things, under condemnation; so the Lord was merciful and gave them a chance to overcome, before He brought them under the law." (Joseph F. Smith, in Conference Report, October 1913, 14.)

Discuss the following questions:

- How does it make you feel to know that you have a loving Father in Heaven who will never give us a commandment that we cannot keep?
- Do you think we are past the time when the Word of Wisdom was a "good suggestion" and that now it is a commandment? Why?

Share this statement: "The simple answer to this question is yes, such commandment has been given and repeated on several occasions. September 9, 1851, President Brigham Young stated that the members of the Church had had sufficient time to be taught the import of this revelation and that henceforth it was to be considered a divine commandment. This was first put to vote before the female members of the congregation and then before the men and by unanimous vote accepted. President Joseph F. Smith at a conference meeting in October 1908, made the same statement, and this has been repeated from time to time." (Joseph Fielding Smith, *Answers to Gospel Questions,* 1:196.)

Doctrine and Covenants 89:5–17
Our bodies are temples of God

Give each of your family members a sheet of paper and ask them to divide it in half. On the top half they should write "Keep out," and on the bottom half they should write "Take in." Invite your family to list, under the appropriate headings, those things they think we should "keep out" and those things we should "take in" our bodies. When all have finished, ask everyone to share their answers.

Hold up a picture of a temple and ask:

- Whose house is this?
- Who can enter into the temples?
- What is required for them to enter?
- According to D&C 109:20, why should no unclean thing enter God's temples?
- According to 1 Corinthians 3:16–17, what else does God consider a temple?
- What does that teach us about what we take in or keep out of our bodies?

Ask your family to silently read D&C 89:5–9 and list all the items God said we should keep out of our bodies. Do the same exercise for those items we should take into our bodies by having family members read D&C 89:10–17.

Some may argue that items not specifically mentioned in the Word of Wisdom can be taken at our own discretion. As examples of the error of this thinking, have your family study and talk about the following statements:

Often when God gives commandments he attaches the phrase: "nor do anything like unto it." (See D&C 59:6; see also D&C 58:26.)

"Some have even used as an alibi the fact that drugs are not mentioned in the Word of Wisdom. What a miserable excuse. There is likewise no mention of the hazards of diving into an empty swimming pool or of jumping from an overpass onto the freeway. But who doubts the deadly

consequences of such? Common sense would dictate against such behavior." (Gordon B. Hinckley, "A Plague on the World," *New Era,* July 1990, 4.)

"The Lord has commanded you to take good care of your body. To do this, observe the Word of Wisdom, found in Doctrine and Covenants 89. Eat nutritious food, exercise regularly, and get enough sleep. When you do all these things, you remain free from harmful addictions and have control over your life. You gain the blessings of a healthy body, an alert mind, and the guidance of the Holy Ghost.

"Never use tobacco products, such as cigarettes, snuff, chewing tobacco, cigars, and pipe tobacco. They are very addictive and will damage your body and shorten your life. Also, do not drink coffee or tea, for these are addictive and harmful.

"Any form of alcohol is harmful to your body and spirit. Being under the influence of alcohol weakens your judgment and self-control and could lead you to break the law of chastity or other commandments. Drinking can lead to alcoholism, which destroys individuals and families.

"Any drug, chemical, or dangerous practice that is used to produce a sensation or 'high' can destroy your physical, mental, and spiritual well being. These include hard drugs, prescription or over-the-counter medications that are abused, and household chemicals." (*For the Strength of Youth,* 36–37.)

Doctrine and Covenants 89:18–21
What promises are associated with the Word of Wisdom?

Bring a treat to scripture study. Ask one family member to do something simple, like pick up a pencil. When the person has finished, give him or her a treat. Continue this process until all family members have earned a reward. Ask family members to explain how this activity relates to D&C 82:10 and D&C 130:20–21. Ask:

- Do all commandments have blessings attached?

- What are some blessings that come from obeying the Word of Wisdom?
- What blessings does God specifically mention in D&C 89:18–21?
- Why do you think those blessings are important?
- What would you say is the greatest blessing coming from obedience to the Word of Wisdom?

Share the following statements:

"We shall be healthy, strong and vigorous: we shall be enabled to resist disease . . . our bodies will become strong and powerful, our progeny will become mighty." (*Times and Seasons*, 3:801.)

"'Treasures of knowledge' extended far beyond material things, out into the infinite areas not explored by many otherwise brilliant people . . .

"Knowledge is not merely the equations of algebra, the theorems of geometry, or the miracles of space. It is the knowledge as recorded in Hebrews by which 'the worlds were framed by the word of God'; by which 'Enoch was translated that he should not see death'; by which Noah, with a knowledge no other human had, built an ark on dry land and saved a race by taking seed through the flood. (See Hebrews 11:3, 5, 7.)

"Of all treasures of knowledge, the most vital is the knowledge of God, his existence, powers, love, and promises." (Spencer W. Kimball, *Faith Precedes the Miracle*, 277–80.)

Share with your family how obedience to the Word of Wisdom has blessed your life.

DOCTRINE AND COVENANTS 90: INSTRUCTIONS FOR THE FIRST PRESIDENCY

Historical background: *"No explanation is given why this revelation was received, but it is one containing information of the greatest importance and may have come through the prayers of the brethren [verse 1]."* (Joseph Fielding Smith, Church History and Modern Revelation, 2:149–50.) *A short time later, members of the First Presidency were ordained. George Q. Cannon wrote, "On the occasion when the ordination was solemnized, the sacrament was administered by the Prophet under the promise that the pure in heart should see a heavenly vision; and after the bread and wine had been partaken of in prayer and humility, the Savior appeared before their eyes, accompanied by concourses of holy angels. It was thus that the faithful were comforted in their meekness and blessed in their devotion." (Life of Joseph Smith, 1907, 130–31.) Watch for the blessings that are available to us because the keys of the priesthood are again on the earth.*

Doctrine and Covenants 90
The "high/low" game

To prepare for this activity, which covers all of D&C 90, you will need a small cup or jar filled with small candies or breakfast cereal. Count the exact number contained in the jar and write it on a piece of paper.

Tell your family that you are going to play the "high/low" game as you study D&C 90. Invite them to pay close attention as they read so they can answer questions correctly. Begin by asking one family member to read aloud the section heading and another the historical background above. Then have your family quickly read D&C 90:1–37, marking words and phrases that impress them.

After the section has been read, begin asking the questions below. When someone correctly answers a question, let him or her guess the number of candies in the jar or cup. Tell the person if the correct number is higher or lower. Through this process of receiving "higher" and "lower" clues, family members should be able to get to the correct amount by the end of the questions. The family member that guesses the correct amount wins the treat (and shares with everyone else).

Some of the questions below have additional information to help you talk about the answers. Feel free to share with your family any additional information you think is important. If you believe the amount of reading is too much for one day, the chapter and questions can be divided into two days. To do this you will need to fill another container of candy to be used later. If necessary, pair young family members with older ones as a team. Only the questions in *italics* are part of the game.

- *How many days after this section was given were the counselors in the First Presidency ordained?* (See the section heading.)
- *What did the Lord say was the reason that Joseph Smith's sins were forgiven him?* (Verse 1.)
- *What was Joseph told would never be taken from him?* (Verse 3.) Discuss the following questions, which are not part of the game: How is what was said in D&C 90:3 different from what was said in D&C 43:3–4? What do you think changed over the past two years of Joseph's life? How can we prove ourselves worthy?
- *What are the oracles of God spoken of in verses 4–5?* (See footnote 4a.) What are some revelations and commandments that some people take lightly? (For example, *For the Strength of Youth* pamphlet.)
- *What happens when we treat the oracles of God lightly?* (See verse 5.)
- *Who is equal with the Prophet in holding the keys of the dispensation?* (See verse 6; the next lesson focuses on keys.)
- *In this dispensation, whom is the gospel to be taught to first?* (See verse 9.)
- *Who will receive the gospel last?* (See verse 10.)
- *What did the Lord say the Prophet should become acquainted with?* (See verse 15. Share

the following statement by Brigham Young: "Let them be educated in every useful branch of learning, for we, as a people, have in the future to excel the nations of the earth in religion, science, and philosophy. Great advancement has been made in knowledge by the learned of this world, still there is yet much to learn." [*Journal of Discourses,* 12:122–23].)
- *What is Joseph warned could become a "snare" or trap, on his mind?* (See verse 17.)
- *What were the members of the First Presidency commanded to keep from their houses?* (See verse 18.)
- *What was the bishop to search for diligently?* (See verse 22.)
- *What three things was the bishop to do so that all things would work together for good?* (See verse 24.)
- *What was Joseph commanded to keep small?* (See verse 25. Share the following quotations: "The counsel to 'let your families be small' has nothing to do with limiting the number of children, because the Lord was speaking of 'those who do not belong to your families.' . . . The term family had been used among Sidney Rigdon's Campbellite congregation to mean a cooperative group consisting of several conventional families." [Richard O. Cowan, *Answers to Your Questions About the Doctrine and Covenants,* 113]. "Lucy Mack Smith and her husband were generous to those who needed help. . . . Later in life Lucy vividly recalled sacrifices that she and Emma had both made for visitors and guests: 'How often I have parted every bed in the house for the accommodation of the brethren, and then laid a single blanket on the floor for my husband and myself, while Joseph and Emma slept upon the same floor, with nothing but their cloaks for both bed and bedding.'" [Karl Ricks Anderson, *Joseph Smith's Kirtland,* 56].)

- *What is the name of the woman who was to go up to the land of Zion?* (See verse 28.)
- *What will angels do when people repent?* (See verse 34. Share the following statement from Joseph Smith: "The spirits of the just are exalted to a greater and more glorious work: hence they are blessed in their departure to the world of spirits. Enveloped in flaming fire, they are not far from us, and know and understand our thoughts, feelings, and emotions, and are often pained therewith." [*History of the Church*, 6:52].)

D&C 90:1–6
The keys of the kingdom

Ask a family member to describe the kind of car they would really like to have. Ask the following questions:

- If I give you the name of someone who is willing to let you have a car just like that at no cost, would you be interested?
- What if he said you could have the car but not the keys? Would you still be just as interested?
- How useful would the car be without the keys?
- What do "keys" represent in this example? (The power to operate the car.)

Read together D&C 90:1–6 and make a list of what the Lord said about keys of the kingdom. Discuss each item on your list using the helps below as needed:

- Verse 2: Keys of the kingdom are a great blessing. Ask your family to name some ways their lives have been blessed because the keys of the kingdom are again on the earth. The following quotation from Elder Merrill J. Bateman might be helpful:

  "The priesthood is the power and authority of God delegated to man. Priesthood keys are the right to direct the use of that power. The President of the Church holds the keys necessary for governing the entire Church. His counselors in the First Presidency and the Quorum of the Twelve Apostles also hold the keys of the kingdom and operate under the President's direction. . . .

  "Priesthood and priesthood keys open the door to the blessings of the Atonement. Through the power of the priesthood, people are baptized for the remission of sins, made possible by the Savior's great act of mercy. A holder of the Melchizedek Priesthood may confer the Holy Ghost. Through the bestowal of the Holy Ghost, members are cleansed with fire, guided into truth, comforted, sanctified, and blessed in many ways as partakers of the fruits of the Atonement. The sealing authority may bind a man, a woman, and their children together forever, making possible exaltations in the world to come—again, a blessing from the Savior." (*Ensign*, November 2003, 50.)

- Verses 3–4: The keys of the kingdom shall never be taken from Joseph Smith. Have your family imagine driving to a destination, stopping, getting out of the car, and returning, only to realize that you had lost the keys. Without the keys, you could not enter the car nor have use of its power to take you home. Testify that in D&C 90:3–4 the Lord promises that He will not allow these keys to be lost before His Second Coming. Or you might share the following testimony of President George Q. Cannon:

  "President [Brigham] Young . . . always said that Joseph stood at the head of this dispensation, that Joseph holds the keys, that although Joseph had gone behind the veil, he stood at the head of this dispensation and that he [President Young] himself held the keys subordinate to him. President Taylor teaches the same doctrine." (*Gospel Truth*, 1:255.)

- Verses 4–5: Our strength depends on how we honor the oracles of God. Share with your family the following testimony of Elder Boyd K. Packer:

  "On one occasion Karl G. Maeser was leading a party of young missionaries across the Alps. As they reached the summit, he looked back and saw a row of sticks thrust into the snow to mark the one safe path across the otherwise treacherous glacier.

  "Halting the company of missionaries, he gestured toward the sticks and said: 'Brethren, there stands the priesthood [of God]. They are just common sticks like the rest of us, . . . but the position they hold makes them what they are to us. If we step aside from the path they mark, we are lost' (In Alma P. Burton, *Karl G. Maeser, Mormon Educator* [Salt Lake City, Deseret Book Co., 1953], p. 22.)

  "Although no one of us is perfect, the Church moves forward, led by ordinary people. . . .

  "I bear witness that the leaders of the Church were called of God by proper authority, and it is known to the Church that they have that authority and have been properly ordained by the regularly ordained heads of the Church. If we follow them we will be saved. If we stray from them we will surely be lost." (*Let Not Your Heart Be Troubled,* 135.)

- Verse 6: The counselors in the First Presidency share in the keys of the kingdom with the president of the Church. Share with your family the following commentary by Elder John A. Widtsoe:

  "The question as to whether the Counselors held the same power as the President was soon debated among the people. What could the Counselors do without direct appointment from the President? These questions were answered in a meeting on January 16, 1836. The Prophet there said, 'The Twelve are not subject to any other than the First Presidency . . . *and where I am not, there is no First Presidency over the Twelve.'* In other words were the President taken, the Counselors would have no authority. The Counselors do not possess the power of the President and cannot act in Church matters without direction and consent of the President. All this defined clearly the position and authority of the President of the Church." (*Joseph Smith—Seeker after Truth, Prophet of God,* 303.)

Share testimonies as a family of when each of you has felt the power of the keys of the kingdom operating through the First Presidency.

DOCTRINE AND COVENANTS 91: APOCRYPHAL SCRIPTURE

Historical background: *"'The Apocrypha' refers to fourteen books which were part of early Greek and Latin versions of the Bible but were not part of the Hebrew Bible.*

"The apocrypha was included in the King James Version of 1611, but by 1629 some English Bibles began to appear without it, and since the early part of the 19th century it has been excluded from almost all protestant Bibles. The American Bible Society, founded in 1816, has never printed the Apocrypha in its Bibles, and the British and Foreign Bible Society has excluded it from all but some pulpit Bibles since 1827.

"From these dates it is apparent that controversy was still raging as to the value of the Apocrypha at the time the Prophet began his ministry. Accordingly, in 1833, while engaged in revising the King James Version by the spirit of revelation, the Prophet felt impelled to inquire of the Lord as to the authenticity of the Apocrypha." (Bruce R. McConkie, Mormon Doctrine, 41.)

Doctrine and Covenants 91:1–6

The Apocrypha—what's that?

Play the game Balderdash with your family. Balderdash requires a person to select the correct definition of a word from several samples. Write the following word and definition on a piece of paper: "Apocrypha: *Secret* or *hidden*." (Bible Dictionary, 610.) Select three family members and give them the paper with the word and definition. Have them make up two additional definitions of the word that are not correct but sound believable. When the three are ready, have each one give one of the definitions (one person gives the correct one and the other two give the ones that are not correct) without telling which one is correct. The rest of the family then tries to guess which definition is correct. After everyone has guessed, reveal the correct answer.

After the game, read together D&C 91:1–2. Invite your family to circle footnote a next to the word "Apocrypha" in verse 1. Then turn to the entry "Apocrypha" in the Bible Dictionary (page 610) and read the first paragraph. As time allows, choose one or more of the books listed and read the information given. Ask a family member what he or she learned about the Apocrypha.

(Note: the word "interpolation" is the "act of foisting [inserting without authority] a word or passage into a manuscript or book." Noah Webster, *An American Dictionary of the English Language*.)

Have another family member read D&C 91:3–6. Ask:

- If people read the Apocrypha, what do they need in order to benefit from it? (The Spirit.)
- What does the Spirit manifest or show us? (Verse 4.)

Invite your family to think of a time when the Spirit manifested truth to them. Give them sixty seconds to think and then have them answer. Testify that the Spirit always testifies of truth. Share an experience when the Spirit manifested truth to you.

DOCTRINE AND COVENANTS 92: WHAT KIND OF A MEMBER ARE YOU?

Historical background: In March 1832, the Lord revealed that there must be an organization to help take care of "the storehouse for the poor." (D&C 78:3.) On April 26, 1832, the Lord instructed Joseph Smith, Newel K. Whitney, Sidney Rigdon, Oliver Cowdery, Martin Harris, and a few others to organize themselves by covenant to manage such affairs. (D&C 82:11–12.) Nearly a year later, the Lord instructed this organization (referred to as the United Order) to add Frederick G. Williams as a member. (D&C 92.) For more information on Frederick G. Williams, see his biographical sketch under D&C 81.

Doctrine and Covenants 92:1–2
Are you a "lively" member?

Before your family comes to scripture study, secretly invite one family member who is a good actor to come acting really tired and sleepy. When the family gathers, invite someone to read D&C 92:1–2. Ask:

- What did the Lord command this organization (known as the United Order) to do with Frederick? (Receive him.)
- What was Frederick commanded to be in verse 2? (A lively member.)
- What do you think it means to be a lively member?
- How would a lively member be different from (your actor's name)?
- How would family scripture study be better if (your actor's name) participated and paid attention? (At this point, be sure to tell everyone that you asked the person to act that way as part of your lesson.)

Share the following statement from President Howard W. Hunter:

"We have a firm belief in the statement that this is the true and living church of the true and living God. The question we have yet to answer is: Am I dedicated and committed, a true and living member?" (*Ensign*, May 1987, 16.)

Have family members look for these two ideas as you sing together "Put Your Shoulder to the Wheel" (*Hymns*, no. 252). Ask:

- Why is it important for a group to "receive"

a new person and for the new person to be a "lively member" of the group?
- Have you ever been new in a class?
- How did you learn to fit in?
- How have you helped others fit in?
- Why is it important to reach out to others?

Ask, "If you had to classify people as just two kinds of people, what would the two kinds be?" After allowing several answers, have family members listen for the two kinds of people described in the following poem:

Leaning and Lifting

There are two kinds of people on earth today,
Just two kinds of people, no more, I say.
Not the saint and the sinner, for 'tis well understood
The good are half bad and the bad are half good;
Not the rich and the poor, for to count a man's wealth
You must first know the state of his conscience and health;
Not the humble and proud, for in life's little span
Who puts on vain airs is not counted a man;
Not the happy and sad, for the swift-flying years
Bring each man his laughter and each man his tears.

No! The two kinds of people on earth I
mean
Are the people who lift and the people who
lean.
Wherever you go you will find the world's
masses
Are always divided in just these two
classes;
And oddly enough you will find too, I
ween,
There is only one lifter to twenty who lean.
In which class are you? Are you easing the
load
Of overtaxed lifters who toil down the
road?

Or, are you a leaner who lets others bear
Your portion of labor and worry and care?

—Ella Wheeler Wilcox

Have a family member read the last sentence of D&C 92:1. Ask, "To whom was the Lord speaking in addition to Frederick G. Williams?" Sing or read the words of "Have I Done Any Good?" (*Hymns,* no. 223) and have family members answer to themselves the questions asked in the hymn.

Read D&C 92:2 again and ask what the Lord promises to those who are faithful in keeping the commandments.

DOCTRINE AND COVENANTS 93:
A REVELATION ABOUT JESUS CHRIST, LIGHT, AND TRUTH

Historical background: *"On the 4th of May, 1833, a meeting of High Priests was held at Kirtland, for the purpose of considering ways and means for the building of a house in which to accommodate [hold] the School of the Prophets (Sec. 90:6–9). Hyrum Smith, Jared Carter, and Reynolds Cahoon were appointed a committee to obtain subscriptions [raise money] for that purpose. The Saints were few and far from wealthy, and an undertaking of that kind must have seemed stupendous [very difficult] to them, but the leaders of the Church were men of God, and their faith was of the practical kind, by which mountains are removed." (Hyrum M. Smith and Janne M. Sjodahl,* Doctrine and Covenants Commentary, *587–88.) Two days later, the Prophet received this section. Notice the power that comes from the light and truth we receive from God.*

Doctrine and Covenants 93:1–5
How is Jesus the Father and the Son?

Ask your family to name people who have seen the face of Heavenly Father or Jesus Christ. Invite a family member to read D&C 93:1. Ask:

- What promise did the Lord give through Joseph Smith?
- How many can have the opportunity to see the face of God?
- What must we do to receive this privilege?

Give a sheet of paper to a family member and

have him or her draw a ladder with five steps. Review D&C 93:1 and label the rungs of the ladder with the steps mentioned in verse 1. Encourage your family to strive to climb this ladder. Share the following statement:

"I have learned that where there is a prayerful heart, a hungering after righteousness, a forsaking of sins, and obedience to the commandments of God, the Lord pours out more and more light until there is finally power to pierce the heavenly veil and to know more than man knows. A person of such righteousness has the priceless promise that one day he shall see the Lord's face and know that he is." (Spencer W. Kimball, *Ensign*, March 1980, 4.)

As you read together D&C 93:2–5, have your family look for ways that Jesus can be considered both the Father and the Son. Ask your family who has heard of the statement "Like father, like son." Discuss what this statement means and how it might relate to the verses just read. Then read John 5:19 and share your testimony that Jesus Christ became like the Father by following the Father's commandments, and that we can do the same.

Doctrine and Covenants 93:6–20
Which John is describing the life of Jesus?

Invite a family member to act as scribe and give him or her a sheet of paper and pencil. As your family takes turns reading D&C 93:6–17, have your scribe write each word or phrase that describes Jesus. Invite your family to mark each describing word or phrase as they are read. When finished, review the list to be sure your family understands what is listed. If needed, use the Bible Dictionary and Topical Guide for assistance.

After reading D&C 93:6–17, your family may wonder which John wrote this account of the Savior. Discuss the following questions:

- Which John do you think is being quoted here, John the Baptist or John the Beloved?
- According to verse 15, what did this John see?
- Which John witnessed the baptism of Jesus?

Share what Elder Bruce R. McConkie said about this:

"There is little doubt but that the Beloved Disciple had before him the Baptist's account when he wrote his gospel. The latter John either copied or paraphrased what the earlier prophet of the same name had written. The only other possibility is that the Lord revealed to the gospel author the words that had been recorded by the earlier messenger who prepared the way before

him." (*Doctrinal New Testament Commentary*, 1:71.)

Read together D&C 93:18–20 and look for reasons why the Lord revealed this account. Ask a family member to share his or her testimony of the Savior.

D&C 93:21–22
What is the Church of the Firstborn?

Write on a piece of paper so your family can see it, "The Church of the Firstborn." Show the paper and ask your family if they have ever heard that phrase before. Have them silently read D&C 93:21–22 and then discuss the following questions:

- Who is the Firstborn?
- According to verse 22, who can become a part of the Church of the Firstborn?
- What do you think it means to be "begotten through" the Savior? (Mosiah 27:24–29.)
- What is the Church of the Firstborn?

To help answer that last question, share the following explanation:

"Members of the Church of the Firstborn are those saints who are heirs of exaltation in the celestial kingdom and who will be joint-heirs with Christ in receiving of the fulness of the Father. In this dispensation only worthy and righteous members of The Church of Jesus Christ of Latter-day Saints could become members of the Church of the Firstborn." (Daniel H. Ludlow, *A Companion to Your Study of the Doctrine and Covenants*, 2:41.)

Encourage your family to strive to be faithful enough so that all of you can be exalted in the celestial kingdom.

Doctrine and Covenants 93:23–39
What is light and truth?

Bring several different light sources to family scripture study—for example, a match, an oil-burning lamp, a flashlight, and a table lamp. Without giving any explanation, make the room as dark as possible and then use the light source that gives out the least amount of light. Then add the next brightest light source and continue on until you use the one that gives off the most light. Ask:

- What happened to the darkness with each new light source? (As the light increased, the darkness decreased.)
- Which light would you prefer if you were alone in the dark? Why?
- According to D&C 50:24, where does all light come from?
- Do you know some people who seem to have more "light" than others?

Read together D&C 93:23–39 and discuss the following questions:

- How would you define truth? (Verse 24.)
- Where does all truth come from? (Verse 26.)
- In what ways is truth similar to light?
- If we want more light and truth, what must we do? (Verses 27–28.)
- What other word is used for "light and truth" in verse 36? (Intelligence.)
- What does the word "forsake" mean in verse 37? (Have someone look it up in a dictionary. *Forsake* means to abandon or turn your back on.)
- According to what we learn in verses 36–37, what power can light and truth give us over Satan's temptations?
- How can we lose light and truth? (Verse 39.)

Show again the different light sources and ask your family to think about which one might best represent them at the present time. Help them know that they can increase their light and truth by keeping the commandments.

Doctrine and Covenants 93:40–53
How to set your house in order

Divide your family into four groups. Assign each group one of the following sets of scriptures: D&C 93:40–43; D&C 93:44; D&C 93:47–49; D&C 93:50. Have each group read the verses assigned and then prepare to give a short report on what they discovered. Allow each group time to report their findings. Ask:

- What can we learn about the importance of setting our families in order?
- According to D&C 93:53, why was Joseph Smith told to translate the Bible? ("For the salvation of Zion." For an explanation of what this translation is, see "Joseph Smith Translation" in the Bible Dictionary, 717.)
- How would Joseph Smith's translation of the Bible help Church members set their families in order?

To help answer that last question, have your family turn to Matthew 7 in their Bibles. Have someone read Matthew 7:1–2 aloud. Then discuss the following:

- Have you ever heard people say, "You're not supposed to judge" when they are told that what they are doing is wrong?
- Do these verses really mean that God does not want us to know and teach others that some actions are right and others are wrong?

Have your family read together footnote 1a, JST Matthew 7:1–2, and discuss how Joseph Smith's corrections of these verses helps us understand what the Lord would have us do.

DOCTRINE AND COVENANTS 94: THREE CHURCH BUILDING PROJECTS IN KIRTLAND

Historical background: By the spring of 1833, the Church in Kirtland had grown to several hundred people, with more Saints gathering all the time. The Lord had earlier revealed that the Church would one day fill the earth. (See D&C 65.) To better prepare the Church to take the gospel to the world, Church leaders and missionaries were commanded to study the gospel and also the learning of men. (See D&C 88:77–81, 122, 127–36; 90:6–9, 14–16.) These circumstances created a need for offices for Church leaders, schoolrooms for teaching adults, and even a printing shop. A committee was appointed to acquire land, and the revelation in D&C 94 appoints and instructs a Church building committee. Notice how much the Lord cares about everything that affects the lives of His children.

D&C 94:1–12

How do the buildings in this revelation represent what is important to the growth of the kingdom of God?

Have your family imagine visiting a foreign country where every city had a sports stadium in the middle of the town, around which everything else was built. Close to every stadium are a concert hall and an art museum. What would these buildings, and their location, tell you about the people of that country?

Share with your family the historical background above. Explain that while the Church had many needs, it was still small and had limited resources to fulfill these needs. With limited money, Church leaders had to be selective about which buildings should be constructed and in what order. Their choices tell us much about the interests and focus of the Church. Ask your family to look for the three main buildings the Saints began to build as they study D&C 94.

Have someone read D&C 94:1–2. Ask:

- What is the first building mentioned in this revelation? ("My house," or the temple.)
- Where was the temple to be in relation to the rest of the city? (The city was to be laid out with the temple as the central building.)

- What does that teach us about how the Lord feels about His house?
- What do you think the Lord is teaching us about the place the temple ought to occupy in our lives?

Share with your family the following statement from President Howard W. Hunter:

"Let us make the temple, with temple worship and temple covenants and temple marriage, our ultimate earthly goal and the supreme mortal experience.

" . . . All of our efforts in proclaiming the gospel, perfecting the Saints, and redeeming the dead lead to the holy temple. This is because the temple ordinances are absolutely crucial; we cannot return to God's presence without them. . . .

"May you let the meaning and beauty and peace of the temple come into your everyday life more directly." (*Ensign,* November 1994, 88.)

As a family, discuss ways you can demonstrate that the temple and temple covenants are central in our lives.

Take turns reading aloud D&C 94:3–9, and have your family mark in their scriptures the second building the Lord commanded the Saints to build in Kirtland. Ask:

- According to verse 3, what significant role

does the First Presidency play in the Church? (They obtain revelations.)

- What other significant role do they have? (They hold and direct the keys of the kingdom in this dispensation—see D&C 112:30–32.)
- What promise did the Lord make about this house in verses 7–9?
- In what ways might that promise apply to our own home?

Explain that when we dedicate ourselves to the Lord and keep our homes physically and spiritually clean, the Lord's presence can be felt there. Nevertheless, this revelation promised a special blessing to the First Presidency. Share the following experience of a Christian minister, Dr. Norman Vincent Peale, who unknowingly felt the power of this special promise as he met with President Spencer W. Kimball and his counselors in the First Presidency's office in the Church Office Building in Salt Lake City:

"We had a pleasant conversation and finally, at the close, I said to the president, because I felt that he was so deeply spiritual, 'President Kimball, will you bless me?'

"He replied, 'You mean you want me to give you a blessing such as I give our people?'

"I said, 'Yes.'

"So he came around behind me with the other two presidents and they put their hands on my head and President Kimball in his quiet, sincere, loving manner prayed for me by name. He asked the Lord to be near to me and love me and to take care of me and to guide me. As he prayed, I began to be very broken up and touched, and then of a sudden I had a wondrous feeling of the Presence and I said to him, 'Sir, He is here; I feel His presence.'" (*Church News,* February 9, 1980, 11.)

Have someone read D&C 94:10–12 and invite your family to mark in their scriptures the third building the Lord commanded the Saints to build in Kirtland. Ask:

- Why might the Lord want the Saints to

BIOGRAPHICAL SKETCH: REYNOLDS CAHOON

Reynolds Cahoon was one of the first people baptized in the Kirtland area by the missionaries who stopped in Kirtland on their way to Missouri in October 1830. The following summer, Brother Cahoon was one of the missionaries called to Missouri to bear record of the land of Zion. (See D&C 52:30; 58:5–6.) In 1838 Reynolds, his wife Thirza, and their seven children were forced to flee their home, lands, and possessions in Kirtland because of persecutions. Later, when the Cahoons lived in Nauvoo, Reynolds served on the building committee of the Nauvoo House, the Mansion House, and the Nauvoo Temple. Eventually, Reynolds settled in the Salt Lake Valley, where he lived until his death in 1861. (See Susan Easton Black, *Who's Who in the Doctrine and Covenants,* 48.)

establish a printing operation even before they had a Church building to meet in?

- What are your favorite Church publications?
- What are some ways your life has been blessed because of publications printed by the Church?

Summarize the significance of this revelation by discussing the following:

- If these three things are central to the mission of the Church (temples, keys of the priesthood, and scriptures and other official publications), how can we more fully give them a central place in our family and in our lives?

DOCTRINE AND COVENANTS 95: A REBUKE FROM THE LORD

Historical background: Concerning the building of the Kirtland Temple, Joseph Smith wrote, "Great preparations were [being made] to commence a house of the Lord; and notwithstanding the Church was poor, yet our unity, harmony and charity abounded to strengthen us to do the commandments of God. The building of the house of the Lord in Kirtland was a matter that continued to increase in its interest in the hearts of the brethren." (History of the Church, 1:349.) *Later on the same day, section 95 was given. As you study this revelation, notice how essential the Lord considers a temple to be.*

Doctrine and Covenants 95:1–3
Can you love someone you chastise?

Read the following case studies and discuss each parent's demonstration of love for their children:

Parents A: When our children disobey, we discipline them in different ways, such as taking away play privileges or sitting them in "time out." It takes much effort to carry out the discipline, but it is important to be consistent. We don't enjoy scolding our children, but we want them to know when we don't approve of their actions. It would be easier to ignore misbehavior, but we want them to grow up to be responsible and to choose the right.

Parents B: When our children do things they should not, we often threaten them with punishment but rarely carry it out. It takes too much effort. It is usually easier to ignore their disobedience and hope they don't do it again. We don't want to tell them they are doing something wrong because we don't want them to feel bad. It is also easier to always take our children's side when there is a conflict with other authority figures.

After your family has discussed the two case studies, read D&C 95:1 and look for how the Lord feels about love and chastisement. Ask:

- What does "chasten" mean? (It would be best to have someone look it up in a dictionary. If that is not possible, explain that it means to reprimand, scold, or chastise.)
- Why would a person chasten someone they love?

- What would it mean if the Lord didn't chasten us?

Invite someone to read D&C 95:2–3 and have your family look for reasons the Lord was chastening the Church at this time. (They had not yet started building the Kirtland Temple.) Read the section heading, historical background, and D&C 88:119. Have your family calculate how long it was between the time the command to build the temple was given by subtracting the date found in the section heading of D&C 88 from the date found in the section heading of D&C 95. (Just over five months.) Ask:

- What can we learn from this experience about the importance of the temple?
- Now that we have many temples built, why is it important that we attend them often?
- How close is our nearest temple?
- How do you think the Lord feels about those who have a temple close but do not attend regularly?

Challenge your family to attend the temple as often as possible.

Doctrine and Covenants 95:4–9
What does the temple have to do with missionary service?

Ask the children in your family to list the five events they think will be most important in their lives. Talk about the events each person listed. Ask:

- Why would a mission be important on this list?
- Is attending the temple something of importance? Why?
- Why should being sealed to your spouse in the temple be on this list? (See also D&C 131:1–3.)

Share with your family what President Howard W. Hunter said on this subject:

"Let us share with our children the spiritual feelings we have in the temple. And let us teach them more earnestly and more comfortably the things we can appropriately say about the purposes of the house of the Lord. Keep a picture of a temple in your home that your children may see it. Teach them about the purposes of the house of the Lord. Have them plan from their earliest years to go there and to remain worthy of that blessing. Let us prepare every missionary to go to the temple worthily and to make that experience an even greater highlight than receiving the mission call." (*Ensign,* February 1995, 2.)

Ask your family to look for reasons the Lord gave for building a temple as they read D&C 95:4–9. Ask:

- What does the word "endow" mean in verse 8? (To give.)
- What does the Lord give his Saints in the temple? (Verse 8.)

Share the following statement by Joseph Fielding Smith:

"The Kirtland Temple was necessary before the . . . elders of the Church could receive the endowment which the Lord had in store for them. The elders had been out preaching the Gospel and crying repentance ever since the Church was organized and many great men had heard and embraced the truth, nevertheless the elders could not go forth in the power and authority which the Lord intended them to possess until this Temple was built." (*Church History and Modern Revelation* 1:405–7.)

Talk about and plan ways your family can bet-ter prepare to serve missions and marry in the temple. Your plans may include starting savings accounts, reading books about the temple, putting pictures of the temple in your home, or other similar goals.

Doctrine and Covenants 95:6–12
Walking in darkness

Blindfold the young children in your family and lead them through different rooms of the house using only your voice (make sure they don't run into anything or get hurt). After returning to your starting point, have them take off the blindfolds. Ask:

- Why is it difficult to walk with a blindfold on?
- Why are you more likely to get hurt when you can't see where you are going?
- How silly would it be to walk around blindfolded if you didn't have to be?

Read together D&C 95:6–8. Ask:

- How is being blindfolded like what the Lord said in verse 6?
- How is failing to obey the Lord's command to begin building the temple like walking in darkness? (See verse 8.)
- How is failing to attend the temple regularly like walking in darkness?
- What kind of "vision problems" can come to those who don't seek the blessings, instruction, and power that come through temple worship?

Read together D&C 95:10–12. Ask:

- What happened in verse 10 that was "grievous" (terrible) to the Lord?
- What happens to the light in your own mind and heart when you are angry and arguing?
- According to verse 12, what do we lose when we don't keep the commandments?
- How is that like walking in darkness?

Share your testimony of how powerful the light is that comes from God.

Doctrine and Covenants 95:11, 13–17
Building a temple

Show your family a picture of the Kirtland Temple, such as Church History photograph 9 in the back of the Triple Combination. Ask:

- How long do you think it would take for our family to build such a big building?
- How long might it take if our whole ward helped us?
- What if we had to do it by hand with no power equipment?

Take turns reading D&C 95:11, 13–17; D&C 109:5. Ask:

- Why was it so difficult for the Saints to build the Kirtland Temple? (The temple was to be grand and beautiful, and the Saints were poor.)
- What did the Lord promise the Saints if they would simply obey? (See verse 11; see also 1 Nephi 3:7.)
- With the Lord helping them, what reason might there be for not building the temple? (Only their failure to be obedient.)
- What sacrifices would you be willing to make to see the power of the Lord help you build His temple?
- What sacrifices could our family make for temples and temple work?

Explain that the Kirtland Temple was not dedicated until March 27, 1836. (See section heading for D&C 109.) How long was that from the time D&C 95 was revealed? What does that tell you about the Saints' attitude toward the temple? Share the following statement:

"Four days after the Lord had rebuked the brethren for their neglect, without waiting for subscriptions [financial contributions], the brethren went to work on the Temple. Elder George A. Smith, a recent convert, hauled the first load of stone for the Temple. Hyrum Smith and Reynolds Cahoon commenced digging the trench for the walls, and they finished the same with their own hands." (Joseph Fielding Smith, *Church History and Modern Revelation*, 1:405–7.)

DOCTRINE AND COVENANTS 96: A DECISION ABOUT THE PETER FRENCH FARM

Historical background: In March 1833, a committee was appointed to obtain land for the gathering Saints and for the buildings the Lord commanded them to build. This committee learned that a man named Peter French would sell 103 acres in Kirtland for $5,000, and the Church purchased it. Purchase of this land included a brick kiln and a house that also served as a hotel. (See Milton V. Backman Jr., The Heavens Resound, *144). As stated in the section heading, the revelation in section 96 came in response to questions about what to do with this land. Look for what we learn in this revelation about God and about how well He knows us.*

Doctrine and Covenants 96: Section Heading
What do we do with the farm?

Invite a family member to read aloud the section heading for D&C 96. Have the rest of the family follow along and look for what the high priests in Kirtland could not agree on. After reading, invite someone to explain what the disagreement was about and what they did to solve their problem.

Talk about a time when your family faced a problem. Share your testimony of the importance of prayer and counseling together as a family to find a solution. You may want to discuss such scriptures as James 1:5 and Abraham 4:26; 5:2–3.

Doctrine and Covenants 96:1–5
What gives Zion strength?

Display some heavy objects for your family to see—weights, stacks of books, or large rocks. Invite a few family members to do some "weight lifting." (If no heavy objects are available, consider having them do push-ups, or similar exercises.) Talk about why exercise or weight lifting makes our bodies stronger. Invite a family member to read D&C 96:1–5. Ask:

- What is to be made strong? (The Kirtland Stake.)
- What do you think the Lord meant by "strong" in verse 1?
- According to verses 2–5, what kinds of things would help strengthen a stake? (Building a temple and publishing revelations.)

Read the following to your family:

"To my brethren and sisters everywhere, I call upon you to reaffirm your faith, to move this work forward across the world. You can make it stronger by the manner in which you live." (Gordon B. Hinckley, *Ensign,* November 1995, 70.)

Invite your family to write in their journals one way they could grow spiritually to help strengthen your ward and stake.

Doctrine and Covenants 96:6–9
How well does God know me?

Invite each family member to take turns sharing a few simple facts they know about each other that friends or neighbors may not know (such as favorite foods or books). Ask, "Why do you know one another so well?"

Have your family read D&C 96:6–7, looking for and marking phrases showing how well God knew John Johnson. Have them share what they found. Ask your family to think about and share a time when they understood and felt that God knew them personally. Read the following statement to your family:

"I bear personal witness this day of a personal, living God, who knows our names, hears and answers prayers, and cherishes us eternally as children of His spirit. I testify that amidst the wondrously complex tasks inherent in the universe, He seeks our individual happiness and safety above all other godly concerns." (Jeffrey R. Holland, *Ensign,* November 2003, 72.) Testify that God knows each of them better than they know themselves.

DOCTRINE AND COVENANTS 97: "ZION—THE PURE IN HEART"

Historical Background: In June 1833, "the First Presidency sent letters of instruction to William W. Phelps, Edward Partridge, and the brethren in Zion, and enclosed plans for the future city of Zion and its temples. . . .

"In the month of July, however, a mob in Jackson County, led by a Rev. Pixley, began to move against the Saints. . . .

"On the 20th of July, the mass meeting convened. Inflamed by falsehood . . . the meeting demanded the [closing] of the printing office" and the store run by Church leaders. "When the brethren refused . . . the mob broke down the printing establishment, seized Edward Partridge and Charles Allen, daubed them with tar from head to foot and covered them with feathers, on the public square. Others were frightened from their homes by threats and yells. On the 23rd, . . . the brethren in Missouri, in order to prevent bloodshed, signed an agreement with the mob leaders to leave the county before the 1st of April, 1834. The brethren immediately sent Oliver Cowdery to Kirtland to report to the First Presidency. He arrived there early in September, 1833.

"The Revelation in Sec. 97 was received before the arrival in Kirtland of Oliver Cowdery, and, consequently, before the Prophet knew any particulars of the storm of persecution that raged in the land of Zion." (Hyrum M. Smith and Janne M. Sjodahl, Doctrine and Covenants Commentary, 608–9.) Notice in this revelation the power of covenants, especially the covenants of the temple.

D&C 97:1–2
A message for the meek

Share with your family the historical background above. Have someone read aloud D&C 97:1–2. Ask your family to imagine they had been asked to deliver this message back to Missouri. Ask:

- Which parts of these first two verses would you have been anxious to share with the Saints in Missouri?
- What would you have said or emphasized to them as you shared it? Why?
- What words and phrases in verse 1 seem to describe what "meek" means?
- How well do these words and phrases describe you?

To help your family learn more specifically what the Lord may have meant in these verses, look up "meek" in your Topical Guide and D&C Index and find scriptures that describe meekness more fully.

Doctrine and Covenants 97:3–9
What are "covenant keepers" promised?

Read together D&C 97:3–5. Ask your family members to think about and answer these questions:

- What phrase does the Lord use to describe how he feels about the school in Zion and Parley P. Pratt?
- Why was the Lord "well pleased" with Parley?

Share this insight from Parley P. Pratt himself about the sacrifice he was willing to make:

"To attend this school I had to travel on foot, and sometimes with bare feet at that, about six miles. This I did once a week, besides visiting and preaching in five or six branches a week." (*Autobiography of Parley P. Pratt*, 75–76.)

Draw a tree similar to the following that will be large enough to show to your family.

See if family members can use all the letters from the fruit of the tree to form a word. (The word is "covenants.") If they are having a difficult time figuring out the word, tell them the word can be found in D&C 97:8. After they have discovered the word, have them read D&C 97:7–9. Then ask how the tree pertains to the message of the verses. Ask:

- What is a covenant? (A sacred promise with God in which God tells us how He would like to bless us and the conditions we must live to receive those blessings. We promise to keep those conditions or commandments.)
- According to verse 8, what should be the condition of our hearts and our spirits?
- What kinds of covenants have we made with God?
- What has God promised if we keep our covenants?

Share the following story from Elder Boyd K. Packer about a recently released stake president who said, "I was happy to accept the call to serve as stake president, and I am equally happy to accept my release. I did not serve just because I was under call. I served because I am under covenant. And I can keep my covenants quite as well as a home teacher as I can serving as stake president."

Elder Packer said, "This president understood the word *covenant*. . . . [He] had learned that exaltation is achieved by keeping covenants, not by holding high position. . . .

"Ordinances and covenants become our credentials for admission into the Lord's presence. To worthily receive them is the quest of a lifetime; to keep them thereafter is the challenge of mortality." (*Ensign,* May 1987, 24.) Ask:

- From what Elder Packer said, how do we achieve exaltation?
- What is the "quest of a lifetime"?
- What covenants do you still need to receive?
- What is the "challenge of mortality"?
- What can you do to better keep your covenants?

Doctrine and Covenants 97:10–28
"My glory shall rest upon it"

Show your family pictures of temples and talk about why we build temples. Divide your family into two groups. Have both groups read D&C 97:10–17, with one group looking for how temples are built and the other group looking for ways temples can bless our lives. Have both groups report their findings. Ask:

- How do these verses explain why we need a recommend to enter the temple?
- What does the Lord promise if we keep the temple undefiled?

Ask family members who have been to a temple to share their testimony of feeling God's presence in that holy place. Have a family member read D&C 97:18 and tell what "these things" refers to. Ask family members how many definitions of "Zion" they can provide. After allowing time for answers, have one family member read the entry for "Zion" in the Bible Dictionary, 792–93.

Read together D&C 97:18–28 and invite your family to identify specific blessings the Lord promised to Zion. Answers could include the following:

- Zion will prosper, spread, and become great and glorious. (Verse 18.)
- The nations of the earth will honor Zion. (Verse 19.)
- The Lord will be Zion's salvation. (Verse 20.)
- Zion will rejoice. (Verse 21.)
- Zion will escape the Lord's vengeance and indignation. (Verses 22–25.)

Have family members mark the word "if" each time it appears in verses 25–27. Ask what Zion must do to receive the promised blessings and what will happen if it doesn't. Share this insight:

"Latter-day revelations provide understanding. They teach that in our day, amidst strife and catastrophe and pestilence, there are two kingdoms locked in grim struggle for the souls of men—Zion and Babylon. More than once they repeat the injunction to 'stand in holy places' for a refuge from these storms of latter-day life (D&C 45:32; see also D&C 87:8; D&C 101:16–23). Prominent among such holy places, and key to all the others, is the temple of the Lord.

"The words *Zion* and *temple* belong in the same sentence together. In August 1833, as Saints attempted against much persecution to establish a geographic Zion in Jackson County, Missouri, the Prophet Joseph Smith was counseled in revelation to build a house unto the Lord 'for the salvation of Zion' (D&C 97:12). The temple is the key to salvation, it said, because it is a place of thanksgiving, a place of instruction, and a place of understanding 'in all things' (see D&C 97:12–14).

Then comes this glorious promise: 'Yea, and my presence shall be there, for I will come into it, and all the pure in heart that shall come into it *shall see God.* . . . Therefore, . . . let Zion rejoice, for this is Zion—THE PURE IN HEART; therefore, let Zion rejoice, while all the wicked shall mourn' (D&C 97:16, 21; emphasis added). For Zion, the pure in heart, the temple holds the key that unlocks holy places—places of rejoicing—while those in Babylon's byways are condemned to mourn." (Lance B. Wickman, *Ensign,* November 1994, 83.)

Explain to your family that unfortunately the Saints did not carry out the Lord's instructions to build a temple in Missouri. They were forced to flee their homes in Jackson County and were later driven from the state. The temple is still to be built. Ask your family what responsibility they feel to seek to bring about Zion. Share the following statement from President Gordon B. Hinckley:

"I see a wonderful future in a very uncertain world. If we will cling to our values, if we will build on our inheritance, if we will walk in obedience before the Lord, if we will simply live the gospel, we will be blessed in a magnificent and wonderful way. We will be looked upon as a peculiar people who have found the key to a peculiar happiness.

"'And many people shall go and say, Come ye, and let us go up to the mountain of the Lord . . . : for out of Zion shall go forth the law, and the word of the Lord from Jerusalem' (Isaiah 2:3).

"Great has been our past, wonderful is our present, glorious can be our future." (*Ensign,* November 1997, 69.)

Discuss as a family specific things you can do to help establish Zion.

DOCTRINE AND COVENANTS 98: LAWS CONCERNING ONE'S ENEMIES

Historical background: Following mob violence in Independence, Missouri, on July 23, 1833, "a number of Church members attempted to settle in Van Buren County . . . but the inhabitants of that county resisted their presence also, and they were forced to return to Jackson County. While the Mormons generally were faithful to their part of the agreement, members of the mob generally were not. Daily, the houses of the Saints were intruded upon and the inhabitants were insulted and threatened.

"Gradually the truth of the situation in Jackson County was made known abroad. The actions of the mob were often decried, and some newspapers began to censure the mob's conduct. The Western Monitor, *heretofore favorable to the demands of the old citizens in Jackson County, now condemned the mob and recommended that the Saints seek redress. But the mob leaders threatened that if the Mormons sought redress by any means, including the law protecting against character defamation or loss of property, they should die.*

"Toward the end of September 1833, Orson Hyde and John Gould arrived in Jackson County. . . . A revelution from the Lord to Joseph [D&C 98] was read to the afflicted saints." (Ivan J. Barrett, Joseph *Smith and the Restoration, 256.) Ask your family to look for how we are to treat our enemies and for how willing the Lord is to forgive His children.*

Doctrine and Covenants 98:1–3
Does God answer our prayers?

Ask family members to compare the intensity of their prayers at times when their lives have been at peace to times when they suffered trial or adversity. Ask:

- Why might our prayers differ during these times?
- Why is it important to pray in both peaceful and trying times?
- According to the section heading and historical background for this section, what do you think the Saints in Jackson County were praying for at this time?
- What do you imagine their prayers were like during this difficult time?

Read together D&C 98:1–3 and discuss the following questions:

- What message of comfort did the Lord have for the Saints at this time?
- What qualities did He identify that we should have when praying?
- Why would it be important to "give thanks" and "wait patiently on the Lord" during hard times?

Ask your family to identify the trials and difficulties they are facing. How would the counsel the Lord gave to the Saints in Missouri apply to our trials?

Doctrine and Covenants 98:4–10
Constitutional law

Write each of the following true/false statements on a separate piece of paper and divide them among your family members:

- T/F Breaking civil laws is acceptable as long as we keep God's commandments.
- T/F God approves of constitutional laws that maintain freedom.
- T/F Laws are important in protecting our freedom.
- T/F If wicked people rule in the government, the righteous are not affected.
- T/F We are responsible to vote and to select good leaders.

Ask each person to read D&C 98:4–10, looking for the correct answer to these statements. When all have finished, ask each person to report on whether the statement is true or false, what the scripture teaches about it, and why it is important. Ask your family how they think the world would be a better place if everyone followed this advice.

Doctrine and Covenants 98:11–22
"Cleave unto all good"

Bring two magnets to scripture study and show your family what happens when you try to put the sides together that repel each other. Then turn one magnet so that the two are drawn toward and attach to each other. Ask your family to imagine that one of those magnets represents God and the other magnet represents your family. Ask:

- Which direction (repelling or attaching) should we face in relation to God? Why?
- What phrase in D&C 98:11 best describes the attached magnets, or what God expects of us? (Cleave unto all good.)
- In your opinion, why is it important to cleave unto God and unto all good?

Take turns reading D&C 98:19–22. Ask:

- How were many Saints in Kirtland doing at "cleaving unto all good"?
- What did God say would happen if they did not repent?

Testify of the importance of choosing righteousness. Emphasize that doing so really is our choice. Share the following statement from Joseph Smith about this principle:

"I teach them correct principles and they govern themselves." (*Millennial Star*, 13:339; see also 2 Nephi 2:27.)

Ask each family member to silently read D&C 98:11–18. Have them identify the following three items:

- What phrase about living righteously and

cleaving unto all good do you most like in those verses?
- Why are you impressed by that phrase, and what does it teach you?
- What could you do in the coming week to better follow the counsel in that phrase?

After all have finished, invite family members to share their answers to the questions above with one another.

Doctrine and Covenants 98:23–48
Play a question and answer game

Explain to your family that the Saints in Jackson County had grown weary of "turning the other cheek." They were ready to retaliate. Read to your family the section heading of D&C 98 and the following petition signed by Edward Partridge and members of the Church in Jackson County, Missouri:

"Influenced by the precepts of our beloved Savior when we have been smitten on the one cheek, we have turned the other also; when we have been sued at the law, and our coat been taken, we have given them our cloak also; when they have compelled us to go with them a mile, we have gone with them twain; we have borne the above outrages without murmuring; but we cannot bear them patiently any longer; according to the law of God and man, we have borne enough. . . . We solicit assistance to obtain our rights. . . . Knowing as we do that the threats of the mob . . . that every office, civil and military . . . had pledged his life and honor to force us from the country, dead or alive . . . we appeal to the Governor for aid." (*History of the Church*, 1:414–15.)

Ask your family how they might feel in such circumstances. Teach them that the Lord gave us instructions about dealing with our enemies in D&C 98. Have family members search D&C 98:23–26, 39–40, 41–47, and become "experts" on the information there.

After everyone is prepared, play a question-and-answer game. Ask the following questions.

Give a small treat to the first person who answers each question correctly.

- What will our reward be when our enemies smite us once, twice, and three times and we don't retaliate?
- What are the consequences to us if we do retaliate?
- When our enemy repents after the first, second, and third offense, what are we to do?
- When our enemy does not repent after the first, second, third, and fourth trespasses, what are we to do?
- If our enemy repents after a fourth offense and repays four-fold, what are we to do and what will our reward be for doing it?
- What does the Lord promise to do with our enemies who come upon us after we have warned them? (Verse 29.)

- How and when can we be justified in retaliation? (Verses 30–31.)
- Name five prophets who lived this law. (Verse 32.)
- When are we justified in going to battle? (Verse 33–36, 38.)
- If we live this law, who will fight our battles for us? (Verse 37.)
- How does it make you feel knowing that the Lord will fight our battles?
- When our enemy repents, how often are we to forgive him? (Verse 40.)
- How can children repent for their fathers? (Verse 47.)
- How does that knowledge bless your life?
- What promise do we have for repentance? (Verses 47–48.)
- How can you apply the Lord's law in your life?

DOCTRINE AND COVENANTS 99: JOHN MURDOCK'S CALL TO SERVE

Historical background: Concerning this revelation, John Murdock said, "I . . . continued with the church preaching to them and strengthening them and regaining my health till the month of Aug. [1832] when I received the Revelation [section 99], at which time I immediately commenced to arrange my business and provide for my children and sent them up to the Bishop in Zion, which I did by the hand of Bro. Caleb Baldwin in Sept [1832]. I gave him 10 Dollars a head for carrying up my three eldest children [Orrice C., John R., and Phebe C.]." (Lyndon W. Cook, The Revelations of the Prophet Joseph Smith, 202–3.) Look for the promises of the Lord to those who receive the Lord's missionaries.

Doctrine and Covenants 99:1–5

Who was John Murdock, and what was he to do?

Before family scripture study, prepare "mission calls" for your family members by writing short letters stating where they will serve, when they will begin, and a brief list of items to bring. Put the letters in envelopes and bring them to family scripture study. Take turns having family members open their call and read the contents to the others. Ask:

- How would you feel if this is where you were really called to serve a mission?
- If you could choose the place you serve, where would it be and why?
- Why is it important to serve wherever and whenever the Lord calls us?
- What could you do to better prepare for a mission?

Explain that D&C 99 is a mission call to John Murdock. Have someone read the biographical sketch on John Murdock and explain why his life was impressive.

BIOGRAPHICAL SKETCH: JOHN MURDOCK

John Murdock was born on July 15, 1792, in the state of New York. In the winter of 1830, four Mormon missionaries stopped in Kirtland. John listened to their message, read the Book of Mormon, and was baptized on November 5, 1830.

Six months after he and his wife Julia joined the church, she died while giving birth to twins. Joseph and Emma Smith, who had also just had newborn twins die, adopted the Murdock Children. Emma was comforted, and Brother Murdock was called to serve a mission. (D&C 52.) The Smiths named the twins Joseph and Julia.

John Murdock marched with Zion's Camp and faithfully served in many church positions, including twice on a high council and twice as a bishop. He followed the Saints to the Salt Lake Valley and later in life served as a patriarch in Utah County. He died at age seventy-nine in Beaver County, Utah. (See Susan Easton Black, *Who's Who in the Doctrine and Covenants,* 203–4.)

Take turns reading D&C 99:1–5 and look for the information pertaining to John Murdock's call. Ask:

- Where was he to serve?
- What kind of an experience could he anticipate having?
- What would happen to those who received John's message of truth?
- Why is it important to receive the gospel as a little child? (See also Mosiah 3:19.)
- According to Mosiah 3:19, what childlike attributes should we strive to obtain?
- What does D&C 99:4 tell us about those who reject the message of truth?

Share your testimony of the importance of being receptive to the gospel message and sharing that message with others.

Doctrine and Covenants 99:6–8
Who is responsible to care for children?

Ask each family member to silently read D&C 99:6–8 and note the phrase "provided for." Talk about why it is important to provide for our families, especially if we were being called on a mission. Read the biographical sketch on John Murdock and learn what he did to help provide for his family after his wife died.

Read the sixth paragraph from *The Family: A Proclamation to the World.* Ask family members to make a list of what God expects of parents in order to obey the command to provide for a family. Share your testimony about the importance of families and talk about ways to strengthen your family today.

DOCTRINE AND COVENANTS 100: LET YOUR HEARTS BE COMFORTED

Historical background: *"On 5 October 1833, Joseph Smith and Sidney Rigdon, accompanied by Freeman Nickerson, started east from Kirtland on a preaching mission. . . . While en route to Upper Canada [the area near present-day Toronto], the party stopped two days in Perrysburg, New York [see Map 3 in Church History Chronology, Maps, and Photographs in the LDS Scriptures], the residence of Freeman Nickerson, who had been baptized the previous April."* (Lyndon W. Cook, The Revelations of the Prophet Joseph Smith, 203.) *The missionaries reached Perrysburg by October 11, 1833, at which time the Prophet wrote in his journal, "I feel very well in mind. The Lord is with us, but have much anxiety about my family."* (History of the Church, 1:419.)

The Prophet may also have been worried about the Saints in Missouri. About a month before this mission, the Prophet asked Orson Hyde and John Gould to travel to Missouri with revelations (such as D&C 97, which was directed to the Saints in Missouri) and give instructions to Church leaders about the persecutions facing the Saints in Zion. It was unlikely that news had traveled the thousand miles from Zion to Kirtland before Joseph left on his mission. (See History of the Church, 1:406–7.)

Doctrine and Covenants 100:1–4
Missionary worries

Ask your family to name some of the things missionaries (both young and old) worry about as they leave home to serve a full-time mission. Have them look in the section heading for D&C 100 for what Joseph Smith and Sidney Rigdon were worried about after about a week away from home. Share with your family the first paragraph of the historical background above to give additional information.

Read together D&C 100:1–4. Ask:

- What did the Lord call Joseph Smith and Sidney Rigdon?
- How do you think that made them feel?
- What did the Lord say about their worries?
- What did He say they should be concerned about and focused on instead?
- What else was said in these verses that you think made them want to follow this counsel?

Invite two family members to do a role-play. One family member should pretend to be so worried about something that he or she is no longer sure about going on a mission. (This could be worries about family, friends, or other home-related concerns). The other family member is to use D&C 100:1–4 in a way that will help resolve the person's concerns and increase his or her faith to go.

After the role-play, share with your family the following counsel given by President Gordon B. Hinckley to the young men of the Church:

"You have missions to perform. Each of you should plan for missionary service. You may have some doubts. You may have some fears. Face your doubts and your fears with faith. Prepare yourselves to go. You have not only the opportunity; you have the responsibility. The Lord has blessed and favored you in a remarkable and wonderful way. Is it too much to ask that you give two years totally immersed in His service?" (*Ensign,* November 1997, 50.)

"Now, my dear young friends, I hope all of you are pointed in the direction of missionary service. I cannot promise you fun. I cannot promise you ease and comfort. I cannot promise you freedom from discouragement, from fear, from downright misery at times. But I can promise you that you will grow as you have never grown in a similar period during your entire lives. I can promise you a happiness that will be unique and wonderful and lasting. I can promise you that you will reevaluate your lives, that you will establish new priorities, that you will live closer to the Lord, that prayer will become a real and wonderful experience, that you will walk with faith in the outcome of the good things you do." (*Ensign,* November 1998, 52.)

Have a family member read D&C 100:12 as well. Ask, "How do you think they felt after this revelation?" Share with your family the following journal entry of Joseph Smith:

"Left Buffalo, N.Y. at 8 o'clock A.M. and arrived at home Monday, the 4th [November 1833] at 10, A.M. found my family all well according to the promise of the Lord, for which blessing I feel to thank his holy name; Amen." (*The Personal Writings of Joseph Smith,* 20.)

Doctrine and Covenants 100:5–8
A promise to teachers

Ask your family to pretend they have been asked to give a talk to a group of young missionaries just getting ready to leave on their missions. They have been asked to answer the following question in their talks: "In order for a missionary to be successful in bringing converts to the Savior and His Church, what must happen in your teaching?"

Invite each person to explain how he or she would answer that question. Then discuss each answer. Tell your family that D&C 100:5–8 gives specific commandments and promises to missionaries as they teach. These commandments and promises are helpful not only to missionaries but to all gospel teachers.

Give each family member a piece of paper. Have them read D&C 100:5–8 and write three phrases they think are most important for all teachers to remember. Have them do this as much by themselves as they can. If needed, encourage them to look up words in a dictionary so they can more clearly understand the verses.

When the family is finished, have them share the ideas they thought were most important. Then discuss the following ideas:

- What does Lord say about where we will get the thoughts we need to speak?
- How does a person declare things in the name of Jesus? (See Bible Dictionary, "Prayer," 752–53 [last paragraph] for an explanation of doing something in the name of Jesus.)
- What is "solemnity of heart" and how does it influence the way we teach, preach, and share the gospel?
- What is "the spirit of meekness" and how can we have it "in all things"? (See Alma 13:28; Moroni 8:26; and D&C 19:23 for some help.)

Tell about a time (or invite other families members to tell) when you have seen the promises in these verses fulfilled.

Doctrine and Covenants 100:9–11
Who is a spokesman and who is a revelator?

Pull two family members aside before scripture study and show them D&C 100:9–11, where the Lord told Sidney Rigdon that he was called to be a "spokesman" for Joseph Smith and that Joseph was to be a "revelator" to Sidney. Ask them to act out the words "spokesman" and "revelator" in such a way that the rest of the family will guess the words. This activity is like charades, and those acting cannot say any part of either word. When all are ready, invite these two family members to act out their words and have the rest of the family guess the words by using D&C 100:9–11.

After the words are guessed, read together D&C 100:9–11. Ask:

- What are the differences between the promises made to Sidney Rigdon and those made to the Prophet Joseph?
- How would you describe the difference between a "spokesman" and a "revelator"?
- How does that keep order in the Church?

Tell your family that although we sustain fifteen men as prophets, seers, and revelators (the First Presidency and Quorum of the Twelve Apostles), only one is authorized to exercise all these gifts—the one who is the chief apostle sustained as president of the Church.

Doctrine and Covenants 100:13–17
What about Zion?

Share with your family the second paragraph from the historical background above. Ask, "What else was Joseph Smith probably worried about besides his family?" Have family members take turns reading aloud D&C 100:13–17. Ask:

- Although the Prophet never wrote about his concerns for Brothers Hyde and Gould in his journal, what does verse 14 tell you about how well the Lord knew Joseph's heart?
- Do you get the feeling that things will be going smoothly in Zion? Why or why not?
- What comfort do you think is in this message?
- Why should they (and we) "let [our] hearts be comforted"? (See verse 15.)
- What do you think this revelation can teach us about trials—even very challenging ones?

DOCTRINE AND COVENANTS 101: THE SAINTS ARE DRIVEN FROM JACKSON COUNTY

Historical background: In D&C 97 the Lord promised that the Saints in Zion would escape trouble if they repented. However, he said, "if she observe not to do whatsoever I have commanded her, I will visit her according to all her works, with sore affliction, with pestilence, with plague, with sword, with vengeance, with devouring fire" (D&C 97:26). The events around the time section 101 was revealed came partly as a result of the Saints' not heeding these warnings.

Despite agreements from the mob, intense persecutions began again in Jackson County on October 31 with a mob unroofing and destroying ten houses, beating the men, and sending the women and children into the cold. Through the week, homes were destroyed and members were forced to leave Independence and surrounding settlements. By Thursday, November 7, hundreds of Saints were camped along the Missouri River as refugees in the cold and rain. The Saints fled to neighboring counties, where in some places they were received with kindness while in others they were not. The revelation in section 101 is given to address these difficult circumstances. Notice how the Lord still promised comfort to His Saints if they would be obedient.

Doctrine and Covenants 101:1–101
What's the object?

To get your family excited to study D&C 101, collect and put as many of the following items as you can find in a box.

- A diamond ring and a piece of coal or charcoal (verses 1–5).
- A picture of a box turtle or a "slow" sign (verses 6–9).
- A toy sword and a cup (verses 10–11).
- A paper heart (verses 13–18).
- Toy animals (verses 24–27).
- A baby doll (verses 28–31).
- A world globe or atlas map of the earth (verses 32–36).
- Salt (verses 37–40).
- Blocks to make a tower, and a picture of the temple (verses 44–62).

- Some wheat or wheat-based cereal (verses 65–66).
- Weed killer or weeds (verse 66).
- A gavel or mallet (verses 81–84).
- A picture of an old woman (verses 81–84).

Have family members take turns selecting items and reading the verses listed by those items. As they take turns, have them explain how the verse and object relate to one another. Also ask them to talk about what those verses teach and why they are important.

Doctrine and Covenants 101:1–10, 35–38
Why do we have difficult trials?

Show your family a pencil and a diamond. Explain that the writing portion of the pencil is graphite, which is a form of carbon, and the diamond is also made of carbon. Have your family estimate the value of the pencil's lead versus the value of the diamond. Discuss why the diamond is significantly more valuable. Explain that scientists believe diamonds were formed millions of years ago when carbon was subjected to great heat and pressure. (Adapted from *Primary Teachers Manual 6*, 172.)

Ask your family to read D&C 101:1–3 and find how these verses compare to the carbon/diamond analogy. (The suffering of the Saints in Jackson County is like the heat, pressure, and time required for carbon to become a diamond.)

Read the section heading and historical background together and look for specific things the Saints suffered. Write "Heat, Pressure, and Time" on a piece of paper. Have your family read D&C 101:4–10 and identify phrases that could be compared to the three things needed to make a diamond. (For example, "They must needs be chastened" could be compared to "Heat." "They who will not endure chastening" may be compared to "Pressure.") Ask your family to share their findings. Then do a similar activity with D&C 101:35–38. The following questions may help with your discussion:

- What were the Saints going through that were like heat and pressure?
- What word in verses 5 and 35 indicates the passage of time? (Endure.)
- How would the trials make them pure?
- How do trials compel us to repent?
- How are these trials of the Saints like Abraham's test?
- How would enduring the trials and remaining faithful cause the Saints to become "jewels" in the Lord's hands?

Talk about some of the trials members of your family are facing. Challenge your family to be faithful no matter what trials they may endure.

Doctrine and Covenants 101:11–22, 65–74
Gathering to Zion

As with an Easter egg hunt, hide some small treats around the room and invite family members to "gather" as many as they can find. When they have finished, talk about what makes a successful gatherer. (For example, works hard, looks carefully, and works quickly.)

Read D&C 101:11–22. Ask:

- What gathering is spoken of in these verses? (The gathering of Israel.)
- Who is Israel? (God's covenant children.)
- Where are they to gather? (Zion and her stakes—verses 18–21.)
- What are some "holy places" (verse 22) the Saints can stand in?
- How can we help gather people to God's kingdom?
- What attributes are important in becoming a great missionary or "gatherer"?

Share the following statements:

"When Joseph first revealed the land where the Saints should gather, a woman in Canada asked if we thought that Jackson County would be large enough to gather all the people that would want to go to Zion. I will answer the question really as it is. Zion will extend, eventually, all over this earth. There will be no nook or corner upon the earth but what will be a Zion. It will all be Zion. I remember that the lady was answered by asking her whether she thought the ark was large enough to hold those that were to go into it in the days of Noah? 'Yes,' was the reply. Then of course Zion will be just large enough to receive all that will be prepared to possess it, as the ark was." (Brigham Young, *Journal of Discourses*, 9:138.)

"In the early days of this dispensation, Church leaders counseled members to build up Zion by emigrating to a central location. Today our leaders counsel us to build up Zion wherever we live. Members of the Church are asked to remain in their native lands and help establish the Church there. Many temples are being built so that Latter-day Saints throughout the world can receive temple blessings." (*True to the Faith: A Gospel Reference*, 189.)

Read the parable in D&C 101:64–75 and discuss the additional insights about the gathering to Zion.

Doctrine and Covenants 101:23–31
The Millennium

Ask your family what they know about the Millennium. Ask each family member to silently read D&C 101:23–31 and identify every item in those verses describing conditions, events, or details concerning the Second Coming or the Millennium. Discuss the findings of the person that found the most items. Invite your family to do a similar search activity while reading D&C 45:55–59; 88:111–15; 133:25.

Doctrine and Covenants 101:32–34
Why and how was the earth created?

Write the words "how" and "why" on a poster or paper and show it to your family along with a world globe or picture of the earth. Explain that many people have questions about the creation, destiny, and purpose of the earth. Ask your family to list some often-asked questions

about the earth, even if they do not know the answer. Some examples may include:

- How old is the earth?
- How long did it take to create the earth?
- When did dinosaurs exist and how do they fit into the events of creation?
- How was man created?

Explain that difficult questions about the earth can often be categorized under "How." In other words, we want to know how God created the earth, or we want to understand how the Church's teachings can coincide with the teachings of science.

Read D&C 101:32–34 together as a family. Ask:

- Does the Lord know answers to all these questions?
- When did He say they will be revealed?
- What is the danger of worrying too much about these answers before He reveals the answers?

Also explain that answers to "why" the earth was created can be found today. These answers are in the scriptures and are the most important for us to know now. We must wait to understand the other difficult questions when the Lord comes. Talk about the following important question and invite your family to search the accompanying scriptures to find answers. Also ask your family to find other scripture references that give additional insights:

- Why did the Lord create the earth? (See Moses 1:39; Abraham 3:24–26.)

Doctrine and Covenants 101:39–42
Why is the Lord calling us "salt"?

Pour a small amount of salt into each family member's hand. Talk about some uses of salt, including the following:

- Flavoring.
- Preservative.
- Antiseptic (germ-killer).
- Essential nutrient.

Read D&C 101:39–42 aloud to your family and notice that the Savior referred to us as "salt." Discuss ways we can be "salt-like" by answering the following questions:

- In what ways can Saints add "flavor" to the world? (Teach the gospel so that people's lives can improve.)
- How can the Latter-day Saints help "preserve" the world? (Gospel and temple ordinances help bring salvation to all people. The sealing power binds families together forever.)
- What can we do to serve as an antiseptic to others? (Preach repentance, and help get rid of evil influences in the world.)
- What would happen to all the people in the world without the gospel? (They could never live with God again.)

Ask any older family members if they know the chemical composition of salt. (Sodium Chloride—NaCl.) Explain that salt is a stable molecule, and doesn't spoil over time. The only way it "loses its savor" is to be contaminated. Ask:

- What could contaminate salt? (Dirt, impurities, etc.)
- What do you think "it is thenceforth good for nothing" means in D&C 101:40?
- How can we "lose our savor"? (Become contaminated with sin.)
- Why is repentance an important principle if we are going to be the "salt of the earth"?

Doctrine and Covenants 101:43–64
Interpret the parable

Give each family member something to draw with. Slowly read D&C 101:43–54 out loud and have your family draw a picture of what they hear. When you have finished, let everyone show his or her picture, and identify each item in the parable. Try and interpret the meaning of the parable by identifying what each item in the parable represents. The following statement will help:

"The settlements of the Saints were the olive trees; the officers of the Church were the watchmen, and the Temple, the site of which was dedicated August 3, 1831, would have been the tower from which the movements of the enemy could have been observed by inspiration. But, as nothing more was done to complete that tower, the enemy [Satan and Missouri mobs] came by night and broke down the hedge, and the servants of the nobleman fled, leaving the enemy in possession (v. 51)." (Hyrum M. Smith and Janne M. Sjodahl, *Doctrine and Covenants Commentary,* 647.)

- Why was building this temple so important?
- Why do you think temples play such a key role in God's kingdom today?
- How can going to the temple help us avoid the temptations and evil efforts of Satan today?

Take turns reading as you study D&C 101:55–64. Look for the solution the Lord offered the Saints at this time. Explain that this solution is also described in D&C 103, when the Lord had many men in Kirtland gather together and travel to Missouri to try to protect and redeem Zion.

Doctrine and Covenants 101:75–95
The Constitution of the United States

Read the following case studies to your family and have them think what they would do under these circumstances:

1. While you were on vacation, someone came into your home and stole many of your possessions.

2. A person, speeding in a car, loses control and drives into your house, causing thousands of dollars in damages.

3. Someone at your school tells you that because you are a Latter-day Saint you are not allowed to stay at school. You are not welcome to learn or study with others.

Ask your family how the following people or things would help if you were faced with the circumstances of the three case studies:

- Police officers
- Laws, courts, and attorneys
- The constitution of the United States

Read the section heading and historical background for D&C 101 with your family. Ask how the three case studies relate to what was happening to the Saints in Jackson County, Missouri, in 1833. Read D&C 101:75–80 together and look for how the members of the Church in Zion were to try to get their lands and possessions back. Read the following statements:

"The Constitution of the United States is a glorious standard; it is founded in the wisdom of God. It is a heavenly banner; it is to all those who are privileged with the sweets of its liberty, like the cooling shades and refreshing waters of a great rock in a thirsty and weary land. It is like a great tree under whose branches men from every clime can be shielded from the burning rays of the sun.

. . .

"We say that God is true; that the Constitution of the United States is true; that the Bible is true; that the Book of Mormon is true; that the Book of Covenants is true; that Christ is true." (Joseph Smith, *HC* 3:304, March 25, 1839.)

"I reverence the Constitution of the United States as a sacred document. To me its words are akin to the revelations of God, for God has placed His stamp of approval on the Constitution of this land. I testify that the God of heaven sent some of His choicest spirits to lay the foundation of this government, and He has sent other choice

spirits—even you who read my words—to preserve it." (Ezra Taft Benson, *Friend,* September 1987, inside front cover.)

Read D&C 101:81–95 and talk about who else the Saints were commanded to turn to for help in these trying circumstances. Ask:

- How rigorously were they to seek help from government officials?
- What government officials in particular were they to seek help from? (Judge, governor, president.)
- What would happen if the government officials did not respond appropriately? (Verses 89–90.)
- What part was prayer to play in seeking help? (Verse 92.)
- When was the last time you prayed for government officials?

Share the following statement by Gordon B. Hinckley:

"I know of no better way to inculcate love for country than for parents to pray before their children for the land in which we live, invoking the blessings of the Almighty upon it that it may be preserved in liberty and in peace. I know of no better way to build within the hearts of our children a much-needed respect for authority than remembering in the daily supplications of the family the President and the Congress and others who carry the burdens of government." ("Except the Lord Build the House," *Improvement Era,* January 1964, 56.)

DOCTRINE AND COVENANTS 102: CHURCH DISCIPLINARY COUNCILS

Historical background: On February 12, 1834, Joseph Smith held a council meeting of high priests and elders. The Prophet taught the brethren about the importance of councils and how they should be conducted. He stated that, "no man is capable of judging a matter, in council, unless his own heart is pure; and that we are frequently so filled with prejudice [narrow-mindedness], . . . that we are not capable of passing right decisions." (Joseph Smith, History of the Church, 2:25–26.) Council members should seek the Spirit as they make appropriate decisions and discipline church members. Notice how the Lord's plan protects the Church and members who are accused of transgression.

Doctrine and Covenants 102:1–2
What is the purpose of a high council?

 Ask your family to answer the following questions:

- What are some reasons people have to go to court?
- How does the court decide what punishment should be given a person who is found guilty? (It depends on the severity of the law that was broken.)
- What happens to a Church member who is accused of serious wrongdoing?

Explain to your family that when members commit serious sin it is sometimes necessary for Church leaders to hold a "disciplinary council." Invite one family member to read aloud the historical background above and another to read aloud D&C 102:1–2. Identify the reasons given for the organization of a stake high council. Explain that as the Church grew, other stakes were organized with high councils. Read the following statement to your family,

"Many high councils exist in the Church at the present time, there being one in every Stake of Zion. . . . The plan of settling disputes . . . among brethren, which the Prophet was then [February 17, 1834] inspired to introduce has grown with the growth of the Church, and the high council has performed an important mission in the years which have followed. . . . The rules which the Prophet established to control its proceedings under divine guidance were delivered to it at the time of organization, and they, speaking of all the high councils which have since been organized, are still governed by them." (George Q. Cannon, *Life of Joseph Smith*, 154–55.)

Discuss as a family ways your high council performs "an important mission" for the members of your stake. If a family member has served on a high council, have him share his feelings about his experience.

Doctrine and Covenants 102:3–23
How is a disciplinary council organized?

Before scripture study cut a sheet of paper into twelve small squares. Label each one with a number from 1 to 12. Place the squares of paper in a bowl. Read together the first part of D&C 102:3 and look for what is needed first to organize a council. Ask:

- Who were the original presidents?
- What does D&C 102:9–10 teach about those who serve as presidents?

Choose a family member to represent the president and have him or her sit at the head of the kitchen table. Then read together again D&C 102:3 and look for what is needed next. Ask:

- How many high counselors are needed?
- What instructions are given to these high counselors in D&C 102:4, 6–7, 12?

Have the other family members sit evenly on each side of the kitchen table as members of the high council. Invite them to imagine that a member accused of serious sin has been brought before them and they have to consider the case. Ask the questions below as your family searches for answers in D&C 102:12–23.

- According to verse 12, what should we do first? Why? (Have family members draw numbers from the bowl.)
- According to verses 13–17, whom will half of you represent? (Verse 17.)
- Why is it important for half of the council to speak for the accused and half against?
- Does the person being accused or the accuser ever get to speak in the disciplinary council? (Yes—see verse 19.)
- After the evidence is heard, who makes the final decision and how is it made? (Verse 19.)
- According to verses 20–23, what will happen if an error is discovered?

Read the following to your family:

"We understand why some feel we reject them. That is not true. We *do not* reject you, only immoral behavior. We *cannot* reject you, for you are the sons and daughters of God. We *will not* reject you, because we love you (see Heb. 12:6–9; Rom. 3:19; Hel. 15:3; D&C 95:1).

"You may even feel that we do not love you. That also is not true. Parents know, and one day you will know, that there are times when parents and we who lead the Church must extend *tough* love when failing to teach and to warn and to discipline is to destroy.

"We did not make the rules; they were revealed as commandments. We do not cause nor can we prevent the consequences if you disobey the moral laws (see D&C 101:78)." (President Boyd K. Packer, *Ensign*, November 2000, 72.)

Testify to your family that a Church disciplinary council is a council of love and is the Lord's way of helping the offender to repent.

DOCTRINE AND COVENANTS 103: "REDEEMING ZION"

Historical background: "The high council of the Church met February 24, 1834, at the house of the Prophet for the purpose of receiving the message . . . from the brethren in Missouri . . . on conditions among the exiles [saints] driven from Jackson County. . . . The brethren there were anxious to know how and by what means Zion was to be redeemed. In Clay County they had been able to obtain food and raiment from the citizens in exchange for their labor, but the idea of being driven from their homes pained them, and they desired to know what the Lord would direct in the matter of reinstating them in their lands." (Joseph Fielding Smith, Church History and Modern Revelation, 1:481–82.) This revelation gives instructions concerning this matter and the organization of what came to be called Zion's Camp. Look for the reasons the Lord gave for allowing the Saints to be driven from their homes.

Doctrine and Covenants 103:1–40
How shall Zion be redeemed?

Write "ZION'S CAMP" in large letters on a paper. Show it to your family and tell them you are going to do an activity to help them learn about Zion's Camp. First have a family member read the historical background above.

Explain that you are going to read statements from D&C 103 that will have missing words and they will be required to fill in the blanks. Each answer begins with a corresponding letter from "ZION'S CAMP." Tell them to figure out the word(s) for each blank, and also identify the verse in D&C 103 where they found the answer. Have the first person to find the answers read the verse aloud. After each verse is read, discuss the accompanying questions and share the quotations provided:

Z—"The Redemption of (<u>Zion</u>) must needs come by power." (Have them look for that phrase and find the missing word. See verse 15.) To help your family understand that verse, ask:

- Who will provide this power?
- Why would the Lord not want the Saints to try and save Zion all by themselves?

Share the following from Orson Pratt: "When we go back to Jackson County, we are to go back with power. Do you suppose that God will reveal his power among an unsanctified people, who have no regard nor respect for his laws and institutions but who are filled with covetousness? No. When God shows forth his power among the Latter-day Saints, it will be because there is a union of feeling in regard to doctrine, and in regard to everything that God has placed in their hands; and not only a union, but a sanctification on their part." (*Journal of Discourses* 15:361.)

I—"After much tribulation, as (<u>I</u>) have said . . . cometh the blessing." (Verse 12.)

- Why do you think the Lord gives us the blessings only after we have faithfully endured the trials?
- You, or another family member, might tell about some adversity or trial you have faced and the blessings received by overcoming it.

O—"Ye shall not go up unto the land of Zion until you have (<u>obtained</u>) a hundred of the strength of my house." (Verse 34.) Ask:

- Did the Lord really need the help of at least one hundred Saints to save those in Missouri from the mobs? Could He save them by Himself? (Of course He could.)
- What does this teach us about what the Lord expects us to do about our problems? (We must do our part. We cannot expect the Lord to do it all for us.)

N—By hearkening to all the words of the Lord "they shall (<u>never</u>) cease to prevail [succeed] until the kingdoms of the world are subdued under my feet." (Verse 7.)

- Write the following sentence on your paper that has "ZION'S CAMP" at the top: "If I am (__), I will succeed in overcoming all my trials." Using what the Lord said in verse 7, have your family suggest what the missing word would be. (Obedient.) Invite them to write that statement or principle in their scriptures or in their journals.

S—"They were set to be a light unto the world, and to be the (<u>saviors</u>) of men." (Verse 9.) Ask, "What can we do in our family to be 'saviors of men'"?

Share the following statement by Elder Carlos E. Asay: "One of the grandest concepts in the gospel of Jesus Christ is the concept that men can and should be more than passive observers in the cause of saving souls. One Church leader taught: 'In our preexistent state . . . we made a certain agreement with the Almighty. . . . We agreed . . . to be not only saviors for ourselves but measurably, saviors for the whole human family. We went into a partnership with the Lord. The working out of the plan became then not merely the Father's work, and the Savior's work, but also our work.' (John A. Widtsoe, *Utah Genealogical and Historical Magazine,* October 1934, p. 189)" (*Ensign,* May 1980, 42.)

C—Saints in Missouri were (<u>chastened</u>) "because they did not hearken altogether unto the precepts and (<u>commandments</u>)." (Verse 4.)

- Read also verses 5–8 and discuss as a family the part obedience plays in the redemption of Zion.
- Remind your family of the principle statement written on your "ZION'S CAMP" paper. (Obedience.)

A—"Let no man be (<u>afraid</u>) to lay down his life for my sake." (Verse 27.)

- Read also Mark 8:34–38 and discuss why we should not be afraid to give our all to the Lord.

M—The Lord "will raise up unto my people a (man), who shall lead them like as (Moses) led the children of Israel." (Verse 16.)

- Ask your family who in the Church is like unto Moses. Share the following insight: "The man like unto Moses in the Church is the President of the Church." (John A. Widtsoe, *Evidences and Reconciliations*, 197.)

P—"All victory and glory is brought to pass . . . through your diligence, faithfulness and (prayers) of faith." (Verse 36.)

- Ask your family what this verse teaches about achieving our righteous goals and desires.
- Show your family again the principle statement written on your "ZION'S CAMP" paper and ask them what they think the Lord is trying to teach us. (Obedience.)

Discuss the kinds of things your family members should do to be more Zion-like so they can be blessed in overcoming all their trials.

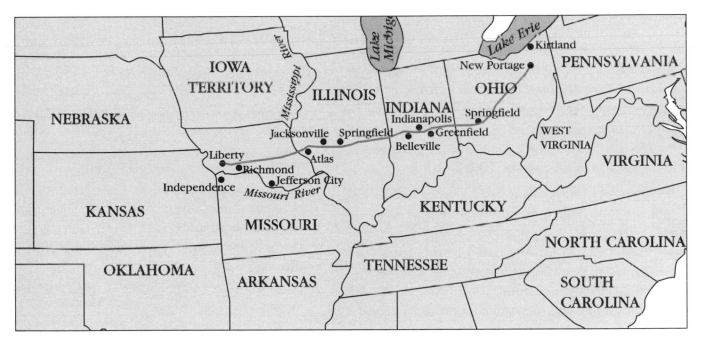

The route of Zion's Camp to Missouri.

DOCTRINE AND COVENANTS 104: THE UNITED ORDER

Historical background: *"The mob spirit in Missouri at the beginning of the year 1834, continued to be most bitter and murderous towards members of the Church, and had reached out and had entered the hearts of many in and around Kirtland. . . .*

"The Church being in dire distress financially, brethren had been sent out to see if they could not collect funds for its relief, both in Kirtland and for Zion. . . . In the minutes of a conference held at Norton, Medina County, Ohio, the deliverance of Zion was earnestly discussed. The Prophet Joseph Smith who was present said in the course of his remarks that 'if Zion is not delivered, the time is near when all of this Church, wherever they may be found, will be persecuted and destroyed in like manner,' that is in the manner in which the saints in Jackson County were destroyed. Destruction in this sense means to be persecuted, mobbed and scattered, their property being lost to them.

"On the 10th of April, a council of the United Order was held. It was there agreed that the Order, as it was then organized, be dissolved, and each member have his stewardship set off to him. Previously to this time, the United Order of Zion and of Kirtland stood as one unit. On April 23, 1834, the Prophet received an important revelation concerning the 'Order of the Church for the benefit of the poor.' ("D&C 104:1")" (Joseph Fielding Smith, Church History and Modern Revelation, 3:22–23.) As you study this revelation look for how the Lord feels about caring for the poor and needy.

Doctrine and Covenants 104:1–10
Blessing or cursing?

Read the historical background for D&C 104 and D&C 78 with your family. Discuss what the United Order was, and why it needed to be dissolved in Kirtland at this time. The following statement may be helpful:

"The United Order is not a communal system; it is not one under which all things are held in common. Rather, after a person has made his consecration, the Lord's agent forthwith reconveys [gives back] to the donor 'as much as is sufficient for himself and family' (D. & C. 42:32), each 'according to his family, according to his circumstances and his wants and needs' (D. & C. 51:3), 'inasmuch as his wants are just.' (D. & C. 82:17.)" (Bruce R. McConkie, *Mormon Doctrine*, 813.)

Take turns reading D&C 104:1–10. Ask:

- What were some reasons the United Order needed to be dissolved at this time?
- What blessings did the Saints sacrifice by not keeping their covenants?

- What are some commandments you are bound to keep today?
- What blessings have you received by keeping the commandments?
- What consequences have you felt when you disobey?
- Why do you think the Lord urges us so strongly to keep our covenants?

Doctrine and Covenants 104:11–18
Who owns the earth and all things therein?

Ask your family to imagine they were to receive a new pet puppy today. Have them make a list of some required duties to care for a pet. Talk about the responsibilities we have to care for our possessions, including our home, bedrooms, cars, and bodies. Ask your family to define the word "stewardship." ("The careful and responsible management of something entrusted to one's care." [*Merriam Webster's Collegiate Dictionary*, s.v. "stewardship."])

Read D&C 104:11–14 and ask:

- To whom do "all things" actually belong?
- Who do we receive our stewardships from?
- To whom do we report about our stewardships?
- If all that we possess really belongs to the Lord, how should we care for everything we have?

Ask each family member to silently read D&C 104:15–18. Ask them to look for the Lord's plan to provide for His children. Ask family members to share one thing from their reading they think is significant and beautiful.

Share your testimony that the earth is full, and there are plenty of resources for everyone, if we will share of our means and use our stewardships wisely. Share the following insight from President Harold B. Lee:

"The rich being made low isn't communistic; it isn't socialistic. It means that those who have leadership, who have skills, who have means, who are willing to contribute, can be put to work with the one who is in need.

"Here are some things that can be done. We can find employment for the unemployed and aid members in times of adversity . . . The ideal is to teach your new priesthood members how to rally round rather than turn the whole job over to some public relief agency.

"Encourage the putting aside for a rainy day in individual homes. That means teaching thrift, frugality, and avoidance of debt. Certainly that is a program that we ought to foster everywhere." (*Stand Ye in Holy Places*, 264.)

Talk with your family about (1) what you can better do to care for your individual stewardships; and (2) what you can do to help someone in need of resources. Make plans to carry out and accomplish your ideas.

Doctrine and Covenants 104:19–46
Who received what stewardship?

Seat your family around a table. Play a matching game with your family by scattering the all the cards outlined below face down on the table. Take turns letting a person turn over two cards. When they do, have them search D&C 104:20–46 to see if the two cards match. If they have a matching pair, they can place those cards in their own "personal pile." If the cards do not match they need to turn them back over. Continue taking turns until every match is found. You could offer a reward for the person that finds the most matches. (Note: The names and stewardships are matched correctly below.)

Write the following names on separate 3 by 5 cards or slips of paper:	Write the following stewardships on separate 3 by 5 cards or slips of paper:
Sidney Rigdon	The lot where he lives plus the tannery
Martin Harris	John Johnson's lot
Frederick G. Williams	The place where he now dwells
Oliver Cowdery	The lot next to the printing office (lot #1) plus the lot on which his father resides
John Johnson	The house in which he lives
Newel K. Whitney	The houses and lots where he now resides, the mercantile plus the corner lot and the ashery
Joseph Smith Jr.	The lot laid off for the building of my house and also the inheritance upon which his father resides

Teach your family that a steward is one who takes care of property or other possessions that belong to someone else. Explain that the individuals listed above were given stewardships by the Lord to manage His affairs on the earth. (For an explanation of "stewardship" see the teaching idea for Doctrine and Covenants 104:11–18 above.)

Talk about these two questions:

- What stewardships (callings) have our family members been given?
- What do you think the Lord expects of us concerning these stewardships?

Doctrine and Covenants 104:47–53
Why was there a division?

Have your family search D&C 104:47–53 and find out what was divided. After they have discovered that "the United Order of the Stake of Zion, the City of Kirtland" was divided from "the United Order of the City of Zion," ask why they think this happened. Have them find the answer in D&C 104:51–52. Read the following statement:

"The brethren in Kirtland were not to suffer on account of the losses inflicted by the mob on the Saints in Zion. As an independent organization, they would be in a position to render financial aid to the exiles. As a part of the organization in Zion, the financial disaster engendered by mob rule would have affected them also, and they might have been unable to come to the aid of their brethren." (*Doctrine and Covenants Commentary*, Hyrum M. Smith and Janne M. Sjodahl, 674.)

Discuss with your family how staying out of financial debt ourselves helps us to be better able to help others in need.

Doctrine and Covenants 104:58–66
The value of the scriptures

 Show your family the scriptures of a family member who has read and marked his or her scriptures a lot and discuss the following questions:

- How much does a set of scriptures cost?
- If you offered someone who had invested a lot of time in his or her scriptures a new set of scriptures if they would give you their marked ones, what do you think they would say?
- Suppose your scriptures were the only ones your family could ever have, how valuable would they be?

Read together D&C 104:58–66 and use the following questions to help your family understand them.

- For what purpose did the Lord command the Church leaders to organize themselves? (Verse 58.)
- For what two important purposes did scriptures need to be made available? (Verse 59.)
- What were Church members to do with the money (called the "avails") that would come from the printing of the scriptures? (It was to go in the "sacred treasury"—see verses 60, 66.)
- What were the funds in the treasury to be used for? (Sacred purposes such as additional printings—see verses 63–65.)

Remind your family of the story of Nephi and his brothers being sent back to Jerusalem to get the plates of brass, which were their scriptures (see 1 Nephi 3–4). Ask your family members if they remember what the Lord told Nephi about the worth of those plates. (They were worth Laban's life—see 1 Nephi 4:13.) Tell your family how you feel about the scriptures and their value to your family.

Doctrine and Covenants 104:67–77
What is the other treasury?

Bring a box or bag of play money to family scripture study. Label your box or bag "Treasury." Give the money to your family in the following denominations: $1.00, $5.00, $10.00,

$20.00, $50.00, and $100.00. Talk to your family about what they would like to do with the money given them. After your discussion, ask them to return the money to the "treasury" and seal it up with tape.

Ask everyone to silently read D&C 104:67–72 and have them tell you how these verses relate to your activity. Ask:

- How is money to be acquired for this treasury? (Verses 67–69.)
- Who does the money in the treasury belong to? (Verses 70–71.)
- Who gives permission for money to be removed from the treasury? (Verse 71.)

Ask everyone to identify one goal they would like to accomplish that will require money. Also ask them to decide how much money it will cost. Unseal the "treasury" and give them what they have asked for.

Invite family members to silently read D&C 104:72–77 and then explain why you gave them what they asked for. Ask:

- How would you feel about living under this system?
- Do you think that there would always be money for you to magnify your calling?
- How is magnifying our callings like taking care of our stewardships?
- Would you be willing to return the excess money to the treasury? Why or why not?
- How would returning excess money benefit others?
- What conditions would have to exist to stop you from obtaining money from the treasury? (Verse 74.)
- How long would you be able to obtain money from the treasury? (Verse 75.)
- How long can the treasurer maintain his job? (Verses 76–77.)

Ask a member of your family to read D&C 104:71–72. Ask what the law of common consent is. Share the following insight:

"A person's inheritance was to consist of personal property, to be operated permanently and freely for the benefit of the person and the family. Should the person withdraw from the order, the inheritance could be taken with him, but the person would have no claim upon surplus donations or possessions initially placed in the common treasury (D&C 51:3–6). At the end of a year or set period, the member who had earned more than needed for his family would voluntarily place the surplus in the common treasury. Substantial profits were to be administered by the group rather than by one individual. Men and women who, despite diligence, had a loss from their operations would have the loss made up by the general treasury for another start, or they might—with consent—be placed in some activity better suited to their gifts. In short, the general treasury was to establish every person in a preferred field and was to care for those unable to profit from their inheritance. The general treasury, holding members' surpluses, would also finance public works and make possible all community enterprises decided upon by the group." (*Encyclopedia of Mormonism*, s.v., "consecration.")

Doctrine and Covenants 104:78–86
Why should we get out of debt?

Make a list with your family of the kinds of things your family is making payments on instead of owning free and clear.

Divide your family into two groups. Ask both groups to search D&C 104:78–86. Ask one of the groups to find all of the reasons why the Lord wants the Saints to pay their debts. Have the other group find all of the blessings that will come to the Saints for working toward and achieving the goal of being debt free. Read the following statement:

"It is a rule of our financial and economic life in all the world that interest is to be paid on borrowed money. May I say something about interest?

"Interest never sleeps nor sickens nor dies; it never goes to the hospital; it works on Sundays and holidays; it never takes a vacation; it never visits nor travels; it takes no pleasure; it is never laid off work nor discharged from employment; it never works on reduced hours; it never has short crops nor droughts; it never pays taxes; it buys no food; it wears no clothes; it is unhoused and without home and so has no repairs, no replacements, no shingling, plumbing, painting, or whitewashing; it has neither wife, children, father, mother, nor kinfolk to watch over and care for; it has no expense of living; it has neither weddings nor births nor deaths; it has no love, no sympathy; it is as hard and soulless as a granite cliff. Once in debt, interest is your companion every minute of the day and night; you cannot shun it or slip away from it; you cannot dismiss it; it yields neither to entreaties, demands, or orders; and whenever you get in its way or cross its course or fail to meet its demands, it crushes you.

"So much for the interest we pay. Whoever borrows should understand what interest is; it is with them every minute of the day and night." (J. Reuben Clark Jr., Conference Report, April 1938, 102.)

Ask these questions:

- What impressed you most about President Clark's statement on the nature of interest?
- Why do you think the Lord wants us to be debt free?
- What did you find in President Clark's message and D&C 104:78–86 that motivates you to be debt free?
- What can we do better in our family to become debt free?

DOCTRINE AND COVENANTS 105: ZION'S CAMP RETURNS HOME

Historical background: *The purpose of Zion's Camp was to help the Saints in Missouri regain the property that had been taken from them. Zion's Camp left Kirtland, Ohio, within the first week of May 1834. They traveled almost 1,000 miles arriving in Missouri in early June 1834. The Governor of Missouri, Daniel Dunklin, had indicated he would help the Saints get their property back, but when Zion's Camp marched into Missouri he broke his promise. Joseph and his men pressed forward until they reached the Fishing River, where they made camp. While there Joseph Smith received the revelation recorded in Doctrine and Covenants 105. Look for what the Lord teaches His Saints about what is required to establish Zion.*

Doctrine and Covenants 105:1–13
Zion's Camp and the redemption of Zion

Choose one family member to read the section heading to D&C 105 and another to read the historical background above. Divide your family into two groups and give one group a sheet of paper labeled *Zion's Camp—D&C 105:7–13* and the other a sheet labeled *Redemption of Zion—D&C 105:1–6*. Have each group read and discuss together the verses listed on their paper and write the Lord's council given on their topic. Have each group report what they learned. It might be helpful to discuss the following questions:

Redemption of Zion—D&C 105:1–6

Ask:

- What stopped the Redemption of Zion? (Verses 2–3.)
- What laws must be lived if Zion is to be built up? (Verses 4–5.)
- Why are the Lord's people chastened? (Verse 6.)

Zion's Camp—D&C 105:6–13 (written to Zion's Camp)

Ask:

- Who was not under condemnation? (Verse 7.)
- What did the Lord counsel Zion's Camp to do? (Verse 9.)
- According to verses 10–12, how can the Saints prepare for Zion? (Invite family members to mark ideas as they find them.)

Discuss as a family how you can establish Zion in your home. Share your testimony that you can establish Zion through obedience to the Lord's commandments.

Doctrine and Covenants 105:14–19
The Lord will fight our battles

Ask your family to think of a time in the scriptures when the Lord helped an individual or His people to win a fight or battle (Samson, David and Goliath, Gideon, Daniel in the lion's den, Nephi and Laban, Israel and Jericho, stripling warriors, and so on). Why does the Lord sometimes fight our battles?

Invite a family member to read the section heading for D&C 105 and then read together D&C 105:14–19. Ask:

- The men in Zion's Camp numbered just over 100. What chance do you think they had to win the battle against hundreds of mobbers in Missouri?
- What promise did the Lord give them? (Verse 14.)
- According to verse 19, why might the Lord fight their battles?
- What was the reason Zion's Camp needed to march all the way to Fishing Run? (Verse 19.)

Share the following story:

"On the morning of the 19th of June, the Prophet feeling that they were in an unsafe place commanded that the camp move forward without delay. They passed through Richmond, where a black woman called to Luke Johnson. He went to hear what she had to say and she said, 'There is a company of men lying in wait here, who are calculating to kill you this morning as you pass through.' The company . . . attempted to continue their journey, but had not gone far before a wagon broke down, the wheels ran off another, and many incidents occurred to hinder their progress. That night they had traveled only to an elevated piece of ground between Little and Big Fishing rivers. While they were making their camp five men with guns rode into the camp and told them they would 'see hell before morning.' This was said with accompanying oaths and blasphemy. They stated that armed men were gathering from Ray and Clay counties to join those from Jackson, and they had sworn the destruction of the camp. During that day about two hundred men from Jackson County made arrangements to cross the Missouri River near the mouth of Fishing River, and be ready to meet the Richmond mob near the Fishing River ford. . . . While this was going on . . . wind and thunder and a rising cloud indicated an approaching storm. Shortly after, it began to rain and hail and the storm increased in intensity. An hour before sundown the mobbers commenced firing a cannon, but when the storm broke they sought shelter under their wagons, in hollow trees and wherever they could hide. Their ammunition became soaked, and when morning came they 'took the back track for Independence, [Missouri].' Very little hail fell in the [Mormon] camp. The brethren found shelter in an old meetinghouse while in the camp of the mobbers hailstones and lumps of ice cut down trees, and crops and trees were twisted out of shape. The water in Little Fishing River rose thirty feet in that many minutes. It was reported that one mobber was killed by lightning and another had his hand torn off when his horse drew his hand between logs of a corn crib. Some out of this wicked mob said if that was the way God fought for the Mormons, they might as well go about their business." (Joseph Fielding Smith, *Church History and Modern Revelation*, 2:1–3.)

Ask:

- How did the Lord fight for Zion's Camp?
- In what ways does He fight for the Saints today?
- What do you think we need to do to be worthy of having the Lord fight for us?

Invite family members to share ways the Lord has fought their battles.

Doctrine and Covenants 105:23–41
Make a "to do" list for establishing Zion in our day

Show a map of the United States to your family (see the map on page 298 of your Triple Combination). Ask your family to point out where the Saints will one day gather and build a latter-day city of Zion. Discuss reasons why the early Saints were not able to establish Zion in their day (see D&C 105:1–6). What do you think members of the Church need to do today in order to establish Zion? Have your family review D&C 105:23–27, 31–32 and mark those things the Lord listed in this revelation to the Prophet Joseph

Smith. Then discuss those things family members marked in their scriptures. You may find the following questions helpful in your discussion:

- How might being "faithful, and prayerful, and humble" help the Saints prepare to establish Zion? (Verse 23.)
- Why do you think it would be a mistake to boast about your religion? (Verse 24.)
- Why does the Lord want the Saints to find "favor in the eyes of the people?" (So "the army of Israel" will have time to become "very great.")
- What will the Lord do to modern Israel that he did for ancient Israel? (Verse 27.)
- According to Verses 31–32, what will the nations of the earth eventually say about Zion?

Read together the Lord's promise found in D&C 105:37. Ask your family what they must do to have the power to build Zion. (They must "follow the counsel" just given.) Have your family create a "To Do" list from the things they marked in their scriptures. Write this list on a sheet of paper and tape it to your refrigerator as a reminder.

DOCTRINE AND COVENANTS 106: MY SERVANT WARREN A. COWDERY

Historical background: In 1834, the Prophet Joseph Smith was commanded to "gather the strength of my house" (D&C 103:22) to participate in Zion's Camp. Parley P. Pratt went with him on this recruiting mission. (See D&C 103:37.) A short time later, in an entry dated "Sunday, March 9," the Prophet Joseph Smith recorded:

"We preached in a school house, and had great attention. We found a few disciples who were firm in the faith; and, after meeting found many believing and could hardly get away from them, and appointed a meeting in Freedom [New York] for Monday the 10th, and stayed at Mr. Warren A. Cowdery's, where we were blessed with a full enjoyment of temporal and spiritual blessings, even all we needed, or were worthy to receive." (History of the Church, 2:42.)

While it is uncertain who was appointed to lead the branch at that time, the revelation in Doctrine and Covenants 106 called Warren Cowdery to be the "presiding high priest" over this growing branch. (See D&C 106:1.) The Prophet Joseph Smith's record may give us the reason this call didn't come earlier. After spending most of the summer leading Zion's Camp to Missouri (see historical background to D&C 105), the Prophet tried to get back to all his duties in Kirtland. He wrote:

"No month ever found me more busily engaged than November [1834]; but as my life consisted of activity and unyielding exertions, I made this my rule: When the Lord commands, do it. . . . I continued my labors daily, . . . and received the following: [D&C 106]." (History of the Church, 2:170.) Notice the several messages of comfort in this revelation.

Doctrine and Covenants 106:1–8
Applying the scriptures

Share the following situations with your family—one at a time. After each, have family members search D&C 106 to find principles providing help, insight, or answers for that situation. Choose one family member to give an explanation as if he or she were talking to the person in the situation, using some part of D&C 106. After each situation, discuss the scriptures and explanation to provide additional insight into the truths found in D&C 106.

BIOGRAPHICAL SKETCH: WARREN A. COWDERY

Warren Cowdery was born in October 1788. He learned about the Church from his younger brother, Oliver, and was baptized in late 1831. (See Susan Easton Black, *Who's Who in the Doctrine and Covenants,* 77.)

From time to time, Brother Cowdery allowed his pride to get the best of him. For example, while serving as branch president in Freedom, he "preferred charges against the Twelve Apostles for their alleged failure to teach the Saints while in Freedom." (Daniel H. Ludlow, *A Companion to Your Study of the Doctrine and Covenants,* 1:548.) Although on this occasion Warren made an apology, he eventually lost confidence in the Church and its leaders and left it about the same time as his brother, Oliver, in 1838. He never returned and died in Ohio in 1851. (See Susan Easton Black, *Who's Who in the Doctrine and Covenants,* 78.)

Situation 1: Jill's bishop asked her to serve as the president of her young women's class. She will probably say yes because she doesn't want to disappoint the bishop. However, she doesn't really plan to do much in this calling since she is in several advanced classes at school and has an after-school job to earn money for college. In fact, she seldom attends the weekly activities because she is at work. She feels like her family's financial situation requires her to put in as many hours as she can and earn as much money as possible for college.

Now invite your family to search D&C 106 for the Lord's counsel that would apply to this situation, for example verse 3.

In addition to D&C 106:3, draw your family's attention to footnote 3a (the promise of the Savior in Matthew 6:33). Ask:

- Is the Lord asking us to ignore temporal matters?
- What is He saying? (That we should make important things our priority, and then the rest will work out.)
- What does the Lord promise us when we trust Him on these matters?

Share with your family the following from President Ezra Taft Benson:

"When we put God first, all other things fall into their proper place or drop out of our lives. Our love of the Lord will govern the claims for our affection, the demands on our time, the interests we pursue, and the order of our priorities." (*Ensign,* May 1988, 4.)

Situation 2: Sam said he didn't intend to go to priesthood meeting because he knew the lesson was going to be on the Second Coming. "I don't even want to think about it," he said. "It just scares me. In fact, sometimes studying about the Second Coming makes me wonder why I should plan ahead in life, save money for the future, or train for a career." (See verses 4–5.)

Have your family cross-reference 1 Thessalonians 5:1–11 to D&C 106:4–5 for more explanation on the phrases "thief in the night" and "children of light" referred to in this revelation. As you read 1 Thessalonians as a family, identify how Paul says the time leading to the Second Coming will be different for "the children of light." You might also want to share the following from Elder Boyd K. Packer:

"We live in troubled times—very troubled times. We hope, we pray, for better days. But that is not to be. The prophecies tell us that. We will not as a people, as families, or as individuals be exempt from the trials to come. No one will be spared the trials common to home and family, work, disappointment, grief, health, aging, ultimately death. . . .

"We need not live in fear of the future. We have every reason to rejoice and little reason to fear. If we follow the promptings of the Spirit, we will be safe, whatever the future holds. We will be shown what to do." (*Ensign,* May 2000, 7–9.)

Assure your family that the Lord will be with and strengthen those who are faithful to him. Although we may not know the exact time of the Savior's coming, it will not overtake us "as a thief in the night" if we are faithful.

Situation 3: David had not kept the commandments as he should and had not been active in the Church for a while. In talking with his home teachers he admitted he wasn't really happy and wished he could change, but believed it was pointless to do so. "I've done too many bad things. What would God think if I came back to Church after all I've done? I don't think I could ever really be a strong member." (See verses 6–8.)

You may want to have your family cross-reference D&C 18:10–13 to D&C 106:6 concerning how the Lord feels about those who repent. The promise in D&C 78:17–18 may also be a second witness to the truth in D&C 106:7–8 that the Lord will have mercy on us, give us greater and greater strength to grow spiritually and stand strong, and that we can ultimately inherit his kingdom—if we will trust Him and receive his grace. Invite your family members to tell what they learned in D&C 106 that impressed them the most.

DOCTRINE AND COVENANTS 107: PRIESTHOOD RESPONSIBILITIES

Historical background: The Twelve Apostles had just been called on their first mission to the Eastern States. Some, feeling unworthy and ill-prepared, asked the Prophet Joseph to inquire of the Lord for them. Section 107 is the Lord's answer. Concerning this section Elder John A. Widtsoe said:

"One hundred years ago this spring great things happened in this Church; the greatest, as an evidence of God's guiding hand over his Church, occurred on March 28th, 1835. . . . On that day The Church of Jesus Christ of Latter-day Saints received a revelation which is one of the most remarkable documents in the possession of man. It stands absolutely unique; there is none like it . . . it sets forth, in plainness and simplicity, the organization of the quorums of the priesthood; the mutual relations of the quorums to one another . . . and there is a wonderful picture of the early history of the priesthood. . . .

"It is so comprehensive in its brevity, so magnificent in its simplicity, that we have found no occasion, up to the present, to wish that it might have been more complete." (Conference Report, April 1935, 80–82.) As you study this revelation, think about how impossible it would be for Joseph Smith to write such a document without the Lord's help.

Doctrine and Covenants 107:1–4
Why is the priesthood called after Melchizedek?

Play the "hangman" game using the word *Melchizedek*. After your family has guessed the word, ask if anyone can explain why the priesthood is called "Melchizedek." Invite your family to read D&C 107:1–4. Ask:

- What was the priesthood called before Melchizedek?
- Why was it changed?

Have your family turn to "Melchizedek" in the Bible Dictionary (page 730) and read it to learn more about this great high priest.

Doctrine and Covenants 107:1–20
What is the difference between the Aaronic and Melchizedek Priesthoods?

Invite your family to suggest a definition for the word *priesthood*. Then read the following: "The priesthood is the power and authority of God delegated to man." (Merrill J. Bateman, *Ensign*, November 2003, 50.) Ask your family to read D&C 107:1 and describe the differences between the Aaronic and Melchizedek Priesthoods. Get two sheets of paper and write "Aaronic" at the top of one and "Melchizedek" at the top of the other. Divide your family into two groups and give each group one of the sheets of paper. Tell each group to search D&C 107:1–20 and write down the important truths they discover. After the groups are finished, invite one person from each group to share with the other group what they learned. The following questions may help your family understand these verses:

- Which priesthood has the right to officiate in all the offices in the Church? (Verses 8–9.)
- Which priesthood has the authority to administer outward ordinances? (Verses 13–14; 20.)
- Who is the presidency of the Aaronic priesthood? (Verse 15.)
- Which priesthood holds the keys to the spiritual blessings of the Church? (Verses 18–19.)
- What blessings that we now enjoy would be unavailable to us if the priesthood had not been restored?

Doctrine and Covenants 107:16–17, 68–70, 76

"Literal descendant of Aaron"

Have your family read D&C 107:16–17, 68–70, 76 and identify what these verses have in common. (They mention the literal descendants of Aaron.) Read the following story:

"I remember a man, . . . came into my office, and after a few pleasantries and a little introduction, he said to me as though to startle me, 'I'm a literal descendant of Aaron.' Well, I said, 'I have always been curious to see a literal descendant of Aaron.' And when he saw that I wasn't too much impressed, he said, 'And I have come to claim my right to be the Presiding Bishop of the Church.' 'Well, now,' I said, 'that is very well, but there is just one little matter that you have overlooked.' And he wanted to know what that was. And then I read to him from the revelations [that] a literal descendant of Aaron may serve without counselors, if called by the President of the Church and ordained to that office (see D&C 68:20; 107:76). 'Now you just go back home and wait until the President of the Church sends for you.' . . . He failed to understand that only through that one man who is His mouthpiece on earth will the Lord reveal instructions for His church." (*The Teachings of Harold B. Lee,* 545.)

Ask:

- Who identifies and calls those who are "literal descendants of Aaron"?
- Why is this important?
- How does the Lord provide a bishop when "literal descendants of Aaron" cannot be found?
- Knowing how your bishop was called, what can you do to show respect for him and his sacred calling?

Doctrine and Covenants 107:21–35

Who is in the presiding quorums?

Before scripture study, obtain a copy of the May or November issue of the *Ensign* magazine (preferably a current one). Find the page with the pictures of the First Presidency, Quorum of Twelve, and General Authorities on one page (usually in the middle of the issue). Show your family this insert of pictures and do the following:

Read D&C 107:22 and ask:

- Who are the three presiding high priests in this picture?
- How are they "upheld"?
- What do we call them?

Read D&C 107:23–24, 33, 35 and ask:

- Who are the Twelve Apostles in this picture?
- How do they differ from other officers? (They are special witnesses of the name of Christ "in all the world.")
- The entire Quorum of the Twelve is equal in power and authority to which other quorum? (The First Presidency—see verse 24.)
- What are some of their responsibilities? (See verses 23, 33, and 35.)

Read D&C 107:25–26, 34 and ask:

- Who are the Seventy in this picture?
- How are they different from the other officers?
- Their quorum is equal in authority to which other quorum? (Quorum of the Twelve—see verse 26.)
- What are some of their responsibilities? (See verses 25 and 34.)

Read together D&C 107:27, 30–31 and list the Lord's counsel to these quorums as they make decisions. Ask:

- How would you describe the Lord's council to these quorums?
- What promise does the Lord give if they make decisions in His way? (See verse 31.)

To help explain the authority of the different quorums, share the following explanation: "There can never be two or three quorums of equal authority at the same time; therefore in the revelation where it reads that the Twelve Apostles form a quorum equal in authority with the First Presidency, and that the Seventies form a quorum equal in authority with the Twelve, it should be understood that this condition of equality could prevail only when the ranking quorum is no longer in existence, through death or otherwise. When the First Presidency becomes disorganized on the death of the President, then the Apostles become the presiding quorum, or council, of the Church with all the power to organize again the First Presidency, when they fall back again as the second ranking quorum of the Church. So with the Seventies, they would become equal only on the condition that the first two quorums ceased to exist." (Hyrum M. Smith and Janne M. Sjodahl, *Doctrine and Covenants Commentary*, 699–700.)

Ask your family to tell about a time when they were in the presence of one of these men or heard them testify and share how they felt. Testify to your family that these are men whom God has chosen to lead us.

Doctrine and Covenants 107:40–57
An account of the priesthood anciently

Ask a family member who holds the priesthood to tell who ordained him. Then ask from whom that person received the priesthood. Have the family member then trace his priesthood line of authority back as far as he can. He may have received the priesthood from his father and his father received it from his grandfather, etc.) Explain that every priesthood holder in the Church could eventually trace his line of authority back to Jesus Christ. An example of such a line of authority is found in D&C 107:40–52. Read those verses together and list each priesthood holder mentioned there, who ordained him, and how old the person was when he received the priesthood. Ask your family what this teaches us about how the Lord controls who receives His priesthood. (See Articles of Faith 1:5.)

Read together D&C 107:53–57. Ask:

- Who did Adam call to an important meeting at Adam-ondi-Ahman? (Verse 53.)
- What did Adam give them?
- Who else came to the meeting? (Verse 54.)
- What was Adam promised? (Verse 55.)
- What did Adam prophesy? (Verse 56.)
- What does this story teach us about the blessings of being a righteous priesthood holder?

Doctrine and Covenants 107:58–67; 85–98
What are a priesthood quorum's responsibilities?

Ask your family:

- What would happen in the United States if for some reason we lost both the President and Congress?
- Why is it important to have leadership at all levels of the government?
- What happens in the Church if we lose the prophet? The bishop?
- Why is leadership important in the Church?

Invite your family to name some important Church leadership positions. (Be sure to include president of the Church, apostles, seventies, stake presidents, bishops, fathers, mothers, etc.) Have your family search D&C 107:58–67 and mark the different priesthood quorums listed there. Ask who family members think the "President" is that is mentioned in verses 65–66. (The prophet and president of the Church.)

Write the following leadership positions on separate pieces of paper: Deacons Quorum President, Teachers Quorum President, Priests Quorum President, Elders Quorum President, and President of the High Priesthood. Divide the papers among family members and have them search D&C 107:85–98 to learn more about the duties of their assigned quorum president. Then have them share what they found. Ask for a volunteer to share a time when he or she saw a quorum president fulfill his duty.

Doctrine and Covenants 107:71–75
Why do we confess to a bishop?

Have your family imagine that they have a friend that has recently joined the Church. The friend cannot understand why a person might need to confess to a bishop. Take turns reading D&C 107:71–75 and look for an answer. Share the following statement:

"Those in sin must confess them. . . . That confession must be made first to him or her who has been most wronged by your acts. . . . If your act is secret and has resulted in injury to no one but yourself, your confession should be in secret. . . . Acts that may affect your standing in the Church, . . . are to be promptly confessed to the bishop whom the Lord has appointed as a shepherd over every flock and . . . to be a common judge in Israel. He may hear such confession in secret and deal justly and mercifully. . . . He that repents thus of his sins and altogether turns away therefrom, to return no more to a repetition thereof, is entitled to the promise of a forgiveness of his sins." (*The Teachings of Harold B. Lee,* 113.)

Have each family member write a letter to "the imaginary friend" explaining why a person would need to confess some sins to a bishop. After your family is finished, have family members read their letters. Testify to your family concerning the bishop's calling as a common judge in Israel.

Doctrine and Covenants 107:77–84
What is the highest council in the Church?

Write each of the following on a separate slip of paper: bishop and counselors; First Presidency and Quorum of Twelve; high council and stake presidency; and Area Presidencies. Scatter these slips of paper on the floor before you or on a table. Have your family place them in order from the lowest council to the highest council (bishop and counselors; high council and stake presidency; Area Presidencies; and First Presidency and Quorum of the Twelve).

Read with your family D&C 107:77–84. Ask:

- Why do you think some cases might be taken to the First Presidency?
- What happens after the First Presidency (the highest council) makes a decision? (It's final—see verse 80.)
- Why does it say that no one is exempt from this council? ("That all things may be done in order"—verse 84.)

Doctrine and Covenants 107:99–100
Do you know what your duty is?

Share the following story with your family:

"It is painful to imagine a shepherd feeding himself and letting the sheep go hungry. Yet I have seen many shepherds who feed their flocks. One was the president of a deacons quorum. One of his quorum members lived near my home. That neighbor boy had never attended a quorum meeting nor done anything with the members of his quorum. His stepfather was not a member, and his mother did not attend church.

"The presidency of his deacons quorum met in council one Sunday morning. Each week they were fed the good word of God by the fine adviser and teacher. In their presidency meeting, those 13-year-old shepherds remembered the boy who never came. They talked about how much he needed what they received. The president assigned his counselor to go after that wandering sheep.

"I knew the counselor, and I knew he was shy, and I knew the difficulty of the assignment, so I watched with wonder through my front window as the counselor trudged by my house, going up the road to the home of the boy who never came to church. The shepherd had his hands in his pockets. His eyes were on the ground. He walked slowly, the way you would if you weren't sure you wanted to get where you were headed. In 20 minutes or so, he came back down the road with the lost deacon walking by his side. That scene was repeated for a few more Sundays. Then the boy who had been lost and was found moved away.

"Now, that story seems unremarkable. It was just three boys sitting in a room around a small table. Then it was a boy walking up a road and coming back with another boy. But years later, I was in a stake conference, a continent away from the room in which that presidency had met in council. A gray-haired man came up to me and said quietly, 'My grandson lived in your ward years ago.' With tenderness, he told me of that boy's life. And then he asked if I could find that deacon who walked slowly up that road. And he wondered if I could thank him and tell him that his grandson, now grown to be a man, still

remembered." (Henry B. Eyring, *Ensign,* May 2001, 38–39.)

Ask:

- How did this young man do his duty?
- How hard do you think it was for him to do it?
- Who was blessed because he did his duty?

Invite your family to read and mark D&C 107:99–100. Ask:

- Where can a person go to learn his or her duty?
- Why is it important to be diligent in our responsibilities?
- What will happen if we don't learn our duties and perform them with diligence?

Identify the responsibilities of each family member and discuss ways you could improve in fulfilling your responsibilities.

DOCTRINE AND COVENANTS 108: "STRENGTHEN YOUR BRETHREN"

Historical background: Entries in the Prophet Joseph Smith's journal for December 25 and 26, 1835, are as follows:

"Friday, 25. Enjoyed myself at home with my family, all day, it being Christmas, the only time I have had this privilege so satisfactorily for a long period. . . .

"Saturday, 26.—Commenced again studying the Hebrew language, in company with Brothers Parrish and Williams. In the meantime, Brother Lyman Sherman came in, and requested to have the word of the Lord through me; 'for,' said he, 'I have been wrought upon to make known to you my feelings and desires, and was promised that I should have a revelation which should make known my duty.'" (History of the Church, 2:345.) The Lord's promise to Lyman Sherman was fulfilled as Joseph received this revelation the same day.

Doctrine and Covenants 108:1–3
Do you resist the Lord's voice?

Ask family members to silently read the first two and a half lines of D&C 108:1, inserting their names in the place of "Lyman." Talk about how it would feel to have the Lord say those words to you. Read together D&C 108:1–3. Ask:

- What had Lyman Sherman done to qualify for forgiveness? ("Obeyed my voice.")
- What was Lyman counseled to do no more?
- In what ways might we sometimes resist the Lord's voice?
- What was Lyman admonished to be more careful about? (Observing his vows.)
- What are vows?

Share the following:

"A vow is a solemn promise or pledge, especially one made to God in which the person dedicates himself to service or a way of life. The word is used in association with words having similar meanings, such as covenants, contracts, bonds, obligations, oaths, and performances. It can be rightly said that every person who has accepted membership into the Church has made vows whereby he will abide by the laws of that kingdom. . . . These covenants are to be observed 'in righteousness on all days and at all times.' (D&C 59:11.)" (Roy W. Doxey, *The Doctrine and Covenants Speaks,* 2:310.)

Ask family members:

- What vows have you made?
- How are you observing your vows? (If you have a young woman in your family you may want her to recite the Young Women theme and then talk about what it means with the family.)
- What was Lyman Sherman promised if he did carefully observe his vows? (Exceeding great blessings.)

Doctrine and Covenants 108:4–8
How can you strengthen your brethren?

Ask your family the following questions:

- What is the kindest thing you can remember someone doing for you?

- What is something another person did for you that helped you become a better person?

Read D&C 108:4–8 and ask what Lyman Sherman was asked to do by the Lord. Invite family members to consider if they are helping or hindering the Lord's work. Tell them that President Gordon B. Hinckley placed a broad application on this verse. In general conference of April 1982, President Hinckley, then a counselor in the First Presidency, quoted D&C 108:7 and said:

"We live in a society that feeds on criticism. Faultfinding is the substance of columnists and commentators, and there is too much of this among our own people. It is so easy to find fault, and to resist doing so requires much of discipline. But if as a people we will build and sustain one another, the Lord will bless us with the strength to weather every storm and continue to move forward through every adversity. The enemy of truth would divide us and cultivate within us attitudes of criticism which, if permitted to prevail, will only deter us in the pursuit of our great divinely given goal. We cannot afford to permit it to happen. We must close ranks and march shoulder to shoulder, the strong helping the weak, those with much assisting those with little. No power on earth can stop this work if we shall so conduct ourselves." (*Ensign,* May 1982, 46.)

Ask family members to list five things they could do to "strengthen" other people. Invite

BIOGRAPHICAL SKETCH:
LYMAN R. SHERMAN

Lyman R. Sherman was born May 22, 1804, in Monkton, Vermont. He later moved to New York and was converted there in 1832. Lyman moved to Kirtland in 1833 and was a member of Zion's Camp. He was ordained as a President of the First Quorum of Seventy in 1835 and was on the high council in Kirtland and Far West.

Lyman Sherman was called to be an apostle in January of 1839 but he died before being notified of his call. (See Lyndon W. Cook, "Lyman Sherman—Man of God, Would Be Apostle," *BYU Studies* 19 (Fall 1978) :124.) Look for the great blessing Lyman received because of his obedience.

family members to do one or two things from their list in the coming week.

(Note: Lyman Sherman was told he would be "remembered with the first of mine elders." However, he died before he was ordained to the apostleship. If you read the historical background and verses 4–8 with your family, you may wish to share the following helpful statements.)

The Lord assured Lyman Sherman he was spiritually clean at this time before his death. (See D&C 108:1.) "Thus, he was worthy to be ordained and included among the first or presiding elders of the church. (See D&C 108:2–6.) He was called to be a member of the Quorum of Twelve Apostles, thus fulfilling the promise extended to him by the Lord in this revelation. He died before he could be ordained and therefore his name does not appear in the list of men who have served in the Quorum of Twelve Apostles.

"Priesthood callings extended to the faithful by the Lord are eternal. Death does not diminish nor take away a man's priesthood calling in the Lord's kingdom. We may be sure Lyman Sherman continues to serve among the presiding elders in the spirit world. (See D&C 124:130; 138:57.)" (L. G. Otten and C. M. Caldwell, *Sacred Truths of the Doctrine and Covenants,* 2:236.)

DOCTRINE AND COVENANTS 109: DEDICATORY PRAYER OF THE KIRTLAND TEMPLE

Historical background: *The long-anticipated day for the dedication of the Kirtland Temple came on Sunday, March 27, 1836. People gathered hours before the service and though they sat two people per seat, still many were turned away. The session proceeded as follows:*

MEETING BEGAN AT 9:00 A.M.

PRESIDING: JOSEPH SMITH

CONDUCTING: SIDNEY RIGDON

READING OF THE TWENTY-FOURTH AND NINETY-SIXTH PSALMS: PRES. RIGDON

CHOIR: "ERE THE VEIL IS RENT IN TWAIN"

OPENING PRAYER: PRES. RIGDON

CONGREGATIONAL HYMN: "OH HAPPY SOULS WHO PRAY"

SPEAKER: PRES. RIGDON, MATTHEW 8:18–20

SUSTAINING OF JOSEPH SMITH AS PROPHET, SEER, AND REVELATOR: PRES. RIGDON

CONGREGATIONAL HYMN: "NOW LET US REJOICE"

CLOSING OF THE MORNING SESSION WITH A TWENTY-MINUTE BREAK

CONGREGATIONAL HYMN: "ADAM-ONDI-AHMAN"

SPEAKER AND SUSTAINING OF OTHER CHURCH LEADERS: JOSEPH SMITH JR.

CONGREGATIONAL HYMN: "HOW PLEASED AND BLESSED WAS I"

DEDICATORY PRAYER (D&C 109) READ BY: JOSEPH SMITH JR.

CHOIR: "THE SPIRIT OF GOD LIKE A FIRE IS BURNING"

ACCEPTANCE OF THE DEDICATORY PRAYER: JOSEPH SMITH JR.

ADMINISTRATION OF THE SACRAMENT

TESTIMONIES SHARED BY THE FOLLOWING:

   JOSEPH SMITH JR.

   DON CARLOS SMITH

   FREDRICK G. WILLIAMS

   DAVID WHITMER

   HYRUM SMITH

HOSANNA SHOUT: CONGREGATION

SPEAKER: BRIGHAM YOUNG

SPEAKER: DAVID W. PATTEN

CLOSING PRAYER: JOSEPH SMITH JR.

MEETING ENDED ABOUT 4:00 P.M.

(Joseph Smith, History of the Church, *2:410–28.)*

Doctrine and Covenants 109:1–5, 12
What took place the day the Kirtland Temple was dedicated?

Before your family gathers for scripture study, arrange the room to look something like the floor plan of the Kirtland Temple.

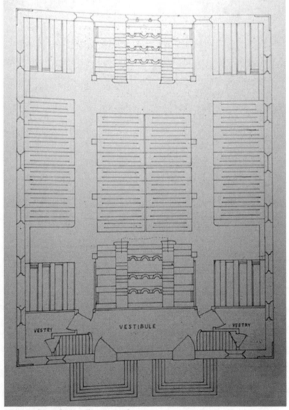

Photo by Alexander Baugh.

As your family enters the room, welcome them to the dedication of the Kirtland Temple. Ask them to remove their shoes and whisper. Once they have been seated, stand (as if at the podium) and share the information from the historical background above. Then read together D&C 109:1–5. Ask:

- Why did the Saints go through great trials to build the temple? (Verse 2.)
- According to verse 4 what did the Saints desire?
- Why was the temple built? (Verse 5.)
- Why would it be important (or significant) to remove our shoes and whisper while in the House of the Lord? (Verse 12.)

Doctrine and Covenants 109:6–20
What is the purpose of a temple?

Select a family member to be a scribe and provide a sheet of paper and pencil. Explain that as the family studies D&C 109:6–20 the scribe will record the family's responses to the questions below. Encourage family members to mark answers as they are found in the scriptures. Discuss the following questions as you study:

- What is the purpose of the temple? (Verses 8–9, 11–13, 14–16.)

- Who is allowed to enter the temple? (Verse 11.)
- What suggestions in verse 8 could help our home become more like the temple?
- Why do you think "no unclean thing" should be allowed to enter the temple? (Verse 20.)
- What can we do to keep ourselves clean so that we will be worthy to enter the temple?

Review those things listed by the scribe and discuss ways your home might be blessed as family members keep themselves clean.

Doctrine and Covenants 109:22–26
Why do missionaries go to the temple before their missions?

Hold up a picture of a temple and ask your family to share one blessing the temple offers to a family (for example, a family can be sealed together forever). Ask:

- How might this eternal outlook help a missionary prepare for a mission?
- How might an understanding of eternal families help missionaries better prepare to teach the gospel?

Take turns reading D&C 109:22–26 and discuss the blessings the Prophet Joseph asked the Lord to give His "servants" (missionaries) when they come worthily to the temple. Ask:

- What will missionaries be "armed with"? (Verse 22.)
- What "may be upon them?" (God's name.)
- Who will go with them to protect them? (Angels.)
- How will the Lord help them against their enemies? (Verse 25.)
- What advantage comes to those who take the Lord's name upon them? (Verse 26.)

Share experiences (your own or any you know about) of blessings of power and protection that come to faithful missionaries.

Doctrine and Covenants 109:27–33
Consequences and blessings

Take turns reading D&C 109:27–33. Have your family find what will happen to those who "rise against this people." Encourage them to mark the consequences they discover. Discuss reasons why such strong language might be used in a temple dedicatory prayer. Read again D&C 109:33 and ask your family to find the reason Joseph asked the Lord to deliver them from their enemies. ("That we might rise up . . . and do thy work.")

Doctrine and Covenants 109:34–38
An answer to a prayer

Take turns reading D&C 109:34–38, first asking your family to watch for specific things Joseph Smith asked for during his prayer. Invite your family to share what they found. Share the following story that took place during a priesthood meeting that was held later in the evening of the Kirtland Temple dedication:

"Brother George A. Smith arose and began to prophesy, when a noise was heard like the sound of a rushing mighty wind, which filled the Temple, and all the congregation simultaneously arose, being move upon by an invisible power, many began to speak in tongues and prophesy; others saw glorious visions; and I beheld the Temple was filled with angels, which fact I declared to the congregation. The people of the neighborhood came running together (hearing an unusual sound within, and seeing a bright light like a pillar of fire resting upon the Temple), and were astonished at what was taking place. This continued until the meeting closed at eleven P.M." (Joseph Smith, *History of the Church*, 2:428.)

Ask your family how this experience was an answer to Joseph's prayer in D&C 109:36–37.

Doctrine and Covenants 109:39–42
What blessings come to those who receive a missionary's testimony?

 Tell your family that you are going to play a game called "Simon Says." To play, tell your family they must follow your instructions, but only if you say "Simon Says" first. For example, "Simon Says bend over and touch your toes." Your family must bend over and touch their toes. However if you say, "Bend over and touch you toes," they should not move, or they are out (cannot participate any longer). As "Simon" your job is to try and get everyone out. The last person who did exactly as Simon said is the winner. After the game is over ask the following:

- What did the winner have to do in order to win? (Listen and obey the proper commands.)
- In what ways can you compare this experience with the gospel? (Only obey if the prophet, the Spirit, priesthood leaders, parents, or scriptures, etc., say to.)

Invite someone to read D&C 109:39–42. Ask:

- How are these verses like the game "Simon Says"?
- What happens to those who obey and accept the missionaries? (Verse 39.)
- What will become of those who "reject" the missionaries? (Verse 41.)

To help your family understand the word "untoward" (verse 41), share the following definition: "Froward; perverse; refractory; *not easily guided or taught*" (*An American Dictionary of the English Language*, 1828, edition, s.v., "untoward"; emphasis added.)

Doctrine and Covenants 109:43–53
How should we treat our enemies?

Have your family turn to and read Matthew 5:44. Then ask:

- What are we to do for our enemies?
- What are we to do to those who curse us?
- How are we to treat those who hate us?
- Who should we include in our prayers?
- Why might doing these things be difficult?

Read together D&C 109:43–53. Have your family look for similarities to the principles taught in Matthew 5:44. Discuss ways your family can apply these principles. To help understand the phrase "seal up the law, and bind up the testimony" (D&C 109:46), share the following insight:

"The law and testimony are the teachings and doctrines taught by God's prophets. To seal or bind them means that the message of warning has been delivered and the message is 'tied up' in preparation for the Lord's destruction." (Donald W. Parry, Jay A. Parry, Tina M. Peterson, *Understanding Isaiah*, 88.)

Doctrine and Covenants 109:54–60
Pray for a soft heart

Bring one metal object (butter knife, or spoon) and a cotton ball to family scripture study. Show your family the two objects and ask them to share ways each object can be like a person's heart. Hold up the metal object and ask: "If a heart is as hard as this metal, in what ways would it be easy or difficult for the Spirit to touch it?" Then hold up the cotton ball and ask, "Why do you think it would be easier for the Spirit to touch a heart that is more like this cotton ball?" Read together D&C 109:54–60. Ask:

- For whom is Joseph praying?
- Joseph is asking Heavenly Father to bless the leaders of the nations with what kind of hearts?
- Why would it be important for a national leader to have a soft heart?
- What might happen to a country if the leaders have hard hearts?
- How might it benefit the Lord's Church for a nation's leaders to have softened hearts?

Doctrine and Covenants 109:61–67
Gathering scattered Israel

Have your family scan D&C 109:61–67 and find the words "children" and "remnants." Then have them find these names (Jacob, Judah, Israel). Ask if anyone can explain the meaning behind these names. If not, draw on a piece of paper an illustration like the one shown here. Explain that, in the Old Testament, Abraham was the father of Isaac, who was the father of Jacob, whose name the Lord changed to Israel. Judah was one of Jacob's sons.

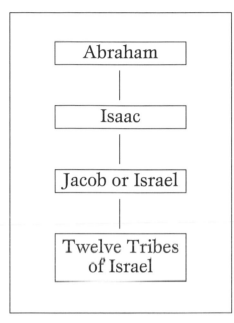

Have your family look again at D&C 109:61–67 and discuss the following questions:

- Who are the "children of Jacob"? (His descendants.)
- Where were they? (Scattered—verse 61.)
- What was Joseph's prayer for scattered Israel?
- What did he ask to happen to Jerusalem, "from this hour"? (Verse 62.)
- What is Joseph asking for the tribe of Judah? (Verse 64.)
- What is Joseph prayer in behalf of all of the remnants of Israel?

If your family members are old enough to understand you might consider sharing the following information. To see how the Lord has answered this prayer concerning the "children of Judah" (the Jews), have a family member read the heading for D&C 109 looking for the date of the revelation. Review the following dates and events with your family to see what has happened since:

1867 First archaeological excavations; C. Warren for Palestine Exploration Fund
1898 Visits of Kaiser Wilhelm II, Theodor Herzl. Theodor Herzl is considered the father of Zionism. Zionism is the gathering of the Jews to Israel.
1917 Balfour Declaration. The Balfour Declaration was put in place by the British and insured an independent state for Israel.
1947 UN vote to partition Palestine; Jerusalem, an "international zone."
1948 Creation of State of Israel; Jerusalem, a divided city.
1967 Six-day War; Israel proclaims a united Jerusalem.
1987 BYU's Jerusalem Center for Near Eastern Studies completed; outbreak of Palestinian Uprising (*Intifada*).

(David B. Galbraith, D. Kelly Ogden, and Andrew C. Skinner, *Jerusalem: The Eternal City*, xi.)

Share the following quotation from Elder Ezra Taft Benson: "The number of Jews has multiplied in recent years in this area [Jerusalem] in a rather remarkable manner. Plans are underway for the incorporation of about a million and a half more during the immediate months ahead, and projected plans call for an eventual population of some four million in this area. (*CR*, April 1950, pp. 72, 74.)" (Daniel H. Ludlow, *A Companion to Your Study of the Doctrine and Covenants*, 1978, 1:561.)

Discuss ways your family can assist in this gathering of Israel.

Doctrine and Covenants 109:68–71
Whom should we include in our prayers?

On a sheet of paper make a list of some of the people your family cares about. Ask which of these we should be praying for and why. Read D&C 109:68–71, first asking your family to look for whom Joseph Smith prayed. (The prophet and his family and other Church leaders and their families.) Discuss reasons why it would be important to pray for Church leaders and their families. Read the following to your family:

"We know that you pray for us, and we appreciate your prayers. They sustain us; they remind us of the great trust which you have placed in us. I want you to know that we pray for you always." (Gordon B. Hinckley, *Ensign,* November 1995, 89).

Encourage your family to pray for the First Presidency, Quorum of the Twelve Apostles, and other Church leaders and their families.

Doctrine and Covenants 109:72–80
Kirtland Temple's dedicatory prayer has roots in the Bible

Explain to your family that you are going to play a matching game. List the following scripture references on a sheet of paper: Song of Solomon 6:10; Luke 3:5; Psalm 41:13; Daniel 2:44–45; Moses 7:56; 1 Thessalonians 4:17; Jude 1:25; Isaiah 6:2; Ezra 6:16–17. Cut them out and spread them face up on a table or the floor. Tell your family that each Bible reference matches a verse in D&C 109:72–80. Give them time to search the scriptures and make their best matches. The list below gives the correct answers:

D&C 109:72   Daniel 2:44–45
"kingdom which thou hast set up without hands may become a great mountain and fill the whole earth"

D&C 109:73   Song of Solomon 6:10
"fair as the moon, clear as the sun, and terrible as an army with banners"

D&C 109:74   Luke 3:5
"rough places made smooth"

D&C 109:75   1 Thessalonians 4:17
"caught up in the cloud to meet thee, that we may ever be with the Lord"

D&C 109:76   Moses 7:56
"crowns of glory"

D&C 109:77   Jude 1:25
"glory . . . majesty . . . dominion"

D&C 109:78   Ezra 6:16–17
"the dedication of this house"

D&C 109:79   Isaiah 6:2
seraphs/seraphims (Isa.)

D&C 109:80   Psalms 41:13
"Amen and amen"

After your family has completed the matching exercise, discuss ways the Bible can be a great inspiration for us just as it was for Joseph. Invite family members to give their own examples of scriptures from the Bible that have inspired them.

DOCTRINE AND COVENANTS 110: PRIESTHOOD KEYS RESTORED

Historical background: *In the New Testament, Jesus promised his apostles that he would "give unto [them] the keys of the kingdom of heaven" so that what they "bind on earth shall be bound in heaven" and what they "loose on earth shall be loosed in heaven." (Matthew 16:19.) A short time later they received these promised priesthood keys during a glorious visit by Moses and Elijah on the Mount of Transfiguration. (See Matthew 17:1–13.)*

On April 3, 1836, Moses and Elijah appeared again in the Kirtland Temple and gave the same keys to the Prophet Joseph Smith and Oliver Cowdery as recorded in Doctrine and Covenants 110. As part of this marvelous manifestation the Savior Himself appeared to accept the Kirtland Temple as His own. (See D&C 110:1–3.)

"It is interesting to note that on the third day of April, 1836, the Jews were celebrating the feast of the Passover, and were leaving the doors of their homes open for the coming of Elijah. On that day Elijah came, but not to the Jewish homes, but to the Temple in the village of Kirtland . . . to two humble servants of the Lord." (Joseph Fielding Smith, Church History and Modern Revelation, 3:84.) Look for the specific powers that were given to Joseph and Oliver by these heavenly visitors.

Doctrine and Covenants 110:1–10
The Savior and His message

Invite your family to tell of characteristics of family members that could be compared to an object or something in nature. (For example, when they smile their eyes sparkle like diamonds.) Explain that the Prophet Joseph Smith and Oliver Cowdery used phrases like these to help describe a vision they had of the Savior in the Kirtland Temple. Write the following phrases on a sheet of paper and show it to your family: "paved work of pure gold," "flame of fire," "brightness of the sun," "rushing of great waters." Have your family guess what each phrase describes in the vision Joseph and Oliver had of the Savior. Then have someone read aloud D&C 110:1–3 and find the comparisons.

Explain that the first three verses describe the Savior's appearance; the verses that follow record what the Savior said. Take turns reading D&C 110:4–8 and discuss the following questions as you read:

- What did Jesus say about himself? (Verse 4.)
- What did He say about Joseph and Oliver?
- What did He say about the Saints who struggled to build the temple?
- What did Jesus promise about the temple itself? (Verses 7–8.)
- Which statement by the Savior do you think was the most comforting to Joseph and Oliver?
- Which one makes the most difference to you?

Read aloud D&C 110:9–10 and ask:

- What did the Savior say would happen as a result of the completion, dedication, and use of the Kirtland Temple?
- In what ways have any of these things been true for you?

Show your family pictures of as many temples as you have access to. Testify that every temple functions as a result of the keys being restored in the Kirtland Temple.

Doctrine and Covenants 110:11–16
What keys did these three prophets bring?

 Write each of the following names of prophets on the top of three separate sheets of paper: Moses, Elias, Elijah. Explain to your family that you will pass the papers around. Each time the paper comes to them they are to write one thing they know about that prophet. See how many facts can be listed without repeating things already listed. Then read D&C 110:11–16 and talk about each prophet in the order they appear in Doctrine and Covenants 110 —Moses, then Elias, then Elijah. The following information might help you discuss each prophet:

Moses

Ask:

- What did Moses bring to Joseph Smith and Oliver Cowdery? (Keys of the gathering of Israel—see verse 11.)
- Why do you think it was appropriate for Moses to bring these keys? (He had gathered Israel once before.)
- How are these keys being used today?

To help answer this last question, share with your family the following statements:

"The President of The Church of Jesus Christ of Latter-day Saints—the man appointed to preside over the whole church, and to be like unto Moses (D&C 107:91)—received keys to gather modern Israel. Even as Moses led ancient Israel out of Egyptian bondage, so the President of the Church was given keys to gather modern Israel into Zion." (Robert L. Millet, *Ensign,* March 1998, 41.)

"The gathering of Israel consists of joining the true church; of coming to a knowledge of the true God and of His saving truths." (President Harold B. Lee, quoting Bruce R. McConkie in *Ensign,* July 1973, 4.)

Elias

If your family wrote very little about Elias in the activity above, in addition to D&C 110:12, read together the reference for "Elias" in the Bible Dictionary, page 663. Ask:

- What do these references teach us about the Elias who appeared in the Kirtland Temple?

- What did Elias bring to Joseph Smith and Oliver Cowdery?

Share with your family the following about what Elias restored:

"Elias restored the great commission, given of God to Abraham our father, whereby the seed of Abraham has power to gain eternal blessings forever through eternal marriage. . . .

"The promises are the provisions of the Abrahamic covenant whereby the seed of the ancient patriarchs are entitled to receive the priesthood, the gospel, and eternal life (including celestial marriage)." (Bruce R. McConkie, *A New Witness for the Articles of Faith,* 508–9.)

Elijah

In addition to D&C 110:13–16, consider also reading Malachi 4:5–6; D&C 2. Ask:

- How do these scriptures show the importance of the keys Elijah restored?
- How are these keys used?

You may want to share the following statements with your family:

"What is this office and work of Elijah? It is one of the greatest and most important subjects that God has revealed. . . .

"This is the spirit of Elijah, that we redeem our dead, and connect ourselves with our fathers which are in heaven. . . . This is the power of Elijah and the keys of the kingdom of Jehovah." (*Teachings of the Prophet Joseph Smith,* 337–38.)

"Malachi plainly outlined the mission of Elijah—to establish a bond of interest between present and past generations . . . to create in the hearts of living men and women an interest in their ancestors." (Mark E. Petersen, *Ensign,* January 1972, 49.)

In summary, invite family members to share one way that the keys revealed by these prophets will bless either them individually, your family, or others.

DOCTRINE AND COVENANTS 111: A TRIP TO MASSACHUSETTS

Historical background: *In July of 1836 William Burgess arrived in Kirtland and told Joseph Smith that he knew of a large sum of money hidden in the cellar of a house in Salem, Massachusetts; a prosperous seaport. He claimed to be the only person alive who knew of the location of the house and where the treasure was hidden.*

At this time in American history, many believed that Spanish pirates had buried treasure in Salem. Later that summer, owing to increasing Church debt, Joseph and others traveled to Salem to find the treasure. Yet they searched in vain for the house with the supposed treasure. Burgess soon departed, explaining that Salem had changed so much since he was last there that he could not find the house.

Though they did not find the treasure they had hoped to find, Joseph and his companions preached the gospel in public settings and became acquainted with many important people. Joseph received D&C 111 in answer to their disappointment. Five years later in Philadelphia, Elders Erastus Snow and Benjamin Winchester were given a copy of this revelation and asked to go to Salem to fulfill it. Within a year there was a branch of 90 members. (See Robert L. Millet and Kent P. Jackson, eds., Studies in Scripture, Vol. 1: The Doctrine and Covenants, *432–36.*)

Doctrine and Covenants 111:1–11
When life hands you a lemon

For this lesson idea, have a lemon or make some lemonade (if necessary, draw a lemon on a sheet of paper). Show the lemon and ask your family what it means when someone refers to a car as being a lemon. Ask them if they have ever felt that life has handed them some lemons before. Share the saying:

"When life hands you a lemon,
Make lemonade."

Consider making a small copy of the quotation for each member of the family. Invite one family member to read the section heading for D&C 111, and another the historical background above. As these are read, have your family look for a lemon that was handed to the Prophet and his companions. Ask, "What do you think Joseph and his companions did to make the situation better?" Read together D&C 111:1–3. Ask:

- What were the "follies" the Lord was referring to? (Looking for buried treasure to pay the Church's debts.)
- Why would it be good to form acquaintances with the people of Salem?

- When was the prophecy of verse 2 fulfilled? (See historical background.)

Take turns reading verses 4–11. Ask:

- How did they know where they should "tarry"? (Verse 8.)
- Why was Joseph to learn about the "ancient inhabitants and founders" of Salem? (Verses 9–10.)
- What other "treasure" might the Lord have had in mind for Joseph to find?

Explain to your family that although temple work for the dead had not been revealed, Joseph had an opportunity to do something else relating to temple work. Share the following:

"In v. 9 the Lord mentioned another kind of treasure, when he instructed the elders: 'Inquire diligently concerning the more ancient inhabitants and founders of this city.' Here, perhaps the Lord was challenging the Prophet and his associates to learn of their ancestors while in the area—perhaps as an introduction to genealogical research. Salem is only a few miles from Topsfield, the ancestral home of the Prophet Joseph Smith. Salem had then and still has today excellent library facilities for genealogy, such as the Essex Institute. While we have no evidence that Joseph Smith did genealogical research in Salem in 1836, the opportunity was ideal and the work needed to be done." (Robert L. Millet and Kent P. Jackson, eds., *Studies in Scripture, Vol. 1: The Doctrine and Covenants*, 432).

Give each family member a copy of the quote you wrote down earlier and have them carry it with them throughout the day. Challenge your family to make the best of bad circumstances by seeking counsel from the Lord as Joseph Smith did.

DOCTRINE AND COVENANTS 112: INSTRUCTIONS TO THE QUORUM OF THE TWELVE APOSTLES

Historical background: Almost a year had passed since the Prophet Joseph Smith received the revelation known as Doctrine and Covenants 111. In May and June of 1837, the United States suffered widespread effects of a financial crash. Referring to this time, Joseph recorded:

"The spirit of speculation in lands and property of all kinds, which was so prevalent throughout the whole nation, was taking deep root in the Church. As the fruits of this spirit, evil-surmising, fault-finding, disunion, dissension, and apostasy followed in quick succession, and it seemed as though all the powers of earth and hell were combining their influence in an especial manner to overthrow the Church at once, and make a final end. . . .

"No quorum in the Church was entirely exempt from the influence of those false spirits who are striving against me for the mastery; even some of the Twelve were so far lost to their high and responsible calling, as to begin to take sides, secretly, with the enemy.

"In this state of things . . . God revealed to me that something new must be done for the salvation of the Church. And on or about the first of June, 1837, Heber C. Kimball, one of the Twelve, was set apart by the spirit of prophecy and revelation, prayer and laying on of hands, of the First Presidency, to preside over a mission to England, to be the first foreign mission of the Church of Christ in the last days" (Joseph Smith, History of the Church, 2:487–89).

On July 23, 1837, the day the missionaries preached the first sermons in England, the Lord gave a revelation through Joseph Smith directed to Thomas B. Marsh who was serving as President of the Quorum of the Twelve Apostles. Look to find the instructions the Lord had for the apostles.

Doctrine and Covenants 112:1–10
What is in *your* heart?

Before family scripture study, get two pieces of paper (preferably red) and cut out two identical heart shapes. Tape, staple, or glue the side edges and bottom of the two hearts together but leave the top open so that it forms a pouch. Write "not well pleased" on several slips of paper and fold them and put them in the heart pouch. This will be used later.

Tell your family that many of the hymns in the hymnbook are based on specific scriptures. Sing or read the first verse of "Be Thou Humble" (*Hymns*, no. 130) and have family members search D&C 112:1–10 for the verse that the hymn comes from. (Verse 10.) Ask:

- What does the Lord promise to those who are humble? (Lead us by the hand and answer our prayers.)
- What does it mean to be humble?

Share this teaching from President Gordon B. Hinckley, "I believe the meek and the humble are those who are teachable. They are willing to learn. They are willing to listen to the whisperings of the still, small voice for guidance in their lives. They place the wisdom of the Lord above their own wisdom." (*Ensign,* January 2001, 2.)

Show the heart pouch to your family and have several family members draw a slip of paper out of the pouch and read aloud what is written. Ask family members to read D&C 112:2 and tell how it relates to what they just did. Have them read D&C 112:1 to see whose heart is being spoken of. Have someone read the historical background above, and another the biographical sketch for Thomas B. Marsh in D&C 31 of this book. Ask:

- What does this tell you about Thomas B. Marsh?
- Remembering D&C 112:10, what do you think might have been some of the things in his heart with which the Lord was not well pleased?

Invite family members to consider if there are things in their own hearts with which the Lord would not be pleased.

Doctrine and Covenants 112:11–15
"Take up your cross"

Have family members look for what Thomas B. Marsh was called upon to do as President of the Quorum of the Twelve that they feel would be good counsel for any quorum president as they read D&C 112:11–12. Then read together D&C 112:12–15. Ask:

- What did the Lord say to all the Twelve in verse 14?

- What do you think it means to "take up your cross"?

To help answer the questions, share the following insights from two latter-day members of the Quorum of the Twelve:

"The Church would grow much faster now, numerically and spiritually, if . . . you and I were better by taking up the Christian cross daily (see Luke 9:23). Part of taking up the cross is denying ourselves the lusts and appetites of the flesh. . . . Thus, the *daily* taking up of the cross means *daily* denying ourselves the appetites of the flesh." (Neal A. Maxwell, *Ensign,* May 1987, 70.)

"Over the centuries, in the minds of millions of people, the cross has been recognized as a symbol of Christianity. But rather than displaying the cross, we prefer to try carrying our crosses. The Lord's message to us is 'Take up your cross.' Take yourself the way you are, and lift yourself in the direction of the better. Regardless of where you have been, what you have done, or what you haven't done, trust God. Believe in him. Worship him as you carry your cross with dignity and determination." (Marvin J. Ashton, *Ensign,* February 1988, 69.)

Invite family members to consider ways they can better carry their crosses.

Doctrine and Covenants 112:16–34
Who has the keys?

For this object lesson you will need a door that can be unlocked with a key (such as your front door). Take your family outside and lock the door behind you. Have someone try to open the door. When the person cannot open the door, ask what is needed. Give someone the key and let him or her open the door. Return to your scripture study and have different family members take turns reading the following verses: D&C 112:16, 19, 21, 28, 30–32. Ask:

- What theme is common to all those verses?
- Who holds the keys?
- What doors can these keys open?

Have your family mark footnote 28b and the reference Mark 16:15. Invite someone to read Mark 16:15. Ask:

- What commission did Jesus give the original Twelve Apostles after his resurrection and before he ascended into heaven?
- Since Jesus gave the commission to the Twelve Apostles in His time and to the Twelve Apostles in Joseph Smith's time, how important do you think it is in our time?

Share this insight from Elder M. Russell Ballard, a latter-day apostle:

"We are living in a most exciting time. What a joy it is to know that the power of the holy priesthood is operating throughout the Church to bless the lives of the Saints. It is wonderful to know that the priesthood vested in the latter-day Apostles has, in this dispensation, opened many nations to the preaching of the gospel. Surely in the future we will see other nations opened in the same remarkable way." (*Ensign*, May 1986, 12.)

Ask your family what they could do to assist in this work. Share the following quotation from President Spencer W. Kimball:

"Every man, woman, and child—every young person and every little boy and girl—should serve a mission. This does not mean that they must serve abroad or even be formally called and set apart as full-time missionaries. But it does mean that each of us is responsible to bear witness [testimony] of the gospel truths that we have been given. We all have relatives, neighbors, friends, and fellow workmen, and it is our responsibility to pass the truths of the gospel on to them, by example as well as by precept [teachings]." (*Ensign*, October 1977, 3.)

DOCTRINE AND COVENANTS 113: QUESTIONS AND ANSWERS

Historical background: *Because of an assassination plot, Joseph Smith and his family fled Kirtland, Ohio, on January 12, 1838, and headed for Far West, Missouri. The Prophet wrote:*

"When I had arrived within one and twenty miles of Far West, the brethren met me with teams and money to help me forward; and when eight miles from the city, we were met by an escort . . . who received us with open arms; and on the 13th of March with my family and some others I put up at Brother Barnard's for the night. Here we were met by another escort of the brethren from the town, who came to make us welcome to their little Zion.

"On the 14th of March, as we were about entering Far West, many of the brethren came out to meet us, who also with open arms welcomed us to their bosoms. We were immediately received under the hospitable roof Brother George W. Harris, who treated us with all possible kindness, and we refreshed ourselves with much satisfaction, after our long and tedious journey, the brethren bringing in such things as we needed for our comfort and convenience.

"After being here two or three days, my brother Samuel arrived with his family.

"Shortly after his arrival, while walking with him and certain other brethren, the following sentiments occurred to my mind: [D&C 113]." (Joseph Smith, History of the Church, *3:9–10.) Notice what a blessing it is to have modern revelation help us understand ancient scripture.*

Doctrine and Covenants 113:1–6
How does God answer our questions?

Ask family members to imagine what it would be like to be able to take a walk with the prophet and ask him any question they wanted. What kinds of questions would you ask? Have one family member read the historical background above, and another the section heading for D&C 113. Explain that today you will study some answers the Prophet gave to questions asked by the Saints.

Make a drawing of a tree stump with roots. Label the tree stump: *stem.* Label the roots: *roots.* Draw a shoot or branch coming out of the stump and label it: *rod.* Invite family members to search D&C 113:1–6 and write on the drawing who the stem, rod, and root represent. You may find it necessary to refer to the definitions listed below taken from *Doctrine and Covenants Commentary,* by Hyrum M. Smith and Janne M. Sjodahl, page 738:

- "Stem] This word means here 'the stock which remains in the earth after the tree is cut down.'"
- "Rod] This means a 'shoot' or branch coming out of the 'stem' of Jesse—a descendant.'"
- "Root of Jesse] A branch from the root. Jesse was the father of David."

For further insight into D&C 113:4, 6, share the following explanation:

"There can be no question that this is describing the Prophet Joseph Smith. By revelation he was told that he held the right to the priesthood (see D&C 86:8–9). That the keys of the kingdom had been given to him is a matter of record; that his labors were to stand as an 'ensign' to which the nations of the earth will gather is also a matter of scriptural promise (D&C 29:4, 7–8; 35:25;

38:33; 39:11; 45:9, 28)" (Monte S. Nyman, ed., *Isaiah and the Prophets: Inspired Voices from the Old Testament,* 18).

Tell your family that even though we can't walk and talk with the prophet today, the Lord has still provided ways for us to find answers to our questions. Discuss as many of these "other" ways you can think of and list them on your drawing. Display the drawing as a reminder throughout the week.

Doctrine and Covenants 113:7–10
What does it mean for Zion to "put on thy strength"?

Invite a family member to make a drawing of a family with chains or heavy ropes around them. Have another family member read aloud Isaiah 52:1–2. Ask your family how the drawing relates to the verses just read. Have your family read D&C 113:9–10 and look for added insight given by the Prophet. Label the chain or rope as the "curses of God." Then read together D&C 113:7–8 and find a way to break the chain (priesthood authority). Discuss ways the priesthood helps families to have strength and enjoy the blessing of God. Have them share specific examples of this strength in your own home. You may want to share the following quotation from Elder Bruce R. McConkie:

"We read in the holy word that Israel will gather to Zion when she forsakes her sins and looses the bands that bind her; that she, being worthy, will receive revelation and come again to know the Lord; that this will be brought to pass by the preaching of the restored gospel; and that the converts who gather to Zion will be perfectly united in belief, in doctrine, in obedience—all to the extent that they see eye to eye in all things" (Bruce R. McConkie, *A New Witness for the Articles of Faith,* 572–73.)

DOCTRINE AND COVENANTS 114: A MISSION FOR DAVID W. PATTEN

Historical background: Elder David W. Patten was an original member of the Quorum of the Twelve Apostles when that Quorum was first organized in this dispensation in March 1835. After participating in the events surrounding the dedication of the Kirtland Temple, Elder Patten moved to Missouri to help build Zion. He assisted Thomas B. Marsh, president of the Quorum of the Twelve, in leading the Church there. (See Lyndon W. Cook, The Revelations of the Prophet Joseph Smith, 226.) Although he had served missions previous to 1838, the call in Doctrine and Covenants 114 was a special one given to the Twelve to open the doors to the nations of the world with the keys they had been given—thus the Lord gave him a year to get ready. Because he was killed in October 1838, Elder Patten was not able to fulfill this mission in mortality. Watch for what the Lord taught here about the need to prepare to serve in the Lord's kingdom.

Doctrine and Covenants 114:1–2
Missionary preparation

Read the historical background for this section to your family and ask them to discover how long David W. Patten had to prepare for his mission with the Twelve Apostles. Ask your family to imagine they have one year to prepare for a mission. Have them make a list of the five most important things they would do to get ready.

Have someone read D&C 114:1. Ask:

- What was the Lord asking David W. Patten to do?
- What "settling up" do you suppose he had to do?
- What kind of preparation does it take to serve a full-time mission today?

Share with your family the following from Elder M. Russell Ballard:

"What we need now is the greatest generation of missionaries in the history of the Church. We need worthy, qualified, spiritually energized missionaries who, like Helaman's 2,000 stripling warriors, are 'exceedingly valiant for courage, and also for strength and activity' and who are 'true at all times in whatsoever thing they [are] entrusted' (Alma 53:20).

" . . . We don't need spiritually weak and semi-committed young men. We don't need you to just

fill a position; we need your whole heart and soul. We need vibrant, thinking, passionate missionaries who know how to listen to and respond to the whisperings of the Holy Spirit. This isn't a time for spiritual weaklings. We cannot send you on a mission to be reactivated, reformed, or to receive a testimony. We just don't have time for that. We need you to be filled with 'faith, hope, charity and love, with an eye single to the glory of God' (D&C 4:5).

"As an Apostle of the Lord Jesus Christ, I call upon you to begin right now—tonight—to be fully and completely worthy. . . . We expect you to be missionaries to match our glorious message." (*Ensign,* November 2002, 46–48.)

Discuss as a family those things you could do or change to best prepare to become the kind of missionary Elder Ballard called for. Read D&C 114:1 again and ask:

- What did the Lord say David W. Patten would "bear" to "all the world"?
- What do you think is so "glad" about the message of the gospel?
- What can we do to better help others recognize that the gospel makes us glad?
- What did the Lord say in D&C 114:2 about those who are not faithful?
- What does that teach us about the need of preparing personally to serve in all of our callings?

BIOGRAPHICAL SKETCH: DAVID W. PATTEN

David W. Patten was born November 14, 1799 in New York. He was interested in religion but did not join any church because he was "looking for the Church of Christ to arise in its purity, according to the promise of Christ," and he believed that he "should live to see it." (*Millennial Star,* 26:406.) Within days of being baptized, he was ordained an elder and went on a mission. After several missions, David was ordained an apostle on February 15, 1835, in Kirtland, Ohio. He continued to serve missions as a member of the Twelve.

As troubles increased in Missouri in the summer of 1838, David was appointed to oversee a small militia. While leading the militia on October 25, 1838, Elder Patten and his men found themselves on the other side of the Crooked River from a Missouri militia who also held prisoners the Saints were trying to rescue. A battle broke out, and David W. Patten was shot. He died later that night. Wilford Woodruff said that David W. Patten had asked the Lord for the privilege of dying a martyrs' death, "at which the Prophet, greatly moved, expressed extreme sorrow, 'For,' said he to David 'when a man of your faith asks the Lord for anything, he generally gets it.'" (In Lycurgus A. Wilson, *Life of David Patten,* 53.)

DOCTRINE AND COVENANTS 115: "THUS SHALL MY CHURCH BE CALLED"

Historical background: *Because of great apostasy in Kirtland, the Prophet was forced to flee Ohio, along with all other members of the Church who would be faithful to Joseph, and gather with the faithful Saints in Missouri.*

"For a brief time, Far West became the headquarters of the beleaguered Church. Between March and July of 1838, seven revelations found in the Doctrine and Covenants were received within its borders (D&C 113; 114; 115; 117; 118; 119; 120). A temple site was dedicated, with the cornerstone being laid according to [the revelation in D&C 115]." (Hoyt W. Brewster Jr., Doctrine and Covenants Encyclopedia, *174.) Because of violence and the expulsion of the Saints from Missouri, the building up of Far West and its temple was never completed. Watch for the great truths that are taught, even in the very name or title of the Lord's Church.*

Doctrine and Covenants 115:1–5
What's in a name?

Ask a family member to say the full name of the Church. Have your family look for the name and underline it while reading together D&C 115:1–4. Explain this is the first time the Lord designated the precise name of the Church in latter-day scripture. Share the following from Elder Russell M. Nelson:

"Surely every word that proceeds from the mouth of the Lord is precious. So each word in this name must be important—divinely designated for a reason. If we study the key words in that name, we can better understand the name's full significance." (Russell M. Nelson, *Ensign,* May 1990, 16.)

Have your family identify the four significant words or parts of the Church's name revealed by the Lord in verse 5 ("the Church," "Jesus Christ," "Latter-day," and "Saints"). The following ideas may help as you talk about the importance of each:

- The Church—How would the significance and the meaning change if the Church's name was "A" Church instead of "The" Church? What insight does JS—H 1:9–10, 19 add to this idea?
- Of Jesus Christ—Why is it significant for the Lord's Church to bear His name? (See 3 Nephi 27:7–8.) In addition, what must the Church be "built upon" in order to truly be His Church? (See 3 Nephi 27:8.)
- Latter-day—How do these words distinguish the Church from the Church of Jesus Christ in other times in the history of the world? Although we live in a different time period, is Christ's Church organized the same way as it was anciently according to Ephesians 4:11?
- Saints—What does the Bible Dictionary say the word "Saint" means? According to D&C 115:5 what can we do to be examples of Saints?

Share the following statement by President Gordon B. Hinckley:

"I believe and testify that it is the mission of this Church to stand as an ensign to the nations and a light to the world. We have had placed upon us a great, all-encompassing mandate from which we cannot shrink nor turn aside. We accept that

Today, the Far West temple site contains several monuments reminding us of the events transpiring there in 1838–39. (Photo by Kenneth Mays.)

mandate and are determined to fulfill it, and with the help of God we shall do it. . . .

"We must stand firm. We must hold back the world. . . .

"We cannot be arrogant. We cannot be self-righteous. The very situation in which the Lord has placed us requires that we be humble as the beneficiaries of His direction. . . .

"Live by your standards. Pray for the guidance and protection of the Lord. He will never leave you alone. He will comfort you. He will sustain you. He will bless and magnify you and make your reward sweet and beautiful. And you will discover that your example will attract others who will take courage from your strength. . . .

"If we are to hold up this Church as an ensign to the nations and a light to the world, we must take on more of the luster of the life of Christ individually and in our own personal circumstances." (*Ensign,* November 2003, 83–84.)

Ask your family:

- What are other names people use for the Church?
- Why don't people always use the full title of the Church?

Share the following excerpts: "As has been emphasized for some years, Church members, news organizations and others are asked to use the full and correct name of the Church—The Church of Jesus Christ of Latter-day Saints—and to avoid use of the term 'Mormon Church' . . .

"When a shortened reference is needed in news reporting or other instances, the terms 'the Church' or 'the Church of Jesus Christ' are encouraged." (*Church News,* week ending March 3, 2001.)

Doctrine and Covenants 115:6, 8
Why is the gathering of the Saints so important?

If possible, set up a tent outside, and study this section inside the tent, or show your family a picture of a tent (see page 96). Begin by asking:

- What does a tent provide for those camping outside? (Shelter or protection.)
- What keeps the tent upright, and helps keep it from blowing away? (Poles, stakes and cords.)
- According to Isaiah 54:2, was the "tent" of the latter-days to become larger or smaller?

Have someone read D&C 115:6 aloud. Ask:

- What does the Lord compare to a tent? (The gathering of the Saints to the stakes of Zion.)
- In what ways does our ward and stake provide safety, peace, and protection?
- According to 2 Timothy 3:1–5, how much wickedness will exist in the last days?
- Why then, is it so important to be under the protection of the Lord's Church?
- What can we do to strengthen our stake and increase the size of the latter-day "tent"?

Read together D&C 115:7–8 and look for the building the Lord wanted constructed in Far West. Talk about how temples provide protection and safety from the evils of the latter-days. (See also D&C 109:24–26.) Explain that Joseph Smith taught:

"The main object [of gathering] was to build unto the Lord a house whereby He could reveal unto His people the ordinances of His house and the glories of His Kingdom, and teach the people the way of salvation." (*Teachings of the Prophet Joseph Smith*, 308.)

Ask your family to notice the word "gathering" in D&C 115:8. Talk about how we "gather" in the latter-days by sharing the following:

"This gathering has commenced and shall continue until the righteous are assembled into the congregations of the Saints in all the nations of the earth." (Bruce R. McConkie, as cited by Harold B. Lee in Conference Report, April 1973, pp. 6–7.)

"Now the gathering of Israel consists of joining the true church and . . . coming to the knowledge of the true God. . . . Any person, therefore, who has accepted the restored gospel, and who now seeks to worship the Lord in his own tongue and with the Saints in the nations where he lives, has complied with the law of the gathering of Israel and is heir to all of the blessings promised the Saints in these last days." (*Teachings of Spencer W. Kimball*, 439.)

Doctrine and Covenants 115:7–19
Far West

Tell your family that you are going to give them a little test about today's scriptures study. As an incentive, you will give a treat to all who answer three or more questions correctly. Read aloud the historical background above and then have your family study D&C 115:7–19 as well as the section heading. Let them refer to their scriptures as needed to answer the questions. (Note: The correct answers below are underlined and indicate where that answer is found.)

1. On what National holiday were the cornerstones laid for the Far West temple? Also remember that one year later, construction was to begin.
   A. Labor Day
   B. Independence Day (Verses 10–11.)
   C. Ground Hog Day
   D. April Fool's Day

2. The leaders of the Church were commanded to not let the First Presidency get into any _____.
   A. Trouble with the Missourians
   B. Dark caves
   C. Debt (Verse 13.)
   D. Legal problems

3. How was the city of Far West to be built?
   A. "Speedily" (Verse 17.)
   B. "Gradually"
   C. "Carefully"
   D. "Cheerfully"

4. Why wasn't the Far West temple built?
A. The Church didn't have enough money to construct it.
B. They could not construct a strong foundation.
C. <u>The Missourians drove the Saints from the state. (Historical background.)</u>
D. The Church decided to build a Visitors' Center instead.

5. What did the Lord say Joseph had received?
A. <u>The keys of the kingdom (Verse 19.)</u>
B. Money to build the temple
C. A home to live in
D. The keys to the wagon

Discuss the following question with your family: Considering the poverty and persecuted condition of the Saints, what does this revelation teach us about the importance of temples?

DOCTRINE AND COVENANTS 116: ADAM-ONDI-AHMAN

Historical background: On Friday, May 18, 1838, the Prophet Joseph Smith, along with many others, left Far West to go exploring with the intention of setting boundaries for stakes of Zion. They came across a place located twenty-five miles to the north of Far West. Some of the brethren called the place "Spring Hill," but Joseph said it was "Adam-ondi-Ahman." (See Joseph Fielding Smith, Church History and Modern Revelation, *2:88–89.) Look for the exciting events that will take place at Adam-ondi-Ahman in the future.*

Doctrine and Covenants 116:1

What is Adam-ondi-Ahman, and where is it located?

Show your family the accompanying map and then read aloud D&C 116:1. Talk about what family members may know about this sacred place, and ask what this verse teaches will eventually happen here. Invite family members to read every scripture reference listed in D&C 116:1 footnote a. Have them find additional information about Adam-ondi-Ahman they could teach the family. When they have finished allow them to share what they have found and discuss these questions:

- Where does this valley get its name?
- What significant events have taken place at Adam-ondi-Ahman?
- What significant people have been or will one day visit this sacred place?
- Would you ever like to visit Adam-ondi-Ahman? Why?

Adam-ondi-Ahman is in Northern Missouri.

Share the following statement by Joseph Fielding Smith:

"Not many years hence there shall be another gathering of high priests and righteous souls in this same valley of Adam-ondi-Ahman. At this gathering Adam, the Ancient of Days, will again be present. At this time the vision which Daniel saw will be enacted. The Ancient of Days will sit. There will stand before him those who have held the keys of all dispensations, who shall render up their stewardships to the first Patriarch of the race, who holds the keys of salvation. This shall be a day of judgment and preparation. Joseph, the Prophet, in speaking of this event, said:

"'Daniel in his seventh chapter speaks of the Ancient of Days; he means the oldest man, our father Adam, Michael; he will call his children together and hold a council with them to prepare them for the coming of the Son of Man. He (Adam) is the father of the human family, and presides over the spirits of all men, and all that have had the keys must stand before him in this grand council. The Son of Man stands before him (Adam) and there is given him glory and dominion. Adam delivers up his stewardship to Christ, that which was delivered to him as holding the keys of the universe, but retains his standing as head of the human family.'" (*The Way to Perfection*, 289.)

Read the words to, or have your family sing Hymn 49, "Adam-ondi-Ahman." Talk about the feelings they have as they think about the words to this hymn. Explain that this hymn was sung at the dedication of the Kirtland Temple.

DOCTRINE AND COVENANTS 117: "THE MORE WEIGHTY MATTERS"

Historical background: "*The departure of the Church leaders from Kirtland [Jan. 1838] had been the signal for a general migration of the Mormons from Ohio to Missouri. Far West was now their gathering place—not their Zion, but only a stake of Zion, as Kirtland had been before. All during the spring and summer of 1838 the exodus continued, until the Saints remaining at Kirtland were very few.*" (Orson F. Whitney, History of Utah, 1:140–41.) *Although this revelation was received at Far West, it was directed to three men remaining in Kirtland, William Marks, Newel K. Whitney, and Oliver Granger. (For more information on Newel K. Whitney see the biographical sketch with section 72.) Notice that* how *we serve is more important to the Lord than* where *we serve.*

Doctrine and Covenants 117:1–9
What are some "weighty matters" that deserve our time and attention?

Have your family look for reasons William Marks and Newel K. Whitney had tarried in Kirtland as you read together D&C 117:1–9. Discuss these questions:

- Which of the Ten Commandments is spoken of in verses 4 and 8? (Thou shalt not covet.)
- What was the object of their covetous desires? (Property—see verse 4.)
- What do you think is the "drop" and what might be "more weighty matters"? (See verse 8.)

Share the following description about verse 8 from Elder John B. Dickson of the Seventy.

"As we examine a drop of water, we observe that it is not permanent and will evaporate. In this case, the men's personal property was important by their standard of measure but was temporary in the sense that it was earthbound and could not pass through the veil with them as they departed this short mortal life.

"In our day, the dwellings we live in are extremely important in most of our social situations. They should be well-kept, comfortable places where our family can be drawn around us, but we need to realize that as we leave this life we

BIOGRAPHICAL SKETCH: WILLIAM MARKS

"At age forty-nine William Marks was baptized and ordained a priest in New York. He soon moved his family to Kirtland, where he established a book and stationery store. . . . On 3 September 1837 he was called to the Kirtland high council, and two weeks later was called to be an 'agent' to Bishop Newel K. Whitney. . . . At a conference on 5 October 1839 at Commerce (later Nauvoo), William was appointed to preside over the stake there. . . . However, by 1844 his faith faltered. [He later left the Church and joined several different factions.] William Marks died on 22 May 1872 at Plano, Illinois, at the age of seventy-nine." (Susan Easton Black, *Who's Who in the Doctrine and Covenants,* 183–85.)

BIOGRAPHICAL SKETCH: OLIVER GRANGER

"Oliver Granger was eleven years older than Joseph Smith and, like the Prophet, was from upstate New York. Because of severe cold and exposure when he was thirty-three years old, Oliver lost much of his eyesight. Notwithstanding his limited vision, he served three full-time missions. He also worked on the Kirtland Temple and served on the Kirtland high council. When most of the Saints were driven from Kirtland, Ohio, the Church left some debts unsatisfied. Oliver was appointed to represent Joseph Smith and the First Presidency by returning to Kirtland to settle the Church's business. . . . He performed this assignment with such satisfaction to the creditors involved that one of them wrote: 'Oliver Granger's management in the arrangement of the unfinished business of people that have moved to the Far West, in redeeming their pledges and thereby sustaining their integrity, has been truly praiseworthy, and has entitled him to my highest esteem, and every grateful recollection.' (Horace Kingsbury, as cited in Joseph Smith, *History of the Church,* 3:174.) During Oliver's time in Kirtland, some people, including disaffected members of the Church, were endeavoring to discredit the First Presidency and bring their integrity into question by spreading false accusations. Oliver Granger, in very deed, 'redeemed the First Presidency' through his faithful service. In response, the Lord said of Oliver Granger: 'His name shall be had in sacred remembrance from generation to generation, forever and ever.' (D&C 117:12.) 'I will lift up my servant Oliver, and beget for him a great name on the earth, and among my people, because of the integrity of his soul.' (*History of the Church,* 3:350.) When he died in 1841, even though there were but few Saints remaining in the Kirtland area and even fewer friends of the Saints, Oliver Granger's funeral was attended by a vast concourse of people from neighboring towns." (Howard W. Hunter, *Ensign,* April 1992, 64.)

cannot take them with us. The same could be said about our automobiles, computers, jewelry, televisions, and thousands of other earthly possessions. As much as we enjoy them and need many of them, they will stay here, remain temporary, and are but a drop when considered from an eternal perspective.

"Our children must be taught that the 'more weighty matters' help them qualify for and ultimately enjoy eternal blessings. While there is nothing wrong with certain possessions and wealth, righteously attained and handled, we must teach our children that the weighty matters include the gospel of Jesus Christ, His Atonement, the family, the priesthood, Christlike attributes, knowledge, and gospel ordinances and covenants.

"We need to teach them never to give up eternal blessings in pursuit of the temporary things of the world. . . . We must teach our children never to give up those things that matter most in pursuit of those things that matter least." (*Ensign*, September 2003, 12.)

Discuss with your family what family priorities may need to be altered in light of Elder Dickson's advice.

Share the following illustration from Elder Harold B. Lee, and talk about how it relates to weighty matters:

"One of the General Authorities had a son working on the railroad that went up Emigration Canyon to the mines in the early days. This boy was found crushed to death under the train. He was working as a switchman. His mother had the feeling that someone had pushed him under the train and taken his life. When the services were held, she was not comforted. But after some weeks, the mother said this boy appeared to her. He said, 'Mother, I've been trying to get to Father to tell him it was just an accident. I had thrown the switch and was running to catch on to the hand bars, but my foot tripped against a root at the side of a rail and I was thrown underneath the train. It was a pure accident. I've been trying to get to Father, but he's too busy at the office. I can't reach him.' President McKay said, 'Brethren, don't you get so busy at the office that spiritual forces are not able to reach you.'" (*Relief Society Courses of Study*, 1979–80, 32–33.)

Doctrine and Covenants 117:10–11
Are you a member in name only?

Have a family member read D&C 117:11 aloud. Ask if anyone has ever heard of a "Nicolaitane band." Read Revelation 2:6, 15 and find out how the Nicolaitanes are described. Tell your family that Elder Bruce R. McConkie indicated "Nicolaitanes" referred to "members of the Church who were trying to maintain their church standing while continuing to live after the manner of the world. . . . the designation has come to be used to identify those who want their names on the records of the Church, but do not want to devote themselves to the gospel cause with full

purpose of heart." (*Doctrinal New Testament Commentary*, 3:447.)

Read D&C 117:10–11 and talk about these questions:

- What do you think it means to "be a bishop . . . not in name but in deed"?
- How might that relate to other callings in the Church?
- What might it mean to be a Latter-day Saint, not in name but in deed?
- What deeds would help show that you are a true Latter-day Saint?

Doctrine and Covenants 117:12–16
"His sacrifice shall be more sacred unto me than his increase"

Ask your family which player on a football team is usually most noticed and gets the most attention (the quarterback). How successful would a quarterback be if the other players did not perform their duties? Share the following from President Howard W. Hunter:

"Like the offensive linemen and other unsung heroes on the football team, most of us may spend much of our lives giving service in relative obscurity. Consider the profound service a mother or father gives in the quiet anonymity of a worthy Latter-day Saint home. Think of the Gospel Doctrine teachers and Primary choristers and Scoutmasters and Relief Society visiting teachers who serve and bless millions but whose names will never be publicly applauded." ("Out of the Limelight," *New Era*, September 1991, 4.)

Ask family members if they know anything about Oliver Granger. Explain that he is an example of someone who was "relatively obscure." Read his biographical sketch to your family, and have your family think about Oliver Granger as you read D&C 117:12–15 together.

Share the following, also from President Hunter: "Though Oliver Granger is not as well known today as other early leaders of the Church, he was nevertheless a great and important man in the service he rendered to the kingdom. And even if no one but the Lord had his name in remembrance, that would be a sufficient blessing for him—or for any of us." ("Out of the Limelight," *New Era*, September 1991, 4.) Invite your family to evaluate how they are doing as members of the Lord's team and if they are doing their best to make it successful.

DOCTRINE AND COVENANTS 118: "CONCERNING THE TWELVE"

Historical background: *Church leaders left Kirtland in January of 1838 to fulfill the command to speedily build up Far West. (See D&C 115:17.) Far West became the central gathering place, and this revelation was given as the Saints began to gather there. (See also the historical background for D&C 117.) Look for whom the Lord calls to fill the vacancies in the Quorum of the Twelve.*

Doctrine and Covenants 118:1
Who fell?

Ask your family to name things that "fall," and how those things could be damaged as a result. (Some examples might include: fruit from a tree, which would become bruised; people who might break a bone; or a plate or cup that could be broken.) Read D&C 118:1 and ask:

- What has fallen? (Some of the early apostles apostatized.)
- What might cause faithful members of the Church to "fall away"?
- How does it affect the Church when people choose to leave it?
- How does it affect the people who leave the Church?

Share the following information about the apostles who fell away from the Church at this time, and those who were called to replace them:

"John Taylor, John E. Page, Wilford Woodruff and Willard Richards, the latter at the time acting as one of the presidency of the British Mission, were called to the apostleship, to take the places of William E. McLellin, Luke S. Johnson, John F. Boynton and Lyman E. Johnson, who had fallen." (Joseph Fielding Smith, *Essentials in Church History*, 179.)

Doctrine and Covenants 118:2–6
What were these apostles called to do?

Write July 8, 1838, on the top of a piece of paper and then make a list of the following names below the date:

Thomas B. Marsh
David W. Patten
Brigham Young
Parley P. Pratt
William Smith
Heber C. Kimball
Orson Hyde
Orson Pratt
John Taylor
John E. Page
Wilford Woodruff
Willard Richards

Show your family this list of names and ask what they think these individuals had in common. (They were apostles on July 8, 1838.)

Fold a large piece of paper in thirds lengthwise. Label the columns like the example below and then ask your family to scan through D&C 118:2–6 and find out some of the things these apostles were asked to do. Fill in the chart with the things you discover. When they are finished, your chart should look like the one on the next page:

Verse	Name of Apostle	Assignment from the Lord
2	Thomas [B. Marsh]	• Stay in Missouri and publish God's word.
3–5	Other apostles	• Preach in all lowliness of heart, in meekness and humility, and long-suffering.
		• On April 26, 1839, leave from the temple site in Far West and go over the great waters—sharing the fulness of the gospel.
		• Bear record of Christ's name.
6	John Taylor, John E. Page, Wilford Woodruff, Willard Richards	• Fill the places of the apostles who had fallen.

Ask some of the following questions:

- What blessings were promised the apostles if they obeyed? (See verse 3.)
- Why do you think the apostles were to gather together before leaving on missions?
- What blessings can come by gathering and counseling with others as we seek to follow the Lord's commandments?
- How has your family been blessed by gathering and counseling together?

Share the following account showing how the Lord fulfilled his promised blessings to these apostles:

When D&C 118 was given, it seemed logical for the apostles to leave from Far West. However, four months later, Far West was attacked and the Saints were driven from the state of Missouri. "The mob, with their apostate allies who had betrayed to them the secrets of the kingdom, had sworn that this revelation should not be fulfilled, and having driven the Saints from their homes, leaving only a few scattered families in and around Far West, and imprisoned the Church leaders, they flattered themselves that their wicked oath had been verified. . . .

"[However on the night of April 25th it] . . . was a beautiful, clear moonlight, Elders Brigham Young, Orson Pratt, John E. Page, John Taylor, Wilford Woodruff, George A. Smith, and Alpheus Cutler, arrived from Quincy, Illinois, and rode into the public square early on the morning of the 26th. All seemed still as death.

"April 26th, we held a conference at the house of Brother Samuel Clark . . . and then proceeded to the building spot of the Lord's house, where, after singing, we recommended laying the foundation, agreeably to the revelation given July 8th, 1839, by rolling a stone, upwards of a ton weight, upon or near the southeast corner." (Orson F. Whitney, *Life of Heber C. Kimball*, 252.) So, the prophecy and promise of D&C 118:5 was fulfilled without any apostles being injured as the mobs had threatened.

DOCTRINE AND COVENANTS 119: THE LORD'S LAW OF TITHING

Historical background: See the section heading for D&C 119. As you study this revelation watch for the Lord's explanation of the law of tithing.

Doctrine and Covenants 119:1–7
What is the Lord's law of tithing?

Ask each family member in turn to mention three or four of their favorite possessions. Then read Deuteronomy 10:12–14 aloud to your family, particularly emphasizing verse 14, and ask:

- According to verse 14, how much of what we have actually belongs to God?
- Why, then, is it important to keep His commandments?
- If He wants us to give something back to Him, should we? Why?

Read the following statement:

"The first rule, and one never to be forgotten, is that *everything* you have or ever will have, individually and collectively, is a *gift from God,* something that he blesses you with, has blessed you with, or will bless you with—you owe it all to him." (Hugh Nibley, *Approaching Zion,* 179–80.)

Now place ten dimes (or other denomination of money) on a table. Explain that even our money is a gift from God. However, He does not require us to pay it all back to Him. What He has commanded is for us to obey the law of tithing.

Invite someone to read the section heading for D&C 119. Ask:

- Where was this section received? (Far West, Missouri. Show your family the map section at the end of the D&C on page 297 of the older scriptures and map number 5 in the new scriptures and point out the location of Far West.)
- What was the question that brought about this revelation?
- Prior to receiving this revelation, what had the Saints understood tithing to mean?

- What law was in place before section 119 was given?

Read D&C 119:1–4 together. Ask a family member to use the money you placed on a table, and demonstrate what "tithing" would be on ten dimes. Discuss the following questions:

- What is one tenth of $100? $1,000?
- Do you think it is harder to pay tithing on a little or a lot of money? Why?
- What is tithing used for? (Building churches and temples, and other church owned buildings, maintenance and upkeep on the buildings, missionary work, paying church employees, and stake, ward, and branch budgets.)
- What blessings have come to you from paying your tithing?

Share the following statements with your family:

"The simplest statement we know of is the statement of the Lord himself, namely that the members of the church should pay one tenth of all their interest annually which is understood to mean income. No one is justified in making any other statements than this." (*Church Handbook of Instructions,* Book 1, 134.)

"I believe that man who pays his honest tithing to God will not only be blessed by God himself, but that the nine tenths will reach farther than the other ten tenths would if he did not obey the law." (Reed Smoot, Conference Report, October 1900, 7–8.)

Share your testimony on the importance of paying an honest tithe. Talk about some blessings you have received as a result. Share some of the Lord's promises by studying Malachi 3:8–12. Also ask your family to study D&C 119:5–7, looking for who is to pay tithing and what consequences will come for those who fail to participate.

DOCTRINE AND COVENANTS 120: THE COUNCIL ON THE DISPOSITION OF TITHES

Historical background: See the section heading for Doctrine and Covenants 119.

Doctrine and Covenants 120:1
Who decides how tithing money is spent?

Have your family imagine having several million dollars. Ask them who they would trust to take care of it for them. Whose advice would they trust regarding how best to use it, spend it, save it, and so forth?

Have family members think of the last time they filled out a tithing donation slip and put donated money into a gray envelope at the Church. To whom are you supposed to give your tithing and offerings? (Members of the bishopric.) Explain that after receiving these offerings, bishops send the money to Church Headquarters. What happens with it then is described in Doctrine and Covenants 120.

Have a family member read D&C 120:1 and find the four participants in the council that decides how tithing money will be used. (The First Presidency, the Presiding Bishopric, the Quorum of the Twelve, and the Lord—by the voice of His Spirit. You may need to explain "the bishop and his council" refers to the Presiding Bishopric of the Church, and "the high council" refers to the presiding high council of the whole Church, or the Quorum of the Twelve Apostles—as described in D&C 107:33.)

From a May issue of the *Ensign* (the April general conference edition), show your family the pictures of those who sit in this council. Also find the "Church Auditing Department Report," which is usually one of the first things presented in the Saturday afternoon session of April's general conference. Find the part that mentions "the Council on the Disposition of the Tithes," and read a portion to your family. Ask:

- Why do you think this is a part of the general conference addresses?
- What does the Lord expect when we use that which belongs to Him?
- How should this process affect the way we use Church funds at our local level in our respective callings and assignments?

DOCTRINE AND COVENANTS 121: REVELATIONS FROM LIBERTY JAIL

Historical background: On October 27, 1838, Governor Lilburn B. Boggs, heeding the false accusations of many apostates and enemies of the church, ordered, "The Mormons must be treated as enemies and must be exterminated or driven from the State, if necessary for the public good." Three days later was the massacre at Haun's Mill. By October 31 state militias had surrounded Far West, outnumbering the Saints five to one. Colonel Hinkle, the commanding officer for the Saints, betrayed the prophet and other church leaders by convincing them that General Lucas of the militia wanted to meet with them in a peace conference. Once they met the General, Hinkle surrendered them as prisoners.

On the night of November 1, 1838, an illegal court was held where the prisoners were not invited. The court sentenced Joseph and his companions to be shot in the Far West town square at eight o'clock the next morning. General Doniphan refused to carry out the sentence saying, "It is cold-blooded murder. I will not obey your order, and if you execute those men, I will hold you responsible before an earthly tribunal, so help me God!" This courageous action saved their lives. Joseph Smith and the others were then taken from one jail to another until settling in Liberty Jail for five months. It was in this setting that the Prophet wrote an important letter from which sections 121, 122, and 123 are taken. Of this letter, Joseph Fielding Smith wrote:

"It is a prayer and a prophecy and an answer by revelation from the Lord. None other but a noble soul filled with the spirit of love of Christ could have written such a letter. Considering the fact that these prisoners had been confined several months; were fed on food at times not fit for a pig, and at times impregnated with poison and once being offered human flesh, evidently from the body of one of their brethren, it is no wonder that the Prophet cried out in the anguish of his soul for relief. Yet, in his earnest pleading, there breathed a spirit of tolerance and love for his fellow man. . . . It was his people for whom he pled, more than for himself." (Church History and Modern Revelation, 3:197.) Watch for how differently the Lord views our troubles from the way we view them.

Doctrine and Covenants 121:1–6
Why?

Ask family members to think of and share one of their greatest trials. Read together the historical background above and the section heading to D&C 121. Compare the trials mentioned by family members with those of Joseph and ask:

- When a person is suffering a great trial, what kind of questions might they ask of God?
- What kinds of questions do you think Joseph Smith might have asked of God?

Invite someone to read D&C 121:1–3 aloud and have your family identify and mark each question Joseph asked. Ask:

- What questions does Joseph ask instead of "why"?
- In what way might asking God "Why?" show a lack of trust in Him or even accuse God of not being there when needed?
- How do questions like, "Where art thou" and "How long," show more faith than asking, "Why"?

Read together D&C 121:4–6 and look for what Joseph requested of the Lord. Ask:

- Who is Joseph requesting the most help for?
- What does it teach us about Joseph's heart that he prays for others more than for himself?

Encourage your family to remember others

during their prayers and challenge them to trust that God has a purpose behind the trials we are given.

Doctrine and Covenants 121:7–9, 29
A relatively "small moment"

Draw a line across a sheet of paper. Have your family imagine that the line represents three periods of time: their pre-mortal life, their earthly life, and their life after death. Ask your family what portion of the line they think represents earth life and mark it with a pencil. Invite someone to read D&C 121:7 aloud. Discuss the following questions:

- According to this verse, what portion of the line might represent the months Joseph spent in prison? (A "small moment")
- How long do you think this "small moment" seemed to Joseph living each day in prison?
- How does it help to know your trials won't last forever?

Read together D&C 121:8–9. Ask:

- What is the difference between "enduring" and "enduring well" the trials we face?
- How do people act who are "enduring well" their trials?
- According to D&C 121:29 how might the way we "endure" trials in this life influence our eternities?
- What promises did the Lord give to Joseph?
- What promise gave Joseph hope that he would not die in Liberty Jail?
- With so much depending on our "small moment" on earth, what should our attitude be toward the trials we face?

Discuss ways your family can help each other to learn how to "endure well" life's trials. Challenge your family members to write in their journals one thing they will do differently to help them better "endure well."

Doctrine and Covenants 121:11–25
The wages of wickedness

Ask your family members to tell what their ideal job would be and why. Discuss the following questions:

- If a job requires work and effort, why would you want a job?
- How does making a wage encourage you to go to work each day?
- Are there some jobs that you think are not worth the wages that are offered?

Write the questions and the references below on separate pieces of paper and divide them among family members. Give your family time to find answers to their assigned questions. Take turns reading D&C 121:11–25 as a family. As you come to verses with an assigned question, have the family member assigned read the question and help the rest of the family discover the answer.

- What will happen to all the efforts made by enemies of the Church? (See verse 11.)
- Why doesn't God immediately punish the wicked? (See verse 12 and also Alma 60:13.)
- How will the actions of the wicked come back to them? (See verses 13–16.)
- Why do the wicked often accuse others of sin? (See verse 17.)
- How bad will the wicked's punishments be? (See verses 20–23.)
- When will the judgments of God come upon the wicked? (See verse 25.)

Ask your family how the results of sin might be considered "wages." Challenge your family to beware of the "wages of sin." (See Romans 6:23.)

Doctrine and Covenants 121:26–33
Look what I found!

Do the activity "Look what I found!" Divide your family into pairs. Invite family members to silently read D&C 121:26–33 and mark those things they find interesting. When all are finished, have them share with their partners the things they found. Then have those family members share with the rest of the family the insight(s) that their partners found.

Doctrine and Covenants 121:34–46
How to make leadership work

Bring the vacuum cleaner to scripture study. Ask your family to list what might happen that would cause the vacuum cleaner to lose the power to clean. Explain to your family that D&C 121:34–46 is important council to those who hold the priesthood. While you read together verses 34–40 have family members mark those things that would keep a priesthood holder from having power in his priesthood. Invite family members to share what they marked and why they think it would prevent someone from having priesthood power. Compare the things marked in verses 34–40 with those things listed that would keep a vacuum from working properly.

Explain that D&C 121:34–40 tells those things the Lord would have priesthood holders avoid, but verses 41–46 tell those things the Lord wants priesthood holders to do. Invite your family to go through D&C 121:41–46 and mark those things that a priesthood holder should do. Have family members share what they found. Discuss as a family individuals you know who are examples of worthy priesthood holders. Ask, "What can we do to follow their examples"?

DOCTRINE AND COVENANTS 122: SUFFERINGS "SHALL BE FOR THY GOOD"

Historical background: This section is also taken from the letters spoken of in the historical background for Doctrine and Covenants 121. As you read this portion of Joseph Smith's letter from Liberty Jail, think about what lessons we can learn from the trials and challenges we face.

Doctrine and Covenants 122:1–4
How do people feel about the Prophet Joseph Smith?

Display a picture of Joseph Smith and ask, "If you were to survey 100 people across the nation and ask, 'what do you think of Joseph Smith,' what answers might you receive?" Have a family member read D&C 122:1–4 aloud and discuss the Lord's response about how people will view Joseph Smith. Ask:

- Why do you think there are such differing opinions of the Prophet?
- How do you think Joseph felt when he received this revelation? (Remind your family that he had been in Liberty Jail for 5 months. He may have been wondering if he would ever get out.)
- How have you seen the prophecy in verse two fulfilled?

Share the following statement from Josiah Quincy, a former mayor of Boston, Massachusetts, who met Joseph Smith while visiting Nauvoo in May, 1844:

"It is by no means improbable that some future textbook for the use of generations yet unborn, will contain a question something like this: What historical American of the nineteenth century has exerted the most powerful influence upon the destinies of his countrymen? And it is by no means impossible that the answer to that interrogatory may be thus written: Joseph Smith, the Mormon Prophet. And the reply, absurd as it doubtless seems to most men now living, may be an obvious one commonplace to their descendants." (As quoted in B. H. Roberts, *Comprehensive History*, 2:349.)

Share with your family your feelings about the Prophet Joseph. Invite everyone to express their feelings about the Prophet in their journals.

Doctrine and Covenants 122:4
"Thy voice shall be more terrible in the midst of thine enemies . . ."

Have a family member read D&C 121:4. Tell your family that the Prophet Joseph knew this promise of the Lord was true because he had experienced it several months earlier, while a prisoner in a jail in Richmond, Missouri. Read the following experience to your family, told by Parley P. Pratt, that illustrates the power the Lord had given Joseph:

"In one of those tedious nights [Winter, 1838–39, Richmond, Missouri, jail] we had lain as if in sleep, till the hour of midnight had passed, and our ears and hearts had been pained, while we had listened for hours to the obscene jests, the horrid oaths, the dreadful blasphemies and filthy language of our guards, Colonel Price at their head, as they recounted to each other their deeds of rapine, murder, robbery, etc., which they had committed among the 'Mormons' while at Far West and vicinity. They even boasted of defiling by force wives, daughters, and virgins, and of shooting or dashing out the brains of men, women and children.

"I had listened till I became so disgusted, shocked, horrified, and so filled with the Spirit of indignant justice, that I could scarcely refrain from rising upon my feet and rebuking the guards, but I had said nothing to Joseph or anyone else, although I lay next to him, and knew he was awake. On a sudden he arose to his feet and spoke in a voice of thunder, or as the roaring lion, uttering, as near as I can recollect, the following words: *'Silence! Ye fiends of the infernal pit! In the name of Jesus Christ I rebuke you, and command you to be still; I will not live another minute and hear such language. Cease such talk, or you or I die this instant!'*

"He ceased to speak. He stood erect in terrible majesty. Chained, and without a weapon, calm, unruffled, and dignified as an angel, he looked down upon his quailing guards, whose knees smote together, and who, shrinking into a corner, or crouching at his feet, begged his pardon, and remained quiet until an exchange of guards.

"I have seen ministers of justice, clothed in ministerial robes, and criminals arraigned before them, while life was suspended upon a breath in the courts of England; I have witnessed a congress in solemn session to give laws to nations; I have tried to conceive of kings, of royal courts, of thrones and crowns; and of emperors assembled to decide the fate of kingdoms; but dignity and majesty have I seen but once, as it stood in chains, at midnight, in a dungeon in an obscure village of Missouri." (*Autobiography of Parley P. Pratt,* 179–80.)

Invite your family to reread D&C 122:4 and find a phrase that best matches this experience. Ask your family if they had been in the room that night, what they might have thought or felt.

Doctrine and Covenants 122:5–8
"All these things shall give thee experience, and shall be for thy good"

Ask members of your family to share a few specific trials they have faced in their lives that they think have been their most challenging. Now compile a written list of the trials your family can remember that the Prophet Joseph Smith experienced. Invite your family to read D&C 122:5–7 and add any other trials you find that the Lord said Joseph Smith would endure. (Find these trials by looking at the "if thou" or "if they" statements in the verses.)

Read the following to your family as an example of how the instruction in D&C 122 was fulfilled in Joseph's life:

"Myself and fellow prisoners were taken to the town, [Far West, Mo.] into the public square, and before departure we, after much entreaty, were suffered to see our families, being attended all the while by a strong guard. I found my wife and children in tears, who feared we had been shot by those who had sworn to take our lives, and that they would see me no more. When I entered my house, they clung to my garments, their eyes streaming with tears while mingled emotions of joy and sorrow were manifested in their countenances. I requested to have a private interview with them a few minutes, but this privilege was denied me by the guard. I was then obliged to take my departure. . . .

"My partner wept, my children clung to me, until they were thrust from me by the swords of the guards. I felt overwhelmed while I witnessed the scene, and could only recommend them to the care of that God whose kindness had followed me to the present time, and who alone could protect them, and deliver me from the hands of my enemies, and restore me to my family." (Joseph Smith, *History of the Church,* 3:193.)

Now, referring back to the list you compiled, ask:

- Which trial do you think was most difficult for Joseph and why?
- Why do you think the Lord would allow Joseph to suffer in that way?
- What important lesson(s) do you think Joseph may have learned through that experience?

Invite a family member to read the following statement, and discuss how our trials, like Joseph's, can help us become more Christ-like:

"I am like a huge, rough stone rolling down from a high mountain; and the only polishing I get is when some corner gets rubbed off by coming in contact with something else, striking with accelerated force against religious bigotry, priestcraft, lawyer-craft, doctor-craft, lying editors, suborned judges and jurors, and the authority of perjured executives, backed by mobs, blasphemers, licentious and corrupt men and women—all hell knocking off a corner here and a corner there. Thus I will become a smooth and polished shaft in the quiver of the Almighty, who will give me dominion over all and every one of them, when their refuge of lies shall fail, and their hiding place shall be destroyed, while these smooth-polished stones with which I come in contact become

marred." (*Teachings of the Prophet Joseph Smith,* 304.)

Invite your family to re-read D&C 122:5–8 looking for reasons why Joseph was tried. Ask your family:

- How do trials help us gain "experience"?
- How can trials be for "our good"?
- What do you think Joseph learned from verse 8?
- What do Alma 62:41 and Alma 36:3 help us learn about enduring trials?
- What have you learned from some of your trials?

Share an experience of your own and testify to your family that trials can work for our good and give us experience.

Doctrine and Covenants 122:8–9
Why did the Savior descend below all things?

Ask your family if they have ever been having a bad day and then talked to someone who was having a worse day. Ask them how their attitudes changed after hearing the other person's experiences. Review with your family, from the historical background for section 121, where Joseph is at the time this section was written and the trial he is going through. Invite a family member to read D&C 122:8–9. Ask:

- What does the Lord want Joseph to understand by what was said in verse 8?
- Why did the Savior need to descend below all things? (See Alma 7:11–12 to help answer this question.)
- What things from verse 9 would have given Joseph comfort?

Explain to your family that sometimes we feel as though no one understands what we are going through—no one. Even though we may feel that way, we know of one who understands perfectly. Invite family members to think quietly of a time when they felt the Savior's love and help for them in a time of need. Testify to your family of the healing influence of the Atonement of Jesus Christ.

DOCTRINE AND COVENANTS 123: MORE COUNSEL FROM PRISON

Historical background: See section headings for D&C 121–23 along with the historical background for section 121 in this book. Look for what actions the Saints were to take after being so badly mistreated in Missouri.

Doctrine and Covenants 123:1–11
Do you know the definition?

Ask family members to scan D&C 123:1–11 and write down each word they do not know or understand. (Note: most of the words they write down will probably be included on the list below.) When they have finished, place the following definitions on slips of paper and spread them out on the floor. Play a simple matching game, seeing if your family can match the correct definition with the unfamiliar word. Give small rewards for each correct match.

When you finish matching all the words, divide the definitions among your family members. Read D&C 123:1–11 aloud and as you come to each difficult word have the family member with that matching slip of paper read their definition in place of the difficult word. This should help your family better understand this section.

- Oppressions—persecutions and mistreatments
- Affidavits—legal statements made under oath
- Libelous—false or misleading
- Concatenation—things linked together in a series or chain; connected
- Diabolical rascality—devilish or dishonest actions
- Nefarious—very wicked; vile or sinful
- Impositions—requirements and expectations that are unnecessary
- Hellish hue—evil and wicked colors
- Imperative—very important and urgent
- Tyranny—power exercised unjustly and cruelly

Have a family member explain the main message of these verses in his or her own words. Ask:

- What does the Lord want the Saints to do?
- What reasons does He give for these commands?
- What specific things does the Lord want the Saints to collect? (See verses 1–5.)
- Why are they to gather and publish these accounts? (See verse 6–11.)
- What phrase is used at the beginning of verses 7, 9, and 11 emphasizing the Saint's responsibility?

What do we learn from these verses that teaches us how the Lord feels about those who persecute His Saints?

Doctrine and Covenants 123:12–17
"We should wear out our lives"

If you have a worn-out pair of shoes or pants with a worn-out knee, show them to your family. Ask, what could "worn-out" shoes or pants represent or symbolize about a person's life. Ask your family to look for how this idea relates to what the Prophet Joseph Smith said in D&C 123:12–17. After reading these verses together, ask:

- Why are there many yet on the earth who do not know about gospel truths?
- What responsibility do you have to share the gospel with others? Why?

Share with your family this example from the life of President Spencer W. Kimball: "'President Kimball was driven to do the Lord's work, and it showed,' says Arthur [Haycock, personal secretary to Pres. Kimball]. His shoes frequently needed resoling because, as he often said to Arthur, 'My life is like my shoes, to be worn out in the service of the Lord.' When he sat on the stand with his legs comfortably crossed, those in the audience could see the soles of his shoes worn right through." (Heidi S. Swinton, *In the Company of Prophets*, 107–8.)

- What phrases in D&C 123:12–17 describe how we should approach the Lord's work?
- What point do you think the Prophet was trying to make in verses 15–16?
- What are some seemingly small things we can do as individuals and as a family to further the Lord's work?
- What kind of attitude should we have as we seek to do all in our power to build the kingdom of God?

Share the following statement by Elder M. Russell Ballard:

"President David O. McKay encouraged every member to be a missionary. President Spencer W. Kimball urged us to 'lengthen our stride.' President Howard W. Hunter affirmed, 'We are at a time in the history of the world and the growth of the Church when we must think more of holy things and act more like the Savior would expect his disciples to act.'

"And now President Gordon B. Hinckley is asking us to carry on, to do better, to do more. He said: 'We have work to do, you and I, so very much of it. Let us roll up our sleeves and get at it, with a new commitment, putting our trust in the Lord. . . . We can do it, if we will be prayerful and faithful.'

"President Hinckley is doing all that he can do to accelerate the work. He is traveling the world to an unprecedented degree to strengthen and edify the Saints and to urge them upward and onward. . . .

"Our President is dynamically out in front, showing the way. The question we must all ask ourselves is, 'Are we keeping pace with him?' Each one of us must be prepared to answer that question." (*Ensign*, November 1998, 6.)

DOCTRINE AND COVENANTS 124: BUILDING UP NAUVOO IN A SEASON OF PEACE AND PROSPERITY

Historical background: "When this revelation was given, this beautiful city, [Nauvoo] . . . had about 3,000 inhabitants. A charter had been granted by the Illinois Legislature, by which Nauvoo was given a liberal municipal government, with authority to form a militia and erect a university. A Temple was about to be built. The scattered Saints were gathering, and the settlements in Illinois were growing rapidly. The mission in Great Britain was highly successful . . . The Church had a moment's rest. There was calm before the next storm." (Hyrum M. Smith and Janne M. Sjodahl, Doctrine and Covenants Commentary, *768.) Notice in this revelation the Lord's continuing instructions on the importance of temples.*

Doctrine and Covenants 124:1–14
A proclamation to world leaders

Ask your family to imagine they wanted to make an announcement or a proclamation to everyone in the world. Have them share ideas about how they might accomplish that. (For example, they might suggest making an announcement on T.V., using the Internet, or making a radio broadcast.) Talk about what kind of technology existed when Joseph Smith was the prophet, and explain that he was commanded by the Lord to make a proclamation. Take turns reading D&C 124:1–11 and discuss the following questions as you read:

- To whom was Joseph to address the proclamation? (Verse 3.)
- What reasons did the Lord give for making the proclamation?
- What was the proclamation to contain? (Verses 5–7.)
- How was Joseph to know what to write?
- How will the Lord prepare the rulers for Joseph's testimony? (Verses 9, 11.)
- What will happen to the rulers who listen to the proclamation and those who do not?

Tell your family: "The Prophet Joseph and others worked on the preparation of this document from time to time until the martyrdom in June, 1844. Following the prophet's death, the Quorum of Twelve Apostles proceeded with the preparation of the proclamation and published it on April 6, 1845. It was then sent to those addressed in the revelation." (L.G. Otten and C. M. Caldwell, *Sacred Truths of the Doctrine and Covenants*, 2:310–11.)

Share the following:

"The Proclamation of 1845 was issued by the Twelve only because at that time there was no First Presidency due to the martyrdom of the Prophet Joseph Smith on June 27, 1844, and a new First Presidency was not organized until December 1847. The Proclamation was apparently made in response to a revelation given January 19, 1841(D&C 124:1–11). It was first printed in a sixteen-page pamphlet in New York City on April 6, 1845, and again in Liverpool, England, October 22, 1845. It was addressed to the rulers and people of all nations. This document announced that God had spoken from the heavens and had restored the gospel of Jesus Christ to the earth. It spoke of blessings and punishments to come, issued a warning voice, and invited all who were interested to assist in the building of the kingdom of God on earth in preparation for the Savior's second coming. On October

3, 1975, President Ezra Taft Benson, president of the Quorum of the Twelve Apostles, spoke of this Proclamation and quoted portions of it in his general conference address. (*Ensign* 15 [Oct. 1975]:32–34.)" (*Encyclopedia of Mormonism*, 1153.)

Ask your family if they know of any official proclamations issued by the Church in their lifetime. Tell them in April 1980, a proclamation celebrating the 150th anniversary of the founding of the Church, was read to the world by President Gordon B. Hinckley, representing the First Presidency and Quorum of Twelve Apostles. (See Conference Report, April 1980, 74.) In September 1995, President Hinckley presented "The Family: A Proclamation to the World" in a General Relief Society Meeting. (See *Ensign*, November 1995, 102.)

Doctrine and Covenants 124:12–21
Does God know you by name?

 Ask your family to answer the following questions:

- Do you think the president of our Church knows the names of every member? Why or why not?
- Do you think the leader of our country knows the name of every citizen? Why or why not?
- Do you think Heavenly Father knows all His children by name? Why or why not?

Define for your family the word, *omniscient.* (All-knowing.) Testify to your family that God is omniscient and does know us each by name.

Tell your family that D&C 124 contains instructions and information to many different people. Assign different family members to read the following verses. After each set of verses has been read, stop and ask what family members learned about the individual(s) listed in the verse(s).

D&C 124:12–14
D&C 124:15

D&C 124:16–17
D&C 124:18–19
D&C 124:19
D&C 124:20–21

Discuss some of these questions:

- Which of the blessings listed in verses 12–21 would you enjoy most and why?
- What character traits enabled these individuals to attain specific blessings?
- Which words or phrases show that God knew each one of these men personally, and knew what promises, blessings, and warnings each needed?
- How does it feel to know that God is omniscient and knows you personally?

Explain to your family that a patriarchal blessing can be compared to personal scripture. In those blessings the Lord can teach us, extend individual promises and warnings, and help us understand His will for us personally. Invite your family to receive their patriarchal blessing at an appropriate time, or if they have received it to read it often.

Doctrine and Covenants 124:22–24, 56–83, 119–22

The Nauvoo House

Briefly tell your family the story of the good Samaritan. (See Luke 10:30–37.) Ask a family member to read Luke 10:27. Ask:

- What does the story of the good Samaritan have to do with loving our neighbor?
- Why do you think it is important to love our neighbors?
- Are our neighbors only those who live next door? Who else is our neighbor?
- What can we do to show love for others, including visitors, strangers, and those of other faiths?

Show your family a picture of the Nauvoo House. Tell your family that the Lord commanded the Saints in Nauvoo to build this house for a

Nauvoo House. (Photo by Kenneth Mays.)

special purpose. Take turns reading D&C 124:22–24, 56–83, 119–22 and find out the name of this house, what purpose it was to serve, and how it would help the Saints to help others. When you have finished, ask each family member to share one important insight they gained from studying about the Nauvoo House. Challenge your family to make your home a place that is devoted to helping and serving others.

It might be of interest to share with your family that " . . . in 1846, when the Saints left Nauvoo, the walls were up above the windows of the second story. . . . It was planned to be the most magnificent hotel in the West, at the time. . . . The unfinished building became the property of the Prophet's widow, and was subsequently claimed by her second husband, Mr. L. C. Bidamon. In 1872 he put part of it under roof and fitted it up as an hotel, known as the Bidamon House." (Hyrum M. Smith and Janne M. Sjodahl, *Doctrine and Covenants Commentary,* 773.)

Doctrine and Covenants 124:25–48

The temple

Have family members scan D&C 124:25–48 and find the word "house" every time it occurs. What is the "house" referred to in these verses? (The Nauvoo Temple.)

Display a picture of a temple—preferably the Nauvoo Temple—and then sing together "I Love to See the Temple" (*Children's Songbook*, 95).

Have your family read D&C 124:25–48 and make a list of the things they learn about the Lord's instructions concerning the Nauvoo Temple. Talk about the following questions:

- In January of 1841, the date of this revelation, what was not found upon the earth? (See verse 28.)
- According to verse 28, what is a major reason we need temples?
- According to verses 30–33, what are the only times the Lord will accept ordinance work for the dead outside of the temple?

Share the following statement from Joseph Fielding Smith:

"In the months when the saints were without a Temple the Lord granted them the privilege of baptizing for their dead in the Mississippi River, but with the understanding that this was a special privilege which would end when they had been given sufficient time to prepare a place in the Temple where this ordinance could be performed. . . . And when that time arrived all baptisms for the dead in the river ceased by divine command." (Roy W. Doxey, comp., *Latter-day Prophets and the Doctrine and Covenants,* 4:265–66.)

Share the following statement from President Howard W. Hunter:

"It should be no surprise to us that the Lord does desire that his people be a temple-motivated people. . . . It would please the Lord for every adult member to be worthy of—and to carry—a current temple recommend . . .

"Let us truly be a temple-attending and a temple-loving people. . . . Let us make the temple, with temple worship and temple covenants and temple marriage, our ultimate earthly goal and the supreme mortal experience.

"All of our efforts in proclaiming the gospel, perfecting the Saints, and redeeming the dead lead to the holy temple. This is because the temple ordinances are absolutely crucial; we cannot return to God's presence without them. I encourage everyone to worthily attend the temple or to work toward the day when you can enter that holy house to receive your ordinances and covenants." (*Ensign,* February 1995, 2–5.)

Re-read D&C 124:42 and ask your family where the plans for the Nauvoo Temple came from. Share the following from the Prophet Joseph Smith:

"In the afternoon, Elder William Weeks (whom I had employed as architect of the Temple,) came in for instruction. I instructed him in relation to the circular windows designed to light the offices. . . . He said that round windows in the broad side of a building were a violation of all the known rules of architecture, and contended that they should be semicircular—that the building was too low for round windows. I told him I would have the circles, if he had to make the Temple ten feet higher than it was originally calculated; that one light at the center of each circular window would

Nauvoo Temple, painting by C.C.A. Christensen.

be sufficient to light the whole room; that when the whole building was illuminated, the effect would be remarkably grand. 'I wish you to carry out my designs. I have seen in vision the splendid appearance of that building illuminated, and will have it built according to the pattern shown me.'" (*History of the Church*, 6:196–97.)

Doctrine and Covenants 124:44–48
Find the principles

Tell your family that one of the greatest blessings resulting from scripture study is the ability to identify principles that guide and direct our lives. One easy way to spot a principle in the scriptures is to watch for the word "if," especially when it is closely followed by a promised blessing. Explain to your family that in D&C 124:44–48 there are four "if/then" statements the Lord gave when revealing information about the Nauvoo Temple. Ask your family to find and mark those four statements. Assign family members to one of those four statements, and have them write in their journal answers to the following about their assigned statement:

- What lesson was the Lord trying to teach?
- Write the statement in your own words.
- How does this statement apply to you and why is it important?

Doctrine and Covenants 124:49–55
Help or hinder God's work?

Ask your family if they have ever wanted to do something for someone in need and were unable to do it because of insufficient time or resources. Read Mosiah 4:24–25 to your family and then ask what they learn there about willingness to serve and ability to serve. Have someone read D&C 124:49 aloud. Ask your family how that verse is like Mosiah 4:24–25.

Make a chart like the one shown below large enough for your family to see. (Be sure to leave off the information in parentheses.)

Have your family search D&C 124:49–55 and list on your chart the blessings for those who serve God in one column and the curses for those who hinder His work in the other column.

Blessings for those who "go with all their might and with all they have—and cease not their diligence."	Curses for those who hinder others from performing God's work.
(If their enemies come upon them and hinder them from performing that work [Jackson County Missouri Temple], then the Lord requires the work no more; accepts the offering—see verses 49–51.)	("The iniquity and transgression of my holy laws and commandments I will visit upon the heads of those who hindered my work, unto the third and fourth generation—verse 50.)
(Save the pure in heart and those slain in Missouri—see verse 54.)	(Judgment, wrath, indignation, wailing, anguish, gnashing of teeth unto the third and fourth generation—see verse 52.)

Have someone read D&C 124:55 aloud. Ask:

- Since temple building in Jackson County, Missouri, was thwarted, what are the Saints to do now to keep the kingdom rolling forth?
- If the Saints build the Nauvoo Temple what will be their blessings?

You may want to share this information regarding the faithfulness of the Saints in building the Nauvoo Temple: "That structure cost more than one million dollars: the Saints were poor, and a great deal of the time the Temple was in course of erection they were harassed by their enemies. The

Prophet Joseph was forced into exile to avoid his enemies who tried to drag him into Missouri, and therefore he could not devote his personal attention to the building of the Temple, as he otherwise could have done; . . . Moreover, the building of that structure was not like building one to-day. The Saints could not order their timber from the lumberyard. . . . There were no iron foundries from which they could obtain the required metal properly prepared; but, on the contrary, every detail had to be performed by the Saints. . . . The whole work had to be supplied out of the tithing of the people." (Joseph Fielding Smith, *Origin of the "Reorganized" Church,* 21.)

Ask family members how they can help with temple building today. Invite them to record in their journals what they will do in their lives to demonstrate their appreciation for temples. Express your gratitude for these early Saints and their examples and then share your testimony with your family of how God continually overcomes evil and moves His purposes forward.

Doctrine and Covenants 124:84–118
Who's who in 124!

Write the following names and references on seven separate sheets of paper:

Almon Babbitt: D&C 124:84
William Law: D&C 124:87–91, 97–102, 107
Hyrum Smith: D&C 124:91–96, 102
Joseph Smith: D&C 124:95, 102, 107
Sidney Rigdon: D&C 124:103–10
Amos Davies: D&C 124:111–14
Robert Foster: D&C 124:115–18

Explain to your family that they will have an opportunity to learn about one or two of the individuals listed on the papers and then report what they have learned to the family. Invite them to choose the papers until they are gone. Give everyone three or four minutes to study the references they have been given and then report on their findings.

You may choose to discuss some of the following questions:

- What do you appreciate about this individual?
- What warnings were given to him?
- What gifts of the spirit did this individual possess?
- How can you emulate this person's good qualities?

The following information may also be helpful in your study:

Almon Babbitt: "His chief ambition was to make money . . . when the Saints left Nauvoo, he was appointed one of the real estate agents in whose hands the abandoned property was left, to be disposed of on the best terms obtainable. . . . Heber C. Kimball [said]: 'My house was sold at $1,700, intended to be used to help to gather the Saints; but Almon W. Babbit put it in his pocket, I suppose.' (*Journal of Discourses,* 8:350.)" (Hyrum M. Smith and Janne M. Sjodahl, *Doctrine and Covenants Commentary,* 784.)

William Law: "When he failed to obey the Lord, even his appointment to the First Presidency could not save him from falling. When he lost the Spirit of God he became one of the most bitter enemies of the Church. Apostates and persecutors rallied around him, and he tried to form a church of his own." (Hyrum M. Smith and Janne M. Sjodahl, *Doctrine and Covenants Commentary,* 785.)

Sidney Rigdon: "He was more or less under the influence of a spirit of apostasy. . . . in Liberty jail, he declared to his fellow-prisoners that the sufferings of the Lord were nothing compared with his." (Hyrum M. Smith and Janne M. Sjodahl, *Doctrine and Covenants Commentary,* 788.)

Amos Davies: "He was slow to obey counsel, and he shunned work. . . . on the 9th of March, 1842, he indulged in abusive language concerning the Prophet." (Joseph Smith, *History of the Church,* 4:549.)

Robert D. Foster: "He was a member of the conspirators who were determined to take the life of the Prophet." (Hyrum M. Smith and Janne M. Sjodahl, *Doctrine and Covenants Commentary*, 790.)

Ask your family how well the Lord seemed to know these men. Ask your family what they think the Lord might say to them in a personal revelation.

Doctrine and Covenants 124:123–45
Church organization and delegation of responsibility

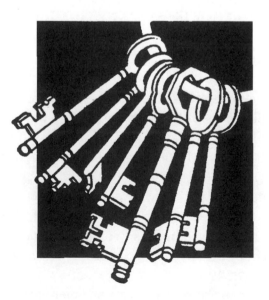 Show your family a set of keys. Read D&C 124:123, 143 aloud to your family and have them find four things those with priesthood keys can do to assist in the Church (see verse 143).

Ask your family to take the following "open book test." Have them scan D&C 124:123–45 as you ask the questions to find appropriate answers:

- What blessing can patriarchs give? (Verse 124.)
- Name four additional titles for the presiding elder over all the Church. (Verse 125.)
- What is the responsibility of the First Presidency of the Church? (To receive "oracles" which means revelations—see verse 126.)

- What priesthood keys do the members of the Quorum of the Twelve hold? (Verse 128.)
- What happens to a man's priesthood when he dies? (Verse 130.)
- What is the purpose of the high council? (Verses 131.)
- According to verses 133–35, what is the purpose of the quorum of high priests?
- What is the purpose of the quorum of elders? (Verse 137.)
- Whose name is the quorum of seventies to bear record of? (Verses 138–39.)
- What is the difference between the quorum of seventies and the quorum of elders? (Verse 140.)
- In which book of scripture can we learn about the bishopric? (Verse 141.)
- Find the names of other priesthood offices mentioned in verse 142.
- Why would it be important to approve or disapprove of individuals holding or being called to priesthood offices in a general conference of the Church? (Verse 144.)
- Where were the holders of these various priesthood offices to meet? (Verse 145.)

Discuss with your family how the authority or keys of the priesthood have blessed your family.

DOCTRINE AND COVENANTS 125: GATHERING TO STAKES

Historical background: *"A major factor that permitted the Saints to gather again after their expulsion from Missouri was the liberal land offer extended to them by Isaac Galland. Dr. Galland . . . offer[ed] thousands of acres of land to the Saints on a twenty-year installment agreement with no interest. During the months of April to June 1839, Church land agents purchased from Galland about twenty thousand acres in Lee County, Iowa, and fifty acres in Commerce, Illinois (Nauvoo) . . . The settlements of Zarahemla, Nashville, Ambrosia, and Montrose were located in Lee County, Iowa, on properties that the Church had purchased from Isaac Galland in 1839."* (Lyndon W. Cook, The Revelations of the Prophet Joseph Smith, 282.)

"Before the arrival of the Saints, there were only 2,839 inhabitants in Lee County. In 1846 the population was estimated at 12,860. So rapidly did the County develop, when touched by the magic wand of 'Mormon' industry." (Hyrum M. Smith and Janne M. Sjodahl, Doctrine and Covenants Commentary, 795.) *Look for the reason why the Lord commands His Saints to gather together.*

Doctrine and Covenants 125:1–4
Why do the Saints of the Lord gather?

Ask your family to count how many places the Saints have gathered to at this point in church history (answers might include, Fayetteville, New York; Palmyra, New York; Kirtland, Ohio; Independence, Missouri; Nauvoo Illinois). Ask why the Lord wants His people to gather together. Share the following quotation: "The Spirit of the Lord Jesus Christ is a gathering spirit. Its tendency is to gather the virtuous and good, the honest and meek of the earth, and, in fine, the Saints of God." (Brigham Young, *History of the Church*, 6:12.)

Invite a family member to read D&C 125:1–4 and look for another location the Saints were to gather. Ask:

- Why were Saints gathering in Iowa? (Verse 2 and historical background.)
- What was the name of this new stake of Zion to be? (Zarahemla—verse 3.)
- If the Lord's people are to gather today as they did in the past, where are we to gather?

The following statements will help answer this question:

"Any person, therefore, who has accepted the restored gospel, and who now seeks to worship the Lord in his own tongue and with the Saints in the nations where he lives, has complied with the law of the gathering of Israel and is heir to all of the blessings promised the Saints in these last days." (*The Teachings of Spencer W. Kimball*, 439.)

"The place of gathering for the Mexican Saints is in Mexico; the place of gathering for the Guatemalan Saints is in Guatemala; the place of gathering for the Brazilian Saints is in Brazil; and so it goes throughout the length and breadth of the whole earth. Japan is for the Japanese; Korea is for the Koreans; Australia is for the Australians; every nation is the gathering place for its own people" (Elder Bruce R. McConkie as quoted by Harold B. Lee in *Ensign*, July 1973, 5).

Ask:

- What do these statements teach us about the gathering of the Saints today?
- What can we do as a family to further the gathering of Zion where we live?
- Will there come a time when we will be called to gather to another place? (Yes—see D&C 45:66–71.)
- How will we know when that time has come? (Follow the prophet.)

Share your testimony on the importance of telling others about the restored gospel so they too can gather to the Lord's kingdom.

DOCTRINE AND COVENANTS 126: TAKE ESPECIAL CARE OF YOUR FAMILY

Historical background: Since joining the Church in 1832, Brigham Young had served many missions for the Church. In 1838 Joseph Smith received a revelation instructing the Quorum of the Twelve to prepare to serve missions to England and to open the work in Europe. Brigham Young departed with his companion, Heber C. Kimball, on September 14, 1839.

"In the month of July, 1841, the apostles began to return to Nauvoo from their missions to Europe, and their coming was a great comfort to the Prophet in his hour of affliction. At a special conference which was held at Nauvoo on the 16th of August, 1841, shortly after the return of the twelve, Joseph stated to the people there assembled that the time had come when the apostles must stand in their places next to the First Presidency. They had been faithful and had borne the burden and heat of the day, giving the gospel triumph in the nations of the earth, and it was right that they should now remain at home and perform duty in Zion." (George Q. Cannon, The Life of Joseph Smith the Prophet, 378–79.) *As you study this revelation, notice how well the Lord knows our situation and cares for our needs.*

Doctrine and Covenants 126:1
How would you respond to a mission call requiring you to leave your family?

Ask your family to rank on a scale from 1 to 10 (1 being low and 10 being high) how difficult the following missionary requirements would be for them:

- Needing to wear a suit, white shirt, and tie every day for two years.
- Teaching others the gospel of Jesus Christ.
- Being in towns and cities away from home.
- Not seeing your family for two years.

Read the historical background for this section and point out to your family that Brigham Young was called to serve many missions, and it was difficult for him, as it is for missionaries today, to leave his family. Read D&C 126:1 aloud and ask your family how the Lord felt about Brigham Young's service and sacrifice. Have someone read Proverbs 3:5–6 aloud and ask what it teaches about how we should react when a call comes from the Lord, even if it means leaving our families for a time.

Share the following story of Brigham Young and Heber C. Kimball. Encourage your family

members to think about and identify the lessons they can learn from these two great missionaries' examples:

"September 14th President Brigham Young left his home at Montrose to start on the mission to England. He was so sick that he was unable to go to the Mississippi, a distance of thirty rods, without assistance. After he had crossed the river he rode behind Israel Barlow on his horse to my house, where he continued sick until the 18th. He left his wife sick with a babe only three weeks old, and all his other children were sick and unable to wait upon each other. Not one soul of them was able to go to the well for a pail of water, and they were without a second suit to their backs, for the mob in Missouri had taken nearly all he had. On the 17th, Sister Mary Ann Young got a boy to carry her up in his wagon to my [Heber C. Kimball's] house, that she might nurse and comfort Brother Brigham to the hour of starting.

"September 18th, Charles Hubbard sent his boy with a wagon and span of horses to my house; our trunks were put into the wagon by some brethren; I went to my bed and shook hands with my wife who was then shaking with a chill, having two children lying sick by her side; I embraced her and

BIOGRAPHICAL SKETCH: BRIGHAM YOUNG

Brigham Young was born in Whittingham, Vermont, on June 1, 1801. He was baptized into the Church April 14, 1832, and ordained an apostle February 14, 1835. He was a member of the first Quorum of the Twelve Apostles in this dispensation. After the martyrdom of Joseph Smith, Brigham Young led the Church as president of the Quorum of the Twelve Apostles for three years. In 1847 he was sustained as president of the Church and served until his death in 1877.

As president of the Quorum of the Twelve, Brigham Young organized and oversaw the exodus of the Saints from Missouri in the winter and spring of 1838–39. In 1846–47 he organized and led the Saints as they were driven from Nauvoo. He entered the Salt Lake Valley on July 24, 1847, and immediately went about the task of building a city. The Salt Lake Valley became the gathering place for the Saints from the nations of the world. Over the next thirty years he directed the settlement of Saints from Idaho to California. (See Lyndon W. Cook, *The Revelations of the Prophet Joseph Smith*, 279–81.)

my children, and bade them farewell. My only well child was little Heber P., and it was with difficulty he could carry a couple of quarts of water at a time, to assist in quenching their thirst.

"It was with difficulty we got into the wagon, and started down the hill about ten rods; it appeared to me as though my very inmost parts would melt within me at leaving my family in such a condition, as it were almost in the arms of death. I felt as though I could not endure it. I asked the teamster to stop, and said to Brother Brigham, 'This is pretty tough, isn't it; let's rise up and give them a cheer.' We arose, and swinging our hats three times over our heads, shouted: 'Hurrah, hurrah for Israel.' Vilate, hearing the noise, arose from her bed and came to the door. She had a smile on her face. Vilate and Mary Ann Young cried out to us: 'Goodbye, God bless you.' We returned the compliment, and then told the driver to go ahead. After this I felt a spirit of joy and gratitude, having had the satisfaction of seeing my wife standing upon her feet, instead of leaving her in bed, knowing well that I should not see them again for two or three years." (Orson F. Whitney, *Life of Heber C. Kimball*, 265–66.)

Discuss the following questions with your family:

- What do you think Brigham Young and Heber C. Kimball were feeling as they left their families? (Concern for their families' condition and wanting to be acceptable before God.)
- How has your life been blessed because of the sacrifice of other family members?
- How could the story of these courageous missionaries help us have a better attitude when we start thinking, "This is pretty tough, isn't it?"

Consider placing some signs with the phrase "Let's rise up and give them a cheer" or "Hurrah, hurrah for Israel!" in some part of your house to serve as a simple reminder.

Doctrine and Covenants 126:1–3
Families and sacrifice

Share with your family the historical background above. Invite them to think about how hard it must have been to serve away from home so often. Ask why they think Brigham

Young was willing to sacrifice so much. Read the following teaching of Joseph Smith:

"Let us here observe, that a religion that does not require the sacrifice of all things never has power sufficient to produce the faith necessary unto life and salvation; . . . it is through the medium of the sacrifice of all earthly things that men do actually know that they are doing the things that are well pleasing in the sight of God. When a man has offered in sacrifice all that he has for the truth's sake, not even withholding his life, and believing before God that he has been called to make this sacrifice because he seeks to do his will, he does know, most assuredly, that God does and will accept his sacrifice and offering, and that he has not, nor will not seek his face in vain. Under these circumstances, then, he can obtain the faith necessary for him to lay hold on eternal life." (*Lectures on Faith*, 69.)

Have a family member read aloud D&C 126:1–3. Ask:

- What did the Lord say about President Young's sacrifice?

- How do you think his family felt about this revelation?
- What did the Lord say was now required of President Young?
- What kinds of sacrifices are involved in caring for one's family?
- Why is it important to take "especial care" of our families?

Share with your family the following commentary on this counsel from Elder Neal A. Maxwell:

"Obviously, family values mirror our personal priorities. Given the gravity of current conditions, would parents be willing to give up just one outside thing, giving that time and talent instead to the family? Parents and grandparents, please scrutinize your schedules and priorities in order to ensure that life's prime relationships get more prime time! Even consecrated and devoted Brigham Young was once told by the Lord, 'Take especial care of your family' (D&C 126:3). Sometimes, it is the most conscientious who need this message the most! (*Ensign,* May 1994, 90.)

DOCTRINE AND COVENANTS 127: BAPTISM FOR THE DEAD

Historical background: *On May 14, 1842, Missouri's former Governor Boggs was shot in Independence, Missouri. Joseph Smith was accused of being involved in the crime by his old Missouri enemies in an attempt to get their hands on the Prophet again. To avoid being falsely arrested by his enemies, Joseph felt it was best to go into hiding for the next five months. It was during this time that he wrote what is today known as Doctrine and Covenants 127 and 128.*

Almost two years earlier, on August 15, 1840, the Prophet spoke at the funeral service of Seymour Brunson. He taught that members of the Church could be baptized for those who had already died. After hearing what Joseph taught, "Widow Jane Neyman asked Harvey Olmstead to baptize her in the Mississippi River in behalf of her deceased son. . . . Many other faithful Saints followed suit and were baptized for their friends and relatives." (Richard Neitzel Holzapfel and Jeni Broberg Holzapfel, Women of Nauvoo, 90.)

Brigham Young said of this time, "In hurrying in the administration of baptism for the dead, . . . people were baptized for their friends and no record was kept. . . . Then women were baptized for men and men for women." (Journal of Discourses, 16:166–67.) *Sections 127 and 128 helped clarify the manner in which baptisms for the dead are to be performed. Notice how Heavenly Father has provided a way for the salvation of all of His children.*

Doctrine and Covenants 127:1–4
How much did Joseph Smith suffer?

Ask your family if they have ever been made fun of by others because they were trying to do something right. Read Matthew 5:10–12 together as a family. Talk about what blessings may come to those who are persecuted. Read the first paragraph of the historical background above. Assign family members one of the verses of D&C 127:1–4. Have them look for a single lesson or idea they learn from Joseph Smith in their assigned verse. After they have had a few minutes to prepare, have them read the verse to the family and then share how the teachings from that verse could help them with the challenges they face in their own lives.

Explain to your family what it means to become "accustomed" to something. An analogy you might use is how it would be difficult to put your hand in a bowl of hot water. However, if you were to put your hand in warm water and then continue to heat the water up slowly, just a bit at a time, you would get used to it, and it would not be so uncomfortable. Tell your family the word "wont" in verse 2 means "accustomed." Have your family tell about some of the difficult trials they remember Joseph Smith facing. Testify how blessed he was, is, and will be because he endured persecution to defend the gospel of Jesus Christ.

Doctrine and Covenants 127:5–10
Do ordinances have to be performed properly to be valid?

Give your family the following case study. Have them identify everything that is wrong. (Note: Improper items are *italicized* in the text.)

John was *seven and a half years old* and was excited to be baptized. He asked his *thirteen-year-old sister* to baptize him. *Just the two of them* went to their *swimming pool* and stood in the shallow end. She *sprinkled* some water on his head and said *"Little brother, you are now baptized."* She *didn't use his name.* John did not feel as good about his "baptism" as he thought he would.

After your family has pointed out what is wrong, ask:

- How old must a person be to be baptized?
- Who can perform a valid baptism? (One holding proper priesthood authority, at least the office of priest in the Aaronic Priesthood.)
- How must it be done? (By immersion.)
- What are the words that must be used? (See D&C 20:73.)
- Does anyone else need to be there? (If no one knows the answer to this question, explain that they will find the answer in D&C 127.)

Now ask if any members of your family have participated in baptisms for the dead. Have them share the experiences they had in the temple and talk about the proper procedures and order for performing baptisms for the dead. When they have finished, read the last two paragraphs of the historical background to your family. Talk about what items were out of order when the Saints first began doing baptisms for the dead. Explain that D&C 127 identifies the proper order for performing this sacred ordinance.

Ask family members to read D&C 127:5–10 and look for the proper order and guidelines Joseph Smith gave the Saints. Discuss the following questions:

- Who is supposed to be a witness to these baptisms? (A recorder, who is to see and hear that the ordinance is done properly—see verse 6.)
- What is the recorder to do after the ordinance? (There is to be a record kept of whose ordinances are performed—see verse 9.)
- What does this teach us about the impor-

tance of the ordinance of baptism? (See verse 7.)

Doctrine and Covenants 127:11–12
Who is "the prince of this world"?

Ask your family if they know who the "Prince of Peace" is and who the "prince of this world" is.

Read D&C 127:11; then share the statement below:

"Just as Christ is the 'Prince of Peace' (2 Ne. 19:6; Isa. 9:6), so is Satan the 'prince of this world' (D&C 127:11) or, rather, 'the prince of darkness, who is *of* this world' (JST, John 14:30; italics added). He reigns in the benighted domain of the world of contention, carnality, and corruption—the world which the Apostle John warned us to avoid (1 John 2:15–17). This 'prince' shall lose his satanical sceptre of power when evil is rejected for righteousness, 'for he hath no power over the hearts of the people [who] dwell in righteousness.' (1 Ne. 22:26.)" (Hoyt W. Brewster Jr., *Doctrine and Covenants Encyclopedia,* 443.)

Ask:

- Why do you think Satan is called the "prince of this world"?
- Why does he have "nothing" in the Savior?

Ask family members to read D&C 127:12 silently and then share with the rest of the family what they learned about Joseph Smith. Ask:

- How does it make you feel to know that a prophet of God prays for you?
- How does the prophet serve us?
- What can we do to serve him?

DOCTRINE AND COVENANTS 128: MORE CONCERNING BAPTISM FOR THE DEAD

Historical background: Read also the historical background for D&C 127. After writing the letter that became D&C 128, Joseph Smith stated, "The important instructions contained in the foregoing letter made a deep and solemn impression on the minds of the Saints; and they manifested their intentions to obey the instructions to the letter." (History of the Church, 5:153.) As you study this section, consider why ordinance work for the dead is so important.

Doctrine and Covenants 128:1–7
Why must Church records be accurate?

Show your family someone's old report card. Look at the date on it and quickly review the grades. Talk about the following questions:

- Why do you think it is important to receive grades?
- Who determines a person's grade, and who fills out the report card?
- Who might want to see a copy of your school grades? (A college, an employer, etc.)
- What if you lost a report card? Could you find another copy of it? Where?
- What is the value of keeping records?

Read Revelation 20:12 aloud to your family. Ask:

- How does this verse relate to report cards?
- What books will we be judged from? Who keeps those records?
- Why would it be important for earthly records to be accurate?

Explain that D&C 128:1–7 includes instructions about record-keeping for baptisms for the dead. Take turns reading these verses. When you have finished, ask a family member to share one important thing learned. Ask each family member to do the same until everyone has had a turn. Continue giving everyone turns until no one can identify any more important principles or doctrines. Talk about why the Lord may feel so strongly about these records. Make plans to attend a temple baptistry or visitors' center to learn more about baptisms for the dead.

Doctrine and Covenants 128:8–18, 24
"Welding" the family of God together

Like links on a chain, have family members make a "link" representing themselves. (Individual links could be made from strips of paper, string, metal clips, or rope.) While each person holds his or her own link, read the following:

"What man or what woman would rejoice or be happy if he could not be associated with his own kindred? What man or what woman would feel that he was enjoying a blessing in the world to come if it were not in the association of his father and his mother? What parent could possibly feel that heaven would be heaven to him unless he could be associated there with his own children? What is true of these immediate connections is true of those that have gone on before. Our fathers and our mothers would never be happy nor feel that they could be exalted and saved in the kingdom of God unless they could be associated with their fathers and their mothers. And so it will be until we connect ourselves and reunite in that one great family, the family of God, united together with that welding link under the new and everlasting covenant." (Elder Rulon S. Wells, Conference Report, October 1924, 42–43.)

Considering that statement, ask family members what the phrase "families can be together forever" means. Ask family members to read Matthew 16:18–19 and Malachi 4:5–6 to find what those verses teach about the power to seal families together. Ask your family to hook their links together. Share your love for your family and your desire to be united eternally.

Now ask your family how many links would be needed if one were made for every person on earth. (World population in 2003 was approximately 6,300,000,000.) Ask:

- For God's family to be complete, how many of them should we be concerned about?
- According to John 3:5, what is required for everyone to enter the celestial kingdom?
- How is it that those who die can be baptized?
- What responsibility lies on our shoulders if this work is to be done?
- How would our efforts benefit them?
- What are some ways we could be blessed by doing this work?

Take turns reading D&C 128:8–18. Stop occasionally and testify of the great importance of this work. Share your feelings about the privilege of doing work for the dead in the temple. Answer any questions that arise, and encourage your family to participate in temple ordinances throughout their lives. You may consider figuring out how long it would take to do temple work for 6,300,000,000 people. Read D&C 128:24 and look for what record will eventually be placed on the temple altar. How many people do you think we will need to do ordinance work for, if the record is to be "worthy of all acceptation"?

Reread D&C 128:11 and emphasize the phrase *"summum bonum."* Explain that this phrase means "highest good." Testify that the highest good we can do to help the human family is ordinance work in the temple. Motivate your family to attend the temple regularly.

Doctrine and Covenants 128:19–23
A reason to greatly rejoice

Invite someone to read D&C 128:19 and mark each time the word "glad" or "gladness" is mentioned. What could possibly cause such great "gladness"? Have a different family member read D&C 128:20–21. Have everyone mark each messenger mentioned that bears glad tidings. When you have finished, make a list of the messengers and what each did to bring glad tidings. Your list may look like the following:

Moroni (verse 20): Revealed the Book of Mormon.

Michael (verses 20–21): Detected Satan.

Peter, James, and John (verse 20): Restored the Melchizedek Priesthood.

Gabriel (Noah, see *Teachings of the Prophet Joseph Smith,* 157) (verse 21): Restored keys.

Raphael (verse 21): Also restored keys.

Read D&C 128:22–23 and look for other indications of glad tidings. Ask your family to answer Joseph Smith's question, "Shall we not go on in so great a cause?" by writing down in their journals one thing they love about the gospel and why it inspires them to "go on." Invite some family members to share their testimony about why it is important to continue in the cause of the faith.

Doctrine and Covenants 128:24–25
"He is like a refiner's fire, and like fuller's soap"

Read D&C 128:24–25 to your family and ask if they know what a "refiner's fire and fuller's soap" is. Ask someone to read the information in the Bible Dictionary under "Refiner" (p. 760) and "Fullers" (p. 676). Ask:

- How is the Savior like a "refiner's fire" and a "fuller's soap"?
- Why does He want us to be purified?
- According to verse 24, what are we to offer in order to be ready for the Second Coming? (Our family history and temple work.)
- In addition to working to save those who have died, what are some other ways we

could offer an "offering in righteousness" on God's altar?

To help answer that question, read the following statement from Elder Neal A. Maxwell:

"The submission of one's will is really the only uniquely personal thing we have to place on God's altar. The many other things we 'give,' brothers and sisters, are actually the things He has already given or loaned to us. However, when you and I finally submit ourselves, by letting our individual wills be swallowed up in God's will, then we are really giving something to Him! It is the only possession which is truly ours to give!" (*Ensign*, November 1995, 22.)

Challenge your family to spend some time thinking about ways they could submit more to God and therefore better prepare themselves for the second coming of Jesus Christ.

DOCTRINE AND COVENANTS 129: MINISTERING ANGELS AND SPIRITS

Historical background: Before Joseph Smith received this revelation, a man came to him and said he had seen an angel, describing his dress. The Prophet told the man he was mistaken because there was no such dress in heaven. The man became angry and commanded fire to come down out of heaven and consume the Prophet and his house. (See History of the Church, 5:267–68.)

Parley P. Pratt had returned from his mission to England just two days before this revelation was received. Parley, having had powerful experiences with spirits on his mission, was anxious to learn more from the Prophet. Joseph Smith had discussed the ministration of angels with the apostles before they were called on their missions (see History of the Church, 3:391–92), *but Parley was absent at the time.*

Doctrine and Covenants 129:1–9
How do you tell if an angel is from the Lord or the devil?

Give each family member a piece of paper and pencil and ask them to draw an angel. Have them show their drawings to the rest of the family and discuss briefly what angels look like. Read the historical background above and tell your family that Joseph Smith taught, "An angel of God never has wings." (*History of the Church*, 3:392.) Have one family member read the section heading and another family member read D&C 129:1–3. Ask:

- What are the two kinds of beings spoken of in these verses?
- What is the difference between "angels" and "just men made perfect"?

Ask a family member to turn to the entry for "Angels" in the Bible Dictionary (p. 608) and read the first paragraph aloud. Ask:

- What is an unembodied angel?
- What is a disembodied angel?
- What is a reimbodied angel?
- What examples can you think of in scripture of angels appearing? Why did they appear?

Tell your family you will pretend to represent an angel. Stand next to someone and say "poof," as if you suddenly appeared. Invite the person to extend a hand for you to shake. Grasp the person's hand and shake it. Have your family scan D&C 129:4–9 and tell what kind of a being you represent. Move next to another family member and say "poof." Have the person extend a hand to shake yours, and as you go to grab it, miss the clasp. Have your family scan the verses and find the kind of being you represent this time. Move to another person and say "poof." This time when the person extends a hand, stand still and do not extend your hand. Say that you are an angel from the presence of God and that you have a message to share. Again have your family look for the kind of being you represent.

Share the following insights concerning the ministering of angels:

"The veil between heaven and earth usually hides the angels from our sight. Yet often in the early stages of our spiritual development, we may experience unmistakable contact with the angels of the unseen world." (Bruce C. Hafen, *Ensign,* April 1992, 12.)

"One of the things that will become more important in our lives the longer we live is the reality of angels, their work and their ministry. I refer here not alone to the angel Moroni but also to those more personal ministering angels who are with us and around us, empowered to help us and who do exactly that (see 3 Ne. 7:18; Moro. 7:29–32, 37; D&C 107:20)." (Jeffrey R. Holland, *Ensign,* January 1996, 12.)

Invite family members to strive to live so they can better discern the importance of angels in their lives, both seen and unseen.

Doctrine and Covenants 129:5–9
Understanding spiritual communication

Share the following statement from Elder Dallin H. Oaks with your family:

"'The word "angel" is used in the scriptures for any heavenly being bearing God's message' (George Q. Cannon, *Gospel Truth,* sel. Jerreld L. Newquist [1987], 54). The scriptures recite numerous instances where an angel appeared personally. . . . When I was young, I thought such personal appearances were the only meaning of the ministering of angels. As a young holder of the Aaronic Priesthood, I did not think I would see an angel, and I wondered what such appearances had to do with the Aaronic Priesthood.

"But the ministering of angels can also be unseen. Angelic messages can be delivered by a voice or merely by thoughts or feelings communicated to the mind. President John Taylor described 'the action of the angels, or messengers of God, upon our minds, so that the heart can conceive . . . revelations from the eternal world' (*Gospel Kingdom,* sel. G. Homer Durham [1987], 31)." (Dallin H. Oaks, *Ensign,* November 1998, 37.)

Explain to your family that in addition to helping us know how to detect true angels when they appear to us, D&C 129 has some principles that can better help us understand the messages we receive from God in unseen ways.

Ask family members to read D&C 129:5–9 and highlight the following phrases:

- "You will feel." (Verse 5.)
- "Come in his glory." (Verse 6.)
- Not "deceive." (Verse 7.)
- "Deliver his message." (Verse 7.)
- "Not feel anything." (Verse 8.)

Have family members identify which of these phrases refers to communications from God, and which of these phrases refer to communications from the devil. Discuss the following questions:

- Spiritual communication from God causes us to "feel" things. What do D&C 8:2 and D&C 9:8 teach you about these feelings?
- When God communicates to us, we feel light and truth. (See D&C 88:11–12.) What do light and truth have to do with "glory," according to D&C 93:36–37?
- Angelic communications from God provide us with messages directly from Him. According to Moroni 10:5, what can we receive messages about from God?
- The devil's communications are often described as empty, dark, or confusing. How do those descriptions compare to the phrase "not feel anything" in D&C 129:8?

Read John 14:26–27 to your family. Testify that the Lord will teach us what we need to know by the power of the Holy Ghost. Invite your family to be sensitive to the promptings of the Spirit and to follow the Lord's direction.

DOCTRINE AND COVENANTS 130: CORRECTING MISUNDERSTANDINGS

Historical background: *Joseph Smith wrote that the information found in D&C 130 was intended to clarify a talk given by Orson Hyde about John 14:23 and the coming of Christ. "At ten* A.M. *went to meeting. Heard Orson Hyde preach. . . . Alluding to the coming of the Savior, he said, 'When He shall appear, we shall be like Him, etc. He will appear on a white horse as a warrior, and maybe we shall have some of the same spirit. . . . It is our privilege to have the Father and Son dwelling in our hearts [John 14:23], etc.'*

"We dined with my sister Sophronia McCleary, when I told Elder Hyde that I was going to offer some corrections to his sermon this morning. He replied, 'They shall be thankfully received.'" (History of the Church, 5:323.)

Doctrine and Covenants 130:1–3
Families in eternal glory

Ask your family to imagine that they are suddenly taken away from home and never allowed to come back or be with their family again. Ask:

- How would you feel to be away from the people you love?
- What would you miss the most?
- Would your mom and dad ever be able to forget about their children?
- Would the children ever really forget about their parents?

Read the historical background above to your family and then have someone read D&C 130:1–2. Use the following questions to help teach about those verses:

- When Orson Hyde talked about the coming of Christ, what part of the Second Coming did he focus on? (Christ coming as a warrior—see historical background.)
- What does the phrase "same sociality" mean in verse 2? (It means the same social structure with family and friends.)
- What will be better about our family relationships after the Second Coming? (They will enjoy eternal glory.)
- What do you think Joseph Smith was trying to teach us by emphasizing glorious family relationships rather than Jesus Christ coming as a warrior?

Joseph Smith also corrected what Orson Hyde taught about John 14:23. Have someone read that verse aloud and then have someone else read D&C 130:3. Ask:

- What did Brother Hyde think the coming of the Father and the Son in John 14:23 meant? (That they would dwell in a man's heart—see historical background.)
- What kind of appearance did Joseph Smith say that would be?
- What does it mean to have a personal appearance from the Savior? (See D&C 93:1; Ether 3:4–14.)

Doctrine and Covenants 130:4–11
What is a Urim and Thummim?

As a family, turn to the Bible Dictionary, page 786, and read the first paragraph under the heading "Urim and Thummim." Discuss together what a Urim and Thummim is and what it used for. Then read together D&C 130:4–11. Ask:

- On what sort of world do angels and God reside? (Verses 6–8.)
- When this earth becomes our celestial home, what will it be like? (Verse 9.)
- What other blessing will be given to those

who inherit this celestial kingdom? (Verses 10–11.)

Ask your family to commit to live to be worthy of the blessings of the celestial kingdom.

Doctrine and Covenants 130:12–13
Additional prophecy on the Civil War

Ask your family if they remember when the American Civil War began? (In 1861.) Ask if they remember where there is a revelation in the Doctrine and Covenants that deals with the Civil War. (D&C 87.) Explain that D&C 130:12–13 refers to the same revelation recorded in D&C 87.

Have your family compare D&C 87:1–4 with D&C 130:12–13 and share insights they find. Point out that Joseph Smith knew about the coming of the Civil War about twenty-eight years before it occurred. (See the teaching idea for D&C 87:1–5 in this book.) Share your testimony of what a blessing it is to have living prophets.

Doctrine and Covenants 130:14–17
When will the second coming of the Savior be?

Tell your family that you are going to play Wheel of Fortune without the wheel and without the fortune. On a sheet of paper draw some dash marks like those below:

"__ __ __ __ __ __ __ __ __ __ __ __ __ __"

Explain that the puzzle your family is trying to solve is an event that has not yet taken place. They can guess what that event is by solving the puzzle. In order to solve the puzzle, they must take turns guessing letters. When they guess a correct letter, write it in the appropriate blank. The event they are trying to discover is the Second Coming. After they have solved the puzzle, ask if they can tell you when the Second Coming will be. Joseph Smith wanted to know and asked the Lord. The Lord's response to Joseph's question is found in D&C 130:14–17.

Have your family take turns reading those verses. Ask:

- According to verse 14, how did Joseph receive his answer?
- What age would Joseph have to live to when he would see the face of the Lord? (Verse 15.)
- What questions was Joseph left to ponder? (Verse 16.)

Share the following insight from Elder Boyd K. Packer:

"Teenagers . . . sometimes think, 'What's the use? The world will soon be blown all apart and come to an end.' That feeling comes from fear, not from faith. No one knows the hour or the day (see D&C 49:7), but the end cannot come until all of the purposes of the Lord are fulfilled. Everything that I have learned from the revelations and from life convinces me that there is time and to spare for you to carefully prepare for a long life.

"One day you will cope with teenage children of your own. That will serve you right. Later, you will spoil your grandchildren, and they in turn spoil theirs. If an earlier end should happen to come to one, that is more reason to do things right." (*Ensign,* May 1989, 59.)

Discuss as a family how you can prepare for the Second Coming. Share your testimony that if we are prepared we never need to fear. (See D&C 38:30.)

Doctrine and Covenants 130:18–19
What can we take with us when we die?

Divide a sheet of paper in half. On the left side write "Things we can take with us after death" and on the right side write "Things we cannot take with us after death." Have your family suggest things they can and cannot take with them while another person records their responses. Invite someone to read verses 18–19. Ask:

- What is one thing verse 18 suggests that we can take with us?

- How do we gain more knowledge and intelligence in this life? (Verse 19.)
- Why might we want to be diligent and obedient in this life?
- How does diligence and obedience to God help us gain knowledge? (Compare D&C 93:36–40.)
- Do you think the Lord could help us learn more about any subject we might be studying?

Encourage your family to include the Lord as they seek diligently for knowledge and intelligence.

Doctrine and Covenants 130:20–21
When we obey God's commandments we are blessed

Ask your family what it takes to get _____. (Fill in the blank with an award appropriate to your family, such as the Young Womanhood or Duty to God Awards, a school diploma, or the Eagle Scout badge, and adapt the following questions accordingly.) Ask:

- Could you get a school diploma if you never passed any of the classes?
- What are some "awards" you would like to get from your Father in Heaven?
- How do you know what the requirements are for those blessings?

Have your family read D&C 130:20–21. Ask:

- If we want a blessing from our Father in Heaven, what must we do? (Verse 21.)
- Will Heavenly Father bless us every time we obey him?
- Does He punish us every time we disobey?

As part of your discussion of that last question, consider sharing this thought from Elder Boyd K. Packer: "Ultimately we are punished quite as much by our sins as we are for them." (*Ensign*, September 1973, 37.) See also Alma 41:10–11.

Encourage your family to be obedient so Heavenly Father can bless them.

Doctrine and Covenants 130:22–23
What is the Godhead really like?

Ask your family if they are aware of how other Christian churches describe the Godhead. (For example, some teach that God is a spirit without a body and that God the Father, the Son, and the Holy Ghost are all one being.) Show your family a picture of the First Vision (such as picture 403 in the Gospel Art Picture Kit). Then read together D&C 130:22–23. Ask:

- What do these verses teach us about the Godhead?
- How does Joseph Smith know what God is like?
- How does knowing that God really is your Father in Heaven make it easier to pray to Him?
- Why is the body of the Holy Ghost different from those of the Father and the Son?
- Why is it important to know what God is really like?

Share your testimony with your family of how knowing what God is really like has helped you have faith in Him and in His Son. Encourage your family to be worthy so that the Holy Ghost might dwell with them.

DOCTRINE AND COVENANTS 131: OBTAINING THE HIGHEST DEGREE OF GLORY IN THE CELESTIAL KINGDOM

Historical background: "On the 16th of May, 1843, a little company, consisting of Joseph Smith, George Miller, William Clayton, Eliza and Lydia Partridge, and J. M. Smith, went to Ramus. The Prophet and William Clayton stayed at Benjamin F. Johnson's overnight. Before retiring, the little party of friends engaged in conversation on spiritual topics. The Prophet told them that 'except a man and his wife enter into an everlasting covenant and be married for eternity, while in this probation, by the power and authority of the holy Priesthood, they will cease to increase when they die; that is, they will not have any children after the resurrection.' . . . Then he spoke of the three heavens in the celestial glory, as recorded in the first four verses of this Revelation.*

"On the 17th of May the Prophet preached a discourse on II. Pet. 1, and showed that knowledge is power. Among the truths announced at this time was that recorded in the 5th and 6th verses of this Revelation. . . .

"He added the truths recorded in the 7th and 8th verses of this Revelation." (Hyrum M. Smith and Janne M. Sjodahl,* Doctrine and Covenants Commentary, *818–19.) Look for the one ordinance God requires for entering into the highest degree in the celestial kingdom.*

Doctrine and Covenants 131:1–4
What is one of the requirements to get to the highest degree of glory in the celestial kingdom?

Take your family into a room where there is only one way in and out. Read to them D&C 131:1–4. Ask:

- What must a person do to go to the highest degree of glory in the celestial kingdom?
- Can you go there in any other way?
- If this room represents the highest degree of glory in the celestial kingdom, what would the door represent? (Celestial marriage.)
- What does this teach you about the importance of being married in the temple?

Return to your normal family scripture study room and have someone read the following story from President Gordon B. Hinckley:

"I leave you a story. It is fiction, but in principle it is true. Can you imagine two young people at a time when the moon is full and the roses are in bloom and a sacred love has matured between

them? Johnny says to Mary, 'Mary, I love you. I want you for my wife and the mother of our children. But I don't want you or them forever. Just for a season and then good-bye.' And she, looking at him through tears in the moonlight, says, 'Johnny, you're wonderful. There's nobody else in all the world like you. I love you, and I want you for my husband and the father of our children, but only for a time and then farewell.'

"That sounds foolish, doesn't it? And yet isn't that in effect what a man says to a woman and a woman says to a man in a proposal of marriage when given the opportunity of eternal union under 'the new and everlasting covenant' (D&C 132:19), but, rather, they choose to set it aside for a substitute that can last only until death comes?" (*Ensign,* July 2003, 3.)

Ask your family:

- Why does that story seem so ridiculous?
- What do you think "an increase" means in verse 4?

To help answer that question, invite a family

member to read what Joseph Smith said about an "increase":

"Except a man and his wife enter into an everlasting covenant and be married for eternity, while in this probation [life], by the power and authority of the Holy Priesthood, they will cease to increase when they die; that is, they will not have any children after the resurrection." (*History of the Church*, 5:391.)

Testify to your family that the only place marriages last and future children are born is in the highest degree of glory in the celestial kingdom. Challenge your children to decide now to remain worthy to marry in the temple and then live true to the promised blessings.

Doctrine and Covenants 131:5–6
"It is impossible for a man to be saved in ignorance"

Invite your family to fill in the blank of the following sentence: "It is impossible for a man or woman to be saved in _____." To help them, read D&C 131:5–6. Ask:

- What does the word "impossible" mean?
- What do you think "ignorance" means? (A lack of knowledge or learning.)
- Why do you think it is impossible for a man or woman to be saved in ignorance?
- Why is it important to gain knowledge?
- What kind of knowledge do you think is more important for our salvation in the eternities, a knowledge of God or a knowledge of math, sports, and music?

After some discussion, read the following statement by Elder James E. Talmage:

"Not all knowledge is of equal worth. The knowledge that constitutes the wisdom of the heavens is all embraced in the Gospel as taught by Jesus Christ; and wilful ignorance of this, the highest type of knowledge, will relegate [reduce] its victim to the inferior order of intelligences." (*The Vitality of Mormonism*, 278.)

Discuss ways your family can gain the most important knowledge.

Doctrine and Covenants 131:7–8
"All spirit is matter"

Before scripture study, write D&C 131:7–8 on a sheet of paper and place it some distance from your house. Make sure it can be seen with the naked eye. (If it is too dark outside, write D&C 131:7–8 in small letters on a piece of paper and tape it onto a wall in your house.) You will also need binoculars. (If you do not have binoculars, at the right time have a young family member pretend to use binoculars and go up and read the paper.)

When your family gathers for scripture study, tell them there is a piece of paper with an important message written on it. Help them see the paper from a distance and have them try to read it. (They should not be able to.) Ask them to explain why they can't read it. Give someone the binoculars and have that person read it. Discuss reasons why the person with the binoculars is the only one who can read the words. Read together D&C 131:7–8. Ask:

- From this scripture, what would the reference on the paper represent? (Spirit that is more fine or pure and we cannot see it.)
- What would the binoculars represent? (Purer eyes.)

Share the following statement from Elder Rudger Clawson:

"The unseen world is much larger and greater and much more important than the world that is seen, the world in which we live. The world in which we live is greatly magnified by the fact that we can behold it with our mortal eyes. The unseen world suffers in this respect, because we do not see it with the mortal eye. Somebody may ask: 'Can it be seen?' Yes, oh, yes, indeed, it can be seen. 'But how shall we see it?' We must look at it through our spiritual eye, or in other words, the eye of faith. There is no doubt that it exists, that greater world, and that it is very substantial." (In Roy W. Doxey, comp., *Latter-day Prophets and the Doctrine and Covenants,* 4:380.)

Ask:

- How can we see the "unseen" world?

- How does knowing that an "unseen world" exists help you want to live your life better?

Invite family members to share examples of those who have seen the "unseen world."

DOCTRINE AND COVENANTS 132: MARRIAGE

Historical background: *"In 1843 the law on celestial marriage was written, but not published, and was known only to perhaps one or two hundred persons. It was written from the dictation of Joseph Smith, by Elder William Clayton, his private secretary, who is now in this city. This revelation was published in 1852, read to a general conference, and accepted as a portion of the faith of the Church. Elder Orson Pratt went to Washington and there published a work called the* Seer, *in which this revelation was printed, and a series of articles showing forth the law of God in relation to marriage." (Journal of Discourses, 14:214.)*

Doctrine and Covenants 132:4–14
Eternal Marriage

Show your family a wedding invitation or some marriage photographs, or share some memories of your wedding day. You may also wish to read them some of your favorite parts of "The Family, a Proclamation to the World."

Ask your family to answer the following questions, on a scale of one to ten (with one being very low and ten being exceptionally high). Also ask them to give reasons for their answers.

- How important do you think marriage is in God's plan for His children?
- How important do you think the decision of whom you will marry is?
- How important do you think it is to be sealed in the temple?
- How important do you think it is for a couple to continue to work on their marriage relationship after being married?

Remind your family what the "new and everlasting covenant" is from your studies of D&C 131:1–4. Show your family a picture of a dam and ask:

(Photo by Kelly Ogden.)

- What does a dam do to the flow of water? (Stops it from progressing.)
- How would that analogy relate to the term "damned" in a spiritual sense?
- According to D&C 131:2–4 and 132:4–6, what would stop us from being able to progress in the highest degree of the celestial kingdom? (Not obtaining an eternal marriage.)

Read D&C 132:7 aloud and explain that not only must we be sealed, but our marriages must be sealed or approved by the Lord in order to actually be valid eternally. Share the following statement from Joseph Fielding Smith:

"The Holy Spirit of Promise is the Holy Ghost who places the stamp of approval upon every ordinance: baptism, confirmation, ordination, marriage. The promise is that the blessings will be received through faithfulness.

"If a person violates a covenant, whether it be of baptism, ordination, marriage or anything else, the Spirit withdraws the stamp of approval, and the blessings will not be received.

"Every ordinance is sealed, with a promise of a reward based upon faithfulness. The Holy Spirit withdraws the stamp of approval where covenants are broken." (*Doctrines of Salvation,* 1:45. See also D&C 132:8–14.)

Doctrine and Covenants 132:15–25
What does it mean to "marry a wife by my word, which is my law"?

To study D&C 132:15–20, assign family members one of three types of marriages. Also assign them to study the accompanying verses:

1. A civil marriage, meaning a marriage performed outside the temple. (D&C 132:15–17.)

2. A temple sealing where one or both spouses do not keep their covenants. (D&C 132:18.)

3. A temple sealing where both husband and wife keep their temple covenants. (D&C 132:19–20.)

While they study their verses, have them look for answers to the following questions. Have them give a report on their findings when they have finished.

- What description does the Lord use for this type of marriage?
- What are the consequences the Lord gives for this type of marriage?
- Why might some choose to enter into this type of marriage?
- Would you like this kind of marriage? Why or why not?

When all have completed their reports, allow everyone to share ideas of how they could prepare to be sealed in the temple, and what things they could do afterward to ensure that the Holy Spirit

of Promise approves their marriage. Talk about the sacrifices needed in order to build successful families. Read D&C 132:21–25, looking for reasons some do not make those sacrifices.

Share your feelings about the joy of marriage. Read the following statement by Parley P. Pratt about the time when he first found out about eternal marriage:

"It was Joseph Smith who taught me how to prize the endearing relationships of father and mother, husband and wife; of brother and sister, son and daughter.

"It was from him that I learned that the wife of my bosom might be secured to me for time and all eternity; and that the refined sympathies and affections which endeared us to each other emanated from the fountain of divine eternal love. It was from him that I learned that we might cultivate these affections, and grow and increase in the same to all eternity; while the result of our endless union would be an offspring as numerous as the stars of heaven, or the sands of the sea shore.

"I had loved before, but I knew not why. But now I loved—with a pureness and intensity of elevated, exalted feeling, which would lift my soul from the transitory things of this grovelling sphere and expand it as the ocean." (*Autobiography of Parley P. Pratt,* 259.)

D&C 132:45–46
Joseph Smith fulfilled ancient prophecy

Read Acts 3:20–21 aloud to your family. As you do, ask them to listen carefully and then answer the following questions:

- Whom did these verses speak about?
- How long did the heavens need to "receive" Jesus? (Until the restitution of all things, which God has spoken by his ancient prophets.)
- What does it mean to restore something?
- Can you give an example of something that has been restored? (A wrecked car, a broken-down home, the gospel.)

- What do we call the time when Jesus Christ returns to the earth, after the restoration of all things has been accomplished? (The Second Coming.)
- According to Acts 2:22, by whom will this restoration take place?

Ask your family to silently read D&C 132:45 and identify what this scripture has to do with what you have been discussing. Ask, "Who is referred to by the word 'you' in this verse?" (Joseph Smith.) "What part did Joseph play in the restoration of all things?"

Read D&C 132:46 and look for one power the Lord restored through Joseph Smith. (See also Matthew 16:18–19; Helaman 10:6–7.) Ask family members to ponder the sealing power for a moment. Ask them to talk about what blessings have come into their lives because there are prophets who hold priesthood keys to seal families together forever.

D&C 132:1–66
Planning for marriage

After studying D&C 132 together as a family, ask unmarried family members to do the following:

1. Compile a brief list of why they think "marriage is ordained of God." (See *The Family, a Proclamation to the World*.)

2. Make a list of attributes they hope their future spouses will possess.

3. Write three questions about successful marriages and how to prepare for them.

Ask your unmarried children to share what they wrote. Also read each of the questions to the married family members and allow them to respond in a panel discussion. Take time to share your testimony, and encourage all family members to work at becoming the best people they can as they seek to find an eternal companion.

DOCTRINE AND COVENANTS 133: PREPARATION FOR THE SECOND COMING

Historical background: *A special conference was held November 1, 1831, to determine if and how to publish the revelations given to Joseph Smith. See the historical background for D&C 1 for more information. After the conference made a decision to publish the revelations and the Lord revealed a preface to the book (now D&C 1), Oliver Cowdery was appointed to take the revelations to Missouri for printing. Before everyone left for home or other assignments, however, Church members had questions for the Prophet. They sought greater understanding of the Lord's work in the last days. Because of their desires, the Prophet sought inspiration and received the revelation found in D&C 133. Since the Lord had given a preface to the Book of Commandments (D&C 1), and since this revelation came at the end of that same conference, shedding further light on things discussed in that preface, this section (D&C 133) was named the appendix and placed at the end of the earliest editions of the Doctrine and Covenants.*

Doctrine and Covenants 133:1–15
Fleeing Babylon and gathering to Zion

Appoint one member of your family to be a scribe. As you read together D&C 133:1–15, stop after each verse and identity what the Lord tells the Saints to *do*. Emphasize that you don't want your family (at this time) to record what the Lord described, or even explanations of why, but just identify what the Saints are commanded to *do*. (For example, in the first verse the scribe would record "Hearken" and "Hear the word of the Lord concerning you.") When you have finished these verses and the list is complete, review as a family the things on the list. Talk about what these commandments might mean to your family, and how you could apply them in your life.

To help your family see the "big picture" of what the Lord commanded in these verses, have your family identify the two places the Lord spoke of that we are to flee from or gather to. (Babylon and Zion.) Have each family member tell one thing they know about either of those places. (You may want to invite them to look over D&C 133:1–15 again and identify things that describe either Babylon or Zion.) After everyone has taken a turn, invite your family to use the Topical Guide to find other references to either Babylon or Zion

that help them understand more fully why we would want to flee the one and gather to the other. Invite them to share their references and what they learned.

Share with your family the following counsel from President Spencer W. Kimball about how we can build Zion:

"This day [of Zion] will come; it is our destiny to help bring it about! Doesn't it motivate you to lengthen your stride and quicken your pace as you do your part in the great sanctifying work of the kingdom? It does me. It causes me to rejoice over the many opportunities for service and sacrifice afforded me and my family as we seek to do our part in establishing Zion. . . .

"Creating Zion 'commences in the heart of each person.' (Journal of Discourses, 9:283.) . . .

"Unfortunately we live in a world that largely rejects the values of Zion. Babylon has not and never will comprehend Zion. . . .

"[Babylon] stands in marked contrast to the Zion the Lord seeks to establish through his covenant people. Zion can be built up only among those who are the pure in heart—not a people torn by covetousness or greed, but a pure and selfless people, not a people who are pure in appearance, rather a people who are pure in heart. Zion is to be in the world and not of the world, not dulled by a sense of carnal security, nor paralyzed by materialism. No, Zion is not things of the lower, but of the higher order, things that exalt the mind and sanctify the heart.

"Zion is 'every man seeking the interest of his neighbor, and doing all things with an eye single to the glory of God.' (D&C 82:19.) As I understand these matters, Zion can be established only by those who are pure in heart, and who labor for Zion." (*Ensign,* March 1985, 3–4.)

To the list you made of things the Lord commanded in D&C 133:1–15, add specific counsel from President Spencer W. Kimball. Post the list where your family will see it often in coming days, or plan to review it often as a family.

Doctrine and Covenants 133:16–35
Events associated with the Second Coming

Have each family member read D&C 133:16–35 to themselves. (You might need to pair younger children with older children.) Give each family member four to six strips of paper. On each strip they are to write one question that can be answered in the verses they read. Encourage them to write questions that have to do with important ideas, events, and truths contained in this part of D&C 133. When everyone is finished, place the questions—folded up so no one can see them—into a bowl or bucket and mix them up. Each person takes a turn drawing a question and trying to give the answer without looking at D&C 133. If he or she cannot answer the question, the person who wrote it shows the family where the answer is in D&C 133.

This activity may bring up questions about some of the things spoken of in these verses. The footnotes will be helpful in obtaining additional context or understanding, since many of the ideas expressed in these verses are related to things spoken of elsewhere in scripture.

Conclude by having family members choose the part of these verses that most impressed them. Invite them to share with the family why it impressed them and what impact they think it will have on them.

Doctrine and Covenants 133:36–45
Who does what?

Divide a poster or large paper into two columns. Write "Who?" at the top of the first column and "Does What?" at the top of the second. (If you don't have poster paper or a whiteboard, have family members make this chart in their own scripture journal or on a piece of paper.)

Take turns reading a verse at a time in D&C 133:36–45. Stop after each verse and ask "Who?" and "Does What?" Record your responses in the columns on your chart. For each thing you record, ask, "Why would they do this?" and talk about the answers. Sometimes, the answer is in that verse or one close by. Other answers will come from what you know about Heavenly Father's plan.

When you get to D&C 133:45, ask your family what they think it means to "wait" for the Lord. As a reminder of the tremendous blessings that await the faithful, you may want to try to memorize this verse as a family. Ask:

- How could reciting this scripture help in a time of doubt or temptation?
- What can you do to increase your faith in this promise of the Lord?

Doctrine and Covenants 133:46–53
Learning about the Savior

Show your family the Harry Anderson picture of the Second Coming of Christ. (Picture 238 or 239 in the Gospel Art Picture Kit.) Ask your family to read D&C 133:46–48 to identify what is not accurate in the picture. Ask them why the Lord will be wearing red at the second coming. (See also Revelation 19:13; Isaiah 63:1–4.)

Explain that while D&C 133:46–53 talks about the appearance of the Lord at the time of His Second Coming, it describes more about Him—his character, attributes, and what he has done—than it does about what will happen. Read those verses together as a family and list everything it teaches us about the Savior. When your list is complete, ask:

- Why are these important things to know about the Lord?
- What difference would it make if we always believe and remember these things?

Since we know that when he comes we will all "mention" His "loving kindness . . . and all that he has bestowed" upon us, challenge your family to make it a habit to find ways to daily speak of the qualities of the Savior spoken of in D&C 133:52. Invite family members to share at least one thing they know about the Savior's loving kindness before finishing your scripture study time.

Doctrine and Covenants 133:57–74
Sharing the gospel message

Have your family imagine that a neighbor or friend asks, "Why does your Church send out so many missionaries, and why do they send them to places where many of the people are already Christian or religious?"

Before anyone gives an answer, explain that D&C 133:57–74 may provide ideas to help them answer. Read these verses together as a family. When you are finished, invite family members to give an answer as if they were talking to the person in the situation above. You may suggest they also consider the ideas in D&C 133:1–15 as they prepare and give their response.

Ask your family to imagine that in response to what you say to this friend or neighbor, the person surprises you by saying, "Actually, I think that believing in God is a kind of crutch for people who don't have personal strength to live their own lives, free from the restrictions of religion." Have a family member read aloud D&C 133:65–74, which is the Lord's answer to such a person. While your family members may or may not decide to share these verses with someone who might say such things to them, have them identify principles contained in these verses. After identifying the principles, have them put the principles in their own words in a way that they might share with someone they know. (For example, one principle found in verses 66–67 is that the Lord has tried on many occasions and in many ways to speak to people, but they do not listen. Verse 67 also contains the principle that the Lord has the power to save us from the judgments and destructions of the last days, and ultimately from death.)

In situations like these, remind your family of the promises in D&C 133:58–59 about those who seem to be weak compared to the strength and wisdom of the world.

DOCTRINE AND COVENANTS 134: GOVERNMENTS AND LAWS

Historical background: *This section of the Doctrine and Covenants is not a revelation but a declaration of belief regarding governments and law prepared by Oliver Cowdery. When it was written, the Saints had suffered mob violence and much persecution in Missouri. The statements in section 134 "were uttered by a people, who, judged by human standards, had every reason to feel that their government had failed [them] and that they might not hopefully and successfully look thereto for their protection." (J. Reuben Clark Jr., in Conference Report, April 1935, 90.) It was "adopted by unanimous vote at a general assembly of the Church held at Kirtland, Ohio, August 17, 1835." (D&C 134 section heading.) Joseph Smith was returning from a mission to Canada at the time it was voted on but approved it a week later. Notice the difference between Church government and man's governments.*

Doctrine and Covenants 134:1–12
What is the purpose of government?

As a family, think of a game or a sport you enjoy playing and list some of the rules. Ask:

- What would happen in the game if there were no rules?
- What if people refused to follow the rules?

Have a family member read aloud the historical background above. Divide your family into two groups. Have both groups search D&C 134, with one group looking for and marking words or phrases that tell the *purposes of civil governments* and the other looking for and marking phrases that describe our *responsibility to the laws of the land.* Allow time for searching and then have each group report on what they found.

Ask your family to look at the footnotes to this section and find the two Articles of Faith referred to. Have family members mark them in their scriptures: (1a: Articles of Faith 1:12; 4a: Articles of Faith 1:11; 7b: Articles of Faith 1:11). Ask if anyone can recite the eleventh or twelfth Article of Faith from memory. If no one can, have someone read them. (They are at the end of the Pearl of Great Price.) If you have small children, you may want to sing "The Eleventh Article of Faith" (*Children's Songbook*, 130) and "The Twelfth Article of Faith" (*Children's Songbook*, 131). Share the following statement:

"To be a Latter-day Saint in very deed is to be one of the best of God's people or children in the world. . . . A good Latter-day Saint will be a good citizen, no matter whether he be a subject of Great Britain, the United States, Holland, Germany or any other country in the world. If he be a good Latter-day Saint he is bound to be a good citizen of the land which gave him birth or which he has adopted as his home. . . . A citizen of God's kingdom should stand foremost among the best of God's people throughout all the world." ("Discourse by President Joseph F. Smith," *Millennial Star*, September 27, 1906, 610.)

Read some or all of the items below and discuss how they might help your family be good citizens and further the cause of good governments:

- Sing your national anthem respectfully.
- Show reverence for the flag of your country.
- Learn more of the heritage and history of your country.
- Campaign for political candidates whose views you support.
- Participate in community service projects and other civic activities.
- Obey the laws of the land.
- Respect public officials and public property.

- Respect political opinions that differ from your own.

(Adapted from *Young Women Manual 2*, Lesson 31: The Law of the Land, 116.)

DOCTRINE AND COVENANTS 135: THE VERY BEST BLOOD OF THE NINETEENTH CENTURY

Historical background: *On June 10, 1844, Joseph Smith and other Nauvoo City leaders ordered the destruction of the press of the* Nauvoo Expositor *that had printed lies about Joseph Smith and other Church leaders. Joseph and seventeen others were arrested. Governor Ford demanded that they be tried in Carthage, Illinois. Upon their arrival, they were illegally charged with treason and taken to jail. On June 27, 1844, a large mob stormed the jail and assassinated Joseph and his beloved brother Hyrum. John Taylor (who was severely wounded) and Willard Richards witnessed the murders and lived to testify of them. (See Ivin J. Barrett,* Joseph Smith and the Restoration, *587–616). As you study this section, notice all the ways your life has been blessed because of the life of the Prophet.*

Doctrine and Covenants 135:1–2
A testimony sealed by martyrdom

Share with your family the following account:

"[Just prior to the martyrdom, John Taylor] sang a song, that had lately been introduced into Nauvoo, entitled, *A Poor Wayfaring Man of Grief, etc.*

"The song is pathetic [sad], and the tune quite plaintive, and was very much in accordance with our feelings at the time for our spirits were all depressed, dull and gloomy and surcharged with indefinite ominous forebodings. After a lapse of some time, Brother Hyrum requested me again to sing that song. I replied, 'Brother Hyrum, I do not feel like singing;' when he remarked, 'Oh, never mind; commence singing, and you will get the spirit of it.'" (*History of the Church*, 7:101.)

Sing with your family selected verses of "A Poor Wayfaring Man of Grief" (*Hymns*, no. 29). Read together D&C 135:1–2. Then take turns reading the following account by John Taylor:

"At four o'clock the [jail] guard was changed. A little after five . . . there was a light rustling at the outer door of the jail, and a cry of surrender, then a discharge of three or four guns. The plot had

been carried out: two hundred of the mob came rushing into the jail yard, and the guards fired their pieces over the heads of the assailing [attacking] party.

"Many of the mob rushed up the stairs while others fired through the open windows of the jail into the room where the brethren were confined. The four prisoners sprang against the door, but the murderers burst it partly open and pushed their guns into the room. John Taylor and Willard Richards, each with a cane, tried to knock aside the weapons. A shower of bullets came up the stairway and through the door. Hyrum was in front of the door when a ball struck him in the face and he fell back saying:

"'I am a dead man.'

"As he was falling, another bullet from the outside passed through his swaying form, and two others from the doorway entered his body a moment later. When Hyrum fell, Joseph exclaimed, 'Oh, my dear brother Hyrum!' and opening the door a few inches he discharged his pistol into the stairway—but two or three barrels missed fire.

"When the door could no longer be held, and when he could no longer parry the guns, Elder

BIOGRAPHICAL SKETCH: JOHN TAYLOR

"John Taylor occupies the rare position of having authored a section in the Doctrine and Covenants (D&C 135). Called to the holy apostleship in 1838, Elder Taylor faithfully served as a member of that quorum of special witnesses and later ultimately served as the prophet and President of the Lord's Church here on earth (D&C 118:6; 124:129).

"It was John Taylor's melodic voice which helped bring peace to the troubled minds of Joseph and Hyrum Smith only short minutes before their lives were brutally taken. Having accompanied the brethren to Carthage, John Taylor had offered to tear the jail down if only Joseph would give the word (LJT, 135). He was severely wounded in the attack which claimed his companions' lives, but he lived to bear powerful testimony of the truth for which the men had earned martyrs' crowns. Of his preservation, Elder Taylor wrote: 'I felt that the Lord had preserved me by a special act of mercy; that my time had not yet come, and that I had still a work to perform upon the earth' (LJT, 150).

"As a young man in England, John Taylor had exhibited an interest in things of the Spirit, including supernatural experiences that led him to America and the restored gospel. One such experience involved seeing a vision of an angel sounding a trumpet to the nations, and having the thought impressed upon his mind that he was to preach the gospel in America (LJT, 28; see Rev. 14:6–7). Upon immigrating to Canada, he became active as a lay preacher, but soon discovered that the doctrines of men did not coincide with the principles of truth taught within the Bible. His conversion was the result of the missionary efforts of Parley P. Pratt, who had received a revelatory blessing regarding the fruits of that mission and their future impact upon the Church (LJT, 35).

"John Taylor joined the Church on May 9, 1836, with the following resolve: 'When I first entered upon Mormonism, I did it with my eyes open. I counted the cost. I looked upon it as a lifelong labor, and I considered that I was not only enlisted for time, but for eternity.' (LJT, 48.)" (Hoyt W. Brewster Jr., *Doctrine and Covenants Encyclopedia*, 578.)

Taylor sprang toward the window. A bullet from the doorway struck his left thigh. Paralyzed and unable to help himself he fell on the window sill. . . . A bullet fired from the outside struck his watch and . . . saved his life. . . .

"Joseph saw that there was no longer safety in the room; and thinking that he would save the life of Willard Richards if he himself should spring from the room, he turned immediately from the door, dropped his pistol and leaped into the window. Instantly two bullets pierced him from the door, and one entered his right breast from without, and he fell outward into the hands of his murderers exclaiming:

"'Oh, Lord, my God!'

"When his body struck the ground he rolled instantly upon his face—dead. . . .

"When Joseph fell from the window the mob on the stairway rushed down and out of the building to find him; and it was this which saved the lives of Willard Richards and John Taylor."

(George Q. Cannon, *The Life of Joseph Smith the Prophet*, 524–26.)

"I felt a dull, lonely, sickening sensation. . . . When I reflected that our noble chieftain, the Prophet of the living God, had fallen, and that I had seen his brother in the cold embrace of death, it seemed as though there was a void, a vacuum in the great field of human existence to me, and a dark, gloomy, chasm in the kingdom, and that we were left alone." (John Taylor in Joseph Smith, *History of the Church*, 7:106.)

Following the reading, invite family members to share their feelings. Then discuss the following questions:

- Why do you think the Lord allowed Joseph and Hyrum to be martyred? (Verse 1.)
- What does the martyrdom teach us about Satan and those who serve him?
- What affect has the martyrdom had upon the Church?
- What affect has it had upon you?

Doctrine and Covenants 135:3
Second only to the Savior

Ask your family members to list as many of the accomplishments of Joseph Smith as they can think of. Invite one person to be a scribe and begin a chart by writing this list in a column on the left-hand side of a sheet of paper. When finished, read together D&C 135:3 and mark the accomplishments of the Prophet listed there. Have the scribe write these accomplishments in a column on the right-hand side of your chart. Invite your family to consider the two lists and tell which accomplishments they appreciate most and why. It might be helpful to discuss the following questions:

- In what ways has Joseph done more, "save Jesus only," for the salvation of men?
- Why do you think it was necessary for Joseph's brother, Hyrum, to also seal his testimony with his blood?

- In your opinion, what was Joseph Smith's greatest accomplishment?

Express your gratitude for Joseph Smith and the contributions he made in behalf of your salvation. You might close by singing "Praise to the Man" (*Hymns*, no. 27) with your family.

Doctrine and Covenants 135:4–7
They knew their fate!

Have your family find the entry for "Prophet" in the Bible Dictionary (p. 754). Have them scan the information and underline the roles and responsibilities of a prophet. If no one mentions that prophets predict or foretell future events, be sure to point it out. Invite a family member to read D&C 135:4–5. Ask:

- What did Joseph know as he went to Carthage?
- Prior to Joseph and Hyrum's departure to Carthage, Hyrum read Ether 12:36–41. How did these verses help prepare him for his death? (See Joseph Fielding Smith, *Life of Joseph F. Smith*, 83.)
- How could Joseph and Hyrum, knowing their future, be "calm as a summer's morning"?
- How do you think Lucy Mack Smith felt when she heard of the death of her sons?
- What do you think Joseph and Hyrum's children felt when they learned of the fate of their fathers?

Ask family members to name famous people of the nineteenth century (like Abraham Lincoln, Ulysses S. Grant, Buffalo Bill Cody, General Custer, Marie Curie, Davy Crockett, Lewis and Clark, John Wesley Powell, Jim Bridger, Robert E. Lee, Olin Winchester, Samuel Colt, Butch Cassidy and the Sundance Kid, Alexander Graham Bell, Steven Foster, John Philip Sousa, Geronimo, Washakie, Wright brothers, Elizabeth Fry, Mayo brothers, Louis Pasteur, Cochise, Nellie Bly, Johnny Appleseed, and Pancho Villa).

Ask your family which person they think was

the best or most important person. Read D&C 135:6–7 and ask how they feel about John Taylor's opinion of the best and most glorious people of the nineteenth century. Ask:

- Why do you think John Taylor referred to Joseph and Hyrum as gems?
- What does "sanctified" mean? (To be made holy.)
- How might the persecution and death of Joseph and Hyrum help make them "gems" of those who are pure and holy? (See verse 6–7.)

Note the following definitions to help explain difficult words in verse 7:

- "Escutcheon" (shield.)
- "Magna Charta" (guarantee of rights and privileges).
- "Under the altar that John saw" (see Revelation 6:9).

Bear your testimony of the Prophet Joseph Smith.

DOCTRINE AND COVENANTS 136: THE CAMP OF ISRAEL MOVES WEST

Historical background: "*The Saints were driven from their homes in Nauvoo under the most trying circumstances and in poverty and destitution in large measure for they had been robbed by their enemies. Therefore it was extremely needful for a revelation from the Lord for their guidance in their journeyings to the Rocky Mountains. The Lord did not fail them in this hour of distress and gave this revelation to President Brigham Young to guide them in their journeyings and admonishing them to keep His commandments. All the members of the Church were to be organized in companies and were required to keep the commandments faithfully that they might have the guidance of His Spirit with them in all their trying circumstances. These companies were to be on the order followed by Zion's Camp in their remarkable march from Kirtland to Missouri, with captains over hundreds, fifties and tens and all under the direction of the council of Apostles.*" (Hyrum M. Smith and Janne M. Sjodahl, Doctrine and Covenants Commentary, 857.) *As you study this section, consider how important it was for the pioneers to follow the Lord's counsel with exactness.*

Doctrine and Covenants 136:1–18
Preparation for migration

Tell your family to imagine that the First Presidency contacted your stake president and told him to organize his stake and be ready to move everyone in one month. Members of your stake will never come back home, and although the destination is still uncertain, it will be at least 1,500 miles away. The instructions say that each family must sell their homes and buy wagons and teams of oxen to carry their possessions. Explain that the early Saints were driven from Nauvoo and faced a challenge that would have been even more difficult than the one just described.

Read the historical background and the section heading for D&C 136 aloud. Ask:

- Imagine it was your family making this trip. What difficulties would you expect to face in a journey of this magnitude?
- Who in your family would have the most difficult time?
- Who might be the most helpful?
- How could relying on the Lord and following His counsel help make the trip easier?

Divide your family into two groups. Ask both groups to read D&C 136:1–18. Have one group make a list of the supplies the Lord commanded the wagon companies to take with them from Winter Quarters. Have the other group write down items of counsel the Lord gave to the Saints who were making the journey. When they have finished, have a spokesperson from each group talk about and describe what they learned.

Ask your family to look closely at verses 11, 17, and 18 and underline the blessings promised to the Saints if they were faithful in doing the Lord's will. Share any pioneer stories your family may know, especially any about your own ancestors. Express your appreciation for the early Saints who were willing to make these sacrifices.

Doctrine and Covenants 136:1–42
Lessons for Latter-day Saints

Have family members turn to their Doctrine and Covenants maps and locate Winter Quarters and the Salt Lake Valley. Have them identify how far the journey was. Talk briefly about how difficult it would be for the pioneers to travel west to the Salt Lake Valley, especially under their difficult circumstances. Read D&C 136:22 and ask:

- What other migration, referred to here, did the Lord lead?
- What are some similarities between the Israelites' journey and that of the Mormon pioneers?

Read D&C 136:2 aloud to your family and explain that the commandments given on this journey would also help "all the people of the Church of Jesus Christ of Latter-day Saints" on another journey. That journey is the journey through mortality as we seek to return to live with our Heavenly Father someday.

Have family members take turns reading D&C 136:1–42. After many or most of the verses, stop and have a family discussion. In your discussion, identify answers to the following questions:

1. What instruction did the Lord give the early Saints in this verse?

2. How would this instruction help them in their particular journey?

3. How could we apply this instruction to our lives today?

4. How would that counsel help us in our journey back to Heavenly Father?

As an example, consider answers to the questions above for verses 3 and 9:

D&C 136:3

1. The Lord instructed the Saints to be organized in companies with captains for each.

2. This would help the people be watched over and cared for by others.

3. We are organized with leaders in stakes, wards, quorums, and families.

4. Our stake, ward, and quorum members help us in our challenges

D&C 136:9

1. The pioneers were to build homes and raise food to assist others who would travel later.

2. This would help the poor Saints to survive. Serving others would also bring blessings.

3. We should use our resources to help make the world a better place for those who are yet to be born.

4. Worrying about others and helping meet their needs is critical to helping fulfill Heavenly Father's plan for His children.

Doctrine and Covenants 136:19–33
What was the Lord's covenant with the Camp of Israel?

Read D&C 82:10 and talk about what that verse has to do with the word "Covenant." Read D&C 136:2, 4 and find the covenant the pioneer Saints made with God for their journey to the Salt Lake Valley. Explain to your family that D&C 136:19–33 indicates a portion of a covenant between the Camp of Israel and the Lord. Give family members two different colored pencils. Take turns reading D&C 136:19–33, looking for and marking Israel's part of the covenant in one color and God's part covenant in another. When you have finished, ask:

- What part of the covenant do you think would be most difficult to obey?

- How confident would you be in God's promises? Why?
- Why would it be important for us to keep those same covenants today?

DOCTRINE AND COVENANTS 137: A VISION OF THE CELESTIAL KINGDOM

*Historical background: Richard O. Cowan writes, "[Section] 137 and 138 were added to the standard works in 1976, at first being assigned to the Pearl of Great Price. Five years later they were transferred to their present position as part of the new 1981 edition of the Doctrine and Covenants. Thus they followed the pattern of 87, which also had been a part of the Pearl of Great Price before it was moved to the Doctrine and Covenants. Both 137 and 138 shed light on salvation of the dead, so their addition to the scriptural canon was timely, coming in an era of unprecedented temple-building activity." (*The Doctrine and Covenants, Our Modern Scripture, 208.)

In 1836 the Saints were living in Kirtland, and the temple was only a few months away from its dedication. This was a great spiritual time for the Saints and for Joseph Smith. As an example, the week before the Prophet received this revelation, he held a special meeting with the Twelve, had a sacrament meeting with a large congregation, married three couples, studied Hebrew, and had sacred experiences in the Kirtland Temple. It was while Joseph was in the Kirtland Temple that section 137 was received. (See History of the Church, 2:381.) *You're your family to watch for the Lord's plan to save all His children, regardless of when or where they lived.*

Doctrine and Covenants 137: 1–9
Joseph sees Alvin in the celestial kingdom

Provide drawing materials for your family and have them draw the scene you will read to them. Read D&C 137:1–4 slowly and give them time to complete their drawings. Then have them show their pictures and describe what they drew. Ask them how they would like to see such a place.

Have someone read D&C 137:5 and identify who Joseph Smith saw in the celestial kingdom besides Heavenly Father and Jesus Christ. Have a family member read the biographical sketch about Alvin Smith. Have another family member read D&C 137:6. Ask:

- Why was Joseph Smith amazed to see his brother Alvin in the celestial kingdom? (Verse 6.)

- What does D&C 137:7–9 teach about those who die without hearing the gospel?
- Who are some people that would fit in that category today?
- What can we do to help them receive the gospel? (We help them by doing temple work on their behalf.)

Share the following situation with your family: A young man has been preparing to serve a mission. Four months before he turns nineteen, he has a terrible accident and is paralyzed from the neck down. He is worried how the Lord will judge him because he can no longer serve a mission. Ask:

- What message from D&C 137:9 could help this young man?
- What does this doctrine teach you about Heavenly Father's love for all of His children?

BIOGRAPHICAL SKETCH: ALVIN SMITH

Alvin Smith was born February 11, 1798. He was the oldest child of Joseph Smith Sr. and Lucy Mack Smith. He was very receptive to Joseph Smith's message of the restoration, and he supported and defended his younger brother.

On November 15, 1823, Alvin became very sick, and the medicine the he was given only made him worse. When he realized that he was going to die, he called the family together, and to young Joseph he said, "I am now going to die, the distress which I suffer, and the feelings that I have, tell me my time is very short I want you to be a good boy, and do everything that lies in your power to obtain the Record. Be faithful in receiving instruction, and in keeping every commandment that is given you." (Lucy Mack Smith, *History of Joseph Smith by His Mother*, 86.)

Doctrine and Covenants 137:10
What happens to a child who dies before age eight?

Have your family guess if the following statement is true or false:

1. A child whose parents are not members of the Church and who dies before age eight will go to the celestial kingdom.

Invite a family member to read D&C 137:10 to find the answer. Also study Moroni 8:22, Mosiah 15:25, and D&C 29:46–47. Ask a family member to share how that makes him or her feel toward God. Testify of your gratitude for God's love and mercy.

DOCTRINE AND COVENANTS 138: VISION OF THE WORK IN THE SPIRIT WORLD

Historical background: The most important background related to the revelation in D&C 138 is explained in the section heading and in D&C 138:1–11. In the opening remarks of the general conference referred to in the section heading, President Joseph F. Smith said, "I will not, I dare not, attempt to enter upon many things that are resting upon my mind this morning, and I shall postpone until some future time, the Lord being willing, my attempt to tell you some of the things that are in my mind, and that dwell in my heart. I have not lived alone these five months. I have dwelt in the spirit of prayer, of supplication, of faith and of determination; and I have had my communication with the Spirit of the Lord continuously." (Conference Report, October 1918, 2.) About six weeks after this revelation, President Smith entered the spirit world he had seen in vision, when he died November 19, 1918.

Doctrine and Covenants 138:1–11
What circumstances led to this revelation?

Ask your family to pretend they are editors for the *New Era* magazine. There is a section in that magazine where advice from teenagers is given for selected questions. Ask your family how they would respond to the following question: "What are some things you suggest to make scripture study more meaningful?"

After talking about your family's answers to that question, read together D&C 138:1–11 after inviting family members to look for what President Joseph F. Smith did during his scripture study. Ask:

- What things did President Smith do that helped him receive revelation on this occasion?
- What two or three words best represent what he did?
- What was he pondering about specifically?

Share with your family the following counsel:

"You need time to meditate and ponder, to think, to wonder at the great plan of happiness that the Lord has outlined for His children. . . .

"I heard President David O. McKay say to the members of the Twelve on one occasion, 'Brethren, we do not spend enough time meditating.'

"I believe that with all my heart. Our lives become extremely busy. We run from one thing to another. We wear ourselves out in thoughtless pursuit of goals which are highly ephemeral [temporary]. We are entitled to spend some time with ourselves in introspection, in development. I remember my dear father when he was about the age that I am now. He lived in a home where there was a rock wall on the grounds. It was a low wall, and when the weather was warm, he would go and sit on his wall. It seemed to me he sat there for hours, thinking, meditating, pondering things that he would say and write, for he was a very gifted speaker and writer. He read much, even into his very old age. He never ceased growing. Life was for him a great adventure in thinking.

"Your needs and your tastes along these lines will vary with your age. But all of us need some of it. I decry the great waste of time that people put into watching inane television. I am not anti-sports. I enjoy watching a good football game or a good basketball game. But I see so many men who become absolutely obsessed with sports. I believe their lives would be enriched if, instead of sitting on the sofa and watching a game that will be forgotten tomorrow, they would read and think and

BIOGRAPHICAL SKETCH: JOSEPH F. SMITH

Joseph F. Smith was born November 13, 1838, a few days after his father, Hyrum Smith (brother to the Prophet Joseph), was arrested by Missourians and put in jail for nearly six months. He was the first child of his mother, Mary Fielding Smith, although she was taking care of Hyrum's five children from his first wife who died in Kirtland, Ohio. Hyrum was killed before Joseph F. Smith's sixth birthday. When young Joseph was ten years old, he helped drive a wagon team for his mother more than a thousand miles to the Salt Lake valley. She died two years later.

When he was fifteen, Joseph was ordained an elder and called on a mission to Hawaii, where he served for nearly four years. He later served another shorter mission to Hawaii after serving in Great Britain for three years. At age twenty-seven he was ordained an apostle and served as an additional counselor in the First Presidency with President Brigham Young. He later served as a counselor to John Taylor, Wilford Woodruff, and Lorenzo Snow. He became the president of the Church on October 17, 1901, and served for slightly more than eighteen years. He had two sons who served in the Quorum of the Twelve Apostles, Hyrum M. Smith and Joseph Fielding Smith (who later became a Church president himself).

ponder." (Gordon B. Hinckley, *Ensign,* February 1999, 5.)

"As I have read the scriptures I have been challenged by the word *ponder,* so frequently used in the Book of Mormon. The dictionary says that ponder means 'to weigh mentally, think deeply about, deliberate, meditate.' . . .

"Pondering is, in my feeling, a form of prayer." (Marion G. Romney, in Conference Report, April 1973, 117.)

Ask your family what impressed them in the counsel of President Hinckley and President Romney and how they will put it into practice.

Doctrine and Covenants 138:11–24
Conditions in the spirit world

Talk about a member of your family who has passed away. Share some wonderful memories you have of that person. Ask your family to consider what the person is doing right now, and what life might be like for him or her in the spirit world. Explain to your family that while we generally know that when we die we go to the spirit world, we do not know much about life

there. Read together Alma 40:11–14 and ask what it teaches about life after death. Explain that D&C 138 gives us perhaps more information than any other place in scripture on this subject, and verses 11–24 tell us mostly about the condition of the spirits in what Alma called "paradise."

Have a scribe write on a two-column chart the following headings (or have family members write it on a page in their scripture study journals): "What they did to be there" and "Words and phrases that describe their condition." Read together D&C 138:11–24. Have family members identify what this passage says about people in paradise and note these truths in the appropriate column on the chart or paper.

You could also do the same for those who were not in paradise (although less information is given) by carefully looking at D&C 138:20–22.

After completing this activity, ask your family what messages are most important for us from our study of the spirit world. Ask why they would rather be among the righteous when they die than the wicked.

D&C 138:25–37, 57–59
The gospel preached to the dead

Read together 1 Peter 3:18–20 and 1 Peter 4:6 (found in D&C 138:7–10) and find what President Smith was pondering about when this revelation came. Have your family find and mark "I marveled" and "I wondered" in D&C 138:25, 28, 29. Then read together verses 25–28 and work together to write one or more questions that express what President Smith "marveled" and "wondered" about. It may take some "reading between the lines," but you should come up with questions like the following:

- How would all mankind be able to accept or reject the Savior when such a relatively small number of people heard Him during His mortal ministry?
- What became of the millions who lived before Christ's mortal ministry and the millions who have lived in darkness since?
- How did Christ preach to all these people in just the three days He was there?

Take turns reading D&C 138:29–37. Ask:

- What are the answers to the things President Smith marveled and wondered about?
- What were those in darkness taught?
- What do these things tell us about what goes on in the Spirit World? (Read also D&C 138:57–59 for additional information and insight.)
- How do these things help us understand the importance of the work we do in the temple?

Discuss as a family how the truths we learn from this revelation can make us less frightened about the next life.

Doctrine and Covenants 138:38–54
Who were among the righteous in the spirit world?

Ask your family, "If you could have anyone from history—except Jesus—teach your Sunday School class this week, who would you want it to be, and why?" After sharing answers and explanations, read together D&C 138:38–53, noting who President Smith saw in the spirit world among those who were appointed to preach the gospel there. Ask:

- Which two people from those noted (including any prophet they might choose from the Book of Mormon as noted in verse 49) would you choose for a teacher?
- Based on what that person did and taught in mortality, what principles of the gospel do you think he or she would be especially good at teaching? (Encourage family members to remember or look up the life and teachings of that person, if necessary.)
- Why would those in the spirit world still need those lessons?

Share with your family that although only one woman is mentioned in this revelation, President Joseph F. Smith taught the following:

"Now, among all these millions of spirits that have lived on the earth and have passed away, from generation to generation, since the beginning of the world, without the knowledge of the gospel—among them you may count that at least one-half are women. Who is going to preach the gospel to the women? Who is going to carry the testimony of Jesus Christ to the hearts of the women who have passed away without a knowledge of the gospel? Well, to my mind, it is a simple thing. These good sisters who have been set apart, ordained to the work, called to it, authorized by the authority of the holy Priesthood to minister for their sex, in the House of God for the living and for the dead, will be fully authorized and empowered to preach the gospel and minister to the women while the elders and prophets are preaching it to the men." (*Gospel Doctrine*, 461.)

Have someone read D&C 130:18–19. Encourage your family to not only prepare themselves to be great gospel teachers in this life but also to never stop learning and growing so that they can continue to teach the gospel in the spirit world. Read D&C 138:57 and ask:

- What does this teach us about what members of our family (or others we know) who have gone on to the spirit world are doing and teaching right now?
- How can we assist in their work?

D&C 138:53–56

What do we learn about the premortal life?

Ask your family how much they remember about their life before they were born on earth. (Probably nothing.) Ask if they would like to know more.

Read D&C 138:53–55 and ask:

- What do these verses say about the timing of these men coming to mortality?

- What, in particular, were they to do while here?
- Who were they before they entered mortality?

Be sure to have your family mark the cross-reference in footnote 55a. Read Abraham 3:22–24 and ask, "What does D&C 138:55 teach about those people Abraham saw?"

Read D&C 138:56 and ask:

- What did these notable prophets do in the premortal life?
- What did they learn, and why?
- Which phrase in verse 56 might refer to you?
- What does it mean to you to know that you may have been taught those things and prepared for those purposes?

OFFICIAL DECLARATIONS 1 AND 2: MODERN REVELATION

Historical background: President Ezra Taft Benson shared the following counsel: *"Let me give you a crucial key to help you avoid being deceived. It is this—learn to keep your eye on the prophet. He is the Lord's mouthpiece and the only man who can speak for the Lord today. Let his inspired counsel take precedence. . . .*

"There is only one man on the earth today who speaks for the Church. That man is the President of the Church (see D&C 132:7; 21:4). Because he gives the word of the Lord for us today, his words have an even more immediate importance than those of the dead prophets. When speaking under the influence of the Holy Ghost, his words are scripture (D&C 68:4).

"The President can speak on any subject he feels is needful for the Saints. . . . The words of a living prophet must and ever will take precedence." (Teachings of Ezra Taft Benson, 134.)

These two official declarations contain descriptions of the revelations received by two latter-day prophets, Wilford Woodruff and Spencer W. Kimball. They also contain information concerning the presentation and acceptance of these revelations by the members of The Church of Jesus Christ of Latter-day Saints.

Official Declaration 1
Do you believe there is modern revelation?

Ask two family members to pretend they are missionaries. Role play with them (pretending you are a sincerely interested investigator) and ask them, "Do you believe in modern revelation? Do you really believe God still speaks to us through prophets today? Why is that necessary if we have the teachings in the Bible?"

After some discussion, ask your family to read Amos 3:7 and D&C 1:17, 37–38 and talk about what these verses have to do with modern revelation. Ask:

- Why do you think it is important to know that God still speaks to us today?
- Why is that important to know when you say your prayers each day?
- What doctrines or principles could the Lord speak to the prophet about?
- Do the words of the current prophet supersede the words of former prophets? Why?

Read the historical background to your family and share your testimony of President Benson's statement. You may also want to take time to scan Official Declarations 1 and 2 to discover what the Lord revealed to President Wilford Woodruff and to President Spencer W. Kimball. Invite family members to share any parts of the declarations they liked or thought were interesting.

Ask your family the following: "Is it possible for the prophet to lead the Church astray? What would happen if he tried? Read the first paragraph under "Excerpts from Three Addresses by President Wilford Woodruff Regarding the Manifesto." Ask family members to describe the message of that paragraph in their own words, and share your testimony that the Lord will never allow His prophet to lead us astray. You may want to sing the Hymn "We Thank Thee, O God, for a Prophet" (*Hymns*, no. 19) or "Follow the Prophet" (*Children's Songbook*, 110).

Official Declaration 2
How do we prepare ourselves to receive revelation?

Ask your family to read the first and second paragraphs of Official Declaration—2. Ask:

- What did President Spencer W. Kimball have to do in order to obtain this sacred revelation?

BIOGRAPHICAL SKETCH: SPENCER W. KIMBALL

Spencer W. Kimball was born March 28, 1895. His mother passed away when he was 11 years old, and at age 19 he served a mission to the Central States. When he returned, he married Camilla Eyring and began working in the banking industry. At age 48 he was called into the Quorum of the Twelve Apostles.

"In 1957 he was diagnosed with throat cancer and underwent surgery to remove his vocal cords in order to save his life. In 1972 he underwent open-heart surgery. Despite these set backs he didn't let it effect his work. On his desk sits a slogan 'Do It.' And that is what he did. Another famous phrase he is known for is 'lengthen your stride.' He became President of the Church on December 30, 1973 and under his leadership not only was the priesthood extended to all worthy males but a major revision of the Standard Works was accomplished. The text was not changed but many helps were added (Topical Guide, footnotes, and Maps, etc.). President Kimball worked diligently until 1979 when his health again failed. He remained very weak from 1981 until he died in 1985." (Richard O. Cowan, *The Church in the Twentieth Century*, 381–82.)

Elder Boyd K. Packer wrote of this great prophet:

"The Lord . . . was not just preparing a businessman, nor a civic leader, nor a speaker, nor a poet, nor a musician, nor a teacher—though he would be all of these. He was preparing a father, a patriarch for his family, an apostle and prophet, and a president for His church. There were testings along the way—examinations in courage and patience, that few would have passed." (*Ensign*, March 1974, 3.)

- How do President Kimball's actions compare with those of Nephi (in 2 Nephi 11:1), Joseph Smith (in JSH 1:11–14), and Joseph F. Smith (in D&C 138:1–2, 6)?

As you discuss what they found, also talk about how we can follow that example in our personal lives. Invite family members to write a paragraph in their journals describing something they have or are worried about. Invite them to receive help from the Lord by following the pattern you discussed. Encourage them to record their experiences in their journals in the weeks that follow.

Point out what President Kimball did after receiving this revelation by re-reading paragraph 2 in Official Declaration—2. Ask:

- Why do you think it was important for President Kimball to present this revelation to his counselors and to the Quorum of the Twelve Apostles?
- To whom was it presented next?
- To whom was it eventually presented on June 8, 1978? (See paragraph 3.)
- How is this action an example of the Law of Common Consent? (See D&C 26:2; 28:13.)
- Why do you think the Lord insists that Church members have the chance to vote to accept His laws?

Share the following statement about this revelation to President Spencer W. Kimball:

"Perhaps nothing has had a greater impact on the worldwide spread of the Church than did the 1978 revelation received through President Spencer W. Kimball extending the priesthood to worthy brethren of all races. For several months the General Authorities had discussed this topic at length in their regular temple meetings. Then, on June 1, 1978, after a three-hour temple meeting, President Kimball invited his counselors and the Twelve to remain while the other General Authorities were excused. He again brought up the possibility of conferring the priesthood on worthy brethren of all races. During the two-hour discussion 'there was a marvelous outpouring of unity, oneness, and agreement in the council.' The President then led the group in prayer on this matter. 'It was during this prayer that the revelation came,' Elder Bruce R. McConkie recalled. 'The Spirit of the Lord rested mightily upon us all; we felt something akin to what happened on the day of Pentecost and at the dedication of the Kirtland Temple.' (*Priesthood,* 128.)

"One week later, the statement known as Official Declaration 2 was released. This is not a record of the revelation itself, but, like Official Declaration 1, is an inspired announcement that the revelation had been received. This may explain why these documents have their present status rather than being numbered sections in the Doctrine and Covenants.

"The impact of this revelation was far-reaching. Faithful Black Latter-day Saints rejoiced as they received long-hoped-for ordination to the priesthood, mission calls, calls to serve in bishoprics or stake presidencies, and the eternal blessings of the temple. Within a few months, missions were opened in the predominantly Black nations of Nigeria and Ghana, and hundreds of converts were baptized." (Richard O. Cowen, *The Doctrine and Covenants, Our Modern Scripture,* 213.)

JOSEPH SMITH—HISTORY

Historical background: "Joseph Smith began dictating the history in 1838. It was finished in 1858, fourteen years after his death, by George A. Smith and Wilford Woodruff, who said of it at its publication: 'The History of Joseph Smith is true, and is one of the most authentic histories ever written.' (Joseph Smith, History of the Church, 1:vi.) The Pearl of Great Price contains extracts from the first forty-four pages of that history." (H. Donl Peterson, The Pearl of Great Price: A History and Commentary, 4.)

Joseph Smith—History 1:1–4, 7
Why write a history?

 Display some of your family's journals and ask:

- Why are journals important?
- Do you think your journal will be more or less valuable ten years from now? Why?
- How valuable do you think your journal will be to your children, grandchildren, and great-grandchildren?

Read the historical background and share your enthusiasm for the chance to read Joseph Smith's history. Ask family members to read JS—H 1:1–2. Ask:

- What reasons did Joseph Smith give for writing the history of the Church?
- When did the writing of the history begin?
- Why are you grateful that Joseph recorded his history?

Give your family a writing assignment to record in their journals the events leading to their conversion, or a spiritual experience from their early life.

Give each family member a piece of paper. Have your family read JS—H 1:3–4, 7 and draw or list each member of the Smith family. Have them include as much information as possible about the family, such as Joseph Smith's birth date, the towns the Smiths lived in, or the religion they belonged to. Talk about what it might have been like to grow up as a member of that family.

Share the following statement from President Brigham Young:

"It was decreed in the counsels of eternity, long before the foundations of the earth were laid, that he, Joseph Smith, should be the man, in the last dispensation of this world, to bring forth the word of God to the people, and receive the fulness of the keys and power of the Priesthood of the Son of God. The Lord had his eyes upon him, and upon his father, and upon his father's father, and upon their progenitors clear back to Abraham, and from Abraham to the flood, from the flood to Enoch, and from Enoch to Adam. He has watched that family and that blood as it has circulated from its fountain to the birth of that man. He was fore-ordained in eternity to preside over this last dispensation." (*Discourses of Brigham Young,* 108.)

Joseph Smith—History 1:5–14
How did the people in Joseph Smith's day feel about religion?

Show your family the telephone directory yellow pages under the heading "Churches." Point out how many different churches there are in your town. Read JS—H 1:5 aloud to your family and have them imagine that all the churches listed in the phone book began coming to your home, wanting you to join them. Ask:

- What kinds of challenges would this situation bring?
- How difficult would it be for you to decide which one to join, if you didn't belong to any church yet?

- Why would this bring confusion into your life?

Explain that JS—H 1:6–14 includes information about how Joseph Smith handled this situation in his life. Invite your family to search those verses on their own and make a list of these things:

- What Joseph Smith did when he was confused or had questions about religion.
- What character traits Joseph exemplified that helped him during this time.
- What proved to be the greatest help for him during this stressful time.

When all have finished, invite family members to share their discoveries. Talk about the pattern Joseph Smith followed, and testify that we can do the same kinds of things when we are confused, seeking a testimony, or need answers in our lives. As part of your discussion, be sure to point out such items as these:

- Joseph Smith did much research concerning his problem. (See verses 7–8.)
- He spent time pondering and reflecting. (See verses 8–10.)
- He studied the scriptures for answers. (See verses 11–12.)
- He prayed for answers. (See verses 13–14.)

Ask family members to talk about any questions they have struggled with in the past, or may be struggling with now. Encourage them to talk about how scripture study and prayer has helped them. Testify that, like Joseph, we can receive answers from God. Have family members mark James 1:5 in their scriptures. Encourage them to memorize that verse.

Joseph Smith—History 1:15–20
The Father and the Son appear to Joseph Smith

Briefly review with your family the story of Moses' vision of the Savior, which was followed by an encounter with Satan, from Moses

1:1–16. Be sure to point out how Moses was able to easily distinguish between the light, power, and majesty of God and the darkness and fear he felt in Satan's presence.

Read together JS—H 1:15–20, pausing during your reading to discuss these questions:

Verse 15

- How was Joseph Smith's experience similar to what happened to Moses?
- What did Joseph learn about Satan from this experience?
- Why do you think Satan tried to kill Joseph rather than lead him astray as he did with Moses?

Verses 16–17

- What did Joseph do to escape from Satan's power?
- What does this teach us about Satan's power compared to God's power?
- What does this teach us about our struggles with Satan?
- Why do you think God allowed Satan to do this to Joseph?
- All his life Joseph had been taught the Christian belief that God was a spirit without a body, and that the Father, the Son, and the Holy Ghost were all the same being. What did Joseph learn about the Godhead from this vision?
- Joseph learned that God knew him by name. Do you think God also knows you by name?

Verses 18–19

- What kind of answer did Joseph expect to get to his question?
- What did Jesus tell him about the churches he had been studying?
- What is so bad about having a "form of godliness" without the "power thereof"?

Verse 20

- How is the effect this experience had on Joseph like the experiences of other prophets? (See footnote a and have your family compare the references there.)
- Since Satan failed to stop Joseph from receiving this vision, what do you suppose he has been trying to do since?

Share with your family your feelings about the Prophet Joseph Smith and the truth of the First Vision. Encourage them to find a time to ponder these verses and pray for their own witness that Joseph was telling the truth. Consider arranging a time (such as in a family home evening) for family members to go where they can be alone to ponder and pray about these things and then return and share their feelings with one another.

Joseph Smith—History 1:21–28
If the boy's testimony is false, why bother to persecute him?

Ask your family what they think it means to "be persecuted for my name's sake" and if any of them feel they have been persecuted for the Savior or the Church.

Ask family members to call out words that would indicate persecution as they follow along while you read aloud JS—H 1:21–28. Ask:

- Why do you think young Joseph openly shared this sacred experience with a Methodist preacher, and why was Joseph "surprised" at the preacher's reaction?
- Do you think that ministers of the day had taught their congregations to pray and read the scriptures? If so, why would they reject a report of an answer?
- How did Joseph feel about his persecution? (Verse 23.)
- Did he ever deny what he had seen? (Verse 25.)
- Why do you think Joseph shared Paul's experience about the testimony of his vision and the results? (Verse 24.)

Invite family members to record an experience in their scripture journal when they were persecuted. Have them include whether or not the persecution came from a friend or an enemy and how they felt about the persecutor. Ask family members to consider what they learned from Joseph Smith about how to deal with persecution. Challenge them to search their hearts and ponder upon their behavior when they were persecuted (for example, were they truthful, innocent, kind, or angry?). Invite them to write a goal about how they can better handle persecution in the future following Joseph Smith's example.

Joseph Smith—History 1:27–29
Joseph Smith wanted to overcome his weaknesses

Share the following statement from Joseph Smith:

"The nearer a man approaches perfection, the clearer are his views, and the greater his enjoyments, till he has overcome the evils of his life and lost every desire for sin." (*Teachings of the Prophet Joseph Smith*, 51.)

Ask your family to say Joseph's statement in their own words and explain what it means. Tell them that even when Joseph was young, he wanted to overcome all his sins, even those that were relatively small. Read JS—H 1:27–29 and identify some of the little things Joseph wanted to overcome. Ask:

- How do the weaknesses Joseph mentioned compare with some of the weaknesses and sins you are trying to conquer?
- Why would it be important for both Joseph and you to overcome these kinds of temptations?
- What were some of Joseph's strengths?
- What was Joseph's "disposition"?
- Is a "cheery temperament" a good thing or a bad thing?

Share the following motto Joseph made for himself later in life. Talk about its similarities with 1 Nephi 3:7, and encourage your family to follow that same motto:

"When the Lord commands, do it!" (*History of the Church,* 2:170.)

Moroni appears to Joseph Smith. (Painting by Tom Lovell.)

Joseph Smith—History 1:30–50
Joseph Smith was visited by Moroni

Show your family the picture of Moroni appearing to Joseph Smith. Have them study the picture as you read JS—H 1:30–33 aloud. When you have finished, ask:

- If you were to paint a picture of this scene, how would you do it differently?
- What details of Joseph's vision stand out the most to you?
- What do you imagine it might have been like to have this experience?
- How is this experience similar to Joseph's vision in the Sacred Grove?

Have your family scan through JS—H 1:30–49 and find how many times Moroni appeared to Joseph in these verses. (A total of four—three during the night, and one the following day. The fifth appearance at the Hill Cumorah will be discussed later.) Read those verses more carefully and discuss the following questions:

- How did Moroni's visits compare to one another?
- What does this repetition teach you about the importance of Moroni's message?
- What did Moroni add to his message in the second, third, and fourth visits?
- What did Moroni warn Joseph about?

Invite your family to study Moroni's message to Joseph. Write the following references on a paper or poster and assign each family member one of them:

- Malachi 3:1–4; 4:1, 5–6 with JS—H 1:37–39.
- Isaiah 11 chapter heading with JS—H 1:40.
- Acts 3:22–23 with JS—H 1:40.
- Joel 2:28–32 with JS—H 1:41.

Have family members study their assigned references and complete the following:

- Compare Moroni's version with the Bible verses, noting any differences.
- Identify what main message the verses teach.
- Draw a picture depicting the message.

When each group has finished, have a group spokesperson show the picture and teach the rest of the family about that portion of Moroni's message.

Joseph Smith—History 1:51–54
The gold plates

Give each member of your family a piece of salt dough. You can make it with one cup of flour, half a cup of salt, half a cup of very warm water, food coloring, and two tablespoons of vegetable oil. Mix the flour and salt, add the water and stir well. Add the food coloring and oil.

Knead for five minutes. Store the dough in a sealed container.

Ask family members to read JS—H 1:51–52. Have them select one of the following objects listed in those verses and mold the object out of dough: the stone box, the stone over the box, the lever, the plates, the Urim and Thummim, and the breastplate. The following descriptions may be helpful:

Lucy Mack Smith stated, "[On the morning of September 22, 1827, after Joseph had returned from the hill, he placed] the article [the Nephite interpreters] of which he spoke into my hands, and, upon examination, [I] found that it consisted of two smooth three-cornered diamonds set in glass, and the glasses were set in silver bows, which were connected with each other in much the same way as old fashioned spectacles. . . . [H]e [Joseph Smith] handed me the breastplate spoken of in his history. It was wrapped in a thin muslin handkerchief, so thin that I could feel its proportions without any difficulty. It was concave on one side and convex on the other, and extended from the neck downwards, as far as the center of the stomach of a man of extraordinary size. It had four straps of the same material, for the purpose of fastening it to the breast." (William J. Hamblin, *Review of Books on the Book of Mormon,* 516–17.)

"The treasure consisted of a number of golden plates, about eight inches long and seven inches wide, about as thick as ordinary sheeting, and bound together in the form of a volume by three gold rings. A large portion of the volume was securely sealed, but on the loose pages were engraved hieroglyphics [expressive] of some language" ("David Whitmer," *Chicago Tribune,* December 15, 1885.)

Read JS—H 1:53–54 to your family and ask:

- When was Joseph to return to the hill?
- What word did Joseph use in verse 54 to describe his meetings with Moroni?
- Why do you think he called them interviews?
- How do you think this preparation would

later help Joseph Smith as he restored the gospel to the earth?

Joseph Smith—History 1:55–58, 62, 75
Joseph Smith faces opposition

Ask a family member to raise his or her arms up and down five times. Have him or her do it again, only this time put your hands on the person's arms and provide some resistance to make it more difficult. Ask:

- If resistance makes something harder to do, is there any value in resistance?
- What will resistance do for your muscles?
- What does 2 Nephi 2:11, 15 teach about this principle?

As a family, read JS—H 1:55–58. Encourage family members to mark everything they find that would have been a challenge for Joseph Smith. (For example, his father's worldly circumstances were limited, Joseph's oldest brother died, he was accused of being a "money-digger," and his in-laws disliked him.) Ask family members to select which trial they feel would have been the most difficult for Joseph to endure and why. Also talk about what blessings may have come to Joseph as a result of suffering this kind of resistance. Ask:

- What can you learn from Joseph's example when you are faced with challenges?
- What do you learn from JS—H 1:62, 75 about Joseph's success in overcoming the dislike Emma's parents had for him?
- Why do you think it is important to resolve family struggles?
- What can we do as a family to overcome the challenges we face?

Joseph Smith—History 1:59–61
Joseph is warned!

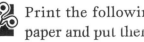 Print the following phrases on strips of paper and put them into a box:

- Joseph is to have responsibility for the plates.

- If Joseph is careless or neglectful of the plates, he will be cut off.
- If Joseph will use all of his endeavors to preserve the plates, they will be protected.
- Joseph is to hide the plates in a bucket in the family's well.
- Joseph is to keep the plates when not being used in a linen bag.
- Joseph is to build a box so the plates can be carried about.

Have family members take turns drawing the papers out of the box until all are taken. Have each person read his or her statement aloud. Have family members put all statements they feel are false back in the box. Have them take all the statements they believe are true and arrange them in the order they think Moroni gave them to Joseph. When they are finished, have them check JS—H 1:59 for accuracy.

Ask your family to scan JS—H 1:60–61 and report:

- Why was Joseph to be so careful with the plates?
- Was Joseph able to keep the plates safe?
- To whom did Joseph give the plates when his work with them was finished?
- Why was it necessary for Joseph and Emma to leave Manchester?
- What does all this teach us about the Lord's wisdom and power?

Joseph Smith—History 1:61–75
Joseph receives assistance

Share the following statement from President Spencer W. Kimball with your family: "God does notice us, and he watches over us. But it is usually through another person that he meets our needs." (*Ensign*, December 1974, 5.)

Ask your family to scan through JS—H 1:61–75 and find and mark "Martin Harris," "Oliver Cowdery," and "my wife's father." Ask family members to read about these three people,

looking for what assistance they offered to Joseph. Ask:

- Why would the assistance of these three men be so important at this time?
- How might the work of publishing the Book of Mormon have been thwarted without their help?
- Has Heavenly Father ever used you to help someone else?
- Why is it important that we try and help others in need?
- What are some things you might do that could offer assistance to the prophet today?
- What are some things you could do to help further the cause of the Book of Mormon?

Joseph Smith—History 1:62–65
What prophecy did Professor Charles Anthon fulfill?

Assign family members the following roles:

- Joseph Smith
- Martin Harris
- Professor Charles Anthon
- Narrator

Ask your family to study carefully and then act out the story from JS—H 1:62–65. Use the narrator to help fill in details of the story, but allow "Joseph," "Martin," and "Professor Anthon" to talk. Those three people could even add some dialogue if necessary to help the story flow well and seem complete.

When the play is finished, have your family turn to Isaiah 29:4, 11–12. Read those verses and identify how Isaiah's words are like what was just shown in your play. Explain to your family that Isaiah wrote this prophecy about 700 years before Christ was born. Ask the following questions, and share your testimony of the truthfulness of the Book of Mormon:

- How would Isaiah have known about these

events with such clarity? (He was a prophet who received revelation.)

- Why do you think it is important to know this story?
- What does it teach you about what God knows?
- What does it teach you about the truthfulness of the Book of Mormon?
- Do you know of other Bible references that refer to the Book of Mormon? (See for example Ezekiel 37:15–17; John 10:16.)

Joseph Smith History 1:68–74
The restoration of the Aaronic Priesthood and baptism

Invite family members to recall their baptism or their ordination to the Aaronic Priesthood and what these ordinances mean to them. Encourage them to share how they feel about the person who performed the ordinance, the significance of the covenants they made, and the potential that these ordinances provide for them.

Tell your family that JS—H 1:68–74 is the story of when Joseph Smith and Oliver Cowdery received these ordinances. Take turns reading those verses and have your family identify the parts of this story that impress them. Discuss some of the following questions:

- What do you learn from Joseph and Oliver about what to do when you have a question while reading the scriptures? (See verse 68. See also Oliver's feelings about these events as found in the first four paragraphs of the footnotes at the conclusion of JS—H.)

- What do you learn about the willingness of Heavenly Father to answer our prayers?
- When was the Aaronic Priesthood restored? (See verse 72.)
- Who conferred the Aaronic Priesthood upon Joseph and Oliver? (See verse 72.)
- Who directed John to do this?
- Why was it important for the priesthood and its ordinances to be restored to the earth?

Share the following statement from President Boyd K. Packer:

"The Church of Jesus Christ of Latter-day Saints is not a remodeled version of another church. It is not an adjustment or a correction or a protest against any other church. They have their 'form of godliness' and their goodness and value.

"John the Baptist returned through the veil to confer the Aaronic Priesthood, 'which holds the keys of the ministering of angels, and of the gospel of repentance, and of baptism by immersion for the remission of sins . . .'

"The Restoration did not come all at once. In a series of visitations, other prophets came to restore the keys of the priesthood." (*Ensign*, November 2003, 24.)

Read with your family the last three paragraphs in the concluding footnotes of JS—H written by Oliver Cowdery. Ask them to compare the feelings they had at the time of their baptism or priesthood ordination with those of Oliver Cowdery. Talk about why it would be important to have a strong appreciation for the gifts of baptism and priesthood that have been given to them.

THE ARTICLES OF FAITH

Historical background: "At the request of John Wentworth, editor and publisher of the Chicago Democrat, *the Prophet wrote a six-page sketch of the rise and progress, the persecution, and the faith of the Latter-day Saints. Wentworth had made this request for a friend named Bastow who was writing a history of New Hampshire. Joseph was pleased that he wanted correct information about the Church and asked that he publish the entire account ungarnished. . . . This original account, generally referred to as the Wentworth letter was printed March 1, 1842, in the* Times and Seasons." *(Ivan J. Barrett,* Joseph Smith and the Restoration, *502.) This letter "is one of the most valuable of our original historical documents, and gives in concise form the very best statement possible of the rise, progress and doctrines of the Church up to the time it was written. . . . It was in that document that the summary of doctrines believed in by the Church appears, commonly known as the Articles of Faith."* (B. H. Roberts, The Seventy's Course in Theology, *First Year, 109.)*

In 1880 at the October General Conference of the Church, members voted to accept the Articles of Faith as scripture. They are now included in the Pearl of Great Price.

Articles of Faith 1:1–13
What are we to do with the Articles of Faith?

Read the following statement from Elder L. Tom Perry to your family:

"What a great blessing it would be if every member of the Church memorized the Articles of Faith and became knowledgeable about the principles contained in each. We would be better prepared to share the gospel with others." (*Friend,* June 1998.)

Below you will find three teaching ideas to help you implement Elder Perry's desires for Church members regarding the Articles of Faith—memorize them, know the principles in them, and share them.

1. Make a mural of principles contained in the Articles of Faith

Divide thirteen sheets of paper among family members. Also assign and divide the thirteen Articles of Faith among your family. Ask family members to write their assigned Article of Faith along the top of their paper, large enough for all to see.

Explain to your family that a principle is a statement of truth by which we can govern our lives. It is a statement that can be applied to all people in a wide variety of circumstances. Read Elder Perry's statement to your family and ask why they think our lives would be blessed by becoming "knowledgeable about the principles contained in" the Articles of Faith. Pass out crayons, markers, and colored pencils among family members. Ask each family member to do the following for their assigned Article of Faith:

- Write a principle the Article of Faith teaches.
- Draw a picture illustrating that principle.

For example, for the ninth Article of Faith they might write, "We believe that God still talks to His prophets today." The drawing might be of the First Vision. (Note: For families with small children, you may want to encourage them to do only the drawings.)

When all of the drawings are finished, have family members read their Articles of Faith and the principles they have written. Tape the drawings together in numerical order and display them as a mural in your home. Encourage family members to use these pictures to help them memorize the Articles of Faith.

2. Memorize the Articles of Faith

Prior to this activity, gather twenty-six 3x5 cards. Write one half of each Article of Faith on a card and the other half on another card. Turn all the cards upside down on the floor or a table and scramble them.

Remind your family that Elder Perry encouraged us to memorize the Articles of Faith. Explain that this memory game will help everyone do so. Have family members take turns choosing two cards one at a time. When someone picks up two cards that have both parts of the same Article of Faith on them, he or she gets to keep the cards and say the Article of Faith aloud. Continue in this manner until all of the cards have been matched.

Set a family goal to memorize one Article of Faith each week for the next thirteen weeks. You could recite an Article of Faith each day at family scripture study or sing one of the songs found in the *Children's Songbook*, pp. 122–33.

3. *"Share the gospel"*

Read the statement from Elder Perry to your family again. Ask them why they think Elder Perry wants us to memorize and know the principles in the Articles of Faith.

Share these stories with your family:

"Our granddaughter Susie lives in an area where her classmates and teacher are not members of the Church, so she wanted to share with them the Articles of Faith. She decided to do this at a time scheduled for sharing something newsworthy. When this time came, eight-year-old Susie stood before her classmates and began, 'We believe in God, the Eternal Father, and in His Son, Jesus Christ, and in the Holy Ghost' (A of F 1:1).

"She continued, but when she got to the seventh article of faith [A of F 1:7], one classmate loudly complained, 'This isn't a current event!'

"The teacher quickly responded, 'Well, it's news to me!'" (Susan L. Warner, "Bear Record of Him," *Friend*, September 1999.)

"One day Julie Ann Christensen, 12, of Arcadia, California, went to visit her friend Lori Bontempo who had just moved across the street. The Bontempo family were sitting around the kitchen table talking about different religions, so Julie told them about The Church of Jesus Christ of Latter-day Saints. When everyone began to question her about the doctrines of the Church, Julie recited the Articles of Faith and explained something about each one. Everyone was amazed that such a young girl knew so much.

"Julie later took them a copy of the Book of Mormon, and she explained that the missionaries would be glad to come and tell them more about the Church. On February 9, 1974, Paul, Carol, Lori, David, and their father and mother were baptized.

"'Julie seemed to radiate something beautiful when she was talking to us about the Church,' Mr. Bontempo said. 'She really has a special spirit about her.'" ("Our Missionary Friends," *Friend*, May 1974, 32.)

Ask your family how memorizing the Articles of Faith, as Elder Perry suggests, will prepare us and help us to share the gospel. Encourage your family to use the Articles of Faith in their conversations with their friends.

HISTORICAL OVERVIEW OF KEY EVENTS

1805–1827

December 23, 1805: Joseph Smith is born to Joseph Smith Sr. and Lucy Mack Smith in Sharon, Vermont.

1811: Young Joseph's infected leg is saved from amputation through a miraculous operation.

1816: The Smith family moves to Palmyra, New York, and later to Manchester.

Spring of 1820: At age 14, Joseph Smith receives his First Vision of God the Father and His Son Jesus Christ, in a grove of trees near his home.
Joseph Smith—History 1:1–28

September 21–22, 1823: At age 17, Joseph Smith is visited by the angel Moroni, who instructs him concerning the Book of Mormon.
Joseph Smith—History 1:29–54
Doctrine and Covenants 2

January 1827: Joseph marries Emma Hale.
Joseph Smith—History 1:55–58

September 22, 1827: At age 21, Joseph is given charge of the gold plates. He begins to translate them through the gift and power of God.
Joseph Smith—History 1:59–62

1828

February 1828: Martin Harris shows a transcript of some Book of Mormon characters to Professors Charles Anthon and Samuel L. Mitchill to verify their authenticity.
Joseph Smith—History 1:63–65

Summer 1828: Joseph allows Martin to take 116 pages of the translation to show to his family. The pages are later lost.
Doctrine and Covenants 3, 10

1829

Doctrine and Covenants 1–5

April 1829: Oliver Cowdery begins work as Joseph Smith's scribe in the translation of the Book of Mormon.
Joseph Smith—History 1:66–75
Doctrine and Covenants 6–12

May 15, 1829: Joseph and Oliver receive the Aaronic Priesthood under the hands of John the Baptist in Harmony Pennsylvania. They baptize each other.
Doctrine and Covenants 13

May or June 1829: Joseph and Oliver receive the Melchizedek Priesthood under the hands of Peter, James, and John.

June 1829: The translation of the Book of Mormon is completed. The Three and Eight Witnesses are shown the gold plates.
Doctrine and Covenants 14–18

1830

Branches of the Church: 4
Total Membership: 280
Doctrine and Covenants 19

March 26, 1830: The Book of Mormon is published in Palmyra, New York.
Doctrine and Covenants 20

April 6, 1830: The Church is organized in Fayette, New York.

Doctrine and Covenants 21–23

June 1830: Joseph Smith begins revising the King James Version of the Bible, including the "Words of Moses."

Doctrine and Covenants 24

June 1830: Samuel H. Smith serves the first mission of the Church to neighboring villages, where he contacts the Young and Kimball families.

Doctrine and Covenants 25–27

September 1830: Many members of the Church are deceived by Hiram Page's false revelations.

Doctrine and Covenants 28

September 1830: Missionaries are called to teach the Lamanites in the West

Doctrine and Covenants 29–34

December 1830: On the way to teach the Lamanites, missionaries teach and convert Sidney Rigdon and his congregation. This nearly doubles the Church membership.

December 1830: The Church branches in the East are commanded to gather to Ohio.

1831

Branches of the Church: 6
Total Membership: 680

February 1831: Edward Partridge is named the first bishop in the Church.

Doctrine and Covenants 41–42

February 1831: Many false revelations and spiritual manifestations are received by those without proper authority.

Doctrine and Covenants 43–48

March 1831: Members of the Church preach to and receive a revelation concerning a religious group referred to as the "Shakers."

Doctrine and Covenants 49–51

July 1831: The Lord reveals to Joseph Smith that the center place of Zion is Independence, Missouri.

Doctrine and Covenants 52–59

August 1831: Sidney Rigdon dedicates Zion for the gathering of the Saints. Joseph dedicates the temple site in Independence, Missouri.

Doctrine and Covenants 60–66

November 1831: Church leaders prepare for the publication of the "Book of Commandments."

Doctrine and Covenants 1, 67–69, 70–72, 133

1832

Branches of the Church: 27
Total Membership: 2661

January 1832: Joseph Smith is sustained as president of the high priesthood at a Church Conference.

Doctrine and Covenants 73–75

February 1832: Together, Joseph and Sidney Rigdon receive a vision of the three degrees of glory.

Doctrine and Covenants 76

Doctrine and Covenants 77–83, 99

June 1832: *The Evening and the Morning Star*, the Church's first newspaper, is published in Independence, Missouri.

June 1832: Elders begin preaching in Canada, the first missionary efforts outside the United States.

Doctrine and Covenants 84–86

December 1832: The Lord gives a revelation concerning war.

Doctrine and Covenants 87

December 1832: The Lord instructs the Saints concerning the building of a temple in Kirtland and the "School of the Prophets."

Doctrine and Covenants 88

1833

Branches of the Church: 23
Total Membership: 3,140

February 1833: The Lord reveals what is today known as the Word of Wisdom.

Doctrine and Covenants 89

March 1833: The First Presidency is ordained and set apart.

Doctrine and Covenants 90–93

Doctrine and Covenants 94–96

June 1833: Work on the Kirtland Temple begins.

July 1833: A mob destroys the Church printing press in Jackson County, Missouri.

Doctrine and Covenants 97–98

October 1833: Joseph Smith and Sidney Rigdon serve a brief mission in Canada.

Doctrine and Covenants 100

November 1833: Mob violence begins to drive the Saints from Jackson County.

Doctrine and Covenants 101

1834

Branches of the Church: 22

Total Membership: 4,372

February 1834: The first stake in the Church is organized in Kirtland, Ohio, with Joseph Smith as president. The first high council is also organized.

Doctrine and Covenants 102

February 1834: The Lord commands Church members to form Zion's Camp to aid the Missouri Saints and help restore Church members to their homes and lands.

Doctrine and Covenants 103–4

May 1834: Zion's Camp begins its march from Kirtland, Ohio, to Missouri.

June 1834: Zion's Camp is commanded to disperse.

Doctrine and Covenants 105–6

1835

Branches of the Church: 22

Total Membership: 8,835

The Church publishes a book of hymns.

February 1835: The Quorum of the Twelve and the First Quorum of the Seventy are organized in Kirtland, Ohio.

Doctrine and Covenants 107

May 1835: Members of the Quorum of the Twelve leave on their missions to the eastern states as apostles.

July 1835: The Church obtains some ancient scrolls of papyrus. Joseph Smith translates the scrolls and learns they contain the writings of Abraham.

The Book of Abraham

August 1835: The Doctrine and Covenants is compiled from revelations that were going to be in the Book of Commandments. It also includes additional revelations and articles of Church doctrine.

Doctrine and Covenants 134

Doctrine and Covenants 108

1836

Branches of the Church: 25

Total Membership: 13,293

January 1836: Joseph Smith Sr. is ordained as the first patriarch of the Church.

March 1836: The Kirtland Temple is finished and dedicated by Joseph Smith.

Doctrine and Covenants 109

April 1836: The Savior, Moses, Elias, and Elijah appear to Joseph Smith and Oliver Cowdery in the Kirtland Temple and give the priesthood keys of their dispensations to the two brethren.

Doctrine and Covenants 110

June 1836: The Saints in Missouri are expelled from Clay County and start to gather to Far West Missouri.

August 1836: Joseph and others travel to Salem, Massachusetts.

Doctrine and Covenants 111

1837

Branches of the Church: 25

Total Membership: 16,282

January 1837: The Kirtland Safety Society begins in Kirtland, Ohio.

July 1837: Heber C. Kimball and others arrive in England. The British Mission, the first mission of the Church, is organized. This opened the first organized missionary effort out side North America. Within eight months two thousand people join the Church and twenty-six branches are organized.

Doctrine and Covenants 112

November 1837: The Kirtland Safety Society becomes bankrupt. Shortly thereafter, many apostatize from the Church.

1838

Branches of the Church: 26

Total Membership: 17,881

January 1838: Joseph Smith's life is threatened by a growing number of apostates in Kirtland. He and Sidney Rigdon flee on horseback to Missouri.

March 1838: Joseph and Sidney arrive in Missouri and are welcomed by the Saints.

Doctrine and Covenants 113–14

April 1838: The official name of the Church is given in revelation.

Doctrine and Covenants 115

May 1838: Spring Hill, Missouri, is named by the Prophet as Adam-ondi-Ahman.

Doctrine and Covenants 116

June 1838: Joseph Smith begins to compile and write the History of the Church, which isn't published in book form until 1902.

July 1838: Those who remain faithful to the Prophet in Kirtland leave the city in a mass exodus to join the Saints in Far West, Missouri. They arrive in October.

July 1838: Because of apostasy, Church leadership is reorganized and the law of tithing is reinstituted, replacing the United Order.

Doctrine and Covenants 117–20

August 1838: During an election in Gallatin, Missouri, a fight occurs between members of the Church and Missourians, increasing tension between the two groups.

October 27, 1838: Missouri Governor Lilburn W. Boggs issues an order stating that the Mormons must be exterminated or driven from the state.

October 30, 1838: The Haun's Mill Massacre occurs. Seventeen Church members are killed and twelve are seriously wounded.

October 31, 1838: A force of soldiers surround Far West and outnumber the Saints five to one. Joseph Smith and others are betrayed and captured. A court-martial orders Joseph Smith to be shot. General Alexander Doniphan defies the order and saves the lives of the prisoners.

November 1838: Joseph Smith and others are imprisoned in Richmond, Missouri.

December 1838: The prisoners are moved to Liberty Jail.

1839

Wards and Branches: 16

Total Membership: 16,460

January 1839: Brigham Young and the Quorum of the Twelve make plans and lead the Saints as they leave the state of Missouri.

March 1839: As a prisoner in Liberty Jail, Joseph Smith writes a letter to the Saints and leaders of the Church.

Doctrine and Covenants 121–23

April 16, 1839: Joseph and his four companions escape from Liberty Jail.

April 1839: The last of approximately 15,000 members of the Church leave Missouri for Illinois. The Church purchases land for the gathering Saints that later becomes Nauvoo, Illinois.

Summer 1839: Members of the Quorum of the Twelve leave for their missionary labors in England.

October 1839: Joseph travels to Washington, D.C., to seek compensation for the wrongs committed against the Saints in Missouri. Joseph meets with various leaders, including the president of the United States, but without success.

1840-1841

Wards and Branches: 19
Total Membership: 19,856

June 1840: The first Church members in England set sail to gather with the Saints in America.

August 1840: The doctrine of baptism for the dead is first introduced to the Church.

December 1840: The Illinois legislature approves a charter for the City of Nauvoo.

January 1841: The Lord commands the Saints in Nauvoo to build another temple and other important buildings in Nauvoo. Hyrum Smith is also ordained as the patriarch to the Church, replacing Joseph Smith Sr., who died the previous September.

Doctrine and Covenants 124

March 1841: The Lord approves other nearby gathering places for the Saints.

Doctrine and Covenants 125–26

October 1841: Orson Hyde dedicates the Holy Land for the return of the Jews.

1842

Wards and Branches: 26
Total Membership: 23,564

March 1842: John Wentworth, a news editor in Chicago, requests information about the Church from Joseph Smith. The Prophet's response is known today as the Wentworth Letter. It contains a brief description of the history of the Church and the thirteen Articles of Faith.

The Articles of Faith

March 1842: Joseph organizes the Female Relief Society with his wife, Emma, as the first president

May 1842: Joseph introduces the temple endowment to a select number of Church members in the upper room in his store in Nauvoo.

August 1842: Joseph prophecies that the Saints will be driven to the Rocky Mountains.

September 1842: Joseph goes into hiding because of false charges that he was involved in an assassination attempt on former Governor Boggs of Missouri.

Doctrine and Covenants 127–28

1843

Wards and Branches: 31
Total Membership: 25,980

Doctrine and Covenants 129–30

May 1843: Joseph and Emma Smith are sealed for time and all eternity.

Doctrine and Covenants 131

July 1843: Joseph writes down a revelation concerning the eternal nature of marriage and the family.

Doctrine and Covenants 132

1844

Wards and Branches: 33
Total Membership: 26,146

January 1844: Joseph Smith is nominated as a candidate for the presidency of the United States.

February 1844: The Prophet organizes groups to explore possible emigration sites in the West for the Saints.

June 1844: The *Nauvoo Expositor* publishes

inflammatory remarks about the Church and its leaders. The City Council declares the paper a public nuisance and orders the press to be destroyed.

June 22, 1844: Joseph and his companions are promised safety by the governor of Illinois. Joseph and his brother Hyrum surrender to officials and are placed in Carthage Jail.

June 27, 1844: Joseph and Hyrum are murdered by a mob while in Carthage Jail.

Doctrine and Covenants 135

August 1844: Sidney Rigdon proposes himself as a guardian for the Church. Brigham Young proposes that the authority to lead the Church rests with the Quorum of the Twelve. Brigham receives the sustaining vote of the Church.

BIBLIOGRAPHY

Anderson, Karl Ricks. *Joseph Smith's Kirtland*. Salt Lake City: Deseret Book, 1989.

Backman, Milton V., Jr. *The Heavens Resound*. Salt Lake City: Deseret Book, 1983.

Barrett, Ivan J. *Joseph Smith and the Restoration*. Rev. ed. Provo: Brigham Young University, 1973.

Benson, Ezra Taft. *The Teachings of Ezra Taft Benson*. Salt Lake City: Bookcraft, 1988

Black, Susan Easton. *Who's Who in the Doctrine and Covenants*. Salt Lake City: Bookcraft, 1997.

Brewster, Hoyt W., Jr. *Doctrine and Covenants Encyclopedia*. Salt Lake City: Bookcraft, 1988.

Burton, Alma P. *Karl G. Maeser, Mormon Educator*. Salt Lake City: Deseret Book, 1953.

Cannon, George Q. *Gospel Truth: Discourses and Writings of President George Q. Cannon*. 2 vols. Edited by Jerreld L. Newquist. Salt Lake City: Deseret Book, 1974.

———. *Life of Joseph Smith the Prophet*. Salt Lake City: Deseret Book, 1986.

Children's Songbook. Salt Lake City: The Church of Jesus Christ of Latter-day Saints, 1989.

Church Handbook of Instructions. 2 vols. Salt Lake City: The Church of Jesus Christ of Latter-day Saints, 1998.

Clark, James R., comp. *Messages of the First Presidency*. Salt Lake City: Bookcraft, 1970.

Cook, Lyndon W. "Lyman Sherman—Man of God, Would Be Apostle," *BYU Studies* 19 (Fall 1978).

———. *The Revelations of the Prophet Joseph Smith*. Salt Lake City: Deseret Book, 1985.

Cowan, Richard O. *Answers to Your Questions About the Doctrine and Covenants*, 113.

———. *The Church in the Twentieth Century*. Salt Lake City: Bookcraft, 1985.

———. *The Doctrine and Covenants, Our Modern Scripture*. Salt Lake City: Bookcraft, 1984.

Doxey, Roy W. *The Doctrine and Covenants Speaks*. Salt Lake City: Deseret Book, 1964–1970.

———, comp. *Latter-day Prophets and the Doctrine and Covenants*. 4 vols. Salt Lake City: Deseret Book, 1978.

For the Strength of Youth. Salt Lake City: The Church of Jesus Christ of Latter-day Saints, 2000.

Galbraith, David B., D. Kelly Ogden, and Andrew C. Skinner. *Jerusalem: The Eternal City*. Salt Lake City: Deseret Book, 1996.

Grant, Heber J. *Gospel Standards*. Comp. G. Homer Durham. Salt Lake City: Deseret Book, 1981.

Hinkley, Bryant S. *Sermons and Missionary Services of Melvin J. Ballard*. Salt Lake City: Deseret Book, 1949.

———. *The Faith of Our Pioneer Fathers*. Salt Lake City: Deseret Book, 1956.

Holland, Jeffrey R. *Christ and the New Covenant: The Messianic Message of the Book of Mormon*. Salt Lake City: Deseret Book, 1997.

Hymns of The Church of Jesus Christ of Latter-day Saints. Salt Lake City: The Church of Jesus Christ of Latter-day Saints, 1985.

Jenson, Andrew, comp. *Latter-day Saint Biographical Encyclopedia*. 4 vols. Salt Lake City: Western Epics, 1971.

Journal of Discourses. 26 vols. London: Latter-day Saints' Book Depot, 1854–1886.

Kimball, Spencer W. *The Miracle of Forgiveness*. Salt Lake City: Bookcraft, 1969.

———. *The Teachings of Spencer W. Kimball*. Edited by Edward L Kimball. Salt Lake City: Bookcraft, 1982.

———. *Faith Precedes the Miracle*. Salt Lake City: Deseret Book, 1972.

Lee, Harold B. *Stand Ye in Holy Places*. Salt Lake City: Deseret Book, 1974.

———. *The Teachings of Harold B. Lee*, edited by Clyde J. Williams. Salt Lake City: Bookcraft, 1996.

Life Sketch of Ann Temperance George Doney, in Daughters of Utah Pioneers Museum archives, Salt Lake City, Utah. Submitted by Ora Lowe Geddes Marstella of Layton, Utah, March 1999.

Ludlow, Daniel H. *A Companion to Your Study of the Doctrine and Covenants*. Salt Lake City: Deseret Book, 1978.

———. *A Companion to Your Study of the New Testament: The Four Gospels*. Salt Lake City: Deseret Book, 1982.

————, ed. *Encyclopedia of Mormonism*. New York: Macmillan, 1992.

Lyon, Jack M., Linda Ririe Gundry, and Jay A. Parry, eds. *Best-Loved Stories of the LDS People*. Salt Lake City: Deseret Book, 1997.

Maxwell, Neal A. *A Time to Choose*. Salt Lake City: Deseret Book, 1972.

————. *Notwithstanding My Weakness*. Salt Lake City: Deseret Book, 1981.

McConkie, Bruce R. *A New Witness for the Articles of Faith*. Salt Lake City: Deseret Book, 1985.

————. *Mormon Doctrine*. 2d ed. Salt Lake City: Bookcraft, 1966.

————. *Sermons and Writings of Bruce R. McConkie*. Salt Lake City: Deseret Book, 1998.

Merriam-Webster's Collegiate Dictionary. 10th ed. Springfield, Mass.: Merriam-Webster, 1999.

Millet, Robert L., and Kent P. Jackson, eds. *Studies in Scripture, Vol. 1: The Doctrine and Covenants*, 432–36.

Nibley, Hugh. *Approaching Zion*. Salt Lake City: Deseret Book, 1989.

Nyman, Monte S., ed. *Isaiah and the Prophets: Inspired Voices from the Old Testament*.

Oaks, Dallin H. *The Lord's Way*. Salt Lake City: Deseret Book, 1991.

Otten, L. G., and C. M. Caldwell. *Sacred Truths of the Doctrine and Covenants*. 2 vols. Salt Lake City: Deseret Book, 1982–1983.

Packer, Boyd K. *Let Not Your Heart Be Troubled*. Salt Lake City: Bookcraft, 1991.

Parry, Donald W., Jay A. Parry, and Tina M. Peterson. *Understanding Isaiah*. Salt Lake City: Deseret Book, 1998.

Pratt, Parley P. *Autobiography of Parley P. Pratt*. Edited by Parley P. Pratt Jr. Salt Lake City: Deseret Book, 1985.

Priesthood. Salt Lake City: Deseret Book, 1981.

Roberts, B. H. *A Comprehensive History of The Church of Jesus Christ of Latter-day Saints*. 6 vols. Salt Lake City: Deseret News Press, 1930.

Robinson, Stephen E., and H. Dean Garrett, *A Commentary on the Doctrine and Covenants*. Salt Lake City: Deseret Book, 2001.

Scraps of Biography. Salt Lake City: Juvenile Instructor, 1883.

Smith, Hyrum M., and Janne M. Sjodahl. *Doctrine and Covenants Commentary*. Salt Lake City: Deseret Book, 1978.

Smith, Joseph Fielding. *Answers to Gospel Questions*. 5 vols. Salt Lake City: Deseret Book, 1957–1966.

————. *Church History and Modern Revelation*. 4 vols. Salt Lake City: Deseret Book, 1947–1949.

————. *Doctrines of Salvation*. Compiled by Bruce R. McConkie. 3 vols. Salt Lake City: Deseret Book, 1954–1956.

————. *Essentials in Church History*. Salt Lake City: Deseret Book, 1979.

————. *Origin of the "Reorganized" Church*. Salt Lake City: Skelton Publishing, 1907.

————. *The Way to Perfection*. Salt Lake City: Genealogical Society of Utah, 1949.

Smith, Joseph. *History of The Church of Jesus Christ of Latter-day Saints*. 7 vols. Edited by B. H. Roberts. Salt Lake City: The Church of Jesus Christ of Latter-day Saints, 1932–1951.

————. *Lectures on Faith*. Salt Lake City: Deseret Book, 1985.

————. *Teachings of the Prophet Joseph Smith*. Selected by Joseph Fielding Smith. Salt Lake City: Deseret Book, 1976.

————. *The Papers of Joseph Smith*. 2 vols. Edited by Dean C. Jessee. Salt Lake City: Deseret Book, 1989–1992.

————. *The Personal Writings of Joseph Smith*. 2nd ed. Edited by Dean C. Jessee. Salt Lake City: Deseret Book, 2003.

Smith, Lucy Mack. *History of Joseph Smith by His Mother*. Salt Lake City: Stevens and Wallis, 1945.

Swinton, Heidi S. *In the Company of Prophets*. Salt Lake City: Deseret Book, 1993.

Talmage, James E. *Articles of Faith*. Salt Lake City: Deseret Book, 1984.

————. *Jesus the Christ*. Salt Lake City: Deseret Book, 1983.

Tate, Lucile C. *Boyd K. Packer: A Watchman on the Tower*. Salt Lake City: Bookcraft, 1995.

Taylor, John. *The Mediation and Atonement*. Salt Lake City: Deseret News, 1882.

Thomas B. Marsh. "History of Thomas B. Marsh, Written by Himself." November 1857. Archives of The Church of Jesus Christ of Latter-day Saints.

True to the Faith: A Gospel Reference. Salt Lake City: The Church of Jesus Christ of Latter-day Saints, 2004.

Webster, Noah. *An American Dictionary of the English Language*. 1828. Electronic edition in GospeLink. Salt Lake City: Deseret Book, 1998.

Whitney, Orson F. *History of Utah*. 4 vols. Salt Lake City: George Q. Cannon and Sons, 1892-1904.

————. *Life of Heber C. Kimball*. Salt Lake City: Bookcraft, 1945.

Widtsoe, John A. *Evidences and Reconciliations*. Salt Lake City: Bookcraft, 1960.

————. *Joseph Smith—Seeker after Truth, Prophet of God*. Salt Lake City: Bookcraft, 1951.

Wilson, Lycurgus A. *Life of David W. Patten*. Salt Lake City: n.p., 1900.

TOPICAL INDEX

Accountability: D&C 29:46–50; 137:1–9
Adam-ondi-Ahman: D&C 27:5–14; 116:1
Administering to the Sick: D&C 42:43–52
Agency: D&C 29:36–39, 45; 73:1–6; 98:11–22
Angels: D&C 129:1–9; 129:5–9
Apocrypha: D&C 91:1–6
Apostles: D&C 18:26–41; 107:21–35; 118:2–6
Apostasy: D&C 118:1
Armor of God: D&C 27:15–18
Articles of Faith: Articles of Faith 1:1–13
Atonement: D&C 19:13–20; 20:17–28, 27:1–4,
    45:1–15; 62:1; 76:39–43; 122:8–9
Authority: D&C 13 section heading; 22:1–4;
    121:34–46

Baptism: D&C 13:1; 20:37; 20:68–84; 22:1–4; Joseph
    Smith—History 1:68–74
Baptism for the Dead: D&C 127:5–10; 128:1–7
Bishop: D&C 41:7–12; 72:1–8; 72:9–19; 85:7–8;
    107:16–17, 68–70, 76; 107:71–75
Bishop's Storehouse: D&C 78:1–7, 14
Blessings: D&C 14:9–11; 31:1–13; 59:1–4, 23–24;
    66:1–3; 89:18–21; 104:11–18; 118:2–6; 124:44–48;
    130:20–21
Book of Mormon: D&C 10:34–45; 10:52–70; 11:1;
    17:2–6; 20:5–16; 84:43–59; Joseph Smith—History
    1:30–50
Booth, Ezra: D&C 71

Cahoon, Reynolds: D&C 94
Celestial Kingdom: D&C 38:16–27; 76:50–70, 92–96;
    88:14–21, 25–26; 130:4–11; 131:1–4; 137:1–9
Chastisement: D&C 28:11–13; 95:1–3; 101:1–10,
    35–38; 121:34–46
Chastity: D&C 63:13–20
Children: D&C 29:46–50; 55:1–6; 74:6–7; 83:1–6;
    99:6–8; 137:10
Church, Lord's true: D&C 1:29–33; 10:52–70; 20:1–4;
    65:2; 115:1–5
Church callings: D&C 9:1–4; 24:1–9; 31:1–13; 36:1–8;
    53:1–2; 53:3–7; 72:1–8; 81 section heading;
    84:106–110; 85:7–8

Church discipline: D&C 42:74–92
Church of the First Born: D&C 93:21–22
Citizenship: D&C 134:1–12
Commandments: D&C 29:30–35; 35:24–27; 42:18–29;
    59:5–8; 61:7–39; 88:118–126
Common consent, law of: D&C 20:60–67; 26:2;
    28:11–13; 104:67–77
Conferences: D&C 20:60–67; 44:1–5
Consecration, law of: D&C 42:30–42, 53–55, 71–73;
    44:6; 48:2; 51:1–19; 82:8–20; 83:1–6
Constitution: D&C 98:4–10; 101:75–95
Contention: D&C 71:7–11
Copley, Leman: D&C 49
Courage: D&C 122:4
Covenants: D&C 3:16–20; 35:24–27; 40:1–3; 63:59–63;
    78:8–22; 82:8–20; 84:31–39; 97:3–9; 98:11–22;
    108:1–3; 136:19–33
Covet: D&C 19:21–41; 117:1–9
Covill, James: D&C 39
Cowdery, Oliver: D&C 6
Cowdery, Warren: D&C 106
Creation: D&C 20:17–28; 88:6–13; 101:32–34

Death: D&C 42:43–52
Debt: D&C 19:21–41; 64:27; 104:78–86
Deception, avoiding: D&C 52:12–21; 129:5–9
Desires: D&C 7:1–8
Diligence: D&C 58:26–29; 69:1–2; 92:1–2; 107:99–100
Disciplinary Council: D&C 102:1–2; 102:3–23;
    107:77–84
Duty: D&C 107:99–100

Elijah: D&C 2:1–3; 110:11–16
Eternal life: D&C 6:1–13; 14:7; 76:113–119
Exaltation: D&C 76:113–119; 93:21–22; 131:1–4
Example: D&C 101:39–42

Faith: D&C 5:1–10; 9:10–14; 27:15–18; 35:7–12; 37:2;
    54:1–10; 63:7–12; 121:1–6
Faithfulness: D&C 58:26–29; 69:1–2; 81:3–7;
    84:106–110; 103:1–40; 117:12–16

Moroni: Joseph Smith—History 1:30–50; 1:51–54
Murdock, John: D&C 99
Music: D&C 25:11–12; 84:98–102

Obedience: D&C 5:21–35; 6:14–24; 16:1–6; 21:4–9;
    27:15–18; 30:1–11; 35:24–27; 38:31–42; 41:4–6;
    42:1–3; 43:8–22; 43:17–35; 51:16–17; 53:1–2;
    64:33–43; 88:22–24, 28–33; 89:1–4; 89:18–21;
    93:23–39; 95:6–12; 98:4–10; 98:11–22; 101:43–64;
    103:1–40; 104:1–10; 105:1–13; 124:44–48;
    130:20–21; Joseph Smith—History 1:27–29
Ordinances: D&C 20:68–84; 84:19–21

Page, Hiram: D&C 28
Parents, responsibility of: D&C 68:13–35; 83:1–6;
    93:40–53; 95:1–3; 99:6–8
Partridge, Edward: D&C 36
Patriarchal blessings: D&C 31:1–13; 39:7–24;
    124:12–21
Patten, David W.: D&C 114
Peace: D&C 19:21–41
Persecution: D&C 71:7–11; 109:43–53; 123:1–11;
    127:1–4; Joseph Smith—History 1:21–27
Peterson, Ziba: D&C 32
Phelps, William W.: D&C 55
Pioneers: D&C 136:1–42
Plan of salvation: D&C 20:17–28; 138:53–56
Pondering: D&C 9:5–9; 76:11–19; 138:1–11
Pratt, Orson: D&C 34
Pratt, Parley P.: D&C 32
Prayer: D&C 6:14–24; 10:46–52; 19:21–41; 23:6–7;
    37:2; 62:4–9; 66:1–13; 67:1–2; 88:118–126; 96
    section heading; 98:1–3; 109:68–71; 121:1–6;
    Joseph Smith—History 1:5–14
Preparation: D&C 1:17–28; 11:12–27; 38:5–9;
    38:10–12; 65:1, 3–5; 88:87–116; 133:36–45
Pride: D&C 5:21–35; 22:1–4; 38:31–42; 67:3–9
Priorities: D&C 106:1–8; 117:1–9
Priesthood, Aaronic: D&C 13; 84:6–30; 107:1–20;
    Joseph Smith—History 1:68–74
Priesthood keys: D&C 13; 27:5–14; 65:2; 81:1–2;
    84:19–21; 90:1–6; 94:1–12; 107:40–57; 110:11–16;
    112:16–34; 124:123–145; 128:19–23; Joseph
    Smith—History 1:68–74
Priesthood, Melchizedek: D&C 84:6–30; 84:31–39;
    86:8–10; 86:11; 107:1–4; 107:1–20; 121:34–46;
    Joseph Smith—History 1:68–74
Priesthood offices and quorums: D&C 20:38–59;
    107:21–35; 107:58–67; 85–98; 124:123–145
Proclamations: D&C 124:1–14
Prophecy: D&C 1:34–39; 87:1–5; Joseph Smith—
    History 1:30–50; 1:61–75
Prophets: D&C 1:8–16, 37–38; 21:1–2; 21:4–9; 24:1–9;

28:1–7, 11–13; 43:1–7; 68:1–11; 74:5; 90:1–6;
    100:9–11; 113:1–6; 127:11–12
Punishment: D&C 19:4–12; 121:11–25

Rebellion: D&C 56:1–11
Record keeping: D&C 128:1–7
Repentance: D&C 1:29–33; 19:13–20; 58:34–43;
    64:1–7; 66:3; 82:2–7; 98:11–22; 107:71–75; Joseph
    Smith—History 1:27–29
Restoration: D&C 1:29–33; 11:1; 14:1–4; 128:19–23
Retaliation: D&C 98:23–48
Revelation: D&C 1:1–7; 6:14–24; 6:5–36; 8:2–4; 9:5–9;
    28:1–7, 11–13; 43:1–7; 48:1–6; 62:4–9; 63:64–66;
    66:1–13; 68:1–11; 76:11–19; 121:26–33; 138:1–11;
    Official Declarations 1 and 2
Reverence: D&C 63:64–66
Riches: D&C 38:16–27; 56:14–20
Rigdon, Sidney: D&C 35
Righteousness: D&C 58:26–29; 76:1–10; 101:39–42

Sabbath day: D&C 59:9–19
Sacrament: D&C 20:68–84; 27:1–4; 27:5–14
Sacrifice: D&C 59:5–8; 64:23–25; 112:11–15; 126:1;
    126:1–3
Sanctification: D&C 20:29–36
Satan: D&C 10:1–33; 29:36–39, 45; 52:12–21;
    76:25–29; 76:30–39; 127:11–12; Joseph Smith—
    History 1:15–20
School of the Prophets: D&C 88:127–141
Scripture study: D&C 1:34–39; 11:21–22; 26:1;
    138:1–11; Joseph Smith—History 1:5–14
Scripture, understanding: D&C 71:1–4; 77:1–15
Scriptures, word of God: D&C 12:1–2; 18:1–8;
    33:1–18; 68:1–11; 72:9–19; 104:58–66
Sealing power: D&C 2:1–3; 110:11–16; 128:8–18, 24
Second Coming: D&C 29:9–29; 34:1–12; 38:5–9;
    38:10–12; 43:17–35; 45:16–59; 63:37–58;
    64:23–25; 65:1, 3–5; 86:1–7; 88:87–116;
    101:23–31; 106:1–8; 128:24–25; 130:1–3;
    130:14–17; 133:16–35; 133:36–45; 133:46–53
Seer: D&C 21:1–2
Selfishness: D&C 56:14–20
Service: D&C 44:6; 53:3–7; 64:33–43; 81:3–7; 86:11;
    104:11–18; 108:4–8; 117:10–11; 117:12–16;
    123:12–17
Sharing: D&C 48:2
Sherman, Lyman: D&C 108
Sin: D&C 58:34–43; 82:2–7; 121:11–25
Smith, Alvin: D&C 137
Smith, Emma: D&C 25
Smith, Hyrum: D&C 11; 135:1–2; 135:3
Smith, Joseph F.: D&C 138